The Native American World Beyond Apalachee

Ripley B. Bullen Series

UNIVERSITY PRESS OF FLORIDA

Florida A&M University, Tallahassee
Florida Atlantic University, Boca Raton
Florida Gulf Coast University, Ft. Myers
Florida International University, Miami
Florida State University, Tallahassee
University of Central Florida, Orlando
University of Florida, Gainesville
University of North Florida, Jacksonville
University of South Florida, Tampa
University of West Florida, Pensacola

The Native American World Beyond Apalachee

West Florida and the Chattahoochee Valley

John H. Hann

Foreword by Jerald T. Milanich

University Press of Florida
Gainesville/Tallahassee/Tampa/Boca Raton
Pensacola/Orlando/Miami/Jacksonville/Ft. Myers

Copyright 2006 by John H. Hann
Printed in the United States of America on recycled, acid-free paper
All rights reserved

11 10 09 08 07 06   6 5 4 3 2 1

Library of Congress Cataloging-in-Publication Data
Hann, John H.
The Native American world beyond Apalachee : west Florida and the Chattahoochee Valley / John H. Hann; foreword by Jerald T. Milanich.
p. cm.—(Ripley P. Bullen series)
Includes bibliographical references and index.
ISBN 0-8130-2982-1 (alk. paper)
1. Indians of North America—Florida—History. 2. Indians of North America—Florida—Antiquities. 3. Indians of North America—First contact with Europeans—Florida. 4. Indians of North America—Chattahoochee River Valley—History. 5. Indians of North America—Chattahoochee River Valley—Antiquities. 6. Indians of North America—First contact with Europeans—Chattahoochee River Valley. 7. Chattahoochee River Valley—History. 8. Chattahoochee River Valley—Antiquities. 9. Florida—History—Spanish colony, 1565-1763.
I. Title. II. Series.
E78.F6H36 2006
975.8'01—dc22   2005058228

The University Press of Florida is the scholarly publishing agency for the State University System of Florida, comprising Florida A&M University, Florida Atlantic University, Florida Gulf Coast University, Florida International University, Florida State University, University of Central Florida, University of Florida, University of North Florida, University of South Florida, and University of West Florida.

University Press of Florida
15 Northwest 15th Street
Gainesville, FL 32611-2079
http://www.upf.com

Contents

List of Illustrations   vii

Foreword   ix

List of Abbreviations   xi

1. Introduction and First Contacts   1

2. The Amacano, Chine, Chacato, and Pacara   22

3. The Chisca and Chichimeco-Westo   52

4. The Pansacola   69

5. The Apalachicoli   79

6. A Hostile Apalachicoli, 1690–1715   121

7. The Yamasee War and Its Aftermath   137

8. The Final Years, 1718 to the Mid-1740s   174

Notes   193

Bibliography   195

Index   219

Illustrations

Tables

1. Spanish and English Versions of Names for Creek Towns, Peoples, and Individuals 6
2. Three Town Lists, 1675–1716 87
3. Village List for 1715 138
4. Statistics on the Indians Just Outside St. Augustine and St. Marks, 1723 176
5. List of the Lower Creek Villages, 1738 181

Maps

1. Locations of West Florida's natives and settlements in the sixteenth and seventeenth centuries 2
2. Late seventeenth-century Indian villages along the Chattahoochee River and surrounding environs 88

Foreword

With this, his fifth book on the colonial period Indians of Florida, John H. Hann has achieved the status of a one-person publishing house. *The Native American World Beyond Apalachee: West Florida and the Chattahoochee Valley* joins John's previous volumes on the Apalachee Indians of the eastern Florida panhandle, the Timucua peoples of north peninsular Florida; the Calusa of southwest Florida, and the Indians of central and south Florida. All have been published by the University Press of Florida in this same Ripley P. Bullen series, and several have won awards.

I cannot say enough good things about John Hann, project historian at Mission San Luis, the Florida Bureau of Archaeological Research's marvelous research and education facility in Tallahassee, and his prodigious scholarly efforts. Hann's books have opened windows into the past through which all of us, whether readers or fellow researchers, can enjoy new views of the American Indians who once lived in Florida.

The focus of Hann's latest volume is the Indians of the western panhandle, the people who in the colonial period lived west of the Apalachee Indians, west of the Ochlockonee River. The tribes of the western Florida panhandle previously had been largely ignored by scholars due to a dearth of easily accessible information. Hann also incorporates information on the adjacent native tribes of the Chattahoochee River drainage in modern Georgia and Alabama. Those groups include some of the predecessors of the Indians later known as the Lower and Upper Creeks.

Hann draws on a host of Spanish (and other) archival sources to tell us about the Amacano, Apalachicola, Chacato, Chichimeco-Westo, Chine, Chisca, Pansacola, and many other peoples who originated in or passed through westernmost Florida from the sixteenth century until the late 1740s. He recounts the first Spanish explorations of that region, then relates the story of the establishment and destruction of the Spanish missions, before taking us well into the eighteenth century.

The information gleaned from Spanish sources will be new to people interested in the Creek Indians and their emergence out of the sixteenth century groups encountered by the expeditions of Hernando de Soto expedition in A.D. 1539–1540 and Tristán de Luna y Arellano in A.D. 1559. There also is fresh information for those studying the appearance of the Seminole Indians in Florida at a later date. In addition, Hann provides new interpretations about the origins of the Uchises and Yuchis, and the impact of the Yamasee War on the movement of Indian towns across the lower Southeast. The aftermath of that war, which involved groups in addition to the Yamasee, had a profound impact on St. Augustine and Spanish Florida, as well as many native peoples in what is now Florida, Georgia, and eastern Alabama.

Into this story, Hann weaves archaeological data as appropriate. It is archaeologists (with some exceptions) who, in the past, provided information on the native peoples of the Apalachicola-Chattahoochee drainage and nearby localities. Hann corrects those previous interpretations as needed.

No one has made better use of Spanish archival materials to learn about the Indians of Florida and adjacent regions during the First Spanish Period than John Hann. This book continues that scholarly tradition.

Jerald T. Milanich
Series Editor

Abbreviations

AGI, IG   Archivo General de Indias, Seville, Indiferente General
AGI, SD   Archivo General de Indias, Seville, Santo Domingo
B.P.R.O.   British Public Records Office
FSU   Florida State University
JTCC   The Jeannette Thurber Connor Collection
JTLC   The John Tate Lanning Collection
NCC   The North Carolina Collection
SC   The Stetson Collection

1

Introduction and First Contacts

Beyond Apalachee

Beyond Spanish Florida's mission provinces among the Guale, Timucua, and Apalachee lay the territories of many Native American peoples with whom Spaniards had at least occasional contact from the sixteenth through the mid-eighteenth centuries. This is true particularly of lands beyond the Spaniards' Apalachee outpost within the limits of modern Tallahassee that stretched westward to Mobile, north-northwestward to Montgomery, Alabama, and north-northeast to the vicinity of Macon. That territory embraces the Panhandle west of the Apalachicola River, much of the eastern half of Alabama, and all of Georgia west of the Oconee River at least, and probably a portion of eastern Tennessee.

This work will focus on the above-mentioned area beyond Apalachee with whose peoples Spaniards established contact during the seventeenth century and the first 60 years of the eighteenth century. In this opening chapter attention will be given briefly to the sixteenth-century contact of de Soto with peoples in the areas delineated. The study will focus principally on the groups that appear most prominently in the Spanish documentation. For much of the earlier part of that period they were largely the peoples from the Oconee Valley westward to the Chattahoochee River who were forebears of the Lower Creeks. In the later years, people of the Tallapoosa, Alabama, and Coosa River valleys, who were forebears of the Upper Creeks, and in a few instances of Lower Creeks, also appear more frequently. Attention will also be given to the identified peoples of west Florida: the Amacano, Chine, Chacato, Chisca, Pacara, and Pansacola.

With the advent of European settlement in the Southeast, some of these diverse peoples experienced highly fluid political alliances, multiple relocations, and internal transformations. Through a series of poorly understood processes, the groups among them living along the Chattahoochee and beyond it eventually coalesced into the tribal entity recognized today as the Creek Confederacy. Much of what is known about the genesis and development of the Upper and Lower Creeks derives from British accounts. This study, however, examines their transformations as seen from the perspective of Florida's Spaniards.

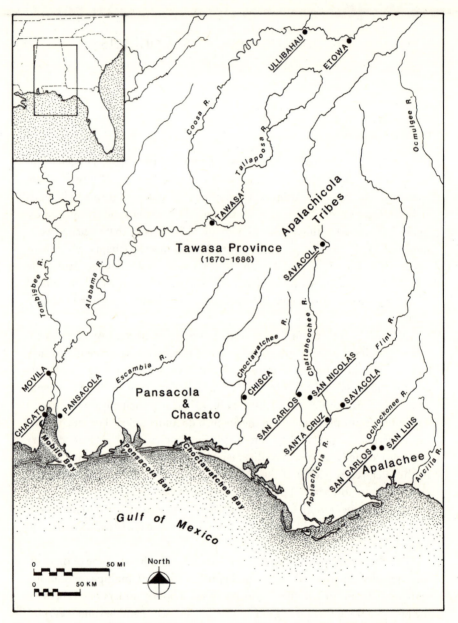

Map 1. Locations of West Florida's natives and settlements in the sixteenth and seventeenth centuries.

Most early historical studies of that region have given scant attention to those native peoples' forebears back beyond the mid-eighteenth century. Until very recently, the few that have dealt with them largely ignored substantial Spanish material that begins in the 1680s, or they have focused more on the Europeans who established the first contacts with the Indian inhabitants than on the Indians themselves. John R. Swanton (1922:172–178, 257) alone among earlier scholars focused on the Native Americans and used the limited Spanish sources easily available when he wrote *Early History of the Creek Indians and Their Neighbors*. His work remains the seminal one on the Creeks' early history, but he tried to do too much with the information available to him. As a result, he went astray at times in his identification and placement of individual towns, establishment of relationships between peoples, and, above all, in his suggestion that the Creek Confederacy existed in Hernando de Soto's time. As Frank T. Schnell (1989:25) observed, Swanton's "views have led to several problems of archaeological interpretation" about where the Creeks first "sat down." Marvin T. Smith (1987:129) remarked more specifically about Swanton's views on the confederacy, "Unfortunately, Swanton never really understood the political reality of the sixteenth-century Southeast. What he mistook for the Creek Confederacy was in actuality one or more complex chiefdoms." Spanish documentation that has become available since Swanton's time dispels some of the mists surrounding his identifications of some of those people.

In *The Governorship of Spanish Florida, 1700–1763* (1964:193–226), John Jay TePaske made substantial use of Spanish sources in his closing chapter on the governors' Indian policy. But his major focus was the governors rather than the Indians. Some of what he had to say about the Indians must be used with caution because of his unfamiliarity with the natives and loose usage at times of terms such as Creek, Lower Creek, and Uchize. His most egregious misstep was identification of the Talapuses as Lower Creeks. More recently Paul E. Hoffman (1990) and Charles Hudson (1990) with Hoffman as a collaborator have done much to remedy the shortcomings of earlier works particularly in the areas in the mountains beyond the Chattahoochee, which is beyond the scope of this work except when its peoples such as the Chisca become actors in the drama farther south in the seventeenth and eighteenth centuries.

Since Swanton's time, archaeologists have added considerably to the body of knowledge about peoples who are recognized today to be among the sixteenth-century forebears of the Creeks and Seminoles. Vernon James Knight Jr., Charles Hudson, David J. Halley, and Mark Williams have published extensively and written reports on these peoples, to mention but a few. That archaeological work has recently been summarized briefly in separate chapters by John E. Worth on the Lower Creeks' origins and early history and by Gregory A. Waselkov and Marvin T. Smith on Upper Creek archaeology. Those chapters appear in *Indians of the Greater Southeast: Historical Archaeology and Ethnohistory*, edited by Bonnie G. McEwan. J. Leitch Wright Jr. is also deserving of mention for his *Creeks and Seminoles: Destruction and Regeneration of the Muscogulge People*. But he focused principally on the first half of the nineteenth century.

Wright (1986:2) observed that the use of the name "Creek" for various groups of Indians originated with the English. Rejecting Alexander McGillivray's explanation that his warriors were known as Creeks because of the abundance of streams in the territories in which his Indian forebears originated, Wright explained that it derived from the native name Ochesee Creek that designated the upper Ocmulgee River. When traders from Charleston stopped there, "they referred to the Indians there as Ochesee Creeks, Ochesees, and eventually simply as Creeks." In the wake of the Yamasee War in 1715, those Indians migrated westward to the Chattahoochee to settle. In post-1715 Spanish records they appear as Uchises. Those Uchises or Yamasee were closely akin to the valley's Hitchiti-speakers, whose forebears had been longtime settlers on that river.

The Lower Chattahoochee Valley in the vicinity of Columbus, Georgia is recognized generally today as the principal ancestral home of the Lower Creeks. It was the location of Apalachicoli Province and of Coweta and Kasihta when that region's towns were first identified by name in 1675, and it was the location of Apalachicoli Province when Spaniards from Apalachee first established contacts with its people in the 1630s. The Hitchiti-speaking towns that constituted Apalachicoli Province per se are believed to be descended from the Valley's prehistoric inhabitants. But people of other regions such as Florida's Panhandle, the Apalachee themselves, and particularly peoples living west, north, and east of the Lower Creek homeland also contributed to the emergence in the seventeenth and eighteenth centuries of the people who came to be known as Lower Creeks. Some were Muscogee speakers like the Coweta and Kasihta while others belonged to diverse linguistic groups.

No such common or stable ancestral home can be identified for the major groups of which the Upper Creeks were formed. Two modern authorities noted: "the term *Upper Creeks* included natives of east-central Alabama who coalesced with a complex amalgam of peoples that formerly lived in eastern Tennessee, northwestern Georgia, and even as far afield as the present state of Mississippi." They commented that the Upper Creek "label was imposed on these diverse groups by English traders and political leaders who either failed to grasp or chose to gloss over the ethnic complexity subsumed by" that all-encompassing term. They remarked that they undoubtedly would have preferred to be known by their town names or "perhaps as Abihkas, Alabamas, Tallapoosas, and Okfuskees, referring to the major regional affiliations of *talwas*" or towns. These major components of the Upper Creeks all spoke Muscogee. In the eighteenth and early nineteenth centuries, Abihkas lived in the lower Coosa Valley, Alabamas around the headwaters of the river bearing their name, Tallapoosas on the lower Tallapoosa River, and Okfuskees farther upstream on the same river (Waselkov and Smith 2000:242–256).

On a broader scale, Vernon James Knight Jr., (1994b:183) observed that the various historic Upper and Lower Creek cultural assemblages "have seemingly clear predecessors in local Lamar-related manifestations" that can be demonstrated in some detail. He posits three regional sub-traditions that "are at home in the Coosa, Tallapoosa and Chattahoochee River drainages respectively." The three are interrelated to a certain degree in being rooted in the Lamar culture and also in their stylistic borrowing and evident interaction with non-Lamar cultures to the west and north. "Indeed," he observed, "some of the phases that lie at the background of Creek culture seem to owe as much to Dallas culture as to Lamar" and several of the stylistic changes are found in all three sub-traditions. "Yet," he concluded, "the local flavor of ceramic development persists through the historic period and accounts for the main regional variation in historic Creek ceramics."

Knight (1994a:378–380) signaled the Coosa, Tallapoosa, and Chattahoochee River valleys as the ones whose people were the most important forebears of the Creeks in general. Speaking from an archaeological perspective, he noted that "for all these areas it may now be said with some certainty that the local variations of Historic Creek material culture are continuous with earlier South Appalachian Mississippian cultures. We can now say more specifically, that the westernmost Lamar cultures are the ancestral populations out of which sprang the nucleus of the later Creeks."

Nomenclature and Spellings

Because Spanish sources used diverse names and spellings to identify rivers, native peoples and towns, and because the Spaniards' names often differed considerably from those the English used, that nomenclature merits attention as a preliminary to this study. Individual Spaniards also applied differing names over time to certain natural and manmade features and to the peoples. There are myriad spellings of Apalachicoli but none so diverse as not to be recognizable. But when Spaniards spoke of the "Apalachicoli River" in the seventeenth century, they intended a stream that combined today's Apalachicola and Chattahoochee. At some point prior to 1740 they also began to refer to the two streams as the "River of the Chacatos" for a people who lived in the vicinity of Marianna until 1675, some of whom had established a village on the Apala-

Table 1. Spanish and English Versions of Names for Creek Towns, Peoples, and Individuals

Spanish Version	English Version
Caueta or Cabeta	Coweta
Casista	Kasihta, Cussita, or Cusseta
Apalachicoli or Uchisi	Cowetas, Kasihtas, Ocheesee Creeks, or lower Creeks
Achito or Euchitto	Echete or Hitchiti
Osuche	Ooseeochee or Hooseche
Tasquique	Tuskegee
Tiquepachee	Tukabatche
Chichimeco or Chuchumeco	Westo or Ricahecrians
Chisca, Uchi, or Yuchi	Uchee, Euchee, or Yuchi
Chacato	Chatot
Tallapoosa towns	Upper Creek
Uchisi, Ichisi, Acjese	Ocheesee, Echete, Hitchiti
Chislacaliche	Cherokeeleechee or Cherokee-killer
Sauocola or Sabacola	Sawokli or Sauwoogelo
Saucola El Menor	Little Sawokli or Sauwoogaloochee

chicola by the 1680s. The two streams were also known at times as the "River of Sauocola." There are myriad spellings of Sauocola also, some of which such as Sawokli and Sauwoogelo, might not be as readily recognizable as the more usual variants Sabacola and Savacola. Although Chacato is the name Spaniards used most commonly, until recently twentieth-century works in English have usually referred to the Chacato as Chatot. The most common Spanish alternate usage was Chacta, which appeared also as the name of a Chacato interpreter in 1675, Chacta Alonso (Hann 1993:54). Occasionally Spaniards used the forms Chactos, Chata and Chatos. But Chata and Chato were also the usual forms Spaniards employed to identify the Choctaw. United States scholars who have not had much exposure to Spanish Florida documentation have used the name Choctaw occasionally for the Chacato. Irving Leonard (1939) is the most notorious example. In his translation, *Spanish Approach to Pensacola, 1689–93*, he used Choctaw exclusively to identify the Chacato, apparently unaware that Chacato and Choctaw were distinct peoples (see Table 1).

For the people we know as Lower Creeks, late seventeenth-century Spaniards used the name Apalachicoli Province to refer to the nine or ten southernmost towns living in the vicinity of the present Columbus, Georgia. Apalachicoli was also the name of the principal town among the southern towns. In the 1680s its chief was spokesperson for all but the four northernmost villages in the province's dealings with Spaniards. Most, if not all the southern towns' residents spoke a language known today as Hitchiti, or one very similar to it like Yamasee.

Hitchiti was the ancestor of today's Mikasuki language, and was so similar to it that James M. Crawford (1975:26), following Mary R. Haas (1978a:282–293), considered Mikasuki a sub-dialect of Hitchiti. Mark Williams (1992:1), quoting Albert Gatschet (1969), noted that "The dialect spoken by the Hitchiti and Mikasuki once spread over an extensive area, for local names are recorded in it from the Chatauchi River ... to the Atlantic Coast." Williams added that it was the language that William Bartram identified as being "known as the *Stincard* tongue." Those southern towns bore names such as Oconi, Apalachicoli, Osuchi, Ocmulque, Achito, and Ocute (Matheos 1686b).

Province of Caueta

Spaniards usually spoke of the four northernmost settlements as the province of Caueta (spelled at times as Caveta or Cabeta) or Casista. These villages were dominant over the rest, north and south. Residents of Caueta, Casista, and Colone (another northern town) spoke Muscogee or Creek, the dominant language among the Upper Creeks, and similar to that of Florida's modern Seminoles (Bartram 1955:365–366; Crawford 1975:25–27, 40; Peña 1716, 1717b:134). Tasquique (the modern Tuskegee) was the northernmost town in the mid-1680s. Diego Peña, who visited the area twice in the wake of the 1715 Yamasee War, described Tasquique's people as Yamasee speakers.

John Worth (2000:271), noting that Tasquique's inhabitants "were later noted to have spoken Koasati," concluded from that that "the town of Tuskegee should probably also be listed alongside the Muskogee towns in 1685." But their being Koasati speakers does not mean necessarily that they were closer linguistically to the Muskogee speakers than to the Hitchiti speakers. Peña's statement, if reliable, definitely links the Tasquique to the Hitchiti. A Yamasee who was in the Apalachicoli country in 1687 spying for Spaniards noted that his language was so closely akin to Hitchiti that he was able to pass for an Apalachicoli when he dressed as they did (Hann 1999:89). There is also evidence that Hitchiti and Apalachee may have been mutually intelligible for experienced speakers. That tie has relevance as well for Koasati speakers inasmuch as Koasati and Alabama are the languages in the Muskogean family, along with Hitchiti, to which Apalachee is supposed to have been most closely related (Haas 1978a:282–293; Hann 1988a:119–120).

It is likely that other Apalachicoli towns of the 1680s were Yamasee speakers as well. If the province's Ocute of the 1680s were descendants of the Ocute whom de Soto found in the Oconee Valley, they also probably spoke Yamasee (Clayton, Knight, and Moore 1993:I, 77, 229, 272–273; Hudson, Smith, and DePratter 1984:70). A cacique of Ocute who migrated to St. Augustine after the

Yamasee War was a Yamasee speaker (Primo de Rivera 1717a). Ocute's absence from the Chattahoochee in 1716 and thereafter suggests that St. Augustine's Ocute and his people came from the earlier town of that name in Apalachicoli Province in the 1680s (Peña 1716).

Occasionally Spaniards alluded to northern as well as southern towns as part of Apalachicoli Province. This probably represents a melding of the unity resulting from Caueta's hegemony and respect for the still surviving preeminence of the chief of the town of Apalachicoli among the southern towns and the degree of independence they still enjoyed under his leadership.

Initially the English referred to all the people of the Chattahoochee Valley as Cowetas and Kasihtas (or Cussitas) for the dominant or Muscogee-speaking towns. But they began to refer to them as Ocheesee Creeks sometime after 1690 because of the migration of some of the towns eastward to the Ocmulgee River, known then as the Ocheesee Creek or River. After the migrants returned to the Chattahoochee in 1716 in the wake of the Yamasee War, the English began to refer to these people as Lower Creeks.

Corkran (1967:3), however, described the derivation of both the names Creek and Muskogee as "uncertain." He noted: "The name 'Creek' seems to have been given them by the English," remarking that the eighteenth-century trader James Adair stated that "the English called them 'Creeks' after the many streams and rivers of their country," while Verner Crane (1918) "derives the name from Ochise Creek . . . on which they lived when the English began to have heavy trading contacts with them."

Uchisi

Spaniards never adopted the name Creek or Lower Creek during this period. They ultimately substituted Uchisi (their version of Ocheesee) for Apalachicoli to refer to the province's southern towns, alluding, for example to "the province of Uchisi and Cabeta" in 1738 (Toro 1738). Peña (1717b:134) used the name Uchisi a generation earlier for the Hitchiti language. Despite this Spanish usage, Swanton (1946:217) somehow concluded that Ochesee "was the name of the Muskogee or true Creek Indians in the Hitchiti language." J. Leitch Wright (1986:2) echoed that sentiment noting that Ochesee was "the Hitchiti word for the intruding Muscogee speakers who settled in traditionally Hitchiti lands." Wright (1986:5), citing Swanton (1946:218), observed that "Muskogee was not a Muskogean word" but from Algonquian, "presumably Shawnee and meant (people of the swampy ground)." Spaniards used Uchisi as early as 1680 to refer to a people who then attacked coastal Guale missions and whose ancestors probably were the Ichisi, Chisi, or Achese who lived on the Ocmulgee River in the vicinity of Macon during the de Soto era. By the early eighteenth century Spaniards were using Uchisi even for Apalachicoli such as the Oconi, whose name's attachment to the Oconee River suggests that in the 1690s migration the Oconi settled on it rather than on the Ocmulgee. In a 1738 document recounting an Uchisi attack on Florida's Pojoy Indians, Spaniards identified those Uchisi as "Ocone." (Clayton, Knight, and Moore 1993:I, 76–77, 229, 270; Hita Salazar 1680d; Toro 1738).

The town of Achito (of Spanish sources) was probably the Echete and Hitchiti of English sources. The link is most obvious in Peña's (1717b:134) rendering of Achito as Euchitto. It is corroborated also by Swanton's and Gatschet's explanations for the derivation of the name Hitchiti from Atcik-ha'ta or Ahi'tcita (Gatschet 1969:77; Swanton 1922:172). But the names Ichisi of the sixteenth century Spanish sources and Uchisi of the seventeenth and eighteenth century ones were the equivalent of the English Hitchiti in reference specifically to the language. Knight (1994b:186) has added a complication with his observation that Ichisi "is evidently ancestral to Ocheese, which in later Creek history was simply a little-noticed Lower Creek town. That these people were originally distinct from the Hitchiti speakers of the Lower Chattahoochee area is suggested by their name, a Hitchiti-language term for 'people of foreign speech' (Swanton 1922:148)." [Swanton actually used the word "different" rather than "foreign."] One might explain the difference by concluding that the earlier "foreign speech" was Yamasee. But, if so, one must then account for Hudson's (1994:178) observation that the chief of Ichisi's gift to de Soto of "a guide who spoke the language of Ocute" implies "that a language difference existed between Ichisi and Ocute," and my remarks in the same vein (Hann 1989:188–189). But it is likely that Yamasee and Hitchiti were closely related languages. Mark Williams, who has worked extensively "with the problem of the Hitchiti-Yamasee distinction posited by Swanton," provided a solution, suggesting "that the Yamasee's language was Hitchiti." That was something that "Swanton (1922:107) himself fell only a little short of saying" in 1922 "in speaking of a nineteenth century fusion of a Yamasee remnant "with the Mikasuki whose language is supposed to have been nearest to their own" (Hann 1989:188–189).

Herbert E. Bolton (1925a:54–56; 1925b:124) created potential for confusion in shortening the native name Uchisi to Uchis as there was another distinct people bearing the name Uchi living along the Chattahoochee by 1716. Diego Peña (1716) characterized those Uchi as having a speech that differed from that of the others and for which there were no more than two or three interpreters. He made those Uchis' distinctness even clearer the following year, observing that the Euchitto, Apalachicoli, and Ocone were of the Uchisi tongue, while the village of Uchi spoke a distinct tongue (Peña 1717b:134). Swanton (1922:288–290) probably was correct in identifying those Uchi as Chisca (Yuchi) and probably Algonquian.

The Sauocola

Spaniards rendered the name Sauocola variously as Sauacola, Sabacola, Sabocola, and Savacola. On English and French tongues, the tribe's name assumed various forms that, at times, bear little resemblance to the Spanish versions. Among them are Bartram's "Swaglaw," Hawkins' "Sauqoogolo," Beverly's "Sowoolla," the DeCrenay map's "Chaoakle" (Fretwell 1980), and Bushnell's (1908:571) and Swanton's "Sawokli." Like Pansacola, the name Sabacola appeared as early as 1657 in Apalachee as the name of a satellite settlement belonging to the chiefdom of Ocuia (Hann 1986b:97).

The Sauocola's Status

The documentation is somewhat equivocal pertaining to Sauocola's status as an integral part of Apalachicoli Province. An unnamed heathen Chacato (1676:62–63), testifying as a witness in a Spanish legal inquiry, provided our sole clear identification of the "village of Sabocola" as belonging "to the Apalachocolos nation." That Chacato was a native of the village that became Mission San Nicolas. He had been living in the Sauocola village when trouble erupted among the Chacato in 1675. Antonio Matheos (1685a), Apalachee's lieutenant in the mid-1680s, referred to the *chicasa* or abandoned site of Big Sauocola as being one and one-half leagues south "of the first place of this province" of Apalachicoli. That statement, of course, might be interpreted as meaning only that Sauocola was no longer the province's first place geographically because of its people's migration far to the south. But its separateness was also implied by another Spaniard who explained to the governor that he was choosing Sauocola Indians to carry a message to the Apalachicoli chiefs "because of their being of the same language" (D. de Leturiondo 1685a). Diego Peña (1716) described the Sauocola's language as distinct from that of the Apalachicoli, while noting that the Sauocola also spoke Apalachee. At least one Sauocola's knowledge of Apalachee was attested to independently, as Domingo de Leturiondo (1685b) chose an Apalachee-speaking Spaniard and a Sauocolan, whom he described as "interpreter for the Apalachina and Apalachecole tongue," for his questioning of two Apalachicoli chiefs. The Sauocola stand apart from the remainder of the Apalachicoli people as the only group who manifested some interest in becoming Christians and in developing close ties with the Spaniards.

There are possible indications of close linguistic ties between the Sauocola and Apalachee in their people's names. Like Pansacola, Sabacola appeared as early as 1657 in Apalachee as the name of a satellite settlement belonging to the Ocuia chiefdom (Hann 1986b:97). It appeared in 1694 as a name borne by at least two Apalachee men, Savocola Caurenti and Savacola Adrian, *eniha* of Ayubale (J. Florencia 1694:214). Juan Ysfane (1685) was the name of Big Sauocola's *osinulo* or "beloved son," who led the messengers alluded to above whom Leturiondo chose to carry messages to the Apalachicoli chiefs. Ysfane appears in the forms Esfan and Isfane as the names of two Apalachee men and one Apalachee girl (Hann 1988a:368–369).

The various indications of a special relationship between the Sauocola and the Apalachee may be reflections from an earlier period when forebears of the Sauocola occupied a site farther downriver than those of the seventeenth-century Apalachicoli, places such as Cemochechobee or Kolomoki. If such were the case, they were merely returning home when they made the first of their seventeenth-century moves southward circa 1674. Perhaps their forebears lived even farther south. If so, that could account for the name Sauocola being attached to the eastern mouth of the river (Milán Tapia 1693:288).

Linguistic Relationships

Documentary evidence indicates that, except for the Chisca, all the seventeenth-century peoples beyond Apalachee who lived within present-day Florida's boundaries spoke the same language or ones that were closely related to the Chacatos' tongue. Chine, Amacano, and Pacara spoke the same language (Fernández de Florencia 1674a:74–75). Their own language was also probably shared by the Chacato in view of Fray Barreda's reference in 1693 to Chief Chine as a Chacato (Leonard 1939:278–279). But, it should be noted that elsewhere Spaniards usually spoke of Chine and Chacato as though they were distinct bands at the very least. Fray Francisco de la Vera identified the Chacato as relatives (*parientes*) of the Pansacola. It is likely that all these peoples were descendants of the earlier inhabitants of Florida's west coast who were part of the Fort Walton culture.

More often the evidence for linguistic relationships is not that straightforward, especially when use or non-use of interpreters is involved. On two occasions in the 1680s when Spaniards spoke with Caueta's chief, they used an Apalachee-speaking interpreter. It is not clear whether that signifies a close linguistic relationship between Muskogee and Apalachee or simply that Caueta's chief had learned Apalachee. In the second instance at least, the chief was Brims, who had an Apalachee wife. Apalachee, of course, belonged to the Muskogean family of languages. Linguists generally place it within that family's eastern division comprised of Alabama-Koasati, Hitchiti, and Creek. But authorities usually have considered Apalachee to be linked more closely to Alabama-Koasati or to Hitchiti rather than to Creek (Caueta's chief 1682; Corkran 1967:62–63; Hann 1988a:119–120; Peña 1716). Worthy of note is Leturiondo's reference above to Apalachee and Apalachicoli as distinct tongues (Leturiondo 1685b). When Apalachicoli chiefs arrived in St. Augustine in 1681 to discuss the friction that resulted from the dismissal of friars whom Governor Juan Márquez Cabrera (1681b) had sent, the interpreter that he used was Diego Camuñas. Camuñas served more commonly as interpreter for communications with the Guale and the Yamasee.

Chisca, Chichimeco, Yuchi

The peoples whom Spaniards identified as Chisca, Chichimeco or Chuchumeco, and Yuchi or Uchi pose other problems of linguistic and tribal relationships about which scholars have disagreed. Swanton (1922:468, 1946:10) considered Chisca and Chichimeco as synonyms a bit too simplistically. This writer believes that Chisca and Chichimeco probably were closely related linguistically. The Yuchi and Uchi (the Uchee of English sources) of eighteenth-century Spanish records beginning in 1716 probably represent the earlier Chisca and Chichimeco, some of whom had joined the Apalachicoli in the late seventeenth century. But Spaniards saw enough distinction between the peoples they called Chisca and Chichimeco to refer to them by separate names even when they mentioned them together. The linguistic tie is suggested by Spaniards' use of Chisca as interpreters for questioning the Chichimeco whom the Spaniards captured in the 1660s (Aranguíz y Cotes 1662; Hann 1988b:75–79; Worth 1998:II, 18–21, 34–35). But their usage may be interpreted otherwise. Spanish sources establish that the Chichimeco who attacked Guale in 1661 had come from Virginia and settled on the Oconee River in Tama-Yamasee territory. Worth (1995:16–17) has corroborated earlier authorities' identification of those Chichimeco with the Ricahecrians or Westo. But that raises a question as to the identity of the people whom Spaniards referred to as Chichimecos as early as the 1620s. Worth, it should be noted, is among those who remain skeptical that Chisca and Westo spoke the same language. It is likely that the Uchee living among the Lower Creeks in William Bartram's time included both Chisca and Chichimeco in view of Benjamin Hawkins' (1982:61) remark that the Uchee "were formerly settled in small villages at Ponpon, Saltketchers (Sol-ke-chuh), Silver Bluff, and O-ge-chee."

Hilibi

Some consider English sources' Hilibi a match for the Apalachicoli town of Alape of the Spaniards. It should be noted, however, that the Hilibi were Upper Creeks and identified as Muskogee speakers by Bartram (1955:366).

Upper Creeks

The Spaniards' Ticopache were the Tukabahchee of English sources. They were recognized later as "the leading town among the Upper Creeks," although Swanton (1922:277–278) believed that its people had been Shawnee originally rather than Muskogee speakers. The Talisi were the Tulsa of English sources (Swanton 1922:230, 243). Talisi appears in the de Soto chronicles as head of a province of that name the head town of which was next to a river just above Casiste. Its chief ransomed the chief of Coosa (Clayton, Knight, and Moore 1993:I, 97, 288). Marvin Smith (1987:16, 97) identified de Soto's Talisi as a Kymulga site in Talladega County, Alabama. The Atasi were once a part of the Tukabahchee but had separated from them at an early time. Swanton (1922:254–257) believed that they were known also as Holiwahali, who were the Ullibahali mentioned by de Soto chroniclers, Elvas and Rangel.

De Soto's Contacts West and North

Hernando de Soto's chroniclers were the first Europeans to identify sixteenth century peoples who are recognizable as ancestors of seventeenth and early eighteenth centuries peoples from whom today's Creeks and Seminoles descended. De Soto does not seem to have learned much, if anything, about the closest sizable group, those living in the Chattahoochee Valley in the vicinity of Columbus, Georgia, during the five months that he wintered in Apalachee. The three reliable accounts by Rangel, Elvas, and Biedma mention only an exploratory maritime expedition that went westward along the Gulf coast. It found a good harbor and a village named Ochus, Ochuse or Achuse. The harbor is believed to have been in Pensacola or Mobile Bay. Garcilaso de la Vega's not very reliable account stated that two small forces of horsemen and soldiers on foot went northward by different routes for 15 or 20 leagues (no more than 50 or 60 miles). Their reported finding of many populous villages in a district "that abounded in food and was free of swamps and dense forest" makes the report suspect. As Charles Hudson (1997:147) noted, the region for a considerable distance north from Apalachee was dominated by pine barrens, which were shunned by the native people and by most animals as well. If they saw any such villages within the distances mentioned it would have to have been close in and inhabited by Apalachee (Clayton, Knight, and Moore 1993:I, 74, 267–268, 270, 273, II, 198).

When de Soto decamped in March 1540, the route that he chose to follow was determined primarily by tales told by two young native captives about a legendary land named Yupaha or Cofitacheque where, they promised, the Spaniards would find the pearls, gold, and other wealth they sought (Clayton, Knight, and Moore 1993:I, 74, 267–268, 270, 273). A four or five-day march brought the army to the place where it crossed to the west side of the Flint River in the vicinity of present day Newton, Georgia. It proceeded northward from there to a small chiefdom named Capachequi located in and around Chickasawhatchee Swamp probably "at the mound site on Magnolia Plantation on Pine Island (9Du1)." Hudson et al. (1984:67) went on to note that Garcilaso possibly was describing Capachequi when he spoke of "a village on a peninsula almost completely surrounded by a swamp with deep mud." Although its Fort Walton ceramics and housing style suggest a cultural affiliation with the Apalachee, Hudson (1997:149) observed that they did not necessarily mean political affiliation. In the next settled region at Toa or Toalli, Elvas (Clayton, Knight, and Moore 1993:I, 75) noted that the houses were different from there on from the ones that the army had seen in Apalachee and other parts of Florida proper, "because those on behind were covered with hay (*feno*) and those of Toalli were covered with reeds (*caniços*) after the fashion of a tile roof" (Ewen and Hann 1998:143). Some had what obviously were wattle and daub walls. Elvas noted that the clay-covered houses were winter dwellings that became hot as an oven from a fire built inside the house. The Indians there had other airier houses for summer. Luys Hernández de Biedma placed the change in housing style at Capachequi, noting that from there on they were like cellars or caves (*cuebas*) below the ground (Clayton, Knight, and Moore 1993:I, 228; Ewen and Hann 1998:164). To reach Toa, the Spaniards traveled through an uninhabited zone for several days after leaving Capachequi. The de Soto chronicles are the only primary historical source that mentions Toalli and Capachequi. That suggests that they did not survive into the seventeenth century when Spaniards and then the English began to frequent the region once more.

Charles Hudson (1997:152) observed that in the Toa chiefdom de Soto found towns that seemed "to them to be larger than any they had seen up to this point" that contrasted "with the small villages of peninsular Florida and the dispersed pattern of Apalachee and Capachequi." These towns were more compact and often walled. Those of Toa Province lay along the Flint River's floodplain from "just below the fall line to about fifteen miles downstream." At Toa they had also entered one of the western fringes of the Lamar area, "a distinctive sub-area of Late Mississippian culture . . . that developed out of an earlier Middle Mississippian culture called Savannah that occupied approximately the same wide geographical range" including what would become known later as the Upper Creek country of the Coosa-Tallapoosa River country and "the upper courses of the Chattahoochee, Flint, Ocmulgee, Oconee, and Savannah Rivers."

From Toalli, de Soto pressed on northeastward to the next chiefdom of Ichisi, which he entered on crossing the Ocmulgee River. Ichisi Province's main town of Ichisi was located near present-day Macon on the floodplain of the Ocmulgee about a mile south of the fall line. It is better known today as the Lamar Mound site or Ocmulgee National Monument. Other than some Apalachee, the Ichisi are the first of a number of native peoples mentioned in the de Soto chronicles whose descendants a century or so later would be part of the emergent Lower and Upper Creeks. Those names include the Altamaha, Ocute, Coosa, Chiaha, Chisca, Itaba, Ulibahali, Talisi, Casiste, and Mabila or Movila. The name Ichisi was reflected in the eighteenth-century Creeks' name for the Ocmulgee River, Ocheesehatche (Clayton, Knight, and Moore 1993:I, passim; Hudson 1997:160–165; Hudson et al. 1984:70; Williams and Shapiro 1990:10–13).

The Ichisi stand out as one of the Indian peoples who proved cooperative despite de Soto's initially hostile encounter with them. As Hudson (1997:159–160) remarked: "This was the first instance in which de Soto and his men were met with gifts of peace . . . in accordance with a ritualized protocol." The Ichisi treated de Soto and his retinue as they would have received one of their own paramount chiefs when he visited his tributaries or allies.

Their neighbors to the east in de Soto's Ocute Province proved equally cooperative. Altamaha, the first of its villages de Soto had contact with, reappeared at the end of the sixteenth century in Spanish documents as the province of La Tama. In the late seventeenth century, Altamaha was mentioned again as the leading town of the Lower Yamasee living in South Carolina. Some Tama lived in Apalachee during the last quarter of that century, probably having come as refugees from the Westos' intrusion into their central Georgia homeland. Similarly, Yamasee had migrated to the Lower Creek country at this time. Ocute were living on the Chattahoochee in 1685–1686. The presence of others there is attested to by the worried remark of an English trader at St. Helena in 1685 "that a thousand or more Yamasee who had been living among the Cowetas and Kuseetaws" had come down with 10 caciques and that more were expected daily (Hann 1996a:68, 76; Méndez de Canzo 1598, 1600; Westbrooke 1684/1685).

Tristan de Luna

The first serious European attempt at settlement of the American continent in the Southeast after de Soto's time was directed toward the Pensacola region in 1559. No people of any importance in the immediate vicinity of Pensacola Bay were documented. When a hurricane destroyed most of Tristan de Luna's supplies before they had a chance to land them, he sent part of his forces into the interior along the river system that reaches the Gulf at present day Mobile. Their search for food drew them eventually as far northward as the former major chiefdom of Coosa where de Soto had received a more or less friendly reception. They did not tarry long there on finding Coosa much diminished compared to what it had been only a short generation earlier (Hudson 1990:68–109; Smith 1987:12–15).

Archaeology's Contribution

In view of the Spaniards' failure to penetrate the Chattahoochee Valley towns prior to the seventeenth century, archaeology offers the sole hope of learning about its people before that time. As Knight (1994a:378, 380) remarked, we are dependent on "connecting historic Creek groups to patterns of archaeological remains and then tracing those patterns backwards in time . . . But as simple as it may sound, the establishment of such histories for the Creeks has proven extraordinarily difficult." Although his remarks as a whole were meant to apply to the Lower and Upper Creeks in general, the last sentence is applicable particularly to the Lower Chattahoochee region because, he noted, "there are simply no eyewitness accounts." That problem has been complicated further by evidence of a most severe post-contact population collapse in the valley, and by the differing interpretations archaeologists have advanced to explain that phenomenon and other changes revealed by archaeological research. Nonetheless, as Worth (2000:266) observed in the most recent synthesis of archaeological evidence: "Archaeological research holds considerable promise as a pivotal source of direct information on the ultimate origins of the Lower Creeks, particularly since many of the earlier transformations of the historic period occurred beyond the light of ethnohistoric documentation." Archaeologists refer to the last broad prehistoric period in the area occupied by the Apalachee and the extensive area to the north of it as the Mississippian period (A.D. 900–1540).

In the Mississippian period, dependence on cultivated plants intensified, leading to population growth and a marked reorganization of social and political structure. This resulted in the emergence of a ranked society and a chiefdom form of government (Smith 2000:13–14).

Archaeologists divide the 400 or so years of the late prehistoric and early historic era into four or five coherent phases, although differing somewhat at times in their nomenclature for them and on the length of the periods. It is during the Singer Phase that the phenomenon known as the Lamar culture appeared in the Lower Chattahoochee Valley.

Singer Phase (A.D. 1300–1400)
Bull Creek Phase (A.D. 1400–1475)
Stewart Phase (A.D. 1475–1550)
Abercrombie Phase (A.D. 1550–1650)
Blackmon Phase (A.D. 1650–1715) (Worth 2000:267–278).

Knight (1994a) and Knight and Mistovich (1984:222–226) extend the earlier Rood phase from A.D. 950 to 1400 in place of the Singer phase. While they acknowledged Frank T. Schnell's advancement of the Singer phase as an "identifiable transition between the Rood phase and the subsequent Bull Creek phase," they had reservations about the use of the name "Singer phase." Although they similarly failed to include Schnell's designation of late Bull Creek as the separate Stewart phase, Knight (1994a:381) later adopted it as based on plausible ceramic evidence.

Perhaps the most striking finding from archaeology pertinent to the origin of the Lower Creeks is the evidence for a population collapse in the lower Chattahoochee Valley in the wake of de Soto's passage up the Flint River and subsequent trek through Upper Creek territory. Knight (1994a:383) observed that surveys in the valley show a 90 percent reduction in site frequency during the Abercrombie phase that is difficult to attribute to epidemics alone. He went on to note: "The dense swath of Stewart-phase Lamar occupation throughout the valley simply vanished, leaving, it seems, just two Abercrombie phase towns, one on either side of the river south of present Columbus, Georgia. Interestingly, both of these compact Abercrombie towns had large platform mounds and may have functioned as mound centers until well into the seventeenth century." But, "By the first part of the succeeding Blackmon phase," Knight (1994a:384) remarked, "a number of large new villages were established nearby, and the regional population rebounded substantially from the Abercrombie decline." That archaeological evidence is very difficult to reconcile with the generally accepted historical evidence and Creek legends that indicate that the Hitchiti speaking Apalachicoli towns, and above all the town of Apalachicoli itself, represented the original inhabitants of the valley.

A dramatic discontinuity between the Stewart and Abercrombie phases is reflected as well in the ceramic assemblages. Worth (2000:268–269) observed that at the few sites that continued to be occupied "a diverse range of new ceramic types appeared, including an entirely new series of shell-tempered types not present in the Stewart phase, but at least reminiscent of contemporaneous Dallas, McKee Island, and Alabama River ceramics from Alabama and eastern Tennessee. These new types included distinctive incised, brushed, black-burnished, and plain shell-tempered wares." Knight and Mistovich (1984:225) observed that Abercrombie Phase sites showed some ceramic continuity with "the earlier Bull Creek phase," but such pottery was far less numerous than the new wares.

Authorities have differed on whether those discontinuities reflect massive population replacement by way of direct immigration or as Worth (2000:269–271) phrased it, whether it "resulted from in situ stylistic evolution among local populations (almost certainly with outside influences) . . . or both." He went on to remark that Knight (1994a, 1994b) concluded "that the 'hybrid' character of the Chattahoochee sequence probably resulted from external borrowing by resident local populations" and that, accordingly, the Abercrombie phase mounds were "'stable political and population centers' that survived the late sixteenth-century population collapse along the Chattahoochee and that served as the basis for local population growth during the subsequent Blackmon phase (Knight 1994a:384)." Conceivably, much of that contraction of settlement resulted partially, at least, from the phenomenon that David G. Anderson (1994:9) characterized as "cycling." He portrayed it as encompassing "the transformations that occur when administrative or decision-making levels within the chiefdom societies occupying a given region fluctuate between one and two levels above the local community." Thus cycling involves a "recurrent process of the emergence, expansion, and fragmentation of complex chiefdoms amid a regional backdrop of simple chiefdoms." After presenting Chad Braley's arguments for a large-scale population replacement as a partial explanation, at least, for the changes observed and noting Braley's positing of similar and simultaneous changes in the Apalachee chiefdom, Worth (2000:271) concluded that the two processes of in situ culture change and population relocation "may have been operating simultaneously." He argued that, "importantly, linguistic and folkloric evidence relating to the Lower Creeks strongly implies dual origins, implying both local population continuity and external immigration."

The first people occupied the Chattahoochee Valley as early as 10,000 to 12,000 years ago, but relatively little is known about their activity until the 4,000–800 B.C. period when fiber-tempered pottery and planting of squash appeared (Scarry 1994:18–19). These developments suggest that people were becoming more sedentary. The Middle Woodland period (300 B.C. to A.D. 500) saw an increase in population and sites, development of ceremonial activity and some minimal use of maize. During this early period there were important settlement centers in the southernmost portion of the Chattahoochee Valley at places such as Kolomoki, Mandeville, and along the length of the Apalachicola River lasting into the 1400s. But they had all been abandoned by the start of the historic era.

The Weeden Island cultures of the north peninsular Gulf Coast region characterized those southernmost portions of the Chattahoochee Valley in the Late Woodland period (500–750 A.D.) with Kolomoki the dominant settlement. But Weeden Island's cultural influence was minimal in the Columbus region as predominantly plain pottery dominated its sites. During the Mississippian Period in this valley (A.D. 1150–1300) a more politically complex culture emerged. The pottery resembled that of Moundville and a sudden appearance of new vessel forms and shell tempering suggests a probable immigration into the valley.

During the 1300s early Lamar pottery types, such as Lamar Complicated Stamped, first appeared in the area. Fort Walton Incised is also recovered, showing influences from Florida's Panhandle (Braley 1998:5–7; Milanich 1994:158–166; Tesar 1980:I, 106–111, 137–139; Worth 1998:4). Braley (1998:7) remarked that from about A.D. 1400 until the mid-sixteenth century, just after de Soto's passage through the Southeast, "the local culture is basically Lamar, with the pottery characterized by wide, folded, pinched rims on jars, curvilinear complicated stamping, and bold incising. The temper is also typical Lamar" consisting of coarse sand grit. Worth (1998:4) observed that during that period (A.D. 1400–1550) those developments "represent the localized stylistic evolution of a typical late-prehistoric Lamar assemblage with continuing influences from the Fort Walton culture to the south."

Schnell (1990:67–68) characterized Bull Creek (A.D. 1400–1475) ceramics as being predominantly complicated stamped (about 60 percent) compared to 35 percent plain; pinched and molded rims were most common. In the Stewart period, plain pottery rose to 55 percent while complicated stamping shrunk to 20 percent. Square houses, individual post houses, and central roof supports were present in both phases, while the Stewart phase also had rectangular houses and clay-daub showing whole-cane wattles. He characterized Bull Creek as having an "unknown form with daub."

Braley (1998:7), citing, Knight and Mistovich (1984) and Schnell, Knight, and Schnell (1993), maintained that Bull Creek ceramics "can be considered as a blend of generic Lamar with generic Fort Walton of this period." He noted that its settlement hierarchy was similar to that of the preceding Rood phase, "although greatly expanded in territory" as they extended "throughout the middle Chattahoochee Valley and into the Piedmont above Columbus." Rood is a pre-Lamar ceramic manifestation contemporaneous with Singer-Moye that appears to be related to those of Mississippian cultures to the west (Schnell et al. 1981:1–3, 240–243).

Schnell (1990:68–69) pushed back the closing date for the Abercrombie phase to A.D. 1625, characterizing it as "Lamar." With regard to pottery, he indicated that, "plain (smoothed, burnished, and polished) predominates. Incising and punctating is more common than complicated stamping. Complicated stamping is less common. Shell tempering is common." He described the following phases, Blackmon (A.D. 1625–1715) and Lawson Field (A.D. 1715–1835) as "Lamar derived," except that "shell tempering is common" and "Grit-tempered-type Chattahoochee Brushed is absent." These are the preconditions, as revealed by archaeology that immediately preceded the beginning of the historic record for the peoples of the Chattahoochee Valley settlements.

First Spanish Contacts Beyond Apalachee

When Spaniards finally returned to Apalachee to stay 93 years after de Soto had departed from his A.D. 1539–1540 winter camp there, they soon gave some attention to Apalachee's immediate neighbors. The few soldiers sent to Apalachee about five years after the first two Franciscans established missions there in 1633 went out from Apalachee to establish peace between the Apalachee and their closest neighbors. Those neighbors who lived on the Lower Chattahoochee River in the vicinity of Columbus were identified as Apalachicoli. The Chacato lived in the vicinity of Marianna and a people identified as the Amacano lived along the coast south and southeast of Apalachee at that time (Vega Castro y Pardo 1639).

The Amacano had become friends of the Spaniards in A.D. 1633 as soon as the first friars arrived. They asked for a friar and promised to go to their land and build a church and convent on learning that a friar was to be sent to them (L. Horruytiner 1633). That friendship was formalized in A.D. 1638 when sergeant-major Antonio de Herrera López y Mesa negotiated a peace agreement between the Amacano and the Apalachee (Vega Castro y Pardo 1639; Worth 1998:II, 18).

When the Amacano were next mentioned in A.D. 1674, they were living with two other peoples identified as Chine and Pacara. Although the three were described as representing distinct "nations," they spoke the same language. As the Chine are believed to have been an autonomous band of Chacato, these three peoples' language was also the same as that of the Chacato (Barreda 1693:279; Fernández de Florencia 1674a:74–75). It is quite possible that the three peoples were living together or associated, at least, in the A.D. 1630s. It is likely that they were remnants of peoples belonging to the Fort Walton Culture that flourished earlier along the Big Bend's coast and in the Apalachicola Valley and farther west along the Gulf coast as far as Fort Walton itself. The Pacara were also referred to at times as Capara.

Little seems to be known archaeologically about these peoples living closest to Apalachee except for the Chacato of the Marianna region. The names of none of the three appear in the Florida Master Site File. By contrast, a number of sites belonging to people who probably were prehistoric precursors of the Chacato in the Marianna Lowlands have been identified and explored. Pottery from the inland heart of the Chacato's historic era territory manifests closer kinship with the Apalachee to the east than with the people of the Pensacola and Mobile bays to the west that comprise the western limits of the Fort Walton Complex's territory. The westernmost peoples had predominantly incised shell-tempered pottery, while ceramics from the Chacato territory eastward were typically coarse sand and grit tempered types with incised and punctated design elements (Gardiner 1966:46–47, 1969:3–4).

While the far western area's economy was oriented mainly toward marine ecology with agriculture minimal at best, the Chacatos' area's subsistence economy was based on land hunting and agriculture like that of Apalachee. Gardiner (1969:1–11) described the Chacato settlement pattern as one of numerous large villages and smaller scattered settlements, but lacking temple mounds. In the loose political-religious organization suggested by their lack of temple mounds the Chacato more closely resembled the westernmost territories of the culture than the area east of the Apalachicola River with its several large temple mound centers suggestive of strong political-religious organization.

Gardiner believed "the size and number of sites with Fort Walton series ceramics [in the Chacato region] attests to some time depth for Fort Walton period occupants in this region." He did not believe that the Chacato lived around the Choctawhatchee Bay area "until extremely late in their history" and dismissed the idea that the bay or the river had been named for the Chacato. He was "inclined to attribute the derivation of these place names to people like the Pensacola who were closely kin to the Choctaws and spoke a closely related language." Not enough is known about any of the west Florida languages to make such a judgment.

For the Apalachicola River Valley, Nancy M. White (2003:1–2) reported after extensive research in the area: "There is a (near) absence of known contact period sites in this valley" based on her two decades of survey there. Yet, she noted, the earliest European explorers "brought various items that somehow did end up there" on at least two sites: the Chipola Cutoff mound "at river mile 42" and the "Thick Greenbriar site at . . . river mile 99" probably. Concerning the single radiocarbon date obtained, she commented: "If . . . the date is correct, it is certainly early for contact—maybe."

2

The Amacano, Chine, Chacato, and Pacara

The four peoples considered in this chapter may all have been the Apalachee's closest neighbors among Florida's non-missionized Indians when two Franciscans launched the formal mission effort in Apalachee in 1633. They were the Amacano, Chine, Chacato, and Pacara, all of whom appear to have been closely related linguistically. The first three were identified in 1674 as "being of the same language (*ydioma*)" (Fernández de Florencia 1674:74–75; Hann 1995a:61). A generation later another Spanish source identified Chief Chine as a Chacato (Leonard 1939:278–279). However, that source's modern translator, Irving Leonard, misidentified the Chacato in question as Choctaw. Both historically and archaeologically, the Chacato are the best known of those four peoples, having been identified as living in the Marianna region in that era and during a protracted period prior to that. The other three people received only scant mention in a few sources and no sites have been clearly identified with them archaeologically.

When the Chine and Pacara were first mentioned in 1674, the Amacano were living with them in a village named Chaccabi. Apalachee's knowledgeable lieutenant, Juan Fernández de Florencia (1674a:74–75), identified Chaccabi as belonging to the Chines and as located 10 to 11 leagues distant from Apalachee in a southerly direction (Hann 1995a:61). But it is not known whether the three peoples were always so closely associated, as the Amacano were first mentioned by themselves almost half a century earlier.

The Amacano

The Amacano were first mentioned in the closing years of the 1620s as a people who occupied an area along the coast of the Big Bend region from the mouth of the Suwannee north along Apalachee's coast. Worth (1998:II, 18) remarked that the Amacano's homeland "is not known with certainty, but they seem to have been located along the Gulf coast, situated between the Tampa Bay Pojoy (pronounced Pohoy), the interior Timucuas of the Suwannee River valley and the Apalachee Province to the northwest." Late in 1628 or early in 1629, Florida's governor had soldiers bring Pojoy's great captain to St. Augustine to negotiate peace between the Pojoy and the Amacano.

When the Apalachee missions were launched, the Amacano asked for a friar. The governor reported that the Amacano had already become friends of the Spaniards and that they "had come close to the province of . . . Apalache." A friar, who arrived in St. Augustine from the western hinterland just four days after the departure of the two friars who established the first Apalachee missions, brought word that the Amacano desired a friar and that they told him that, on learning that they would be given one, "they will go to their land and build a church in which they can say Mass and a convent as a dwelling" (L. Horruytiner 1633).

It is possible that a mission was attempted among the Amacano at this early date. Worth (1998:II, 18, 208, n. 44) implies that one of his sources, Francisco de Ocaña (1635) spoke of a mission having been established among the Amacano by 1635. Worth discounted the validity of Ocaña's report, observing that "it probably describes the missionization of Apalachee itself in 1633." Worth seems to have based his judgment in part on the governor's having sent a soldier west and northwestward late in 1638 to establish peace agreements between the Apalachee and their non-Christian neighbors, the Chacato, Apalachicoli, and Amacano. Worth noted that during "the fall of 1638 raiding parties had been sent from both Apalachee and Timucua provinces . . . to take vengeance for the earlier murders of Christian Indians in both provinces." The raiding parties had killed many of their enemies and brought back a number of prisoners, who were being held in Apalachee. The governor sought to prevent escalation of such warfare and to promote peace negotiations by returning the prisoners and convening a meeting of the leaders. Governor Damián de Vega Castro y Pardo (1639) reported success in this enterprise in August 1639. Worth did not make it clear, however, whether Amacano took part in the hostilities of the late 1630s. Their friendliness with the Spaniards in 1633 would seem to rule that out as also does Ocaña's seeming belief that a mission had been established among them. But if such a mission was established, it appears to have been short-lived.

The next mention of the Amacano occurred in 1674 in the Apalachee lieutenant Juan Fernández de Florencia's report of a mission created in the Chine village of Chaccabi where Amacano were then living with their linguistic relatives, the Pacara and Chine. From that point on the Amacano were usually mentioned by name in the general listings of the missions until the end of the century. But that bare mention is the only such documentary attention they seem to have received from 1674 on. The Chine always received top billing in the references to the mission. The Amacano were mentioned for the last times in 1702 and 1704. The governor mentioned the Amacano and the Pacara at the beginning of November 1702 as he reported the growing threat to survival of Florida's missions represented by the increasing hostilities waged by the Apalachicoli, encouraged and supported by the English. He wrote in the wake of a disastrous rout suffered by a large Apalachee force in an ambush on the Flint River as it was marching northward to retaliate for an attack earlier that year on the Timucua mission of Santa Fée (Zúñiga y Zerda 1702b).

Swanton's (1922:95, 119, 1946:88, 119, 208) identification of the Amacano as possibly Yamasee can be dismissed out of hand as it seems to be based on nothing more substantial than a superficial resemblance in sound between the two tribes' names and a rough contemporaneity between the establishment of missions (in Apalachee) among the Amacano and the Tama-Yamasee. He does not seem to have been aware of the Amacano's linguistic tie with the Chine, whom he equates with the Chatot or Chacato with more justification.

The Chine

The account of the founding of that mission early in 1675 appears to contain the first mention of the Chine under that name. They probably were the most numerous of the three groups that inhabited the mission at Chaccabi. Even when the mission's site was moved, the village continued to be referred to as "the place of the Chines." The name Chine seems to have derived from the name of their chief or vice versa. The Chine's knowledge of the coast westward from Apalachee all the way to Mobile is the salient feature that seems to have distinguished them in the eyes of the Spaniards.

Spaniards employed them as pilots and guides on at least two maritime expeditions along that coast and in a 1677 overland expedition against the Chisca of west Florida. When the first reports of French activity on the Gulf coast near the Mississippi reawakened Spanish interest in that region, it had become an unknown land to the Spaniards themselves despite their earlier explorations there. Apalachee's lieutenant indicated the village of the Chine as a source of pilots who were experienced in going by canoe from St. Marks to the place of Pansacola (Matheos 1686d). Seven years later in 1693 Chief Chine and his son served as pilots for the ketch that functioned as the maritime arm of Governor Laureano de Torres y Ayala's exploratory expedition to Pensacola and Mobile bays. The source is a statement Fray Rodrigo de Barreda made in his journal from the 1693 expedition to Pensacola Bay. He spoke of questioning "Chief Chine and the rest of the Choctaw Indians" (Leonard 1939:278–279). Irving Leonard mistakenly identified the Chacato as Choctaw in his translation of the documentation from that expedition that he published. Fray Barreda should have known whereof he spoke as he worked among the Chacato in 1674 and 1675. Governor Torres y Ayala also seems to identify Chief Chine and his son as Chacato. Chief Chine's prior acquaintance with the region between Pensacola and Mobile bays is reflected clearly in the journals on the expeditions written by the governor and Fray Rodrigo de Barreda (Leonard 1939:241, 249, 278–279).

Beyond Barreda and the governor's testimony in 1693, the evidence concerning the Chine's tribal ties to the Chacato is equivocal or, as in the matter of their linguistic ties with the Amacano and Pacara, raises more questions. Elsewhere Spaniards used the separate names of Chine and Chacato in speaking of those peoples even when the Chine and Chacato were serving together on the 1677 expedition. There is no indication in the account of the 1677 expedition that the Chine joined the Chacato in their plans to desert the expedition or that they were included in the Apalachee leaders' offer to the Chacato to excuse the Chacato from having to participate in the attack because there were Chacato living in the Chisca village (Fernández de Florencia 1678).

The 1694 visitation record provides other equivocal linguistic evidence. Despite the availability of a Chacato interpreter, Ubapt Gaspar, whom, the visitor used to talk to the refugee Chacato then living at the Apalachee mission of Escambé, the visitor used the same Apalachee-speaking interpreter he relied on to converse with the Apalachee at their missions when he spoke with the people at the Chine mission (J. de Florencia 1695:162–164, 177). But it is likely, of course, that the Chine and others had learned the Apalachee's language after having lived among them for almost a generation.

The master of the ketch on which Chief Chine served as pilot in 1693, on passing what seems to have been the mouth of the Ochlockonee River, noted that "this river is called Claraquachine in the Apalachina tongue" (Leonard 1939:283). It is not clear whether the "*chine*" in that name signified a link between the Chine people and that river or its mouth. Claraquachine was not the usual native name for that river used by Spaniards. They generally called it "Rio Lagna" or some variant thereof. Rio Lagna means "Yellow River."

Population Figures

Apalachee's lieutenant, Fernández de Florencia (1675a) gave the population of the three nations that lived at Assumpción de Nuestra Señora in mid-1675 as 300, apparently seriously understating their number as he is known to have done for other missions on that list. A census of adults made in 1681 suggests that the figures for 1675 included only adults or reflect some other similar limitation. The census listed 158 adults consisting of 45 married men, 29 single men, 45 married women, and 39 single women. Fourteen of the single men and 31 of the single women were non-Christians (Worth 1998:II, 136). A 1689 listing put the population at 30 families indicating a population of about 150 individuals (Ebelino de Compostela 1689).

Documentation on the destruction of the Apalachee missions and settlements in 1704 provides no explicit information on the fate of the Chine mission's inhabitants. Governor Zúñiga y Zerda (1705) listed Ayubale, Tomole, Capoli, Tama, and Ocatoses [Tawasa] as the five places whose people Colonel James Moore had carried off. Inasmuch as the Chine's village was relatively close to Tama and Tomoli, a case could be made that it would have been a likely target as well. That likelihood is illustrated in B. Calvin Jones' (1972:27) map of the province and his depiction of the probable thrust of Moore's attack. But the Chine mission was closer to San Luis and its garrison than were Tama and Tomoli and that closeness might have provided a margin of security. Therefore the fate of the Chine mission's people remains an open question.

The Chine Mission's Location

When Fernández de Florencia (1674) spoke of the founding of the Chine mission back in 1674, he located Chaccabi "ten to eleven leagues distant from Apalachee in a southerly direction." He certified that the Franciscan provincial Fray Alonso del Moral established a mission and erected a church there dedicated to St. Peter the Apostle. Fray Moral said the first Mass in it on Saturday, April 21, 1674. He left Fray Francisco de la Barreda there to begin the instruction of its people.

The roughness of Fernández de Florencia's estimate (10 to 11 leagues) of the distance of the new mission from Apalachee (presumably meaning San Luis where he was based) suggests that Chaccabi lay off the beaten path rather than on the trail to the port of St. Marks about which he would have had precise knowledge. The name Chaccabi suggests a possible association with the Rio Chachave depicted on the Alonso Solana map of 1683 in view of the seventeenth-century Spaniards' penchant for interchanging b and v. The Rio Chachave is the modern Spring Creek opposite Piney Island (Hann 1995a:61–62).

If such was the case, the new mission had been moved to another location less than a year later when Bishop Gabriel Díaz Vara Calderón (1675) conducted his visitation of Apalachee. Both he and Fernández de Florencia (1675a) gave the mission's name in 1675 as Assumpción del Puerto or Assumpción de Nuestra Señora. Assumpción was only six leagues from San Luis at most. The bishop described the path southward from San Luis as one league to Tama, another one to San Martín de Tomoli, and four from Tomoli to Assumpción. Fernández de Florencia described Assumpción merely as "on the path to the sea from San Luis" without giving the distance.

The mission's name had reverted to San Pedro by 1680, being referred to then as San Pedro de los Chines (Márquez Cabrera 1680). It appeared the following year in a mission census as San Pedro de Medellín (Worth 1998:II, 136). The 1683 map placed Medellín close to the headwaters of the Wakulla River a short distance from the eastern bank (Hann 1995a:62, Figure 1). The mission's name had changed again by 1695 to San Antonio de los Chines (J. de Florencia 1695:177). That name change undoubtedly reflects another move in the mission's location. A 1697 listing put the "Place of the Chines" inland from Tomoli and only half a league from Tama, apparently very close to San Luis (Torres y Ayala et al. 1697). Through all these changes, it appears to have retained its diverse population.

Accounts of Narváez's 1528 visit to Apalachee mention a village toward the coast name Aute as does Garcilaso's account of de Soto's exploits 11 years later. The eight or nine day's travel that Narváez's men allegedly spent to go from their Apalachee to Aute seems to rule out Aute's being in the vicinity of the Rio Chachave. However, Garcilaso's placement of Aute only "two days journey of six leagues each . . . over a very good road" is very compatible with a Rio Chachave location. As none of the more reliable de Soto chroniclers mention Aute, there is no way of knowing whether the Inca's account is trustworthy. Aute was not mentioned in any later accounts (Nuñez Cabeza de Vaca 1964:26; Clayton, Knight, and Moore 1993:II, 199).

The Pacara or Capara

The Pacara were, if anything, even more faceless than the Amacano. They were first mentioned, it seems, in 1674 in the record of the establishment of the mission at Chaccabi. Their name reappeared only a few times thereafter on mission lists or in passing references. There are no references to individuals, the Pacara's activities, or customs or numbers within the total populations given for the mission. The only anomaly is Fernández de Florencia's (1674, 1675a) rendering of their name as Capara on his 1675 listing of the missions after having used the Pacara form in 1674. Elsewhere Pacara was the form invariably used.

During one of the last mentions of the Pacara and Amacano in 1702, they were described as being among the heathens living then in Apalachee along with Savacola, Chacato, and Tabasa or Catases, (whose name was rendered elsewhere as Ocatases) (Zúñiga y Zerda 1702b). Tabasa are better known as Tawasa, who lived in the vicinity of Montgomery, Alabama in the de Soto era. They seem to have had ties of friendship, at least, with the Chacato by the 1670s. Chacato who sympathized with the 1675 attack on the friar working among them sought refuge among the Tawasa, who were still living in the Montgomery region in that year. But some Tawasa had moved into Florida, possibly, by the 1690s (Hann 1988a:68, n. 9). Conceivably, they had migrated with the Chacato who had returned in the 1680s from their exile in the land of Tawasa near Montgomery, Alabama.

The Chacato

Among the people of the world beyond Apalachee in the seventeenth century, the Chacato remain the best documented and best known for that time period. Still they have received very little attention over the last three decades or so in work published on Indians of the Southeast in general or on the natives of Florida in particular. So little known were these people a generation or so earlier that a scholar translating documents pertaining to Spain's approach to Pensacola in the years 1689–1693 could identify the Chacato who participated in the venture as Choctaw. Among broadly focused works, Swanton's (1922:134–137, 1946:107–108) remain the most informative published sources on the Chacato and other natives of west Florida. But his accounts do not exhaust the potential of the records that are available.

First Contacts

The Chacato were first mentioned by name late in 1638 when Florida's governor sent sergeant-major Herrera Lopez y Mesa to end an ongoing war between the Apalachee and Chacato. The governor remarked that this achievement was extraordinary with respect to the Chacato because they had never before been at peace with anybody (Vega Castro y Pardo 1639; Worth 1998:II, 18).

The next governor visited the Chacato and the Apalachicoli in 1646, describing both peoples as having asked for friars at that time (Rebolledo 1657 in Hann 1986b:111). That governor had ambitious plans for expanding the Spanish presence in the deep western Florida hinterland. He installed the first deputy governor at San Luis in Apalachee in 1645. He himself began a sizeable wheat-growing and cattle operation on western Timucua's border with Apalachee on lands loaned to him by the cacique of Asile on the pretext that they were needed for the king's service. That governor's death in 1651 from the epidemics that began in 1649 ended whatever chances of success his farming operations had. A more lasting legacy was his introduction of the deputy-governorship and the beginning of trade between Spaniards based in Apalachee and the Apalachicoli (F. Menéndez Marqués and Horruytiner 1646:322; Ponce de León 1651; Reyna 1656; Royal Officials 1647; Ruiz de Salazar Vallecilla 1647; Zuniga y Zerda 1705).

The Chacato asked for friars again at the beginning of the 1660s (Díaz Vara Calderón 1675). The occasion was probably provided by an early 1660s expedition headed for the Choctaw (*Chata*) country led by Apalachee's deputy gov-.

ernor, Pedro de Ortes. The Choctaws' country was then believed to lie beyond Apalachicoli Province. But Ortes advanced only as far as Casista, then the farthest away of the settlements in that province (Ramírez 1687).

Establishment of Chacato Missions

Spaniards finally granted the Chacato's request for friars in mid-June 1674 thereby beginning regular contact with at least some among the Chacato. The launching of this mission effort only two weeks or so after establishment of the mission at the Chine's Chaccabi raises the possibility that it was not merely a coincidence. But there is no hint of that in the documentation from 1674 except for the statement of the two distinct officials who oversaw and certified the establishment of the Chine and Chacato missions that they were doing so "by order of the señor governor." The separate missions' establishments are somewhat unique because of the detail provided about those events. There is no ready explanation for the degree of detail provided as Apalachee's lieutenant apparently had absented himself from the province shortly after certifying the establishment of the Chine mission on April 28, 1674. Adjutant Andrés Perés (1674:75), lieutenant of Timucua Province (describing himself as "assistant in the one of Apalachee"), wrote up the formal certification of the establishment of the two Chacato missions.

The Chacato's principal village, the name of which Péres gave as Achercatane, was a four-day journey toward the northwest from Apalachee. The provincial arrived there on Monday, June 18th with three soldiers, and three other friars. After the cacique and leading men gave their consent, a church was built there and dedicated to St. Charles Borromeo on the following Thursday, June 21. After saying Mass in it and baptizing an infant son of the chief and two sons of leading men, the friars and other Spaniards traveled to the second village that same day. Péres gave its name as Atanchia. On the following day, Friday, the provincial erected another church, dedicated it to St. Nicolas de Tolentino, said Mass in it, and solemnly baptized an infant nephew and heir of the village's cacique. The provincial left the three friars to instruct the people of the province. Péres was still in the province when he drew up his certification on June 23. The third friar probably was destined for a third settlement that eventually became a *visita*. When the principal village's name was mentioned anew, it was given as Yatcatane.

One of the three friars does not seem to have remained very long in Chacato territory. The first subsequent documentation, from early September 1674, identified Miguel de Valverde and Rodrigo de la Barreda as the two friars working then among the Chacato. The friars claimed at that time that more than 300

Chacato had become Christians, including the caciques of San Carlos and San Nicolás. But they seem to have taken too forceful an approach to their work as their over zealous pressure tactics had stirred up trouble as well.

Three feared warriors protested that they were being pressured to become Christians against their will. They threatened their chiefs with trouble at the hands of their Chisca friends living in the mission villages and in a Chisca settlement relatively nearby. In response to the friars' appeal for support, Apalachee's lieutenant brought a few soldiers and 25 harquebus-armed Apalachee to restore calm. During the soldiers' eight-day stay at the two missions, the three troublesome warriors became at least nominal Christians along with 50 additional Chacato. The lieutenant expelled the Chisca living at the two missions (Valverde and Barrera 1674:34–35).

The Chacato Precursors

The prehistoric precursors of the Chacato were Fort Walton culture peoples who occupied the Marianna Lowlands, and possibly some of the peoples who occupied the Gulf coast from the mouth of the Aucilla River to St. Andrews Bay or even farther west (Milanich 1994:358–359). The Chisca village mentioned in the Chacato documents, probably located on the Choctawhatchee River, had Chacato and Pansacola contingents (Fernández de Florencia 1678). The name Choctaw attached to that river suggests that its banks once were considered Chacato territory as the river's name doubtless reflects Anglo confusion of the Chacato with the Choctaw. Although considerable archaeological research has been conducted on sites believed to be associated with historic era Chacato, no recognized mission-era structural remains have been identified to date.

This result is not surprising in view of the short life of the two Chacato missions in the Marianna region and the haste with which they seem to have been erected. If Andrés Péres's (1674) certifications are accurate, the church at San Carlos was built in two days at the most; the one at San Nicolás sprang up overnight. If they were built by the natives and no nails or other iron hardware were employed, they might leave no trace other than postmolds. They need not have been large. Bishop Díaz Vara Calderón (1675) estimated San Carlos's population as "few more than a hundred" and that of San Nicolás as "few more than thirty." Writing about six months later, Apalachee's lieutenant put their respective populations at 300 and 100, while observing, "both missions are no more" (Fernández de Florencia 1675a). The low figures given by the bishop may have resulted from his having visited them in winter when many of the people were dispersed in the woods hunting or on the coast fishing.

After working at the Waddells Mill Pond site (8Ja65), William M. Gardiner (1966:57) was "reasonably certain that Ja 65 is indeed the village of San Carlos," although he cautioned that no historical material was found on the site. B. Calvin Jones (1973, 1975, 1987), on the other hand, after considerable work on 8Ja65 rejected the possibility that it was the site of San Carlos. But he considered it to have been an important ceremonial mound site and possibly the center for the 25 to 30 prehistoric settlement sites that he had located in the vicinity of Marianna. Jones believed (as did Gardiner) that some of those sites were probably occupied until the beginning of the historic era and that their inhabitants may well have been ancestors of the mission-era Chacato. Jones observed, however, that the intensity of the human occupation of that region bore no comparison to that of the Apalachee region.

Mark F. Boyd (1958:260) placed San Nicolás in the vicinity of Rock Arch Cave in the Florida Caverns State Park. Fray Rodrigo de Barreda (1693:267–268) in a record of a trip that he made overland from Apalachee to Pensacola Bay noted that the then abandoned site of San Nicolás was adjacent to a cave. "Here we spent the night in the hollow of such a beautiful and unusual rock that I can state positively that more than 200 men could be lodged comfortably within it; inside there is a brook which gushes from the living rock. It has plenty of light and height with three apertures buttressed by stonework of unusual natural architecture. Around it are level plots of ground, groves of trees and pine woods." But Jones (1987), based on his surface survey, rejected Rock Arch Cave as the site of San Nicolás, noting that no archaeological evidence of the Spanish presence of 1674–1675 had been found to date anywhere in the region. The limited nature and brevity of the Spanish presence there were doubtless factors contributing to that result.

Trouble among the Chacato

The Spaniards' use of force in September 1674 to quell some Chacato warriors' protests over the friars' pressure tactics did not permanently resolve the underlying tensions between the new and the old ways. They resurfaced in a more serious form in less than a year as the implications of religious conversion became more evident to the elements that had resisted it earlier or had not fully understood them, particularly as the friars made it clear that nominal conversion would not satisfy them.

During the summer of 1675, three noted warriors, Juan Fernández de Diocsale, Luis Ubabesa, and Juaquín, forged a conspiracy, phrased euphemistically at the start as envisioning only expulsion of the bothersome Fray Barreda, who was alone in the province at that time at San Carlos. Presumably, they were the same recalcitrants who had threatened trouble in 1674. Diocsale almost certainly was one of the initial trio. The friars' report that Juan Fernández de Florencia served as godfather for one of them suggests that Diocsale was the man in question in view of his Spanish surname, Juan Fernández, and the involvement anew of the Chisca. As will be seen below, Diocsale was the son of a Chisca woman and a former chief (Fernández de Florencia 1675b; Valverde and Barrera 1674).

As in Guale in 1597, a culture clash over sexual mores was at the heart of the matter. Diocsale, already angered at being chided by the friar over irregular attendance at Mass and the need to send away three of the four women with whom he had been living before his baptism, was pushed to thoughts of murder when the friar had three of the women removed from Diocsale's house. The friar insisted that the 84-year-old warrior marry (in a Catholic ceremony) the woman among the four with whom he had lived the longest. In view of Diocsale's reputation for having Chisca at his house for meals regularly, loss of those three women's culinary services was a hard blow, not to mention the loss of status that it probably entailed for a man who had once been chief of San Carlos.

Nevertheless, according to testimony given during an inquiry into the tumult held in the fall of 1675, it was Ubabesa and Juaquín who initiated the conspiracy to kill the friar after Barreda had reprimanded Ubabesa publicly for an adulterous affair with a Christian Chacato woman while her husband was absent in Apalachee. When the aggrieved husband's complaint moved Barreda to punish the woman and scold Ubabesa at Sunday Mass, Juaquín allegedly broached the idea of killing the priest. It should be noted, however, that during an inquiry held in St. Augustine about a year later into a second conspiracy involving Diocsale, a number of witnesses listed the "prime motivators" of the 1675 tumult as Diocsale, the San Carlos *eniha* Cutca Martín, the cacique of San Antonio, an unidentified elderly Indian who had died since 1675, and the heir to the chieftainship of San Carlos. One witness from the 1676 inquiry included "Chiscas from San Nicolás" (Cacique Miguel 1676; Cutca Martín 1676; Diocsale 1676; Pedro, son of Diocsale, 1676; unidentified Chacato Indian, 1676:60–68).

The conspirators' rapid winning of widespread support indicates considerable discontent. But another factor difficult to gauge was alleged fears aroused by the conspirators' bullying threats that they would have the Chisca come to kill everyone who did not follow them (Fernández de Florencia 1675d:43–44; Nicolás, fiscal, 1675; Phelipe, *usinulo,* 1675:46–49). The cacique of San Carlos (1675:49–50) testified that Diocsale had frightened all the people of San Carlos and San Nicolás. San Carlos's *usinulo* certified that Diocsale, as a brave, had all the Chacato "subject to his will and also because of the fear of the Chiscas" and that "Diocsale made himself feared because of being the son of a Chisca woman." Other Chacato corroborated the chief's testimony about Diocsale's sway over the Chisca. In his opening statement for the inquiry into this tumult, Fernández de Florencia (1675c:43–44) accused Diocsale of having assembled some Chisca and some caciques to support him. But all the inquiry's witnesses cited above were people who had remained ostensibly loyal to the Spaniards. Subsequent events in 1676, particularly the Chiscas' moving of their village from its site at the mouth of the Apalachicola River to one deep in west Florida as a prelude to their beginning of hit-and-run attacks against people of Apalachee and Timucua, indicate that the Chisca represented a potential threat at least (Pedro, son of Diocsale 1676:60–62).

Except for the one witness from the 1676 inquiry who implicated Chisca from San Nicolás, there is no other corroborating evidence that the Chisca as a people participated in this movement during the summer of 1675, as they had taken part in 1647 in the revolt among the Apalachee. The opposite is suggested in an August 2 note to the governor by Apalachee's acting deputy-governor, Andrés Péres (1675a:39). In it Péres reported that he had summoned the interpreter for the Chiscas "in order to dispatch him to speak to the Chisca caciques, asking them not to give support to the Chacatos, because if they give it, sir, we are going to have our hands full because there are many Chiscas." The Chacato conspirators' talk of the Chisca may have been no more than a psychological ploy. Diocsale also claimed that the Apalachicoli were at his disposal, a claim that was patently false (Cacique Carlos 1675:49). The rebels' plans from the start—to flee to a refuge among the Tawasa once they had killed Fray Barreda and the friar at Santa Cruz de Sauocola rather than remaining to defend their villages—suggests that the enterprise did not enjoy much support from the Chisca, at least initially (Fernández de Florencia 1675d:43–44).

The conspirators first spoke only of expelling Fray Barreda when they approached the leading Indians at San Carlos, asking for a contribution of two deerskins from each to bring that about. San Carlos's leaders refused them, objecting that only the Franciscan provincial could remove the friar and making it clear they would resist any attempt to expel or harm him. Only then did the conspirators resort to threats and reveal the full scope of their plans (Ebanjelista 1675; Nicolás, fiscal 1675; Phelipe *usinulo* 1675:44–49). The loyal element that spurned the initial invitation included all the known leaders at San Carlos except Diocsale. At San Nicolás it included the cacique and the *eniha*, although San Nicolás's young cacique seems to have wavered from the start. Juaquín, the fiscal at San Nicolás, was a ringleader among the conspirators. The 80 men of the out-village or *visita* of San Antonio had been quick to join the movement.

The loyal element set up a guard at San Carlos to protect Fray Barreda on learning of the threat to him. The friar dispatched San Nicolás's "principal *eniha*," Santiago, to San Luis some time after the crisis erupted with an appeal to the acting lieutenant for aid. Under the pressure from the conspirators, Cutca Martín, the *eniha* at San Carlos and San Nicolás's cacique, Miguel, soon defected. Prior to that, Cacique Miguel had declined a request by Fray Barreda that he accompany him to San Luis with his harquebus. As the loyal element shrank, Cutca Martín panicked most of San Carlos's remaining inhabitants by affixing a shield at the edge of San Carlos's plaza and spreading a report that the Chisca were on their way to kill all those who remained to defend the friar. That news impelled the loyal Chacato to advise the friar to try to save himself by fleeing to Santa Cruz. Seemingly unaware that Cutca Martín had joined the conspirators, the *eniha* was permitted to choose two young men who were to guide the friar, as that responsibility fell normally within the *eniha's* purview. Cutca instructed the guides to kill the friar at the first opportunity. That San Carlos's cacique did not accompany the friar himself or send warriors from the guard force whom he could trust raises a suspicion that Pilate-like, he was washing his hands of the affair.

The young guides made their attempt only a short distance out on the trail from San Carlos after asking the friar for a light for their tobacco. As Barreda bent over to retrieve it from whatever baggage he carried, one of the young men struck him on the head and then in the face with a hatchet, felling him. The stunned and wounded friar was able, nonetheless, to grab the musket that he carried and kill his assailant. The second Indian then fled to bring news of the failure to San Carlos (Cacique Carlos 1675:49–50)

Although the friar had to pass San Nicolás on his way to Santa Cruz, the conspirators do not seem to have made any move to intercept or overtake the friar despite the short lead that he must have had. Diocsale himself, on arriving at the house of San Carlos's cacique not long afterward to inquire of the chief's wife whether news had arrived as yet of the friar's death, on being told that the friar had killed the Indian, allegedly contented himself with an idle boast. He remarked that, if he had not been late and if he had made the attempt as he was supposed to have done, the friar would not have escaped and he would have split the friar's skull like a pumpkin with his first blow (Cacique Carlos 1675:49–50; Elena, wife of Carlos 1675:50).

The Spanish Response

On receiving Fray Barreda's appeal for aid, acting deputy governor Péres immediately dispatched ensign Antonio Herrera with five soldiers and nine Apalachee drawn from San Luis and Escambé to supplement the protection the Chacato were providing until the regular deputy governor should return to determine what was most appropriate. He was not able to send more Indian warriors at that moment because of the pressure of farm work resulting from the rains having been late. He noted that the second hoeing had not yet been completed in some fields. Three hoeings was the normal routine. But word from Fray Juan Ocon at Sauocola that Fray Barreda's Chacato guard had shrunk to 20 men moved Péres to dispatch 24 archers "who were to catch up with the soldiers." Word of Barreda's arrival at Sauocola that same day led Péres to dispatch 11 gunmen with orders to Herrera to bring the two friars to San Luis with all the forces he had sent (Barrera 1675:40; Herrera 1675:40–41; Péres 1675a, 1675b:37–40).

In response to news of those developments, Governor Pablo de Hita Salazar sent Pedro de Florencia to Apalachee in mid-August 1675 with a few soldiers and the munitions he could spare to assist his brother Juan Fernández who had already returned. They were to study the problem together to find the most appropriate solution (Hita Salazar 1675b, 1675c:41–43). But even before Juan Fernández had reassumed his post, the friar at San Luis, Juan de Paiva, convinced Péres to offer the Chacato who had fled to Tawasa that if they returned to their settlements, the lives of all those involved in the tumult would be spared. At once Péres and Paiva dispatched Santiago, the *eniha* of San Nicolás, to offer those terms to the fugitive Chacato at Tawasa. When Santiago stopped at San Carlos, its chief and the 30 or so people who were there endorsed the idea.

Initially, Santiago met reproaches from San Nicolás's cacique and others among the conspiracy's leaders for having carried Fray Barreda's appeal for aid to Apalachee's lieutenant and taunts about the reward they presumed he expected to receive for his loyalty to the Spaniards. Ubabesa told him flatly that neither he nor his relatives would return to their land. Shortly thereafter, a messenger from Paiva brought word that Apalachee's lieutenant had seconded the offer in the name of the king and the governor, allegedly swaying many to consider returning to their land. But when Cutca Martín, *eniha* of San Carlos, arrived from Florida, he dissuaded many of them from accepting the offer. He asked what reason they had to return inasmuch as the soldiers and the Apalachee had destroyed their fields. Cutca had returned to San Carlos to retrieve his wife and children who had not accompanied him on the earlier exodus. As Paiva and the lieutenant arrived at San Carlos while he was there, the lieutenant gave his permission for the departure of his family, urging him to bear witness to the good treatment and pardon Juan Fernández was giving them. As no other source corroborates the destruction of the Chacato's crops, it seems unlikely that they would have been destroyed in the light of the lieutenant's statement to Cutca (Santiago, *eniha* of San Nicolás 1675:52–53). Among the leaders in the conspiracy who fled to Tawasa, the cacique of San Nicolás and its fiscal, Juaquín, along with Diocsale himself accepted the offer and returned.

Questioning and Sentencing of the Leaders

Fernández de Florencia began a formal investigation of the rebellion at San Carlos on October 3, 1675, with an opening address stating the charges against Diocsale, the cacique of San Nicolás, and others alleged to have been involved, and his determination to learn the truth about it and punish the leaders. For the questioning of the witnesses, all of whom were Chacatos, the lieutenant employed a two-man interpreting team. It consisted of Chacato Alonso, who translated the Chacato's testimony into Apalachee, and Diego Salvador, an Apalachee-speaking Timucua from Acuera's Ibiniuti, who translated the Apalachee into Spanish. In an unusual safeguard, the lieutenant (who also was fluent in Apalachee) appointed his brother Pedro and another soldier, ensign Joseph de Salinas, also described as interpreters for the Apalachee tongue, to talk to and listen to Diego Salvador to check on the validity of his rendering of the testimony into Spanish (Hernández de Florencia 1675d:43–44).

Six witnesses testified. They were Juan Ebanjelista, an interpreter for the Chacato tongue; Phelipe, *usinulo* at San Carlos; Nicolás, its fiscal; Cacique Carlos; the cacique's wife, Elena; and Santiago, *eniha* of San Nicolás. They provided details on the involvement of Diocsale; Cutca Martín; Ubabesa; Juaquín, the fiscal; the cacique of San Nicolás; Bacta Diego, who was the father of Ubabesa; and others not named (Juan Ebanjelista; Phelipe, *usinulo*; Nicolás, fiscal; Cacique Carlos; Elena, wife of Carlos; Santiago, *eniha* of San Nicolás 1675:44–50, 52–53).

The lieutenant closed the inquiry at San Carlos on October 12, 1675, with an address to all the people. He explained that, even though those who followed the leaders of the uprising had committed a crime in doing so, those who returned to their settlements would be granted the pardon that Fray Paiva had promised them in the name of the governor and of his majesty. He also ordered the detention of the three leaders present who were involved in the uprising, Diocsale, Cacique Miguel, and Juaquín. Even though their lives were to be spared as had been promised, they were to be brought to Apalachee under arrest. He would receive their confessions there and then impose a corporal punishment on them (Hernández de Florencia 1675d:53).

The lieutenant took the statements of the three detainees and imposed their sentences at San Luis on October 20–21, 1675. When Diocsale was questioned about the testimony pertaining to his involvement in the uprising, he admitted only to having gone along with the idea of expelling Fray Barreda when

Ubabesa broached the idea to him. He denied having had anything to do with ordering the killing of either of the friars, stating that it was the *eniha* Cutca Martín who had ordered that Fray Barreda be killed. He admitted having asked the wife of Cacique Carlos if Fray Barreda had been killed, but maintained that when she replied, no, all that he had said was that, despite his age, if he had put his hand to it, he would have split him open like a pumpkin. He attributed his flight to Tawasa to his fear of the Spaniards and to his wife's crying because of her similar fear (Diocsale 1675:54). Cacique Miguel denied the truth of all the testimony against him except that pertaining to his flight to Tawasa. He attributed his flight to his fear of the Apalachee (Cacique Miguel 1676:54–55). Juaquín (the fiscal) (1675:55–56) denied having suggested the killing of Fray Barreda, or that he had said anything to him about Ubabesa's adulterous affair other than to ask him to overlook it on that occasion, remarking that he could punish him if he did it again. Cacique Miguel attempted to explain away his reproach to the *eniha*, Santiago, by saying that it was prompted by everyone's having said that Santiago meant to deceive the Spaniards and that this belief had motivated his reproach.

Juan Hernández de Florencia (1675e:56) sentenced Diocsale to perpetual exile from his village. He gave Cacique Miguel and Juaquín four years of labor in the royal works, one year without pay, the rest with pay. He also reserved his right to proceed against the other four guilty parties, namely Luis Ubabesa, Bata (sic) Diego, Cutca Martín, and Coquita Luis, who were in Tawasa. All four were former residents of San Carlos. The lieutenant remanded Diocsale to St. Augustine for what seems to have amounted to house arrest. Cacique Miguel's sentence was commuted in less than a year at Fray Paiva's request and the cacique reassumed his leadership of the people of San Nicolás (Hann 1988b:67, 1993:57–58). As will be seen below, Diocsale's exile and commutation of Cacique Miguel's sentence did not bring a quietus to the tumult. A new probe would begin in less than a year involving Diocsale, Cacique Miguel, Cutca Martín, and attacks by Chisca on mission villages' inhabitants.

The second inquiry would identify a few new malefactors as prime movers of the 1675 tumult and omit mention of some of those accused in 1675 of being prime instigators. Diocsale and Cutca Martín continued to be identified in 1676 as having been prime movers in 1675. The new figures so identified were the cacique of San Antonio, an unnamed elderly native then deceased, the heir to the San Carlos chieftainship, and some Chiscas from San Nicolás. Cutca Martín (1676:66–67) accused Cacique Carlos and two of Carlos's sons of being among the prime instigators in 1675, but that aspect of his testimony is suspect as their involvement was not mentioned by any of the others who testified in the 1676 inquiry. In 1676 there was no mention of Ubabesa or Juaquín the fiscal (Cacique

Miguel 1676; Diocsale 1676; Pedro, son of Diocsale 1676; unidentified Chacato Indian 1676:60–65). Ubabesa and Juaquín's lack of rank may account for their exclusion.

The Chacato's Abandonment of Their Homeland

Little is known about the status of the Marianna region Chacato population in the wake of the inquiry held at San Carlos in the first half of October 1675. There is no indication that any friar ever returned to work at the mission sites in that region, or exactly how long the Chacato themselves remained there. San Carlos was still occupied apparently when Chisca attacks inspired by Diocsale began, probably early in 1676. Governor Pablo de Hita Salazar (1677c:69–70), in his mid-1677 re-sentencing of Diocsale, charged him with not having spared even the inhabitants of the place where he was born in his instigation of the Chisca attacks on the Christian native villages. Both San Carlos and San Nicolás had been abandoned by their inhabitants some time before September 1677, a fact reported by the leaders of an Apalachee attack force that passed through there in that month on their way to retaliate against the Chisca (Fernández de Florencia 1678). The Chacato whom the Apalachee had compelled to accompany them as guides were then living within the jurisdiction of the chief of San Luis de Talimali. The Chacato had probably migrated into Apalachee territory to escape the Chisca attacks. Their settlement was half a league west of San Luis. Its location is depicted on the 1683 Alonso Solana map (Hann 1988a:44).

Chisca Attacks

During Diocsale's confinement at St. Augustine, he apparently was permitted visitors. At some point he began sending messages through those visitors to his friends among the Chisca, urging them to attack the Christian native settlements, especially those of Apalachee, and telling his friends that he expected that the Spaniards would execute him. Commencement of those attacks in 1676 is reflected in Fray Paiva's Apalachee Ball Game manuscript. The governor's 1676 inquiry into Diocsale's renewed hostile activity mentioned that some Apalachee were killed during Chisca raids at Ivitachuco, Patale, Bacuqua, Escambé, and Ayubale, and in the territory between Sauocola and the Apalachicola River.

Informants that Juan Fernández de Florencia had in Apalachee attributed the Chisca raids to instigation by Diocsale from his exile. (It should be noted, however, that Yamasee, mistaken for Chisca, were responsible for some of the raids in Apalachee and Timucua, and particularly at Patale. See Hann 1991a:154). By the time the lieutenant heard of Diocsale's machinations, Cacique Miguel had been released at Fray Paiva's request and Cutca Martín had been pardoned after returning from Tawasa. Miguel left for St. Augustine soon thereafter, ostensibly to visit the governor. The lieutenant warned the governor that his informants had told him that Miguel and his party were planning to try to free Diocsale and bring him west to lead the Chisca in a full-scale war against the Christian native provinces. The warning prompted the governor to detain Cacique Miguel and his party and to hold an inquiry into the whole affair at St. Augustine. The lieutenant was to do the same in Apalachee with his informants. It is not known whether the lieutenant did so as no further mention of that inquiry or record of it have been located as yet (Hann 1993:57–58).

The Second Inquiry

The governor's witnesses included Pedro, a Christian native from San Nicolás, who was identified as a son of Diocsale; an unnamed non-Christian native from San Nicolás; Cacique Miguel of San Nicolás; and the San Carlos *eniha*, Cutca Martín. There was a delay in the questioning of the *eniha*. While he was being held in the fort at St. Augustine, he escaped "after having dug out underground under the guardhouse," managing to get outside by way of a bastion at ten o'clock at night. Soldiers sent to search for him eventually found him in the woods (Hann 1993:58; Hita Salazar 1676b:65–66).

The testimony of Diocsale's son Pedro proved to be the most damning in linking his father to the inciting of the 1676 Chisca attacks against the Christian native provinces. Pedro was a credible witness, having been identified by others as one who communicated with the Chisca, understood their language, and had visited the new Chisca settlement west of his Chacato homeland. He cleared Cacique Miguel of the charge that he had come to St. Augustine to carry off Diocsale so that the Chisca and Chacato might make war jointly on the Apalachee and Timucua, testifying that he was present when Miguel visited his father and that his father did not give Miguel any message for the Chisca or Chacato. Pedro blamed his father and Cutca Martín for the 1676 troubles, stating that he was not aware that Miguel was an accomplice as had been rumored. He asserted further that his father had met with Chisca who visited St. Augustine and sent word to the Chisca caciques to make war on the Christians because he was certain that the Spaniards were holding him there with the intention of killing him and that his father had said the same to him. Pedro identified the prime movers of the 1675 uprising as his father, Cutca Martín, the cacique of San Antonio, and an Indian who had died since then. He also revealed that days before the 1675 uprising Diocsale had spoken with the Chisca about going to war against the Christians and that Cutca had participated in those discussions (Pedro, son of Diocsale 1676:60–62).

The unnamed Chacato witness stated that he was living in the "village of Sabocola of the Apalachocolos nation" when he heard about the 1675 uprising. He identified its motivators as Diocsale, the cacique of San Antonio, the *eniha* "Ocuta" Martín, an old man then deceased, the heir to the chieftainship of the village of San Carlos, and Chiscas from San Nicolás. He was questioned only about the movement of 1675 (unidentified Chacato Indian 1676:62–63).

Cacique Miguel's subsequent behavior suggests that there was validity to the charges against him that Apalachee's deputy- governor had reported, but none of the governor's witnesses implicated him. Miguel himself claimed that he had come to St. Augustine only to see the city and visit the governor. That claim appears specious in the light of his recent stint there in the royal works. Either he had kept his intentions to himself or there was a conspiracy of silence among the other witnesses to protect him. Miguel testified that he knew for certain that Chisca were responsible for the killings that had occurred in Apalachee. He reported having heard that the Chisca were fortifying their new village with the intention of making war on Christian villages and on other enemies (Cacique Miguel 1676:63–64).

Cutca (rendered as Cutta on this occasion) Martín identified Cacique Carlos, two of Carlos's sons, and the *eniha* of San Carlos in 1676 as having been prime movers in the 1675 revolt along with Diocsale and the cacique of San Antonio. His charge against the chief was probably an exaggeration, but it adds probability to circumstantial evidence that suggests that Carlos may have been aware of the threat Fray Barreda faced from his guides. Cutca Martín (1676:66–68) testified that Diocsale wanted to leave St. Augustine with Cacique Miguel's party and that Diocsale gave him a message for the Chisca chiefs asking them to make war on the Christians.

Diocsale (1676:64–65) initially denied that he had given any order to the Chiscas to make war on the Christians and insisted that his son Pedro and Cutca were lying when they made their charges against him. But under cross-examination he finally admitted his guilt. When questioned at the beginning of his testimony about his role in 1675 in the attempt on the friar's life, he replied without equivocation that he had intended to kill the friar because of the friar's removal of three of his wives. He also implicated the cacique of San Antonio and an *eniha* as his co-conspirators in 1675. The *eniha* doubtless was Cutca Martín.

For Diocsale's part in the mischief that occurred in 1676, the governor sentenced him to perpetual exile in Mexico and remanded him to the custody of the archbishop-viceroy of New Spain. The governor sentenced Cutca Martín to six months of service on the construction of the stone castillo that was then underway. Cacique Miguel and the remainder of his party, who had been detained for questioning, were set free because of the lack of any credible evidence against them (Hita Salazar 1677a, 1677b, 1677c:68–70).

After Cacique Miguel returned westward to reassume his chieftainship, he took off with six or seven of his tribesmen, saying he was going to gather together his people of San Nicolás to bring them back, presumably to Apalachee. Instead, by his mediation, some Chacato made peace with the Chisca with the intention of joining them in harassing the Christian provinces. Governor Pablo de Hita Salazar (1677d) accused Miguel also of soliciting Pansacola participation in those attacks even though the Pansacola had been at peace with, and had maintained friendship with, the Spaniards. This suggests that the Apalachee lieutenant's informants' reports about the hostile intent of Miguel's party's visit to St. Augustine had probably been reliable, and that Miguel had concealed his plans skillfully. It also shows that the 1677 Apalachee expedition against the Chisca was not as entirely spontaneous on the part of the natives as a reading of the native leaders' report on it in isolation might lead one to conclude. The native leaders of San Luis and Escambé, who provided almost all the warriors for that strike force, received encouragement, at the very least, from Apalachee's lieutenant, if not outright instigation from the governor. Repercussions from the expedition would be felt at least five years later in the form of a Pansacola attack in 1683 on the Sauocola mission on the Apalachicola River (Márquez Cabrera 1683). A few Sauocola and their Chief Balthasar had joined the expedition as it passed through their village and stopped there to rest and re-supply. The Pansacola became involved because some of them along with some Chacato were residents of the Chisca village at the time the Apalachee struck (Fernández de Florencia 1678).

Documentation generated by the troubles of the 1674–1676 period provides our only significant glimpse at the daily life of the Chacato, their political leadership, customs, linguistic affiliation, and other aspects of their culture. What it can tell us is very limited in most respects.

Chacato Leadership

On the whole, the titles used to identify Chacato leaders duplicate those used for the Apalachee, namely, cacique principal, cacique, *eniha principal*, *eniha*, *usinulo*, and *chacal* or *fiscal*. The chiefly titles of *mico* and *holahta* do not appear in this documentation. Omission of *holahta* is not meaningful. Spaniards rarely employed *holahta* for the Apalachee and Timucua, preferring the term cacique, which they had become habituated to in the Caribbean. Our knowledge of

Apalachee use of *holahta* comes mainly from literate chiefs who used it when signing their name. Among the Chacato, San Carlos's chief was the only one referred to as *cacique principal*. *Tascaia*, the term for warrior, is the same as the one for Apalachee. But allusions to Diocsale as a "great warrior" together with the following that he had suggests the Creek institution of the *Tustunnuggee thlucco* described by Benjamin Hawkins (1982:72) rather than anything known from the Apalachee.

Evidence about chiefly succession among the Chacato is very limited and somewhat equivocal. There is only one reference that identifies a chief's nephew as his heir, thereby indicating a matrilineal line of succession similar to that among the neighboring Apalachee. But other documentation suggests that matrilineality was not sacrosanct or even that patrilineality may have been more common in practice. Cacique Carlos's own father had been the village's chief. Carlos's father was then succeeded by Diocsale whom Carlos's father had raised in his household and to whom he had given the status of adoptive son. It is worthy of note that Diocsale (1676:64–65) identified himself in his testimony as a Chacato rather than as a Chisca, the tribe of his mother (Cacique Carlos 1675:49–50). Repeated allusions to Diocsale being a feared warrior and as having the troublesome Chisca at his command may have been a consideration in his elevation to the chieftainship. There are references to Diocsale "protecting" the Chacato from greater harassment than what they were forced to endure from the Chisca. Generational considerations may also have been a factor in Diocsale's elevation and stepping down, as Cacique Carlos was 20 years or so younger than Diocsale who was about 80 in 1675 (Ebanjelista 1675:44–46; Fernández de Florencia 1675e:54). It is worthy of note that Diocsale may have adopted Carlos as his son at some point before stepping down in his favor. San Carlos's *eniha* Cutca Martín (1676:66) referred to Carlos as a son of Diocsale. That might, of course, simply reflect the Indians' looser use of terms such as "son" than is usual among Europeans.

Linguistic Affiliations

Documentary evidence suggests that with the exception of the Chisca, all the peoples living between Apalachee and Pensacola Bay at the beginning of the last quarter of the seventeenth century within the limits of present day Florida were closely related linguistically or even spoke the same language. Fray Rodrigo de Barreda (Leonard 1939:278–279) spoke of questioning "Chief Chine and the rest of" the Chacato Indians. As we have seen, Chine, Amacano, and Pacara all spoke the same language.

If Swanton's (1922:95, 119, 1946:88, 107, 119, 208) seeming guesses about the linguistic identity of those peoples have any validity, this linguistic unity may have extended northward to include the Apalachicoli inhabitants of the Chattahoochee Valley as well as other Hitchiti-speaking peoples living east of them along the Flint, Ocmulgee, Oconee, and Altamaha rivers. He identified the Chine as a band of Chatot, meaning Chacato, but he offered no evidence for that assertion. Swanton does not seem to have been aware of the Spanish identification of the Chine, Amacano, and Pacara as linguistic brothers. He equated the Amacano with the Yamasee and the Pacara or Caparaz with de Soto's Capacheque, based apparently on nothing more than their names' rough resemblances and without suggesting that the Chacato and Chine were closet Yamasee as well. When one considers the geographic propinquity of all those peoples to one another, and their Fort Walton and Lamar cultural affiliation that conclusion assumes a certain reasonableness, even though it is not obvious that Swanton reached such a conclusion explicitly.

However, Spanish authorities' use of both Apalachee and Chacato interpreters during the inquiries into the Chacato troubles indicates that the two native peoples' languages were distinct to some degree at least. During the 1675 inquiry, Chacato interpreter, Chacta Alonso, translated from Apalachee to Chacato and vice-versa. Diego Salvador, who had been royal interpreter in Apalachee for at least 20 years, handled Apalachee to Spanish and vice-versa. Interestingly, he was Timucua by birth, an Acueran from Ibiniuti's village of Moscoso, who had grown up in Apalachee (Hann 1996b:206). His Moscoso origin suggests the possibility of de Soto-era overtones, especially in view of the rank of sergeant-major that he held. To ensure that Salvador transmitted the questions and answers faithfully, Pedro de Florencia, an Apalachee-speaking Spaniard, monitored the process, having been dispatched by the governor when he learned of the troubles because of Salvador's experience in Apalachee and language capabilities. His monitoring of the inquiry hardly seems to have been needed. Pedro's brother, the deputy governor Juan Fernández, who was directing the inquiry, also was conversant with that tongue. Their father, Claudio, was Apalachee's first deputy governor, who died at the hands of the Apalachee in 1647 (Hann and McEwan 1998:36).

Apalachee and Chacato may have been related closely enough, however, to permit a degree of mutual understanding of each other's languages without an interpreter. During the 1677 expedition against the Chisca, the Apalachee were sufficiently conversant with the speech of their Chacato guides to understand the discontented Chacato's talk among themselves of deserting the expedition (Fernández de Florencia 1675b, 1678). The incident, of course, might also indicate merely that these western Apalachee had had sufficient contact with the Chacato to have become familiar with their tongue.

For the governor's 1676 inquiry held in St. Augustine, he chose a Spanish soldier named Marcos Delgado, who understood the Apalachee language, and an Apalachee named Juan Alonso, as interpreters (Hita Salazar 1676a:59–60). During the 1677 visitation of Apalachee there was no mention of the Chine or Chacato settlements. At the Tama village, Diego Salvador served unassisted as the interpreter. But at the Tocobaga place he was joined by an interpreter for the Tocobaga's tongue. During the 1694 visitation, Hubabaq Gaspar, interpreter for the Apalachee, performed the same function at the Chine village and at that of the Tama (J. Florencia 1694:176, 177). But to speak with the Chacato who were lodged at the San Cosme and San Damián de Escabí mission at the time of the 1694 visitation, a special interpreter for their language was provided (J. Florencia 1694:163). The Chacato's lack of linguistic adaptation can be attributed to their having been living in isolation from the Apalachee in a mission on the Apalachicola River until earlier that year when the Sauocola and others had attacked the Chacato mission. That community also probably included some of the Chacato who had gone into exile in 1675 at Tawasa or beyond. Some of them had returned and resubmitted to Spanish rule during the latter half of the 1680s.

Settlement Pattern

The documentation for the Chacato tells us little else about their daily life, games, architecture, or settlement pattern. References to the abandoned village sites in the Marianna region in the report on the 1677 expedition against the Chisca suggest vaguely that the villages were compact rather than spread out like the Apalachee settlements. Both San Carlos and San Nicolás had a church and convent. The convent at San Carlos was mentioned in terms that suggest that it may have been a two-story structure similar to that of the later Creek chiefs' summer house. The granary at San Carlos was definitely an elevated structure that was large enough and close enough to the convent to function as the guard post, housing the warriors who were protecting Fray Barreda in 1675 when his life was threatened. Most striking, perhaps, is the absence of any mention of a council house in the records of the inquiry that Fernández de Florencia (1675b:43–56) held at San Carlos in 1675, coupled with mention of the council house at San Luis when the final phase of the inquiry was transferred there. When the lieutenant spoke to the assembled people of the village, the "*plasa*" was identified as the scene of that function. On hearing of that contrast, Gary Shapiro suggested that it might indicate that the Chacato's plaza was the equivalent of the Creeks' square ground.

Epidemics

Despite the known impact of epidemics on Florida's native peoples from Apalachee eastward, particularly during the decade that began in 1649, the Chacato leadership in 1675 contained a surprising number of individuals of mature age whose presence suggests that the Chacato's relative isolation from Spaniards until then protected them to a degree. Diocsale was eighty plus. Cacique Carlos was 60, Juaquín the chacal was 55, Nicolás, San Carlos's fiscal, and San Nicolás's *eniha*, Santiago, were 45. The *usinulo* Felipe was 40. San Nicolás's Cacique Miguel, at 30, was the youngest whose age was recorded. Bacta Diego, father of Ubabesa, was fit enough to carry some of the deerskins he collected to Tawasa as a present, as was a brother of Juaquín (Fernández de Florencia 1675b:43–56).

The Exile Communities

Little is known about the Chacato in the wake of their abandonment of their Marianna area homeland, and particularly about the timing of the various moves that they made in the wake of the events of 1675 and 1676. The exodus to Tawasa territory occurred at the time of the attempt on the life of Fray Barreda. That exodus probably included all the people of San Antonio, most of those from San Nicolás, and an undetermined number from San Carlos. Some of the fugitives may have gone westward at that time to seek refuge with the Pansacola. Prior to the 1677 expedition, a group of Pansacola and Chacato in west Florida opened a trail inland from the coast so that they might join up with Chisca who had just established a settlement on the Choctawhatchee. Those Chisca had been living in a settlement that was described by Cutca Martín (1676:66) as "close to the river of Sabacola" apparently on harmonious terms with the Spaniards. Francisco Milán Tapia (1693:288) identified the river of Sauocola as the eastern mouth of the Apalachicola River in 1693, which was where an earlier Spanish map showed that Chisca village to have been located. The Chisca moved to far western Florida in the hope of being able to respond with greater impunity to Diocsale's appeal to them for raids against the settlements of Indians allied to the Spaniards. An undetermined number of the fugitives to Tawasa had responded favorably to Fray Juan de Paiva's offer by the end of September 1675 of a relative amnesty and no executions even for the ringleaders. The *eniha* of San Nicolás had been Paiva's envoy. Diocsale himself, Cacique Miguel, and Juaquín the *chacal* were among those who returned (Fernández de Florencia 1675d:53; Hita Salazar 1675d:51).

It is likely that the Chacato loyal to the Spaniards moved to a village site in Apalachee on lands about one league west of San Luis. They were at least under the direction of San Luis's chief some time in 1676, after the Chisca began their raids, if they had not made the move earlier. It is not known how long the Chacato remained at the location shown on The Alonso Solana map of 1683 as the mission of San Carlos, which was still in existence at the site (Hann 1988a:44, 68). In 1681, San Carlos had a population of 216, of whom 200 were Christians, which included 63 Christian married couples. All but seven of 55 single men were Christians, as were all but nine out of 35 single women (Worth 1998:II, 136). It is probable that the above population listing did not include the mission's children.

The Chacato probably abandoned their site in Apalachee soon after the drafting of the 1683 map. Domingo de Leturiondo (1985b), sent by the governor late in the fall of 1685 to conduct a visitation of Apalachee and Timucua, noted that there were then two places "that are on the River of Apalachicoli, Chacatos and Sauocolas, which are fourteen leagues distant from this province." He warned the governor that pursuit of his policy of hostile action against the Apalachicoli and Coweta would put those two new settlements in danger of obliteration. The Chacato mission probably was moved to that location to provide support for the Sauocola, who had decided to move downriver once more so that they might receive a friar because the Caueta chief was opposed to having friars work within the territory under his jurisdiction (Hann 1996a:72–73). Documents associated with the Marcos Delgado expedition of 1686 again show the presence of both the Chacato and the Sauocola on the Upper Apalachicola River at that time (Boyd 1937:14–15).

Prior to Delgado's departure, Tawasa's chief had visited Apalachee bringing 24 Christian Chacato (men and women) who had been living in his territory, apparently since 1675. Others were still living there (Matheos 1686d). It is possible that Delgado's visit to Tawasa led to the return of additional fugitive Chacato. There appears to have been trouble in that region. Delgado reported hearing of a Christian Chacato named Clemente, who was killed in a raid by the Movila. He identified the village of Ogchay (Okchai) in Tiquepache Province just beyond the province of Tawasa as inhabited by Chacato. But he gave no indication that they were Christian or recent immigrants to that region (Boyd 1937:15, 25).

Resurrection of San Nicolás

Such an influx might account for the reappearance of a mission named San Nicolás de los Chacatos which had 70 families, or about 350 individuals. It is possible that the Sauocola mission also housed some Chacato as its name was given in 1689 as San Carlos de Çabacola. It held 30 families or about 150 individuals (Ebelino de Compostela 1689). In a 1690 listing of the convents that had friars, the latter village's name was given, however, as Çavacola Chuba or Big Savacola. As the Chacato mission was mentioned among the many villages that did not have a friar at that time, it is probable that one of Sauocola's two friars served the Chacato mission (Luna 1690).

The Sauocola mission appears to have vanished prior to mid-1693. Journals recording a newly arrived governor's overland trek from San Luis to Pensacola Bay in mid-1693 made no mention of the Sauocola mission. In mentioning the crossing of the river at the Chacato village, Governor Laureano de Torres y Ayala (1693b:230) referred to the Chacato village as "the most outlying mission post and curacy of his Majesty in this region." Fray Barreda (1693:267) also mentioned only the Chacato mission, placing it on the river's west bank a little over nine leagues beyond the Ilcombe (Escambé) mission located then a league west of the Ochlockonee River. The parting with the Sauocola apparently had not been a friendly one. In 1694 Sauocola participated in the attack on the Chacato mission that produced the refugees whom the visitor, Joaquín de Florencia (1694:187) encountered at Escambé in December of 1694.

The Chacato Contract

At that meeting, the Chacato asked formally for permission to reoccupy the site near San Luis where they had lived earlier. To that end, a contract was drawn up between the chief of San Luis and the Chacato refugees spelling out the Chacatos' rights and establishing restrictions on their hunting and gathering. As this is the only such contract known to have survived, it is not clear whether such contracts were traditional among the natives or something Spaniards had introduced after the first establishment of the Chacato village there to lessen conflicts.

Under this contract the Chacato were to hunt for bear only in conjunction with the Apalachee and only on occasions when the Apalachee went out on such hunts. All the bearskins were to be given to San Luis's chief. The Chacato were to receive only the meat from the breast, stomach, and back of bears that they killed. But they were to be allotted enough meat from the better cuts to enable them to provide their priest with some and meet other such obligations. They were to give the skins of any panthers that they killed to San Luis's chief. Hunting of an unidentified white bird was prohibited. If they killed one, they were to present it at the San Luis council house and pay compensation. They were to harvest grapes and nuts only in unison with the Apalachee but they could keep all that they themselves gathered on such occasions. The hunting of deer, other animals, and birds, as well as the gathering of other fruits, was "free and unencumbered." They were free to cultivate the lands as their own (J. de Florencia 1694:187–188). Before moving to that site, the Chacato refugees planned to make a trip to some unidentified place.

Fifty Sauocola, Apalachicoli, and Tiquepache were responsible for the 1694 attack. It was but one incident in the warfare that followed Spanish placement of a fort garrisoned by Spanish soldiers and Apalachee warriors in Apalachicoli territory in 1689 to halt those peoples' trade with the British. In 1693, Governor Torres y Ayala (1693a:218–225) noted that Apalachicoli "has had wars with all the Indians of San Luis de Apalache for two years now," observing that "though they are still engaged in hostilities, it is not with the same intensity as before." In the 1694 attack, the fifty-man assault force killed five of the Chacato and carried off 42 to sell to the Carolinians as slaves (Torres y Ayala 1695b).

Expedition to Pensacola Bay

During Governor Torres y Ayala's 1693 expedition to Pensacola Bay he employed five Chacato and five Apalachee to care for the 100 or so horses he had acquired in Apalachee (Torres y Ayala 1693b:238). The Chacato's familiarity with horses is reflected in the 1694 visitation record for Escambé. A Chacato named Chuguta Mariana complained that Escambé's "cacique don Vicente owed him three riding horses that he had sold to him" for which he had not received payment (J. de Florencia 1694:163–164).

When the Torres y Ayala expedition arrived in Pensacola Bay, two small encampments of Chacato constituted the only Native Americans whom it encountered there. The larger one held five men, six women, and four children, who were Christians. The second one held only one couple and three children (Torres y Ayala 1693b:238, 241). Governor Torres y Ayala (1693a:221, 1693b:259) mentioned finding the remains of only one Pansacola village. The Indians who accompanied him told him that they had been all but wiped out by continuous warfare with the Movilas. Fray Barreda (1693:280), however, reported two abandoned Pansacola Indian villages at which there was a vast number of oyster shells. His Chacato informers attributed their disappearance to wars with the Apalachicoli as well as the Movila. The whereabouts of the few survivors was unknown.

The Last Days in Apalachee

There is no documentation that indicates whether the Chacato reoccupied the site near San Luis. However, they remained in or near Apalachee until early in 1704 apparently, as there is occasional mention of them down through the beginning of the destruction of the Apalachee missions. For the construction of the Spanish settlement on Pensacola Bay in 1698, Chacato as well as Apalachee were recruited to assist with the cutting of lumber and other such projects. In view of their acquaintance with west Florida's terrain, some also probably participated in the cattle drives from Apalachee that provided much of the meat for the new settlement in its early days. Some Chacato, doubtless, were among the native workers known to have succumbed to an epidemic introduced in 1702 by people newly arrived from Veracruz.

During the winter of 1698–1699, 40 Chacato from the community in or near Apalachee were responsible for the treacherous murder of a number of peaceful Indians from the province of Tasquique who were killed while on their way to San Luis to trade. The Chacato were out on a buffalo hunt with a disreputable Spaniard who had been exiled to Apalachee from St. Augustine. The hunters killed 16 out of the 24 Tasquique traders, attacking them as they slept and seizing their trade goods (Hinachuba 1699). Possibly the Chacato considered that attack as justified revenge for the assault on their Apalachicola River village four years earlier.

Christian Chacato were mentioned as being anxious in mid-1702 to join 800 Apalachee who were clamoring for permission to attack the Apalachicoli in revenge for the latter's treacherous murder of three Apalachee traders in their midst and for the attack on Timucua's Santa Fé mission earlier that year (Zúñiga y Zerda 1702a:36–38). The Chacato who took part in that expedition in early October are likely to have suffered serious losses. Only about 300 straggled back out of an 800-man force composed of Apalachee, Chacato, and Timucua (Romo de Urisa 1702; Zúñiga y Zerda 1702b). They walked into an ambush on the Flint River set up by an Apalachicoli force that had been on its way to attack Apalachee and which had been alerted to the coming Apalachee attack by dissident elements among the Apalachee. The Chacato killed two of the enemy. In retaliation for that loss, the Apalachicoli burned a Timucua and some Apalachee whom they captured.

In this era, conceivably, some Chacato were still hostile to the Christian natives. The Spanish commander of the routed force from Apalachee, Francisco Romo de Urisa (1702), reported that, in all the attacks on the Christian provinces, not one Yamasee had been involved, "only Chiscas, Chichimecos, Apalachicolos, Chatas, and Uchizes." In Mark F. Boyd's (1953:470–472) translation of this document he rendered "Chatas" as Chacatos. That rendering is conceivable but it does not seem to be appropriate here. Elsewhere in the document, Romo de Urisa used the conventional spelling, "Chacatos," to designate that people. By using "Chatas" here, I believe Romo intended its more usual meaning of "Choctaw." Boyd also went astray here in transforming "Uchizes" to "Yuchis."

One of Romo de Urisa's other uses of the name "Chacata" in this document is his recounting of the often-told tale of a Chacato woman from Apalachee, who had been living in Achito with her Sauocola mate for about a year. Shortly before the Christian Indians' rout on the Flint, she had witnessed a meeting of leaders from various Apalachicoli towns in which the Apalachicoli discussed a plan to attack St. Augustine and the Christian provinces in conjunction with the British. As soon as she was able to escape from Achito, she hastened to Apalachee to warn the Spanish authorities. On the way she passed through the scene of the recent battle, availing herself of some of the food the defeated force had left behind (Solana 1702:468–470).

The Chacato were among the people of seven missions in Apalachee who survived and who remained in Spanish territory when Colonel James Moore withdrew from the province in January 1704. But the Chacato, Tawasa, and some Apalachee appear to have set out overland for Pansacola not very long thereafter (Junta de Guerra 1705).

After Moore had captured Apalachee's wounded deputy-governor and a number of soldiers in an encounter in the wake of his capture of the Ayubale mission's defenders, the Carolinian sent an offer to the fort at San Luis. He wanted to exchange the deputy-governor and a few of the soldiers for Apalachee's Chacato population. That ransom offer doubtless was made by Moore to please his native allies so that they might avenge the Chacato's killing of the Tasquique traders five years earlier. The fort's interim commander rejected the offer, even though a brother-in-law was among Moore's soldier-prisoners. He informed Moore that such a trade was out of the question because the Chacato were subjects of the king. After the commander refused a monetary ransom, Moore again demanded the handing over of the Chacato, threatening war without quarter if his terms were not accepted by 9:00 the following morning (Córcoles y Martínez 1709).

Migration to Pensacola and Mobile

Most of the surviving Chacato who migrated to Pensacola did not remain there very long. Like the Apalachee from San Luis and Escambé, they continued on to Mobile to live with the French. Writing 20 years after the event, Bienville placed the number of immigrant Chacato at about 250, one-half the number of immigrant Apalachee. In his report to Pontchartrain soon after they had begun to arrive, he placed the Apalachee immigrants at 400 and the Chacato at about half that number (Bienville 1704:27, 1726:535–536). Bienville noted on various occasions that the Chacato came from St. Josephs Bay or from near Pensacola rather than from Apalachee. The Chacato were assigned lands at the mouth of the river at a site then called Oigonets, which the French would take for themselves in 1711 when they moved the town of Mobile to its present site (Higginbotham 1977:192–193). The Chacato were then moved farther down the bay to Dog River. Their new site was one-quarter of a league up that river (Higginbotham 1977:459). By 1725 the original 250 people had been reduced to 40 (Bienville 1726:526–527, 535–536; Higginbotham 1977:193–194).

There is little mention of the Chacato in the French records. The French valued them as warriors and viewed them as good Catholics. They were mentioned as speaking a dialect distinct from Apalachee, but their speech, like that of the Apalachee, was heavily larded with Spanish (Bienville 1726:535; Higginbotham 1977:310, 313). There was mention of one of them in a Mobile newspaper as late as the early 1850s (Higginbotham, personal communication).

Recently archaeologists have explored areas along Dog River occupied by the emigré Chacato from 1711 on. Gregory A. Waselkov and Bonnie L. Gums (2000:184) suggested that the limited archaeological evidence generated by their research there indicates that the Chacato "lived in widely settled households, all part of a single village but dispersed throughout the entire lower Dog River drainage" rather than in a compact settlement on one or both banks as is suggested by colonial-era maps.

Some Chacato migrants may have lived among the Apalachee in the Mobile area or, at least, provided pottery to them. Ann S. Cordell in her study, *Continuity and Change in Apalachee Pottery Manufacture,* found that there was considerable similarity between the pottery of the Apalachee at Mobile and that which they had made at San Luis de Talimali. But to explain an absence of grog temper in sand and grit-tempered vessels, Cordell suggested that the most likely explanation is that such vessels were made by Chacato refugees (Cordell 2001:29–30).

3

The Chisca and Chichimeco-Westo

First Contacts

The Chisca were likely sixteenth-century immigrants to Florida proper rather than prehistoric aboriginal inhabitants. Their name first appeared in the de Soto accounts as that of a people living in the southern Appalachians. It recurred a generation or so later in connection with the Juan Pardo expeditions into the same country where de Soto learned of the Chisca. The name also appeared during an inquiry held in St. Augustine to gather information about the lands and natives of the Tama region and the hinterland farther north visited by Pardo and his lieutenant, Hernando Moyano. By the sixteenth century's closing years, a people bearing the name Chisca had appeared in western Florida. The continuity of the Spaniards' use of that name and other circumstances suggest that Florida's Chisca were related, at least, to those encountered earlier farther north.

Two of de Soto's chroniclers placed the province of the Chisca to the north of Coste. Coste is believed to have been on Bussell Island, in the mouth of the Little Tennessee River (Hudson 1997:205). Rangel noted that at Coste, de Soto was told of a province called Chisca "which was rumored to have great wealth." The Fidalgo observed that de Soto had asked Coste's chief "if he knew of any rich land." In reply the chief identified Chisca as a place that had a foundry for copper and another finer but softer metal of the same color. The Inca also mentioned the name Chisca but obviously confused it with Quizquiz, which lay farther west in the vicinity of Memphis (Hudson 1997:280–282; Clayton, Knight, and Moore 1993:I, 89, 284, II, 385 and note 26).

Early in 1567 Juan Pardo's lieutenant Moyano attacked a Chisca town, killing many of its people and burning their houses. Charles Hudson (1990:27) speculated that the Chisca's territory "appears to have been in and to the other side of the mountains north of Joara, including the area along the upper course of the Nolichuky River," while admitting that its location is unknown because Moyano left no description of the route he and his men "traveled to this first Chisca town." Francisco Martínez (1566:317–321), who wrote the account that Hudson used, claimed that fifteen Spanish soldiers killed more than one thousand of Chief Chisca's Indians in that engagement and burned fifty huts.

During the inquiry held in St. Augustine in 1600, a Hispanicized Indian woman named Teresa Martín, whom Moyano had brought out from the Joara hinterland when she was a very young girl, described the Chisca in mythic terms as Indians who "go about clothed and are very white, ruddy, and blue-eyed, after the fashion of the Flemish, because the hair that they have is like a little bit of gold." Teresa Martín (1600) described the Chisca as the source of gold *chaguales* her people used in their dances and little gold pipes they wore. She placed the home of the Chisca on a mountain three or four days journey from her village. Luisa Menéndez (1600), whom Moyano had brought out as a girl, repeated the tale of gold *chaguales* her people had acquired through trade with people "from some mountains that they called of Chisca." That land's Indians were "very white and blue-eyed and red-haired." She gave the name of her village as Manaytique. But her husband, Juan de Ribas (1600), rendered the name as Guanaytique. He had been sent with Pardo into the hinterland as a young man of 17 or 18 and was left there with one of the chiefs to learn the languages so he might serve as an interpreter. Florida Spaniards' early association of this people with tales of wealth and gold doubtless etched their name deeply in their minds.

First Chisca in Florida

The birth of the Chacato Juan de Diocsale to a Chisca mother in the Marianna region by 1595 provides the first evidence of a Chisca presence within Florida's modern boundaries. Worth (1998:II, 19) dates their first recorded presence in quantity to the governorship of Juan de Salinas (1618–1624). A soldier testified in 1635 that, on orders from Salinas, he had gone more than 60 leagues into the interior to punish the Chisca and Chichimeco Indians. The soldier described them as ferocious people who were robbing and killing Christian Indians of Timucua and Apalachee.

The soldier's use of the distinct Chisca name for one group of those raiders, rather than the generic catch-all term Chichimeco, suggests that the Chisca were (or at least were believed to be) a known quantity linked to the sixteenth-century possessors of that name from Tennessee's Appalachian Mountains. It also raises an intriguing question about the identity of the people masked under this early use of the term Chichimeco for Florida of the 1620s. Chichimeco is a name derived from Nahuatl that Spaniards in Mexico applied to the warlike nomads of northern Mexico's interior.

People Spaniards referred to as Chichimeco in the early 1660s have been convincingly identified as the Westo or Ricahecrians of English sources (Bowne 2005:31–35, 54–55; Worth 1995:17, 27). But identification of the Spaniards' Chichimeco of the 1659–1662 period and thereafter as the Westo or Ricahecrians does not by itself resolve the problem created by allusions to Chichimeco attacks on Spanish Florida mission territories in the 1640s and 1620s (see Hann 1996b:238–239; Worth 1998:II, 19). Attempts to identify the people referred to earlier as Chichimeco as actually being Chisca fly in the face of Spaniards' use of both names together in referring to the incidents of the 1618–1624 period. They clearly viewed them as distinct peoples and considered the Chisca a known quantity. In 1662, Spaniards' requested Chisca interpreters in order to question four Chichimeco whom they had captured in Apalachicoli territory. This suggests that by then at least, if not earlier, Spaniards had some knowledge of the Chichimeco-Westo's tribal identity and probably that they were related to or had prior acquaintance with the people whom they called Chichimeco in the 1620s.

The speculation that the Ricahecrians of the mid-1650s Virginia represent a branch of the Erie provides a potential explanation that links the Spaniards' Chichimecos of the 1620s to the Ricahecrians of the 1650s. The name Ricahokene appears on Albemarle Sound in John White's 1585 map of Virginia (Cumming 1998:Plate 12) as one of four Weapemeoc villages on that sound's north side. It is the southernmost of two villages on the eastern side of an inlet. Significantly, the name Ricahokene does not appear in subsequent depictions of the Weapmeoc's territory. William Green (1998:3–6) provides an explanation for their disappearance, noting that John Smith in 1608 placed their "town of 'Righkahauck' on the Chichahominy River in Virginia." Green (1998:10–12) observed further that by 1621 Smith placed them on the James River under the command of Itoyatin, brother and successor of Powhatan. Green suggests that after Powhatan's uprising was quelled "some of the Rickohockans may have fled over the mountains where they are shown on subsequent maps" such as the one by Lederer Cummings (1998:Plate 36). Green attributes this early Erie presence in the south to this band of Erie's having acted "as middlemen, obtaining shell from Virginia and transporting it back" to their northern homeland in Huron territory. Their mobility as traders provides a possible explanation as well for their contacts with the Chisca that enabled some of the Chisca to learn their language. The Iroquois's 1656 defeat of the Erie probably brought another major influx of Erie (known in the north as Riquehronnon or variants thereof) into Virginia, where they already had fellow tribesmen. The Rickohockans had good reason to leave Virginia in 1656 after having killed the Pamunkey's king Totopotomoy, an ally of the English (McCartney 1989:175). Green has identified the Westo as having been a band of Erie. A more recent work, *The Westo Indians: Slave Traders of the Early Colonial South*, by Eric E. Bowne (2005:42, 44, 50–53, 69–70), has much more convincingly identified the post-1656 Spanish Florida references to Chichimecos as definitely being bands of Erie. Bowne also verified the validity of Spanish claims that these post-1650s Chichimecos were "man-eaters." But it was merely a ritual cannibalism linked to those northern Iroquoian speakers' mourning-war tradition. As Bowne (2005:26, 69–70) noted, such "alien practices likely added to the group's reputation as formidable warriors," while their "ready access to firearms" gave them "a military superiority over bow-and-arrow Indians" in the South.

Chisca in Timucua

Chisca next appeared in a 1639 letter by a governor who referred to them as "a quantity of Indians called Ysicas or Chiscas, a warlike people who pride themselves on that, who roam freely through these provinces." He viewed them as potentially valuable allies who might be useful for hunting down fugitive Christianized natives or assisting the Spaniards against any enemies who might appear. He hoped to persuade them to settle down and to that end he suggested to them a place ten leagues from St. Augustine beyond the Rio Blanco and near a village of Catholic Timucua (Vega Castro y Pardo 1639). As Worth (1998: II, 19–20) has remarked, the governor's plans "met with only mixed success." That might possibly be phrased more strongly as "scant success." In 1647 one group of Chisca played a significant role in precipitating the 1647 revolt among the Apalachee in which three friars and the deputy-governor and much of his family perished and seven out of eight mission churches were burned. Worth noted that Chisca rebels became a serious problem in Timucua's neighboring Yustaga Province in the immediate wake of the pacification of Apalachee as they "stationed themselves along the roads and river crossings in order to ambush soldiers and Christian Indians."

In response, Spaniards issued an ultimatum on September 5, 1647, ordering the Chisca to settle down in the towns of Christian caciques within two months or they would be ejected from Spanish Florida. Worth (1998:II, 34–35) interpreted the acting governor's dispatch of soldiers to Ibiniute Province two months later as "indicating that the main body of the Chisca was definitely in the upper St. Johns River valley by that date (and very probably earlier)." But it could also mean only that the Ibiniute region harbored the recalcitrants among the Chisca. Worth believed that "a *reducción* of the Chisca" went forward after 1647, although he offered no documentation to support his conclusion. He noted, however, that "documents dating to 1650 and 1651 reveal that the Chisca had not effectively assimilated into the towns of the Christian Timucua," and were noted in 1650 to be "rebellious and risen up."

By 1650–1651 Chisca intruders became a problem anew for missions both in Ibiniute and Timucua provinces, killing some Indians and carrying off many men, women, and children. Spaniards then perceived them as a potential threat to missions among the Guale of coastal north Georgia. Worth identified the Chisca as then having encampments at the Santa Lucia de Acuera mission along the middle St. Johns River and at the "abandoned sites of Tocoy and Moloa along the . . . lower St. Johns River" from which "they had continued preying upon the Christian Indians." Worth (1998:II, 20) identified the Chisca's targets in Timucua Province in several raids in the spring of 1651 as the town of Napofai belonging to the Santa Fé mission, the Tarihica mission, and the La Chua hacienda. Almost 30 years later Captain Matheo Luis de Florencia recalled having participated in a 1651 campaign against the Chisca in which soldiers endured many toils and risks until they had expelled the Chisca from the land (Charles II 1682; Hann 1996b:238). Another soldier, Juan Bauptista Terrazas (1678) was sent as a scout with six soldiers (and, presumably, with Indians as well) to track down the same Chisca intruders. He reported that he had caught up with one of the Chisca bands, killing many of them, after which the rest fled leaving the province free of them.

Potential Chisca raids against Guale were a concern as well during this time. In the first half of 1651 the governor instructed a soldier he sent to Guale with supplies for its friars to inquire of the Guale leaders if they had any reports of Chisca Indians in or near their lands. If he heard any reliable reports, he was to assemble all the Guale warriors he felt were necessary and set out with them and the soldiers under his command to capture and kill the intruders and liberate their captives (Ponce de León 1651). Worth (1998:II, 21) has concluded that, although these Chisca and Chichimeco raids of the first half of the seventeenth century may have been only sporadic as compared to those of the late seventeenth century, they were a factor, nonetheless, in the interior Timucua missions' ongoing population decline.

Chisca Settlement

By the time the Chisca were next mentioned in 1661 at least some of them had settled down in the vicinity of Apalachee and were on apparently friendly terms with the Spaniards. The occasion was the appearance of a new group of Chichimeco, the ones identified today as the Westo or Ricahecrians, who attacked Guale that same year. Spanish forces' capture of four of those Chichimeco led the governor to instruct his deputy in Apalachee to enlist some Chisca to serve as interpreters for his questioning of the Chichimeco prisoners. At that time those Chisca probably were living in a settlement at the mouth or delta of the Apalachicola River that appears on a Spanish map. But, despite the change in relations, the Chisca, like the Chichimeco, still enjoyed a bad reputation in the eyes of Spaniards.

Spanish Assessment of the Chisca

Because of the Chisca and Chichimeco's predatory activities, both may have gained a worse reputation than they deserved. Bishop Díaz Vara Calderón's description of the Chisca living near the Apalachee is typical of this "bad press" and probably echoed what Florida authorities believed as revealed in a 1675 letter by Governor Pablo de Hita Salazar (1675c). The governor described the Chisca as "our enemies, rebellious people, untamed and brought up licentiously without the moderating effect of culture or other advantages, devoted solely to the hunt, which is their sustenance." The bishop described them as living "in encampments (*rancherías*) without any fixed settlements and sustaining themselves with the hunt, nuts, and roots of trees." He characterized them as numbering over 4,000 (Díaz Vara Calderón 1675). Yet, when trouble erupted among the Chacato in mid-1675, Spanish relations with the Chisca were good enough for acting deputy-governor Péres (1675a:39) to inform the governor that he had "sent to summon the interpreter (*atiqui*) for the Chiscas in order to dispatch him to speak to the Chisca caciques, asking them not to give support to the Chacatos," commenting, "because, if they give it, sir, we are going to have our hands full because there are many Chiscas." Their culture (in the present day) is closely related to that of the Creeks and to the Shawnee and other Northeastern peoples (Jackson 1998:32).

The Chichimeco-Westo

The Chichimeco of Spanish Florida records from the late 1650s are generally recognized today as having been the Westo or Ricahecrians of English sources, who are the Riqueherrons of French Canadian sources. The Westo were remnants from the Erie town of Riguj, which an Onondaga force had overwhelmed early in 1656. Steven C. Hahn (2000:63–68) suggested that some of the survivors fled south into Virginia, where they soon formed an alliance with expansion-minded Virginians who hoped to use the predatory newcomers to capture Indians of the southern tribes whom the English might use as slaves in the then expanding tobacco plantation economy.

In August 1657 Governor Diego de Rebolledo mentioned that a Franciscan newly arrived from Guale brought reports of "a new people of war . . . present . . . in Jacan" [Virginia], accompanied by Englishmen, were fortifying themselves in the region known as Tama [in the vicinity of present-day Macon] (Rebolledo 1657:114). By the fall of 1659 a band that seems to have represented the same people had begun their slave raids in the service of the Virginia planters. In October of that year a new governor recorded the movement through Apalachicoli and Chacato provinces of an unidentified force of about 1,000 men consisting of white blond people accompanied by "many warrior Indians with striped faces" who possessed firearms and were "laying waste to the land" (Worth 1995:15–17). The size of that Chichimeco force suggests that the newly arrived Erie refugees from Riguj's numbers had been enhanced by joining forces with Erie Indians already long established in Virginia, namely the Rickohockans mentioned earlier, who had killed the Pamunkey's king in 1656. Accounts of a Chichimeco attack two years later on the Guale missions eventually led to identification of the attackers as Chichimeco, and established that they represented the same people as those of the "striped faces" of 1659.

In 1661 a force later identified as Chichimeco descended the Altamaha in 200 canoes and rafts, accompanied by some Englishmen, and attacked the Guale mission of Santo Domingo de Talaje, forcing its abandonment. But when the attackers moved against the mission on Sapelo Island in a boat improvised from boards from Talaje's church and convent, the current on the bar of Ospogue swept their craft out to sea where they soon drowned in sight of those left behind. Other Chichimeco died in encounters with the Guale. Pursuing Spanish forces wounded still others as they were retreating upriver. During the next year Spaniards, based probably in Apalachee, captured four Chichimeco in Apalachicoli Province. Their questioning of them, using Chisca from the Apalachee region as interpreters, confirmed that these Chichimeco had come from Jacan and revealed that they were then living in the provinces of Tama and Catufa. But by the spring of 1663 and possibly a little earlier, the Chichimeco had moved farther into the interior to the Savannah River valley, possibly to the same location on the middle Savannah River where Henry Woodward encountered them in 1674 (Worth 1995:15–19).

In May of 1675 the Chisca living in the vicinity of Apalachee were sufficiently friendly toward the Spaniards to send word to Apalachee's lieutenant about a recently formed league between the Chichimeco and the English. The English were encouraging the Chichimeco to make war against the mission Indians and other Indians who had rendered obedience to Spain's king. The source of this intelligence was a Chisca woman who had been captured and enslaved by the Chichimeco. Eventually she was brought to Charles Town to be sold to the English for a shotgun (*escopeta*). She escaped and made her way back to her village, bringing news that Englishmen in the Chichimeco village were teaching the Indians to use firearms with the purpose of the Chichimeco's attacking St. Augustine and destroying the Christian Apalachee and Timucua (Hita Salazar 1675a; Reding 1925:174).

It is debatable how much training the Chichimeco needed in 1675. When

Henry Woodward visited the Westo town in 1674, supposedly the first Englishman to have done so, he was greeted with a volley from 50 or 60 small arms (Woodward 1674). As Worth (1995:17) noted, that incident indicates "that not only were the Chichimeco in possession of firearms prior to contact with the Carolinians, but also powder and shot, which could only have been supplied on a regular basis by English traders to the north." Their acquaintance with firearms may have been long-standing.

The Chisca Turn Hostile Anew

Relations between the Chisca and the Christian Indians had been sufficiently peaceful that even when the Chisca's hit-and-run strikes in the night against the Christian settlements began, Spaniards and Indians did not immediately attribute them definitively to the Chisca. In the Apalachee leaders' report to the deputy governor on their expedition against the Chisca, they explained that when the attacks began many years earlier they did not know whether the culprits were Chisca or Chichimeco. But finally in 1676 they learned that Chisca were responsible for some of the attacks from killings that occurred at Ivitachuco and at the Chine's place and at Cupaica. The detection of Chisca responsibility, it is worthy of note, followed the sentencing and detention of Diocsale and his appeals to his Chisca friends for revenge. As the alarms continued into 1677, the Apalachee decided to respond once the crops had been harvested for that year. Diocsale's son, Pedro, provided further confirmation of his father's and the Chisca's culpability in his testimony during the second trial of his father late in 1676. He stated that he had "heard that the Chiscas have killed some Apalachee people between Sabacola and the river of Santa Cruz [the Apalachicola River] and that they inflicted two other deaths in Vitachuco" and others in Patale, Bacuqua, Escanbé [Cupaica], and Ayubale (Pedro 1676:60–62).

The New West Florida Settlement

On deciding to accede to Diocsale's plea, the Chisca's first move was to abandon their settlement in the Apalachicola delta for one farther west that probably was located on the Choctawhatchee River. During Pedro's questioning he was asked: "whether he knows that the Chiscas abandoned a place that they occupy (*toman*) alongside of (*junto*) the river of Sabacola and went two days journey farther away beyond the Chacato villages where they made an enclosure (*corral*) for their defense." Pedro responded that he knew and had seen that the Chiscas had abandoned that site "and that they had built an enclosure of wood two and one-half *estados* of a man in height [about sixteen feet three inches] with the intent that if they came to make war on them, not to have their women, sons, and daughters in it and the men of valor to defend them." The Apalachee referred to that "enclosure" as a palisade. The *estado* was a measure equivalent to 2.17 yards.

Pedro's testimony indicated further that the Chisca's intent in building that palisaded site was to make war not merely on native provinces that were Christian, but also on many of the rest of the native peoples who were within their reach. He stated that he knew for certain "that their having made it has been with the intent of making war against the provinces of Apalache, Timuqua, Apalachicoli, Chacatos, Sabocolas, Casistas, Oconi, Usichi, Ayjichito, and other provinces and places of consequence."

In a 1677 order Governor Pablo de Hita Salazar spoke of the Chisca nation then as appearing "to be on the Rio Pansacola divided into two settlements and [noted] that the Chacatos *se alimaron* [? bordered on] the Pansacolas." When the Chacatos' chief of San Nicolas fled with six or seven of his people, the governor reported that they had done so with the evil intent of returning to attack the Christian provinces, noting that the Chacatos had made peace with the Chiscas in order to do so and that he was also courting the Pansacolas [who were then at peace with the Spaniards] to win their support for that project. The governor ordered his son to journey to Apalachee to confer with Fray Juan de Paiva and with the governor's lieutenant there, Juan Fernández de Florencia (Hita Salazar 1677d).

When the governor asked Pedro how many people it appeared to him "it would be possible to assemble in the said palisade (*palenque*) for war," the witness testified that it appeared to him that it would hold 700 fighting men at the most "besides children (*hijos*), women, and young people (*muchachos*)." On this occasion Pedro provided more architectural details about the palisade. He noted: "that on the inside of the said enclosure they have placed some supports (*muletas*) and some boards (*tablas*) on top of them in order to be able to fight standing on top of them, and at intervals they have bonnets (*bonetas*) above and below on all sides (*por todas partes*)." The exact nature of this last feature is not clear to this writer. Luis Arana and Albert Manucy (1977:61) described a bonnet as "a cap or V-shaped work, raised in front of the fortification salient to shield it from frontal fire." What Arana and Manucy (1977:60) had in mind apparently was a glacis. In an illustration they show the bonnet outside the moat in front of a bastion.

The Apalachee Attack of 1677

Pedro's testimony and the Apalachee's experience in their early fall encounter with the Chisca at their palisade indicates that those Chisca were handicapped by a lack of firearms. He stated that, although he had not seen their firearms, he had heard it said that they possessed two, which they obtained while fighting with the Chichimecos. It is probable that such intelligence was made available to the Apalachee as they prepared for their expedition. Although the Apalachee's 190-man force probably were seriously outnumbered, the 15 gunmen out of the 85 warriors whom San Luis contributed, and another 15 out of Cupaica's 70-man contingent, helped to overcome that handicap. The psychological impact of that imbalance in weaponry was illustrated most dramatically as the Apalachee began their withdrawal on the third day after their arrival and capture of the Chisca settlement. As they departed from the burning remains of the village in two columns, carrying their wounded in the middle, a Chisca troop came out on the trail in sight of them. When two quick shots by Cupaica's Chief Don Bernardo and San Luis's *eniha* Bip Bentura killed two of the Chisca instantly, the rest of them fled.

The only other attempt the Chisca made against them involved sympathetic magic or what Spaniards referred to as witchcraft. About half a league farther on, the expeditionaries entered "a clearing with four snail shells and some pots with boiled herbs." The Apalachee, unfamiliar with their portent, asked their Chacato guides what those signified. The Apalachee leaders reported that the Chacato told them "that it was witchcraft that they had put on us, so that we would not find our way back to our lands and so that they might kill us with this." The leaders concluded their account remarking: "But it pleased God that, after eight days we should enter the abandoned village of the Chacatos, very happy and with our wounded, carrying them on *poriguelas*." After having met a group from Apalachee the next day, who were bringing them food, they reported that they "continued on very content and entered into Apalache on the fifth day of October of the said year of 1677 by the favor of God and of the Virgin our Lady of the Rosary." As their own Christian sympathetic magic, they had carried her standard with them on that expedition (Fernández de Florencia 1678).

On the Apalachee's trek westward to attack the Chisca, they had followed that same trail as far as the abandoned site of San Carlos, the westernmost of the two Chacato missions in the Marianna region. Although the trail continued on westward to the Chisca's new village, the Apalachee calculated that the Chisca would maintain sentries on it. In the hope of surprising the Chisca, the Apalachee leaders reported that they had left the trail at San Carlos "going toward the south until we picked up a trail that comes from the sea to the Chiscas' settlement. The Chacatos and Pansacolas who had settled by the sea had opened this trail." At the time of the attack, however, those other two peoples were living with the Chisca.

After reaching that new trail, as they came within sight and sound of the

Chisca village, they "noticed then that the trail was well beaten down from the people who lived towards the sea who had gathered in the palisade of the Chacatos, Pansacolas, and Chiscas." As they approached it after nightfall, they heard yells and a drum and saw big fires. The inhabitants maintained fires both within the palisade and outside of it (Fernández de Florencia 1678).

The Apalachee leaders' account of their force's attack on the village provides considerably more architectural detail about the village to supplement that provided by Diocsale's son, Pedro. They portrayed the palisaded enclosure as very large with each of its four sides over 300 paces in length. Its size made them forego trying to encircle it with their meager force, and they concentrated their attack against one side. Three large houses stood within the palisade. They were equipped with loopholes from which the defenders could shoot their arrows. Once the attackers penetrated the palisade, many of the Chisca retreated into those houses to loose volleys of arrows that the Apalachee described as being so thick that "it looked like very thick smoke." Five Apalachee died and 40 were wounded during the attack. The sides of those houses were covered with boards apparently, as the Apalachee spoke of smashing many boards with the bar-shot that they carried. They mentioned the palisaded area as also having "high platforms" and corncribs. Many of the women and children, who had taken refuge in both types of elevated structures, were burned alive when the buildings were ignited by the cartridges. There seem to have been other houses in addition to the three large ones, as the Apalachee mentioned that there was a "tree there that caught fire from the firearms and burned many houses with its leaves."

The settlement appears to have been on the east bank of a river where it passed through a gorge. The wounded inhabitants and others who were able to flee did so by leaping into the river and swimming to the other side. The river was narrow enough that arrows the Chisca shot from the other bank reached to where the Apalachee were in the settlement. The cultivated fields were at some distance from the village. Because the food supplies the Apalachee found within the palisade were scanty, they sent a force of 30 men out to the fields to gather more. To reach them they had to pass through woods. There was at least one storehouse near the fields. The Apalachee reported that a Chisca, "who was in a storehouse, fired at and wounded one of our men after he had gathered some food supplies." Another member of that troop, who insisted on going back to the palisade early by himself, was ambushed and killed as he went through the woods (Fernández de Florencia 1678).

A Spanish expedition to Pensacola Bay in 1693 provides additional information that the river on which the Chisca's village was located was indeed the Choctawhatchee. Francisco Milán Tapia (1693:291), who led that expedition's maritime wing, referred to a river that could only be the Choctawhatchee as "a river called the Chicasses." Chicases was the Spaniards' usual name for the Chickasaw. But, conceivably, the name was misspelled or miscopied by Leonard and meant to be "river called the Chiscas."

Spanish Misrepresentation of the Chisca

The Apalachee leaders' account of the 1677 expedition indicates that Spanish depiction of the Chisca as strictly hunter-gatherers may not have been accurate. It is possible, of course, that Chacato or Pansacola were solely responsible for the planting of that village's fields. At the very least, maize had become part of the Chisca's diet in that village. While the Apalachee were hacking their way through the woods between San Carlos and the sea-trail on the way out, one of their scouting parties found three Chisca smoking meat. The main contingent was able to surround them, killing two of them when they assumed a defensive posture. Those Chisca had ears of corn with them for sustenance. The meat they were smoking probably was buffalo. On the day before, scouts had seen buffalo tracks and the tracks of people who were following them. A few days prior to that the Apalachee had seen many buffalo tracks, and on the following morning the Chacato among them killed a buffalo cow.

The Chisca's Linguistic Identity

The one possibly significant clue to the Chisca's linguistic identity is the Spanish governor's request to the West Florida Chisca in 1661 for interpreters when Spanish forces captured several Westo-Chichimeco. It is not clear, however, whether he sought out the Chisca because they spoke the same language as did the Westo, or because the Chisca had interpreters who could handle the language. Identity or similarity of the two languages would seem to be the more probable alternative. The Spaniards probably had some record of the identity of the Chiscas' language from the presence of Chisca among the Apalachee in the 1640s. Those Chisca helped spark the 1647 revolt of the Apalachee against the Spanish presence in their territory. Spaniards described the Chisca in the 1640s as "especially warlike and nomadic, wandering freely through the entire area then comprising Spanish Florida. At that time a group of them reportedly journeyed 200 leagues to St. Augustine to render obedience to the Spanish monarch (Vega Castro y Pardo 1643)" (Hann 1988a:16).

The many ways in which the Chisca resembled the fearsome and troublesome Westo-Chichimeco suggests a possibility, at least, that they came ultimately from a similar milieu whether or not they were united by ties of blood and/or language. The fear that the Chisca inspired in the Chacato mirrored that which the Westo instilled in the natives of coastal Carolina where the first English settlers reported that the natives were more afraid of the Westo "than the little children of the Bull beggers in England." Like the Chisca, the Westo were described as a "rangeing sort of people" (Crane 1956:6, 12–13). Both were accused at times of cannibalism, charges that seem to have been unfounded. Bishop Díaz Vara Calderón (1675) described the Chichimeco as killing their fellow Indians, Christian and non-Christian, wantonly without regard for "age, sex, or estate, roasting them and eating them." As late as 1700, St. Augustine's pastor occasionally referred to the Chisca as Caribs (Hann 1986a:177). Both surrounded their villages with palisades.

It was such considerations, doubtless, that led Swanton (1946:212–214) to identify both the Chisca and the Westo with the people of the eighteenth century known as Yuchi or Uchee who were recorded then as living among the Apalachicoli. The absoluteness of Swanton's identification of the three peoples has frequently been challenged. This writer believes that it is probable that Chisca and Westo-Chichimeco spoke the same or a closely related language. It is clear, however that the Yuchi or Uchee of the eighteenth century were descendants of the Chisca. And if Chisca and Chichimeco spoke similar languages it is reasonable to suppose that the small number of Westo who survived the Carolinians' war against them were eventually absorbed by or amalgamated with the more numerous Chisca-Yuchi. From Diego Peña (1716) to Benjamin Hawkins at the end of the eighteenth century, the Chattahoochee River Uchee were noted as having a language diverse from those of the people among whom they were living.

On the other hand, however, Hawkins' (1982:61–62) favorable portrayal of the Uchee challenges the idea that they were descendants of the Chiscas whom Spaniards characterized as bandits, untamed nomads, and of the Carolinians' fierce and bloody Westo. Hawkins described the Uchee as more civil, orderly, and industrious than their Creek neighbors, remarking that their women were more chaste, their men better hunters, and that "the men take part in the labors of the women, and are more constant in their attachment to their women, than is usual among red people." He noted as well that they had clung to their original customs and laws, having adopted none from the Creek. That is a tradition that their descendants today (still living among the Creeks) maintain (Jackson 1996:121). A partial explanation may be my already noted suspicion that, for the Chisca at least, the earlier assessments were overdone. There is also the consideration that peoples' character can change over a century or under the influence of a change in lifestyle.

One potential challenge to the identity of Chisca and Yuchi that can be dismissed out of hand is that represented by Boyd's (1953:470) translation of a

1702 document that lists Chisca and Yuchi as distinct peoples. Boyd simply mistranslated Uchizes as Yuchis. The document's author, Francisco Romo de Urisa (1702), stated that the attackers of the Spanish provinces during that period had not included a single Yamasee and were composed solely of "Chiscas, Chichimecos, Apalachicolos, Chatas, and Uchizes." Boyd transformed Romo's Chatas into Chacatos and his Uchizes into Yuchis. In this instance Romo de Urisa's "Chatas" probably were Chacato as Spaniards occasionally used that form to identify the Chacato, though the term usually identified the Choctaw.

In reporting some of the same events as Romo de Urisa, Apalachee's lieutenant, Manuel Solana (1702) cited a Chacato woman recently arrived from Achito as having informed him that the forces that had defeated Romo de Urisa's warriors on the Flint consisted of "four hundred Chisca and Apalachicolo men assembled in the same place of Achito without any other nation involving itself except only ten Chichimeco men and three Chichimeca women . . . and one other Abalachicola woman and an Englishman as squad leader." As her account was transmitted to us through the Spaniard's letter, we do not know whether Chichimeco was the term she used in referring to the Westo. But it is obvious that she made a distinction between Chisca and Chichimeco, whatever term she may have used to identify the latter. Solana's use of the "b" in spelling Abalachicola suggests that he spoke Apalachee and may not have had to use an interpreter in speaking with her. In my experience that spelling of "abalache" has been associated unfailingly with people, native or Spanish, who were familiar with the Apalachee language.

Chisca Ballgames

Based on modern practice, the Chisca have two ballgames. The game played most commonly has two goals on the north and south ends of the field. But they also share a single pole stickball game with the Creek, Seminole, and other Indians. The two-pole game pits women against men. Its goal consists of two green branches that are set into the ground to form an arc five feet high and six feet across. The women may carry the ball, throw it in the air, or pass it along the ground by kicking or rolling it. Men can only kick or roll it and may not run with the ball as can the women. Their game has a ritual purpose and there are special ceremonies to be observed before the first game of the year (Jackson 2000:38–43).

Presently, each year after winter has passed, each of the three Yuchi chiefs opens the new ritual season for his ceremonial ground with the skyward toss of a handmade ball to open the new season. Jackson (2000:33, 37, 50, 57) observed that "their three ceremonial grounds remain the most prominent institution of Yuchi social life." They encompass both the secular and religious life of the local Yuchi settlement. "Spring football games launch a ritual season that climaxes with the midsummer Green Corn Ceremonial." Usually the game is played to eight points. Today's Yuchi game, comparatively, "is closest in form and significance" to the Oklahoma Shawnee and Delaware's game. Jackson sees the Yuchi "as mediating cultural contacts between Northeastern and Southeastern groups." The Yuchi, he notes "are the only modern ceremonialists practicing both football and the single-pole stickball game in their ritualized forms. While the single-pole game points to an affinity with their Creek neighbors, the form and significance of the football game connects the Yuchi strongly to their longtime allies, the Shawnee." Jackson concludes: "Scholars interested in Yuchi culture have long seen it as a permutation of Creek patterns. Consideration of the football game, along with other patterns of social organization, bilingualism, social interaction, and ritual practice, point to ties with Central Algonkian groups that Yuchi people have always recognized but which are only recently being noticed by students of Woodland culture history (cf. Callender 1994)."

Chisca Population

The Chisca appear to have been the most numerous group in west Florida in the second half of the seventeenth century. Díaz Vara Calderón (1675) put their population at more than 4,000. A large population was indicated as well by acting lieutenant Péres's (1675a:39) remark that, if the Chisca were to join the Chacato in the 1675 revolt, it would mean real trouble because of their numbers. The 4,000-plus figure suggests that there were other settlements in addition to the one attacked, or the two seemingly on the Choctawhatchee that Governor Hita Salazar (1677d) alluded to in a muddy fashion as being on the Rio Pansacola.

The Chisca After 1677

It is not known whether the Chisca who survived the 1677 attack rebuilt their destroyed settlement at that site. Diocsale (1675:54) had stated at his initial trial that his reason for sending presents of deerskins to Atasi and Tawasa was so that they would not harm the Chisca who were going to that province to settle. The possibility that the Chisca had made some such move is suggested by Marcos Delgado's report on his 1686 trip to the Upper Creek country. While he was in the province of Cossate (Koasati), he summoned various chiefs from downriver provinces as far away as the land of the Movila. During his speech to them, Delgado reproached the chiefs from Movila about a "report brought by Christian Indians from Mobila of the killing of the Chisca Indians who were brothers coming to see us" (Boyd 1937:27–28). The 1693 overland expedition from San Luis to Pensacola Bay apparently saw no natives at all during their trek except for the few Chacato they met on the bay. If Delgado's report about the Chisca was reliable, it suggests that there had been a rapprochement with the Chisca since 1677.

A friar stationed at the Chattahoochee River village of Sauocola remarked on May 19, 1681: "Today it is better; that they do not have either Chuchumecos or Chiscas among them. On the contrary, most of the places are at war with them, according to what is said." But he implies, possibly, that Chisca had been living among them earlier. As to the Chuchumeco-Westo, the friar noted in a postscript that the son of Caueta's chief had just brought news to Sauocola that many Chuchumecos [or Chichimecos], then being harried by the English of Charles Town and their Indian allies, had come to Caueta to live (Gutiérrez de la Vera 1681).

It is clear that the Chisca had made peace with the Apalachicoli and joined forces with them sometime before 1702. It is likely that such a development was spurred by the growing rift between Spaniards and the Apalachicoli in the latter part of the 1680s in the wake of an Apalachee lieutenant's burning of the four northernmost settlements of that province early in 1686. Alliance with the Apalachicoli offered the Chisca a chance to avenge the Apalachee attack of 1677, particularly once the Apalachicoli opted for open war after the establishment of a Spanish-Apalachee fort on the Chattahoochee in the midst of the Apalachicoli's settlements in 1689. But the alliance was not immediate. Apalachee's deputy-governor, Matheos, spoke on August 21, 1686, of the Apalachicoli as then at war with the Chiscas, who had recently killed 12 Apalachicoli men. The Apalachicoli were also momentarily at odds with the English, according to Hahn (2000:160–161), believing that the English had not done enough to assist them against the Chiscas.

That alliance was clearly in existence by 1702. After Spanish withdrawal from Apalachee in 1704, Governor Zúñiga y Zerda (1704) spoke of Chichimeco and Chisca involvement in the destruction of the province, attributing to them the traditional charges of cannibalism: "The fear and terror that the English and the heathen were wont to instill in them with the burning alive of the Indians, the roasting of others, and the Chichumeco and Chisca Indians' eating of them and in [their] catching in small wooden bowls (*enbatiguelas*)[1] the blood that ran from the wounds and [their] drinking of it in the sight of the wretched sufferers and other inhuman atrocities that they inflicted on them." Those charges were resurrected in a somewhat different form during testimony in a 1705 inquiry about events of the last days of the Spanish presence in Apalachee in the previous year. One of the soldiers, son of a lieutenant of Apalachee, repeated hearsay gleaned from natives captured by the forces that accompanied Colonel Moore who had escaped later. In telling of atrocities inflicted on those who were tortured to death, the soldier, Manuel Solana (1705), testified that the Indians "cut the breasts from the women and roasted them on some long, large stakes. And it appears to him that he even heard the prisoners say that the Indians of the Chichimecos and Chiscas nation cut off pieces when they were half roasted and were eating them. This in the battle of Ayubaly."

About two generations later Spanish records from Pensacola identified Chisca as inhabitants of a Spanish mission in the vicinity of Pensacola in 1747. Ronald Wayne Childers (1998) believes that the mission may have existed as early as 1639. Childers noted as well that Chisca were living in 1760 "somewhere on the road to Apalachee . . . about 20 or 30 leagues from Pensacola." Spaniards' continued use of the name Chisca at that late date definitely undermines the belief that the Chisca and the Yuchi were the same people.

The earliest mention of Chisca involvement in the Apalachicoli's attacks on the Spanish-allied Indians dates from the October 1694 attack on the San Carlos de los Chacatos mission on the Apalachicola River. The 50 or so attackers were identified by women captives who escaped as consisting of four Sauocola, and two Chisca, while the rest were drawn from the Caueta, Apalachicoli, and Tiquepache (Torres y Ayala 1694).

The Chisca resurfaced in 1715 in the Spanish documentation under the name Yuchi and persist down to today under that name still living among Lower Creeks in Oklahoma. Jason Baird Jackson (1996:122) observed that "*Yujiha* is their name for themselves in their own language," remarking that "Euchee is their preferred spelling when writing English" and that "Yuchi is the form adopted by scholars." He might have added that the usage reflects the spelling that appears in the Spanish records of the early eighteenth century. Although they are "incorporated politically with the much larger Muskogee (Creek) Nation," within it they maintain a separate identity and "an autonomous existence to the degree that their condition as a socially encompassed community has permitted." Thus they maintain "uniquely Yuchi form of community organization, ritual practice and cosmological belief" in their three major settlements in Oklahoma (Jackson 1996:121–122).

4

The Pansacola

First Contacts

The Pansacola are the least known of west Florida's natives because Spaniards had almost no contact with them until the 1680s, and even then the contact was fleeting. Narváez and his men may well have seen Pansacola as they sailed along west Florida's coast in 1528. De Soto's men probed along the same coast possibly as far as Mobile Bay, and Tristán de Luna landed in Pensacola Bay, established a short-lived settlement there, and found a few natives living along the Escambia River. But none of them mentioned the Pansacola by name or left any useful description of the people whom they met or saw at a distance. The sole fruit of de Soto's agents' exploration along the coast was identification of a town named Achuse or Ochuse on a very good sheltered harbor 60 leagues west of Apalachee and six days journey from the Indian town of Mavilla (Clayton, Knight, and Moore 1993:I, 73–74, 104, 228, 268, II, 246). Most authorities agree, as did Luna that Ochuse was located on Pensacola Bay (Hoffman 1990:91, 96, 101; Hudson 1997:220; Milanich and Hudson 1993:222, 237, 241). Even the documents of the last quarter of the seventeenth century in which the Pansacola were first mentioned tell little about this people for whom the bay was named.

First Mention by Name

It is worthy of note that even Bishop Díaz Vara Calderón (1675) failed to mention the Pansacola, even though he listed many other tribes much farther away deep in the interior such as the Choctaw, Movila, and Tawasa. Spaniards' earliest surviving mention of the Pansacola seems to have been made in a July 1677 order by Governor Hita Salazar (1677d). Pansacola, of course, was a name they had been familiar with since their return to Apalachee early in the century. It was the name of an Apalachee satellite settlement belonging to the chiefdom of Aspalaga (Rebolledo 1657:95). It also appeared with some frequency as a name used by individual Apalachee (Hann 1988a:366–369). The governor's order shows that Spaniards had had some contact with the Pansacola prior to mid-1677, possibly through groups such as the Chine, who were reputed to be familiar with the Gulf coast as far west as the Mobile area (Matheos 1686d). He described the Pansacola as being at peace and as having shown themselves to be friends of the Spaniards. It is not clear what impact the Spanish-inspired Apalachee attack on the Chisca village just two months later had on the Pansacola's attitude. That settlement had housed Pansacola and Chacato as well as Chisca (Fernández de Florencia 1678). Pansacola does not seem to have been mentioned again until the mid-1680s by which time Pansacola were once again well disposed toward Spaniards, if they had turned hostile in the wake of the events of 1677.

The Unknown Coast

The lack of contact and apparent disinterest was part of the general torpor that accompanied Spain's decline throughout the century. Strange as it may seem today, Spanish officials in Florida, Mexico, Seville, and Madrid at the beginning of the 1680s knew little or nothing about the vast expanse of the coast between Apalachee Bay and the port of Tampico in northern Mexico, even though they jealously regarded it as part of Spain's domain. Much of the geographical knowledge acquired by the early sixteenth-century explorers from Alonso Álvarez de Pineda to Francisco de Coronado had faded from the corporate memory of Spanish officialdom. Pineda had mapped the shoreline from Apalachee Bay to Yucatan in 1519. He gave the name Amichel to the stretch between Apalachee Bay and Tampico that still remained unsettled by Europeans in 1680, and named the Mississippi "river of the Holy Spirit." But subsequent explorers created a potential for confusion by attaching the name Holy Spirit to other features of the Gulf coast. De Soto gave that name to the bay where he landed, today's Tampa Bay.

About all that remained of that early knowledge was the existence of a great river flowing into the Gulf somewhere along its coast and of a magnificent bay that bore the same name. A confused belief arose over the years that the river and bay must be associated, in short, that the great river flowed into the great bay. That belief stymied efforts to identify anew the great river on which René-Robert Cavalier de la Salle was supposed to have established his settlement in the 1680s (Weddle 1973:ix-x, 25).

Investigations in Florida

The first signs in Florida of a desire to end the prevailing ignorance appeared in the 1670s, stirred by concern over pirates operating in the Gulf. Governor Hita Salazar advocated exploration of the coast between Apalachee and Mexico as preliminary to settlements along that coast to forestall Spain's enemies from doing the same. In response, the Crown bestirred itself enough in 1678 to order Mexico's viceroy to establish the location of the supposed river and bay of the Holy Spirit on the Gulf's northern coast. But, as of the summer of 1685, when Mexican authorities first received knowledge of La Salle's sailing from one of La

Salle's former men when he was captured in a Spanish naval force's encounter with pirates, Mexico's viceroy had done nothing to carry out the king's orders.

That neglect was brought to the king's attention early in August 1685 when Martín de Echagaray, a naval captain and pilot with long service at St. Augustine, asked the king for authorization to explore for Holy Spirit Bay to determine its region's suitability for settlement and to learn whether Frenchmen had occupied the region. Before Echagaray left for Spain, he had spent time in Apalachee gathering intelligence from its native inhabitants about the lands west of Apalachee. The Holy Spirit Bay Echagaray had in mind was the one that was supposed to be at the mouth of the Mississippi (Dunn 1971:20–30, 43; Weddle 1973:7).

As Robert Weddle (1973:26) has remarked: "There is no explanation for his prescience. . . . He had left St. Augustine for Spain in July of 1683—a year before La Salle sailed from France to establish his ill-fated settlement." For reasons not yet established, Juan Márquez Cabrera, who assumed Florida's governorship at the end of 1680, also showed a seemingly prescient interest in establishing the location of Holy Spirit Bay and in learning about the route or trail that went to the bay. Sometime in 1685 (prior to official word of Mexico's authorities' receipt of definite news about the La Salle venture), Márquez Cabrera instructed his lieutenant in Apalachee to send him a report "about the trail that goes to the bay of the Holy Spirit." Around November 1685 apparently, after having made inquiries, the lieutenant, Antonio Matheos, composed a report based on what he had learned, mentioning rivers, places along the way, and distances from one to the other.

But he did not forward the report to the governor at that time. Matheos used as a pretext, in an explanation later to the governor, his alleged fear that it was not clear enough for the governor to understand it. Matheos (1686d) told the governor of the report's existence only about six months later in May of 1686. Instead (back in November apparently) he asked the governor for the mission given later to Marcos Delgado. Matheos had proposed going overland to Movila Bay by way of Apalachicoli Province, Pansacola, and thence on to Estanani on Mobile Bay. He promised that he could come and go in a month and that he would be certain to bring back reliable information on the location of Holy Spirit Bay.

On informing the governor of the unsent report in May 1686, Matheos chided him for not having responded favorably to his earlier request, observing that his burning of four villages in Apalachicoli Province ruled out use of such an overland route. As an alternative, he noted that one could go to Pansacola by canoe from St. Marks, using pilots familiar with that coast who were available in the Chine village. Matheos felt that the Movila surely could provide information about the bay and river of the Holy Spirit. He explained that it was necessary for him to go to Movila himself because an ongoing war between the Pansacola and the Movila prevented his communicating with the Movila via the Pansacola. The Chine and Chacato living in Apalachee apparently had been the channel through which Florida's Spaniards maintained contact with the Pansacola and gained what little knowledge they had of the coast to Pansacola and Movila.

Pansacola Visits to Apalachee

As a result of those contacts, some Pansacola had come to Apalachee to visit Matheos probably some time in 1685, receiving an arquebus as a gift. Matheos (1686f:12–13) reported the arrival of ten more Pansacola at San Luis on August 19, 1686 to barter for powder and balls for that gun. As the Marcos Delgado expedition was about to depart on its search for the Mississippi, Matheos asked the visitors to assist the expedition with canoes and to re-supply them with provisions when they reached the Pansacola's village. After a lengthy and heated discussion with a leading man among the Pansacola group who insisted that his village lacked the food resources to provision the number of people whom the expedition would involve, Marcos Delgado, the expedition's leader, told Matheos to desist. Delgado resolved to follow a more northwesterly track to Tawasa, located then in the vicinity of present-day Montgomery, Alabama.

Badgered by Matheos and desiring the powder and balls they had come for, the Pansacola promised to meet Delgado with canoes at a point on the Choctawhatchee. Four of the Pansacola were to hasten home to arrange for the canoes and the rest were to wait for Delgado at the Chacato settlement on the Apalachicola River. When Delgado received no report on the promised canoes during his stopover at San Carlos, he pressed on toward Tawasa (Boyd 1937:5–6, 12–13).

Barroto's Visit to Pensacola Bay

A little over six months earlier the Pansacola villages' inhabitants had warmly welcomed a seaborne expedition that had set out from Apalachee on January 30. It was the Juan Enríquez Barroto expedition commissioned by Mexico's viceroy on learning of the existence of the La Salle colony. This expedition, mounted in Havana, had stopped in Apalachee to hire native pilots at the Chine village who might serve also as interpreters. When some of the Spaniards landed at the village in Pensacola Bay, natives led them to the chief's house where Indians brought out a cross for the Spaniards to kiss. They were served maize tortillas and the Spaniards distributed glass beads as gifts. The Pansacola reported that many of their people had died in attacks by Indians from Mobile Bay, who also had destroyed their planted fields. When the Spaniards asked whether they had seen or heard of any white people, they stated that earlier their fishermen had come upon ten white men almost starved to death. After treating those strangers hospitably, they had guided them as far as the Apalachicola River, whence Christian Indians had brought them on to Apalachee (Reina 1686:13–14).

The Pez Expedition

Historical sources provide little other reliable information about the life and customs of the Pansacola while they remained residents of Florida. Leonard (1939:15, 18–19) observed that "Barroto is known to have taken detailed notes of his observations . . . though these records have not come to light." Two subsequent expeditions sailed along the same coast in 1686–1687 and 1688, but neither one entered Pensacola Bay. Thus when Andrés Matías Pez wrote his enthusiastic Memorial in 1689, he had never been in the bay himself. His enthusiastic boosterism about the potential of the bay and its inhabitants reflects that of Barroto and Pez's own career-advancement interests. As Barroto visited Pensacola Bay in the winter of 1686, he would not have been likely to have seen Pez's "little patches of corn, beans, squash, tomatoes, chili, and many other products characteristic of the Indies" at the Indian village there. Most other accounts remarked on the infertility of the bay's sandy soils and suggest that the Indians lived inland where better soils were to be found and maintained only seasonal fishing camps on the coast.

That is the import of the following passage from Carlos de Sigüenza y Góngora's description of the bay from his visit there in the spring of 1693 in the company of Admiral Pez. "In the estuary and the previous one there are many oysters; judging by the tumble-down *bohios*, or fishermen's huts, on the banks, it is doubtless much frequented by the Indians in the summer time, which is the season when they come down to their fisheries on the seacoast after preparing their inland cornfields" (Leonard 1939:172).

The Pez expedition of 1693 surprised two small parties of unidentified Indians along an inlet or stream while they were preparing a midday meal. The Indians fled at the sight of the Spaniards and Mexicans, leaving their food and other possessions behind. Barcia presented Sigüenza y Góngora's description of the meal in preparation as follows:

> They found a fire lit and a poorly made earthen pan placed by it with some tastelessly stewed buffalo lungs and some pieces of meat that had begun to roast on wooden spits; on one, some fish were stuck like tidbits; it had in reed baskets (that the Indians call *Uçate*) some maize [and] pumpkin seeds; (*Hallaron lumbre encendida y puesto un Barreño mal hecho á ella, con unos Livianos de Cibola desabridamente guisados y algunos pedaços de*

carne empeçada a tostar en asadores de palo, en uno estaban atrevessados Peces como Chuchos; tenia en cestas de caña (que llaman Uçate los Indios) algun Maiz, pepitas de Calabaças) (González Barcia Carballido de Zúñiga 1723:309; 1951:336).[1]

At the second campsite the Mexicans found a variety of pemmican in addition to half-roasted buffalo meat. Sigüenza described it as buffalo meat "pounded into a very fine, evil smelling powder in wooden mortars." There was a large quantity of it, recently prepared as the still intact buffalo's head lay nearby. They also found baskets at this camp that contained "roots like those of lilies or ginger, fiberless and sweet; others when taken in one's hands, stained them a pinkish color, then turned purple and, finally bluish" (Leonard 1939:162).

Sigüenza considered this group's earthenware to have been of a better quality than the stew pan found at the first site. He described it as "numerous, not badly shaped pots and pans with gourd dippers and ladles of buffalo horn in them." There were 10 or 12 tanned buffalo hides nearby and "uncured pelts of martens, foxes, otters, and many deer" (González Barcia Carballido de Zúñiga 1723:309; 1951:336).

They found quantities of buffalo hair at both campsites, some in balls and some "on cross-shaped distaffs of *otate*" (González Barcia Carballido de Zúñiga 1723:309; 1951:336). At the first campsite they found buckskin bags filled with the hair of buffaloes and other animals, along with mussel shells, bones, roots, and other odds and ends. "Little buckskin bags" in the second camp contained "beaver hair, soft, white feathers . . . wooden combs . . . not badly made, leather shoes like buskins, pieces of brazilwood, dittany roots, claws of birds and animals, and a thousand other small objects." The second campsite also had earthen pigments for body-painting. At a charnel house they found some of the buffalo hair converted into a "very well-woven sash" (González Barcia Carballido de Zúñiga 1951:336).

The first campsite had feather headdresses placed for safekeeping between carefully tied pieces of tree bark. The headdresses were made from feathers of turkeys, cardinals, and various other birds. It also had a small iron hatchet with its handle reversed. The other camp contained a well-worn handleless hoe and an iron adze. It had two huts fashioned with a single sloping roof covered with "bark stripped from pine trees with considerable skill" to keep each piece intact. A medium-sized fishing craft there contained an "indefinite number of bows and arrows." The arrows were made of "a shaft of hard wood tipped with bone" (González Barcia Carballido de Zúñiga 1951:336–337).

Sigüenza described the charnel house as a "hut built on four stakes with a covering of palm leaves." It contained a deerskin, the buffalo-hair sash alluded to earlier, a yard and one-half long piece of tattered blue cloth of Spanish manufacture, hanging baskets of little shells of mother-of-pearl, fish scales, animal bones, and tufts of hair. In Leonard's probably careless translation, the bones of a human body lay "on a reed mat at the base of a very handsome pine near by." Barcia placed those remains in a container that was more complex than Leonard's "reed mat." According to Barcia, "At the foot of a great pine they saw in a chest a decayed cadaver that appeared that of a woman" (*Al pie de un gran pino vieron en una Petaca un cadaver carcomido que parecia de Muger*) (González Barcia Carballido de Zúñiga 1723:310). Barcia's *petaca* has the sense of a trunk or hamper covered with hides or leather, such as one that would be put on the back of a mule or horse for carrying cargo. His *carcomido* could be rendered also as "gnawed upon." The flesh still clung to the hands and feet and in Sigüenza's account the hands and feet were the features that led Sigüenza to identify the remains as those "of a woman or a lad" (Leonard 1939:160–162, 167).

The Apalachee Expeditions of 1693

Twin expeditions that went from Apalachee by land and sea a few months later in the summer of 1693 also found no trace of the Pansacola except remains of two of their villages, but they spoke to a few Chacato whom they encountered there. Consequently, it is likely that the Indians who fled from Pez and Sigüenza were also Chacato, but their flight from the Spaniards is puzzling unless they did not recognize them as such. But, conceivably, they were Pansacola and afraid of the Spaniards because of Pansacolas' involvement in an earlier attack on the Sauocola mission. One of the two abandoned village sites was on the extreme eastern edge of the bay where Governor Torres y Ayala set up camp after reaching the bay (Torres y Ayala 1693b:236–237; Barreda 1693:280).

The Pansacola's Fate

The Chacato told the visitors that the Pansacola had been killed off largely in the course of their wars with the Movila and the Apalachicoli. They knew nothing about the whereabouts of the survivors. Leonard (1939:66) believed that "The Pansacolas . . . had been practically annihilated, it appeared, in tribal wars with the neighboring Mobilas, and the few remnants were scattered about the hinterland of their former domain." But it is more probable that the surviving remnant had made peace with the Movila and sought refuge in their midst. Jay Higginbotham (1977:42) cites solid evidence that Pansacola had a village on Mobile Bay by 1700 and a misdated document by Governor Torres y Ayala that may indicate that the move occurred earlier. While Charles Levasseur was exploring the Mobile River in 1700, he spent a night at a Pansacola village at the mouth of the Tensaw River, the eastern arm of the Mobile. It is probable that the Movila were equally anxious for peace by then, influenced perhaps by the losses they, as well as the Pansacola, had been suffering at the hands of Indians allied to the English. These raids had been intensified by an English demand for Indian slaves.

Whatever was the size of the remnant Pansacola population that migrated to the Mobile region, the Pansacola seem to have maintained their identity through the period of French control in that region. Crawford (1975:30) observed that "the Pensacola and Mobile bands maintained a separate existence until at least 1758" and that they moved westward when the territory was ceded to Britain. About 1725 Bienville noted that the Pansacola and the Biloxi then had villages on the Pearl River, remarking that "These nations now have only forty men who are very laborious and good hunters" and who "furnish an abundance of meat to all the French who are near enough to trade for it" (Rowland and Sanders 1932:III, 535).

Archaeology's Contribution

Even archaeology's contribution to our knowledge of the Pansacola's culture is somewhat limited. For archaeologists, the name Pansacola identifies a cultural complex found from Choctawhatchee Bay westward along the coast as far as Louisiana. But as Knight (1984:201) observed, it is not "a tight coherent unit" throughout that stretch, but characterized by "regional and temporal variants" involving ceramics, settlement types and patterns and other considerations. Consequently, he concluded: "It seems clear that we are dealing here with a number of societies under the Pensacola rubric with potentially separate histories and that we cannot properly speak of Pensacola as a single prehistoric system" (1984:201).

Nonetheless, as Milanich (1995:96–97) remarked, it is recognized generally that the Pansacola peoples' culture "bears affinities to assemblages farther west along the Gulf coast, such as the Mobile Bay region." But he also observed that most archaeologists view the western panhandle's Pensacola culture as a late addition inasmuch as Pensacola materials at many sites overlie Fort Walton materials. Consequently, evaluation of what is known has been muddied occasionally by confusion over what is Pensacola and what is Fort Walton. Although the famous Fort Walton site is the type site for a culture that is distinct from the Pensacola culture, Milanich (1994:381) noted that despite this the Fort Walton site "is associated mainly with the Pensacola culture as it is defined today." It flourished in the western panhandle from Choctawhatchee Bay through Mobile Bay on into Louisiana. It lasted in Florida "from A.D. 1200 into the colonial period," and it followed "the early Fort Walton-period culture" in the western panhandle (Milanich 1994:380–381). Although it was characterized by shell-tempered pottery, it also had some that was sand-tempered.

Although Milanich (1994:381) observed that Pensacola culture on the whole is poorly known archaeologically in Florida, enough work has been done for Knight (1984:200, Fig. 8.1) to suggest regional variants for the Choctawhatchee Bay and Pensacola Bay regions. He placed the Hogtown Bayou-Point Washington variant at the easternmost edge of the Pensacola distribution and the La Casa variant to the west in the region of Perdido Bay (Milanich 1994:381). Most of the Pensacola sites found to date have been on or near the coast rather than in the uplands. European artifacts found at sites around Choctawhatchee Bay indicate that the Pansacola continued to occupy that region through the middle and late sixteenth century. Although archaeologists have differed on the importance of agriculture among the Florida Pansacola, the consensus favors those who have maintained that "cleared-field agriculture was not important to the subsistence of the Florida Pensacola peoples" (Knight 1984:206–215; Milanich 1994:381–383).

The Pansacola's Language

As virtually nothing is known about the Pansacola's language, it is not possible to say anything about its affinities with certainty. Circumstantial evidence suggests that it was very similar to or related to that of the Chine and Chacato; the Pansacola were identified as relatives of the Chacato. It is all but certain that the two Indian guides whom the Enríquez Barroto expedition engaged at Apalachee early in 1686 were Chine inasmuch as the Chine were identified by Apalachee's lieutenant, Matheos, as people who were knowledgeable about the Gulf coast westward as far as Movila. But it is not clear whether, in serving as interpreters for Barroto in his contact with the Pansacolas, those guides used their own language (Leonard 1939:12–13).

It is certain, however, that Swanton's (1946:173) seeming rationale for his assertion that the Pansacola's "language and customs seem to have been almost identical with those of the Choctaw" can be dismissed out of hand, whatever one may think about the validity of the thesis itself. If Swanton's evidence is that cited in his earlier work (1922:13), it provides a weak foundation for so sweeping a statement. That evidence was, basically, that the Pansacola's name "is plainly Choctaw and signifies 'hair people'" together with "Adair's statement to the effect that the Choctaw were *Pansfalaya*, 'long hair,'" and Cabeza de Vaca's having met several chiefs in an area Swanton believed to be near Pensacola Bay who wore their hair long. On those grounds one might say that the Apalachee also were Choctaw as they wore long hair and used the name Pansacola, although they are not known to have applied it to themselves as a people. Swanton's statement illustrates the perils of building such bridges on the basis of meaning or similarity of names. Others have suggested an alternate meaning of "bread people" for Pansacola. There is also the consideration of Matheos's statement: "The Estananis and Pensacolas are enemies of the Chata" (Boyd 1937:13), even though it was not unknown for linguistic brothers to war against one another.

5

The Apalachicoli

Origins

Archaeologists believe that ancestors of some of the peoples in the Chattahoochee Valley in the seventeenth and eighteenth centuries had first occupied it long before that time, possibly as long as 12,000 years ago. In the late Middle Woodland period around A.D. 300–500, settlement centered on large sites such as Kolomoki in southwestern Georgia and continued centered there during the Weeden Island period (A.D. 500–760). The Mississippian-era Rood phase (A.D. 1150–1300) was characterized by the appearance of new vessel forms and a change to shell tempering which suggests a radical cultural change and probably an influx of new people. Through the ensuing 350 or so years, until the arrival of the first Europeans, the valley experienced the various cultural phases of the region as a whole. Archaeologists maintain that during the one hundred year period that began in 1550, the valley suffered a ninety percent reduction in site frequency. As Vernon James Knight Jr. (1994a:383) observed, the earlier "dense swath of Stewart phase Lamar occupation throughout the valley simply vanished, leaving, it seems, just two Abercrombie phase towns, one on either side of the river south of present Columbus, Georgia." Both those sites had large platform mounds. Knight speculated that the sites may have functioned as mound centers until well into the seventeenth century, a phenomenon, he noted, that had not yet been documented for the Coosa or Tallapoosa regions.

As to the lateness of the valley's recovery, he may have overstated the case a bit. Just five years after Spaniards established a permanent presence in Apalachee in 1633, Apalachicola Province was vital enough to induce Spaniards to reach out to establish amicable relations with it's people and for a new Spanish governor to visit it in 1645 when he traveled to Apalachee (Hann 1988a:16). For the historic era in the wake of the catastrophic losses, Knight (1994a:384) saw the two surviving Abercrombie phase settlements as probably being "stable political and population centers during the first half of the seventeenth century." He then observed cautiously that "By the first part of the succeeding Blackmon phase (ca. A.D. 1650–1715) a number of large new villages were established nearby, and the regional population rebounded substantially from the Abercrombie decline." Nonetheless, even though "most of the local population disappeared," he saw "clear signs of cultural, social, and political continuity from the sixteenth through the seventeenth centuries" (Knight 1994a:385).

On the topic of origins for the valley's people, Knight (1994a:375) noted that "prominent Muskogee origin myths portray these peoples as arising out of an alliance between Muskogee-speaking towns from the west (Kasihta and Coweta) and an autochthonous Hitchiti-speaking town" on the Apalachicola River. The latter, of course, would be the town of Apalachicola. On that issue Knight commented perceptively: "at some level this may be close to the truth." But then, referring to the "Creek Confederacy," he insisted that there was no documentary evidence that that broader alliance existed prior to the eighteenth century as earlier authorities such as Swanton maintained. However, it may have been foreshadowed or intimated prior to that time in documentation that has become available since Knight took that stand.

Other linguistic elements also settled in the valley and elsewhere such as immigrant Apalachee during the seventeenth and eighteenth centuries. Most prominent among these immigrants were a people who appear in Spanish records as Yuchi or Chisca or Ysicas. Chisca in Apalachee played a significant role in the Apalachee's 1647 revolt. Chad Braley (1998:13) placed them in Apalachicoli territory "at least as early as 1662." But he dates their main arrival on the Chattahoochee as probably having taken place "during the early eighteenth century following the Yamasee War." But it is likely they first arrived on the Chattahoochee at least as early as they appeared in Apalachee.

Spanish sources, from the beginning of the seventeenth century until 1763, never used any equivalent of the modern names, "Lower and Upper Creek," for the peoples of the Chattahoochee Valley and those living in the Coosa-Tallapoosa region. They referred to the former most commonly as Apalachicoli or Cauetas and to the Upper Creeks as Talapuses when alluding to them in general. But clearly, linguistically distinct people such as the Yuchi were alluded to by their particular name or a variant of it.

Documentation from at least as early as 1680 or so established clearly that Emperor Brims enjoyed a position of overall leadership among his fellow Lower Creek chiefs. On a visit to St. Augustine, he made an official disclaimer to Spanish authorities that his sway extended beyond the twelve principal towns of the Lower Creeks at that time. But his need to make that disclaimer indicates that there were people then who were making that claim. That reality suggests, at the very least, that he may have already enjoyed influence beyond those peoples of the Chattahoochee Valley (Hann 1996a:68–70).

First Contacts

Seventeenth-century Spanish contact with the Apalachicoli began in the late 1630s, but a quarter of a century was to pass before Spanish sources provided any substantial information about the people of that province. That first contact was part of Governor Vega Castro y Pardo's (1639) late 1638 initiative entrusted to sergeant-major Herrera López y Mesa to establish a general peace between the Apalachee and their Amacano, Apalachicoli, and Chacato neighbors. He had succeeded by mid-1639 (Horruytiner 1640; Worth 1998:II, 18).

There is no indication that the Apalachicoli gave obedience to the Spanish Crown at this time or during the ensuing quarter century or that any Apalachicoli leader went to St. Augustine to visit the governor at that time. The Apalachicoli would meet the next governor early in his term in the mid-1640s, but it was because the governor visited Apalachicoli Province while he was in Apalachee. The governor does not seem to have provided any details about his trip or the leaders of that province.

Although Spaniards traded regularly with Apalachicoli from the 1650s on, Spanish sources did not identify any of the Apalachicoli towns by name until 1675 except Casista. Apalachee's lieutenant, Pedro de Ortes, traveled as far as Casista in the early 1660s on an expedition that was supposed to have taken him as far west as the Choctaw country. He identified Casista then as the last place in the province in the geographic sense (D. de Leturiondo 1672; Ramírez 1687; Rebolledo 1657). Ortes's placement of Casista on the Chattahoochee early in the 1660s rules out the speculations of Swanton (1922:216–220) and others that Casista was Henry Woodward's Cofitachequi or that Casista was located near the upper Savannah River in 1670 (Corkran 1967:49).

Historical sources fail to indicate whether Apalachicoli Province included Muskogee speakers such as the Coweta and Casista in the 1630s. On the basis of Creek migration legends, the Hitchiti speakers are considered to be the earlier inhabitants of the region and the Muskogee-speakers relative latecomers. Their later arrival is reflected, probably, in Antonio Matheos's (1686b) reference to the people of the four towns that he burned early in 1686 (Caueta, Casista, Colone, and Tasquique) as being "from other places." Several versions of Creek and Casista migration legends portray the Creek, in general, and the Casista, Coweta, and Chickasaw, in particular, as having originated in the west and, specifically, on the Red River. It is commonly believed that they moved eastward gradually, fighting a series of wars with other peoples and eventually reaching the Tallapoosa and Coosa Rivers.

The Casista allegedly achieved their leading ranking on the Coosa River after meeting the Abihka in that region. According to the legend, the four peoples agreed that the one among them who gained the most scalps in a four-year war against a common enemy would achieve primacy. Casista won out, followed by Caueta. From that time only those two towns could raise the red or scalp-pole. According to legend, the Casista-Caueta moved on later to the Chattahoochee. The Casista allegedly established hegemony there over a people who practiced head deformation and who were in possession of mounds. The Casista established themselves in the vicinity of the mounds. If that portion of the legend has any validity, the flat-headed people probably were ancestors of the Apalachicoli. Swanton (1922:129) noted that the village of Apalachicoli's former importance is reflected in the Creek name that it bore, *Talwa lako*, meaning "Big Town," and from William Bartram's statement that it was "the leading White or Peace town." The legend maintained that the Casista-Caueta eventually moved all the way to the coast until the white people drove them back to the Chattahoochee (Gatschet 1969:214–251).

That last part of the legend may reflect the 25-year period beginning circa 1690 when the Casista-Caueta and some of the Apalachicoli migrated eastward to settle on central Georgia's Ocmulgee and Oconee rivers. The migration of some of the people of the town of Apalachicoli to the lower Savannah River could be construed as a move "all the way to the coast." Those peoples' post-Yamasee War return to the Chattahoochee River valley could represent "the white people's driving them back to the Chattahoochee." For the early part of this period from 1670 into the 1750s the legend is not reliable in giving primacy to Casista. Caueta clearly enjoyed primacy during that period under Emperor Brims, Brims' brother Chiquile (the Chigelly of English sources), Brims' son Malatchi, and the latter's son Togulki (Corkran 1967:15).

The legend is possibly borne out historically to the extent that the de Soto chroniclers mention a large village named Casiste in the Tallapoosa River region that could have been Casista's predecessor, although Casiste was not a paramount town in the 1540s and was in the chiefdom of Talisi (Clayton, Knight, and Moore 1993:I, 95, 202, n. 157, 288).

A Migration of the Early 1670s?

Spanish sources speak cryptically about a mysterious migration of new natives into the Apalachicoli country in the early 1670s in connection with a request for friars. Although those migrants had come from afar, they were alluded to as though they were part of the Apalachicoli people. They are supposed to have come from a location over 100 leagues away, but there is no indication as to the direction of the migration. When two friars were provided, there was reference to a second migration seemingly from the Chattahoochee to today's Apalachicola River or to an affluent of it, although that also is not entirely clear (Moreno 1673; Somoza 1673).

There is scant evidence for interest in friars among the Apalachicoli proper prior to the mid-1670s and some of that evidence is of dubious validity. Apalachicoli were alleged to have requested friars during the governor's visit in the mid-1640s (Reyna 1657:428–430). Fray Juan de Medina reported around the mid-1660s that, while he was visiting Apalachee as provincial, chiefs had come from Apalachicoli settlements to ask for friars and that they had done the same with his predecessors (Melgar 1673).

The earliest expression of such an interest on the part of the Apalachicoli in the 1670s appears in a report that Domingo de Leturiondo (1672) wrote at the end of December 1672 while he was in Madrid. Leturiondo seems to refer to it cryptically at the beginning of the following passage that is concerned principally with Apalachicoli who had been living on the Chattahoochee since Spaniards established contact with them in the 1630s.

> Relative to the exploration that the said Father Fray Juan Moreno proposes, what can be said is, that there are eighty leagues of entirely Christian Indians from the fort of Florida to Apalache; and that from Apalache to Apalachicolo there is an equivalent area of pagan Indians who have given obedience to His Majesty and who are very submissive to the governor's lieutenant in Apalache. Soldiers are accustomed to go from there to their villages and dependencies. That one can trade among them with full security. Governor Benito Ruiz de Salazar Vallecilla went to their land personally about twenty-three years ago. And it is reported that since then all those peoples have been very docile and affable and that the most remote of them desire contact with the Spaniards.

Only nine days later the Franciscans' Commissary General in Madrid spoke of "a pressing need for religious for the new settlements that are being formed in Apalachicoli to where the Indians came to make settlements at the advice of the Father Provincial of Florida, on seeing the strong requests that they were making for ministers and the difficulties that he recognized in their living at a distance of more than one hundred leagues from the farthest conversions, which are those of Apalachee, they came to the land of Apalachicoli to dwell solely with the objective of obtaining Holy Baptism" (Somoza 1673). As a stopgap measure, the provincial brought Frays Alvaro de Navia and Andrés de Armas to Florida from the convent in Havana to serve these newcomers and promised to try to find two others to serve them.

The Commissary General went on to remark:

> Not only will God be greatly served that these Indians of Apalachocoli should have the necessary ministers so that they may teach them, but also that once these [natives] have been thoroughly infused with the knowledge

of our holy law, the religious will be able to make new *entradas*, because there are infinite [numbers of] Indians in that region, and, according to the reports, they are all docile, of good character, and we can promise ourselves that they will be easily converted. For it is not known that they have any particular rite or ceremony, or that they offer adoration to any idol, which is usually the greatest difficulty that the religious encounter in the missions. Because when they have some particular law of their own or when they have adorations pertaining to heathenism, they receive the word of the gospel with much greater difficulty (Somoza 1673).

Fray Juan Moreno (1673) of Florida, who was in Spain in early 1673 to recruit friars, reported that the newcomers had then moved down to "the borders of their land [to an area] that was three days distant by trail from Apalachee, where they formed nine settlements that three or four thousand Indians occupied on the bank of a river that they call of Apalachee, which is six leagues distant from the sea toward the direction of the setting sun, a placid site, delightful, and suitable for harvesting a great deal of wheat and corn." Moreno noted further that "the distance from village to village is two leagues, and from the first to the last, eight." The spacing is remarkably similar to the first and last of the Apalachicoli settlements on the Chattahoochee (Junta de Guerra 1673).

Much of the rest of Fray Moreno's letter clarifies what Leturiondo had in mind when he spoke of the exploration that Moreno proposed. The friar saw this conversion as a prelude to establishment of easy overland communications with Mexico, remarking:

The distance is so short that separates Apalachicoli from the live conversion of Tampico, *custodio* of the province of the Holy Gospel of Mexico, 200 leagues more or less, and 80 from there to Mexico City. With this [result], that, on exploring this land (even though the Indians are many, they are docile, as has been stated and where resistance will not be encountered), the viceroys of Mexico can send messages to Spain with facility when the situation demands it, in having ships in Florida. And they will come with more security than by way of Vera Cruz. For in Florida they will find themselves disembogued already and free of the risks of the gulf and of the Bahama Channel and of the enemies that ordinarily infest the coasts of Havana, with another great benefit flowing from this for that presidio [St. Augustine]. It is that, as there are no more than 300 leagues from Mexico to Florida, the *situados* can go by the mainland, avoiding the risks that they have experienced on many occasions that the enemy has caught them because they came by sea (Moreno 1673).

There appears to be no other evidence for such a massive migration into or from Apalachicoli territory in the early 1670s or late 1660s. Although the account's detail suggests verisimilitude, one is tempted to view the story told by Moreno and the commissary as propaganda in support of Moreno's request for badly needed friars. Yet, other evidence validates the statements about two friars having been brought from Cuba on an interim basis to serve the newcomers (Moral et al. 1673). And if it were mere propaganda, the Crown had a reliable witness at hand whom it could question about these matters in the person of Leturiondo. He had been Apalachee's deputy-governor in 1670. Much, if not all, that Moreno said about the feasibility of communications overland between Mexico and Florida was doubtless based on the reported experiences of an Indian whom Leturiondo had sent westward in 1670 to explore the land (Moreno 1673; Somoza 1673).

One possibly ostensible thread of reality that at least partly corroborates those early 1670s migration accounts appears to be the move southward of Sauocola to the Apalachicola River by 1674. But that affected only one village and the numbers affected were small. The rest of Moreno's account appears to reflect nothing more solid than an expectation similar to the better known one that Bishop Díaz Vara Calderón (1675) expressed two years later that the rest of the Indians of Apalachicoli Province would move downriver as had the Sauocola.

Nonetheless, it was a time of migrations into Apalachee by Tama-Yamasee, Chine, Pacara, Amacano, and Tocobaga. And a decade or so earlier a governor reported a similar phenomenon for Apalachicoli and Chacato territory, noting that in those provinces "bordering on that of Apalache, people are coming in great quantity." The newcomers included "many warrior Indians, their faces striped, and who use firearms." The governor identified some of those invaders two years later as Chichimeco who had ensconced themselves in the Tama country along the Oconee River. Worth (1995:16–17) has identified these Chichimecos as the Westo or Ricahecrians of English sources. Depredations by the Chichimecos undoubtedly were responsible for some of the migrations such as those of the Tama-Yamasee, whose presence in Apalachee was first mentioned in the mid-1670s (Díaz Vara Calderón 1675; Hann 1993:32, Fig. 2, 58, 60–61, 74–75, 117–119, 1995a:61–64). Ocuti could well have moved to the Chattahoochee when the Chichimeco entered the Oconee Valley.

Although Hahn (2000:71–73) suggested tentatively that Apalachicoli themselves, who were longtime residents of the Chattahoochee Valley, were among the people requesting friars at this time, presently, the documentary evidence this writer has seen suggests that recent Tama-Yamasee migrants into the valley are the best candidates for the people whom Moreno mentioned. Their presence in such numbers in the Apalachicoli country is suggested by the worried remark of an English trader at St. Helena in 1685 "that a thousand or more Yamasee who had been living among the Cowetas and Kuseetaws" had come down with 10 caciques and that more were expected daily (Westbrooke 1684/1685). The Westo's intrusion in that era into the heart of the Tama-Yamasee lands of central Georgia provides a motivation for such migrations. And the Tama-Yamasee are documented as being closely enough related to the Hitchiti-speaking original inhabitants of the Chattahoochee Valley to pass for Apalachicoli. There is evidence from the 1680s for a considerable Yamasee presence in the region, not to mention Matheos' (1686b) less specific reference to the people of the four towns that he burned early in 1686 as being "from other places." There is also the archaeological evidence mentioned in Chapter 2 that indicates massive depopulation of the valley during the century following the de Soto *entrada*. It calls for some such influx to account for the number of towns that were present in the 1680s. In this sense the Tama-Yamasee were as ubiquitous as the Chisca and a much larger element in the stew than the Chisca. But one is left to wonder why those migrating peoples were never identified as Tama-Yamasee, people with whom Florida Spaniards had been familiar for almost a century.

Moreno thus possibly told the truth and the migration went unrecorded in any other source that has survived because the stay of some of the migrants on the Apalachicola was ephemeral. There is evidence for the presence of marauding Yamasee bands that were mistaken for Chisca on the fringes of Apalachee in the spring of 1675 and earlier (Hann 1991a:152–158). But there is also a striking resemblance between Moreno's description of the migrating settlements of the early 1670s and those described in the Lamhatty manuscript. David I. Bushnell (1908:568–574), who first published the Robert Beverly version of the account, and Swanton (1929:435–438), who republished that version along with a second one by John Walker, both identified the main river system depicted on the Lamhatty map as the Apalachicola-Flint-Chattahoochee (Hann 1988b:94). But, the migration Lamhatty recorded supposedly occurred a generation or so after 1672.

In the spring of 1675 the governor also received intelligence provided by a Chisca chief from the Panhandle and from a friar working among the Chacato of the Marianna region. They reported on English activity in the hinterland of north Georgia and of the dispatch of a ship from Charles Town to spy upon the Apalachee garrison. That doubtless increased Spanish interest in establishing a more permanent presence among the Apalachicoli. The Chisca chief informed the Spaniards that Englishmen in the Westo's village were training them in the use of firearms so that they might attack western Timucua and Apalachee, and about an English spy-ship heading for the Gulf Coast. The friar reported word

Table 2. Three Town Lists, 1675–1716

1675	1685–1686	1716	Warriors
Chicahûti	Sauocola chicasa	Chilacaliche	80
Sabacôla	Talipasle	Sauocola	84
Oconi	Ocôni	Apalachicolo	113
Apalachôcoli	Apalachicoli	Achito	54
Ylapi	Alape*	Ocomulque	58
Tacûsi	Tacussa*	Uchi	106
Vsachi	Osuchi	Tasquique	28
Ocmûlgui	Ocmulque	Casista	64
Ahachîto	Achito*	Cauetta	62
Cazîtho	Casista**	Chaugale	46
Colômme	Colone**		
Cabita	Caueta**		
Cuchiguâli	Tasquique**		
	Ocuti*		

* Towns for which the 1685–1686 documents provide no explicit locational information.
** Northernmost towns in 1685–1686.

from another tribe that Englishmen had arrived at a village only five days distant from his Chacato mission (Reding 1925:170–175).

Apalachicoli Towns on the Chattahoochee

Two listings of the names of the Apalachicoli towns exist for the years 1675 and 1685–1686. A third listing from 1716 identifies the towns that were then reestablished in the Chattahoochee Valley in the wake of the Yamasee War. Bishop Díaz Vara Calderón (1675) identified 13 towns by name in 1675. A decade later distinct sources gave the number of Apalachicoli towns as 11 and 12, but then identified at least 14 settlements by name. The correct number at that time probably is twelve. Early in 1682, Caueta's chief (1682), then the paramount chief, stated that he had 11 villages (presumably in addition to Caueta) under his jurisdiction. It may be that Chicahuti of the 1675 list was only a transitory settlement as nothing even remotely resembling it appears on the subsequent lists of the villages along the Chattahoochee. Hahn (2000:79) observed that in 1686 a Spanish soldier [Marcos Delgado] on "a diplomatic mission to the Tallapoosa River reported that he had made peace with a chief of Chicahuti. Two of the 14 villages named in the 1685–1686 period were probably satellite settlements rather than the principal ones to which the numbers 11 and 12 presumably referred, or possibly settled there only transitorily. The listing from 1716 identified only 10 towns, two of which do not appear on the earlier listings. Table 2 contains the three lists of towns, the tentative locations of which are provided in Figure 2.

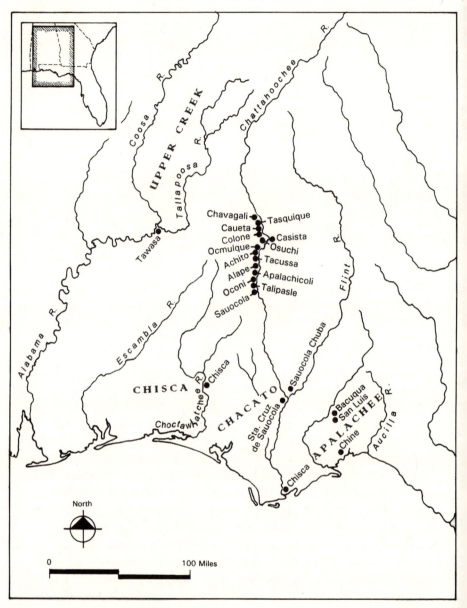

Map 2. Late seventeenth-century Indian villages along the Chattahoochee River and surrounding environs.

The bishop's listing is a formal one and may represent the south to north location of the towns along the river, although the bishop did not indicate that such was the case. The 1685–1686 sources' placement of the towns, whose location relative to their neighbors is known, supports such a conclusion. Names marked with a single asterisk are ones for which the 1685–1686 documents provide no explicit geographic information. Double asterisks identify the northernmost towns in 1685–1686. In 1686 their leaders refused even to meet with Apalachee's lieutenant to pledge a severance of ties with the British traders from Charles Town. Although Ocuti was south of Casista in 1685, I placed it last not only because its immediate neighbors were not indicated, but also because it is absent from the 1675 list. Its insertion among the towns south of Casista would have made the matching of the progression of the towns from Oconi northward on the two lists less obvious. Ocuti's absence from the 1675 list is linked, no doubt, to its well-authenticated Yamasee identity (Primo de Rivera 1717b). In 1675 they were probably one of the still roaming bands of Yamasee who had been driven from their ancient homeland in central Georgia. The same may be true of the Tasquique (also absent from the 1675 list) whom Diego Peña (1716) also identified as Yamasee-speakers, although I am not entirely convinced of the reliability of Peña's identification.

My presentation of the 1675 list reflects the order in which the bishop presented the names of those thirteen villages. Before listing them, the bishop mentioned the existence of a fourteenth village thus: "a place of heathens called formerly Santa Cruz de Sabacola the lesser and today, la Encarnación a la Santa Cruz de Sabacola because of the church having been dedicated to this so sovereign mystery on Thursday the twenty-eighth of February of the present year where the head chief of that province became united with his vassals of Sabacola the greater, which has become reduced to our holy faith and [which] will be a great settlement and conversion when the same thirteen Apalachecole places have offered to do the same." The bishop went on to note: "which are at the bank of the river [the Chattahoochee] at a distance toward the north of thirty leagues" (Díaz Vara Calderón 1675). The bishop then proceeded to identify them as above as "Chicahuti, Sabacola, Oconi, etc."

The river in question here is regarded today as two rivers, the Apalachicola and the Chattahoochee. But seventeenth-century Spaniards applied the name Apalachicola to both streams.

John Worth (2000:276) speculated (as I had earlier) that the bishop "apparently lists the Apalachicola towns in south-north order along the river." In his list of possible sites for the towns the bishop mentioned, Worth put question marks opposite Chicahûti and Cuchiguâli to indicate that he had found no site to match with either, in contrast with all the rest. While placing Chicahûti among the towns "of uncertain linguistic affiliation and origin," Worth thought that "it might be classified as Hitchiti... based solely on its southern geographic location."

For Sabacola the identity question is further complicated by the existence of an Apalachee village bearing the name Sabacola. A further element of mystery as to the Sabacola's ultimate origin arises from a document indicating that the Apalachicoli Sabacola spoke Apalachee in addition to their own language. Worth (2000:271) suggested that the Hitichiti speakers "appear to have included at least Hitchiti [Achito], Apalachecole, Sawokli, Ocmulgee, and Oconnee." He considered Osuche inhabitants, as did I, to be other possible Hitchiti speakers (Hann 1996a:66).

The name Ocone was shared also by one of the Apalachee's principal villages. And most obvious, of course, is the two neighboring provinces' sharing of the name Apalache. As to the implication of that sharing, Swanton (1922:130) felt that in spite of it, he was "inclined to think that there was only a remote relationship between the two peoples." But in view of the relatively meager information that has survived about the Apalachicoli or about the language of either people, there is really no basis for making such a judgment.

It is worthy of note that names of three of the late seventeenth century Lower Creek villages appear in the de Soto narratives in areas distant from the Chattahoochee Valley. They are Ylapi, Ocuti, and Casista. The sixteenth century Ilapi and Ocute were well to the east of the valley. Rodrigo Rangel described Ocute as a "great chief" who lived in the region before the extensive uninhabited zone de Soto crossed to reach the kingdom of Cofitachequi. While de Soto tarried at Cofitachequi, he sent about half of his army to Ilapi because its "chieftainness had a large supply of corn stored there." Garcilaso gave twelve leagues as the distance between Ilapi and Cofitacheque (Clayton, Knight, and Moore 1993:I, 272, 279–280; DePratter 1994:200).

Hudson (1997:183) placed Ylapi of the de Soto era near present-day Cheraw, South Carolina, on the Peedee River not very far south of the North Carolina border. Hudson et al. (1984:70) identified de Soto's Ocute with the Shoulderbone archaeological site; the latter was "a large site with at least five mounds. The largest was twelve m. high and the diameter of its base was about 55m." Smith and Kowalewski suggested that "the site was the capital of a powerful province with several other large mound sites including Shinholser [de Soto's town of Altamaha] subject to it." For the Ocute, the move to the Chattahoochee would not have involved a very great trek. But the trek would have been considerably greater for Ylapi's people. The third village, Casiste, in de Soto's time was on the Coosa River some distance north of that stream's junction with the Tallapoosa (Hudson 1997:148, map 6). Swanton (1946:49) had placed Casiste "on the bank of the Altamaha River." More recently, Knight (1994a:374) described it as "merely one of the towns subject to the minor chiefdom of Talisi." But Elvas described it as "a large town" (Clayton, Knight, and Moore 1993:I, 95).

Linguistic diversity is perhaps the most obvious characteristic of the towns on these lists. The inhabitants of Apalachicoli itself and those of other towns such as Ocone and Ocmulque were Hitchiti speakers and are believed to be descended from much earlier settlers in the region. The people of Tasquique and Ocute were Yamasee speakers whose language was apparently closely akin to Hitchiti (Hann 1996a:66–68). Worth (2000:271–272) also placed the Saucola among the Hitchiti speakers. But it should be noted that Diego Peña, after remarking that most of the southernmost towns spoke the same language (Hitchiti), remarked that Sabacola has a distinct language and added that they also spoke Apalachee (Boyd 1949:25). Peña gave no reason for their bilingualism. Savacola was a name borne occasionally by Apalachee men and also in 1657 it was the name of an Apalachee satellite village that was under the jurisdiction of the chief of San Joseph de Ocuya (Hann 1988a:29, Table 2.2, 367, 368). These coincidences suggest the possibility of an earlier intimate tie between the Apalachee and the Saucola. Worth also listed Osuche as possibly "Hitchiti speaking, if for no other reason than its early location in the southern part of Apalachicola." He also identified the people of Chicahuti, Talipasle, Ylapi, and Tacusa as Hitchiti speakers based on their supposed southern location, although he qualified that by remarking that they were among those he regarded as being of "uncertain linguistic affiliation and origin" (Worth 2000:272). The sixteenth-century Ilapi's proximity to Ocute raises the possibility that its inhabitants were Yamasee-speakers (Quiroga y Losada 1688c). It is unlikely that Ilapi was the Upper Creek town of Hillabee as Swanton (1922:258–259) and, more recently, Hahn (2000:79) have suggested. And the 1685–1686 list's mention of Alape refutes Hahn's (2000:79) statement that "Ilapi no longer appeared on the Chattahoochee after 1675."

Caueta and Casista (and probably Colone as well) were Muscogee speakers. Worth included the Tasquique (Tuskegee) among the Muscogee speakers (as Koasati speakers) and, based solely on their northern location, the Chuchiguale/Chavagale as well. The Yuchi or Westo, who were living in one or more of those towns as refugees were yet another linguistically distinct group. They spoke a language that was probably related to Algonquian. Worth (2000:280, Figure 10.2) published a tracing of an "anonymous map ca. 1715" showing them as having a village of their own during the Lower Creeks' sojourn on the Oconee and Ocmulgee rivers and points east. The town's name appeared as "Ewches." Their language was probably Algonquian.

From the 1680s on, if not earlier, immigrant Apalachee represented yet another Muscogee-related group living among Apalachicoli Province's peoples.

One of those immigrants (probably from an earlier period) was Emperor Brims' wife named Qua, who was from a leading family of Mission San Luis. A son of Brims also had an Apalachee wife (Hann 1988a:172).

The 1675 list, compiled by Bishop Díaz Vara Calderón (1675) apparently lists the villages in a south to north progression. He presented their names as follows: Chicahûti, Sabacôla, Ocôni, Apalachôcoli, Ylapi, Tacûsa, Vsachi, Ocmûlgui, Ahachîto, Cazîtho, Colômme, Cabita, Cuchiguâli." At that time, if not earlier, there were two villages of Sauocola, which the bishop referred to as Sabacola the lesser and Sabacola the greater. In 1675 the people of Sabacola the lesser were living at a mission located on the Apalachicola River due west of San Luis de Apalachee (Díaz Vara Calderón 1675). There is no further mention of Chicahuti after 1675.

At the time of the chief of Caueta's first recorded visit to Apalachee and St. Augustine at the beginning of 1682, in the wake of his expulsion of the friars and the soldiers protecting them, the friar at Bacuqua gave the chief a letter he had addressed to the governor. In it, Fray Rodrigo de la Barreda (1681) spoke of "sixty-six places that have communication with this province of Apalache" as rendering vassalage to Caueta's cacique, "not to mention other provinces, like the one of Chiaha, the Chickasaw, and many others" that did the same. But the cacique himself, on being questioned under oath on this subject by the governor, stated firmly that only the eleven villages of the province of Apalachicoli were under his dominion (Chief of Caueta, n.d. [1682], notes by Connor or her transcriber). Verner W. Crane (1956:34) identified Caueta as the "war town" and Casista as the "peace town," noting that both became the strongholds of English influence among the Lower Creeks.

As Vernon James Knight Jr. (1994a:385–386) observed, "Seventeenth-century annexations of refugee groups by Muskogees and Hitchitis were accomplished not by a nascent Creek Confederacy but by regional polities, which were not yet mutually allied at the close of the century. These were the Tukabatchee polity on the Tallapoosa River, the Abihka polity on the Middle Coosa River, and the Apalachicola polity on the Chattahoochee River, the latter known by the English as the Cowetas. Here are the three coalescent districts we have identified as nodes of stability through the seventeenth century, now identified by name as the result of re-established contact by European nations. Each one was in a very real sense descended from a corresponding Mississippian chiefdom extant in the sixteenth century" (Knight, 1994a:385–386).

Peña (1716) stated explicitly that the province had 10 villages in 1716; that his listing represented a south to north progression; and that six leagues or about fifteen and one-half miles separated Apalachicoli and Caueta. His failure to mention Oconi and Osuchi does not mean that they had disappeared permanently from the river. They reappeared on later lists as towns located along the Chattahoochee (Hann 1988a:364). Peña (1717b:134) mentioned Oconi as early as October 1717 as one of six towns that had agreed to move southward into Apalachee during the following winter. Peña's Chilacaliche, usually rendered as Chislacaliche by Spaniards and as Cherokeeleechee or Cherokee-Killer by English speakers, was well to the south of the other towns, located just above the confluence of the Flint and Chattahoochee rivers on the site of a 1680s-era Sauocola mission (Hann 1988a:48–49).

Beyond placing Casista on the Georgia side of the river and Coweta and Tasquique, and probably Colone as well, on the Alabama side in the 1685–1686 period, Spanish documentation for those years provides no specific information as to the location of the rest of the towns except for the distance between certain towns and indications of the order, south to north, for many of them (Matheos 1685a, 1686a, 1686d). But, using archaeological evidence, John Worth (2000:Figure 10.1) has placed eight of the towns on the Alabama side in 1685 and five on the Georgia side, including Colone, which documentation seems to place on the west bank. The other towns he located on the east bank were Alape, Tacusa, Hitchiti (Achito), and Casista. Worth (2000:275) placed the town of Apalachicoli as "very likely at the Patterson site (1Ru66) based on that site's proximity to the known site of the Spaniards' fort near the town of Apalachicoli in 1689–1692." But he did not rule out the possibility that it was (1Ru65) just downriver from it, which William Bartram described as its early eighteenth century location.

Late in the eighteenth century, Caueta, Uchee, Ooseeoochee, Cheeauhau, Palachoocle, and Big Sauocola were all on the Alabama side, while Cussetuh (Casista), Hitchetee, Oconee, Little Sauocola, and Eufala were on the Georgia side (Hawkins 1982:53, 55–56, 61, 63–66). Hawkins gave Welaunee Creek as the location of Big Sauocola but identified it as a new settlement.

There is no indication that Bishop Calderón's travels took him to the Apalachicoli country except for his visit to the Sabacola (Sauocola) mission on the Apalachicola River in the vicinity of the present Chattahoochee State Hospital. Consequently one cannot know how up-to-date the source of his information was or that all the towns that he mentioned were still in place in 1675 when he made the first surviving record of their existence except for Casista. That is not much of a problem, as all the towns he listed appear a decade later with the exception of Chicahuti and Cuchiguali. Chicahuti had moved to the Upper Creek country by 1686 (Hahn 2000:79). Whatever the reason for the failure to mention Cuchiguali in the sources from 1685 and 1686, it reappears in 1716 as Chaugale. The resemblance between the two forms clearly undermines the attempts by Mark F. Boyd (1949:25), Mark E. Fretwell (1980:105–107), and others to identify

Peña's Chaugale as a variant of Sawokli. Boyd's listing of Apalachicoli's population of warriors as 173 in his translation of Peña's report may be a typographical error. The number is spelled out clearly as *ciento y tres*, or 103, in the Stetson Collection's Photostatic copy of Peña's report. The only mention of Talipasli occurred in the 1685–1686 documents unless its inhabitants are a branch of the Tali mentioned elsewhere (see Swanton 1922:212–213). One of the Tali towns, Tahogale, has an interesting resemblance to Chaugale. An even more intriguing resemblance to Chaugale is presented by the DeCrenay map's Chaouakle, which Fretwell (1980:107) believed represented Sauocola.

Their Clothing and Appearance

Writing about the non-Christian Indians in general, namely, the Lower and Upper Creeks (Uchises and Talapuses, Yamasees, and Chickasaws), Pedro Sánchez Griñan (1756) described their dress as made of skins. It consisted of a leather jacket (*cuera*) that reached to the mid-thigh (*medio-muslo*), without sleeves; a strip of cloth (*lista de pano*) or leather a third of a yard in width with which they cover their private parts; boots and sandals of deerskin, when they are traveling. They were "of great stature, of a somewhat dark color (*algo moreno*), valorous, much inclined to war, but cruel and inclined to drunkenness." He noted that "they made war in troops of 50 and 70 to 100 men and more, always by way of ambush and never in open battle." They painted their face and their body with various very fine colors that they extract from plants.

Food and Medicine

Sánchez Griñan described their diet as meat of bear, buffalo, deer, and cakes of maize. When they exhausted those on their travels, they replaced them either with palm hearts (*palmitos*) or various roots of great sustenance. They planted only a little bit of maize and some vegetables, which did not produce in proportion to the land's richness because of the scant cultivation they gave it. He observed that they lived in the countryside most of the time engaged either in warfare or in the hunt. They had many medicinal herbs, "some of marvelous power for curing fevers, wounds, and convulsions" (or lockjaw—*pasmos*). Through all the years of Spanish contact with the ancestors of the Creeks and Seminoles, it is surprising that Spaniards seemingly made no reference to the most important of their seasonal ceremonies, the Green or Great Corn Ceremony. According to Swanton (2000:546), it became known to English-speakers as the "busk," which was a trader's corruption of the native Creek term *poskita* or *boskita* meaning "a fast."

Character

The Spaniard was skeptical about the motives of those who sought baptism, observing that they did so "not from any interior calling but rather out of interest in the gift that the god-parents are accustomed to make." As to trusting in their word, he noted that, despite the gifts that they were given in Florida, they often broke the pacts of friendship that they contracted by making frequent raids "especially the Chickasaw" (Sánchez Griñan 1756).

Mission Attempts Among the Apalachicoli

The first attempt at missionization among the Apalachicoli involved the Sauocola and may be linked with the mysterious migrants of the early 1670s who had allegedly requested friars. As a preliminary to the launching of a 1679 mission to the Apalachicoli country, Governor Hita Salazar (1679) informed the Franciscan provincial that he had received no reports since he assumed the government about the Apalachicoli desiring to become Christians other than the one "fray Moreno gave about Apalachicoli." He identified the report as one Moreno made to the king that the Indians of Apalachicoli "were very docile and friendly and during the past year of 1674 insinuated their willingness to be reduced." This could be what led to establishment of the first mission among the Sauocola in 1674.

Nothing specific is known about the circumstances of the Sauocola's migration southward to the site the bishop visited early in 1675 or about the mission's existence prior to that. He is the first Spaniard known to have spoken of the Sauocola by name. That omission contrasts with the recording of the founding of the Chine and Chacato missions in April and June of 1674 similarly situated in regions west and southwest of Apalachee (Hann 1993:74–75, 1995a:61–63). The Sauocola mission's existence prior to the bishop's visit is implied in his remark that it was "a place of heathens formerly named Santa Cruz de Sabacola the lesser" (Díaz Vara Calderón 1675). Although the bishop spoke of this Sauocola as representing "Little Sauocola," a decade later both Domingo de Leturiondo (1685a) and Matheos (1685a) spoke of the middle-Chattahoochee River site of "Sauocola el Grande" or "Big Sauocola" as also being abandoned at that time. Worth (2000:277) identified the site of this original Big Sauocola as the Blackmon site (1Br25).

The demise of the mission and the Sauocola's abandonment of that site is equally as obscure as its founding. The mission held less than 30 men in mid-1675 when the Chacato in the Marianna-region missions rebelled. The leader of the soldiers sent to deal with the trouble reported that Santa Cruz's chief intended to leave with all his people once that soldier withdrew Santa Cruz's friar unless the chief was given three soldiers. Although the soldier advised against providing such aid and there is no evidence soldiers were sent, the chief was still there two years later in September 1677 when the expedition against the Chisca stopped at Santa Cruz. Chief Baltasar and six of his men joined the expedition (Fernández de Florencia 1678; Hann 1993:39–41). It is probable that the Sauocola retreated upriver to the Apalachicoli heartland soon thereafter to escape retaliation. There is no indication of further Spanish contact with the Sauocola or Apalachicoli until late in 1679 except a notice in 1680 that Sauocola's chief had come to Apalachee many times to ask for friars (Hita Salazar 1680c).

That 1674–1677-era village was on the west bank of the Apalachicola River about 15 leagues from San Luis a little below the confluence of the Flint and Chattahoochee according to Governor Torres y Ayala's (1693b:230) journal of his trek from Apalachee to Pensacola Bay. Interpretation of some of the data on the location of this mission has been marked by considerable confusion. Mark F. Boyd (1958:215–217) began by observing equivocally, "While his [the bishop's] statement indicates that Sabacola El Menor was adjacent to the bank of a river, it is not evident that this could be the bank of the present restricted Apalachicola River." He then suggested more positively that the bishop's Sabacola was located above the confluence of the Flint and Chattahoochee near the site appropriated by Cherokeeleechee in 1716, concluding, "In further confirmation, it is known that the Sabacola of Peña was west of the Flint River." Mark E. Fretwell (1980:104) spoke even more forthrightly of: "Bishop Calderón's sojourn at the Forks of the Flint and Chattahoochee at the heathen village called formerly Santa Cruz de Sabacola el Menor. His new mission church was located on the west side of the Flint River near the mouth of Spring Creek a few miles above the forks now covered by Lake Seminole." Both confused the short-lived Calderón-era mission with a later Sauocola mission that was located just above the forks.

Careful comparative reading of the 1677 anti-Chisca expedition account and the journals kept by Governor Torres and Fray Barrera in 1693 makes it clear that both expeditions followed the same trail as far as the Marianna region. It is also evident that the bishop's Sabacola mission occupied the same position on the west bank of the Apalachicola River as did the later mission of San Carlos de los Chacatos until it was attacked by the Sabacola among others. The 1677 expedition did not cross any stream that could be construed as the Flint to reach the village of Sabacola on the west bank of a stream identified as the river of Santa Cruz (clearly the Apalachicola). Seventeenth century Spaniards never used any name other than *Pedernales* (Flint) to designate the Flint River (Fernández de Florencia 1678; Leonard 1939:230, 266–267).

The bishop himself described the location of the site clearly enough to have ruled out such confusion. He described it as "two leagues from San Luis to the

River Agna (the Ochlockonee), which separates the provinces of Apalache and Apalachicoli, and at a distance of twelve to the bank of another large and heavy flowing one that takes the name of that province and runs through it from north to south" (Díaz Vara Calderón 1675). He made that point even more clearly in describing the "thirteen Apalachicoli places" as being on the banks of the same river 30 leagues to the north.

The bishop went on to state that he had changed the village's name from "*Santa Cruz de Sabacola the Lesser to la Encarnación a la Santa Cruz de Sabacola*" to commemorate the day on which he dedicated its church, February 28, 1675. He then noted, in a potentially confusing passage, that on that occasion "the great Cacique of that province joined in (*se agrega*) with his vassals from Big Sabacola (*Sabacola el grande*), who has been reduced to our Holy Faith and it will be a great town (*Población*) and conversion especially when (*quando*) the thirteen Apalachicoli places have offered to do it likewise (*hazer los mesmo*)." The chief whom the bishop designated "head Chief (*Cacique mayor*)" was the chief of Big Sauocola, not the province's paramount, the chief of Caueta. Although Lucy L. Wenhold's rendering of "*quando*" in this passage was "as" rather than "when" is an acceptable translation, its reliability is questionable in the absence of any other evidence that they had done so (1936). The bishop was not above embellishing the truth a bit, as he probably did, in claiming an active role in the mission's foundation, although he probably did no more than to consecrate its church.

The Sauocola mission of Santa Cruz did not live up to the expectations that Bishop Calderón had for it in 1675. Its population remained small and none of the other upriver settlements' peoples showed any disposition to move downriver. Despite that unpromising lack of interest, a second mission attempt was launched in 1679. Three friars were sent to a Sauocola settlement in the heartland of the Apalachicoli country without any preliminary contact with the leaders of the province to gauge whether the friars' arrival there would be welcome or not. The primary impetus for the launching of the mission at that moment appears to have been the arrival of a new mission band of 23 friars in June of 1679 and the governor's growing awareness of the desire of the English at Charles Town to establish communications with the Apalachicoli. Governor Hita Salazar observed in a letter to the Franciscan provincial that, because of the Englishmen's desire, it had become important "to move more quickly (*antisipar*) on that effort to send religious to the province of Apalachecola" as he had already suggested privately (Hita Salazar 1679).

As the provincial was about to visit Apalachee, the governor suggested that he consult the friars with long service there, as well as the province's leaders about the neighboring heathen provinces' desire to become Christians. He confessed that he had received no reports other than the ones Fray Juan Moreno had given about the Apalachicoli, presumably those referring to the mysterious migrations of the early 1670s, and insinuations in 1674 about their willingness to be reduced. Spanish sources from the early 1670s speak cryptically about a migration of new natives into the Apalachicoli country along the Chattahoochee River in connection with a request for a large contingent of new friars. Although the migrants had come from places more than 100 leagues distant from Apalachee, they were alluded to as though they were part of the Apalachicoli people. But the sources gave no indication as to the direction from which the migrants had come. The Tama-Yamasee seem to be the most likely candidates as many of them had been driven from one of their traditional homelands in central Georgia by raids of the firearm-bearing and fierce Westo and the Tama-Yamasee were closely related linguistically with the Hitchiti-speakers among the Apalachicoli. However, in view of Florida Spaniards' familiarity with Tama and Yamasee since the era of Hernando de Soto, it is strange that these documents from the early 1670s do not identify these migrating peoples, except for those who settled in Apalachee, some of whom were Tama-Yamasee.

Interestingly, there is archaeological evidence corroborating such a migration. As I have noted earlier, archaeologists' research indicates that there was a massive depopulation of the Chattahoochee River valley during the century following the de Soto *entrada*. That depopulation seems to call for some such influx to account for the number of towns known to have been present there in the 1680s.

In one of these documents, Fray Juan Moreno (1673) of Florida, who was in Spain in early 1673 to recruit friars, reported that the newcomers had then moved down to "the borders of their land [to an area] that was three days distant by trail from Apalache, where they formed nine settlements that three or four thousand Indians occupied on the bank of a river that they call of Apalache which is six leagues distant from the sea toward the direction of the setting sun, a placid site, delightful and suitable for harvesting a great deal of wheat and corn." Moreno noted further that "the distance from village to village is two leagues and from the first to the last, eight." That spacing is remarkably similar to that of the first and the last of the Apalachicoli Province settlements on the Chattahoochee in the 1680s.

The first of these documents also throws a dramatic new light on the missionization of Apalachee. It speaks of the missionization there as "being newly begun" during the period. The remark suggests that there had been a hiatus in the province's evangelization since 1656 when five of the friars working there perished on a ship sailing for Cuba that was lost enroute. Alarmed by the unrest stirred up initially among the Apalachee by Timucua agitators looking for support for the 1656 revolt by the hinterland Timucua, those friars died while fleeing to Cuba (Hann 1996b:212). Apparently, they were not replaced immediately.

The provincial does not seem to have followed the governor's advice very zealously, remarking only in his postmortems that he had relied on advice from the lieutenants of Apalachee and Timucua and his alleged interpretation of the governor's remarks as having led him to understand that the Apalachicoli "were asking for conversion." As a result, he concluded, when the three friars arrived, whom he had dispatched, "so sudden a coming without any notice to them or their consent caused surprise and trouble among the natives," with the popular uproar obliging the friars to withdraw to Apalachee (Barreda 1692) only three days after their arrival (Hita Salazar et al. 1680).

The governor attributed the mission's failure primarily to the opposition to it by the chief of Caueta and the lack of money in the Indian fund to permit gift-giving that would make the friars' efforts more acceptable to the leaders who mattered. When Apalachee's lieutenant suggested the use of force to locate the trouble-makers and bring them back, Governor Hita Salazar (Hita Salazar et al. 1680) did not consider that an appropriate reaction "because this business of conversion is one of evangelical preaching and, in the beginnings among the barbarians, more a matter of gift-giving." He felt that if the Indian fund had provided its usual goods as part of the *situado*, "he would have conquered their wills with those [goods]." The friars had been well received by some on their arrival but, on the third day, Indians from neighboring places harassed those who had welcomed the friars with the result that they then stated unanimously that they did not wish to become Christians. The instigators threatened the welcomers and the friars with the bogeyman of the "Chuchumecos" if the friars should stay on. The governor felt that those opposed to the friars' presence were already in communication with the English at Charles Town and on good terms with the Chichimecos. The provincial, Fray Barreda (1680), indicated as part of the problem "their coming so unexpectedly, without any notice to them and without their consent," noting that "this caused surprise and consternation among the natives and as a result of a popular disturbance (*alboroto*)" the friars were obliged to withdraw. The Sauocola chief's absence from his village at the time of the friars' arrival also contributed to the outcome, as it was he who had been asking for friars. On his return home that chief sent regrets that he had not been present to overcome the difficulties (Hita Salazar et al. 1680).

Hita Salazar (1680a) advised the provincial that his policy would be one of awaiting a better occasion "when God should open paths" to permit the friars to return. To achieve that outcome, Apalachee's lieutenant was to continue friendly communications with the Apalachicoli, to welcome them warmly when they came to visit, and to make no reference to their expulsion of the friars, treating it as if it were something that had not occurred. The lieutenant followed those orders when Sauocola's chief came to visit. He did the same with another unidentified chief who probably was the town of Apalachicoli's old Chief Pentecolo. That chief seems to have served regularly as Apalachicoli Province's point man for dealings with the Spaniards in times of stress (Hita Salazar et al. 1680).

The next governor, Juan Márquez Cabrera, adopted a more truculent approach. Having entered Florida by way of Apalachee, he met there with Sauocola's chief. Attributing the 1679 mission's failure to its not having been accompanied by soldiers, the new governor returned two friars to Sauocola in March 1681, backed initially by 12 soldiers, although their number was soon reduced to eight. The friars baptized 36 people between children and adults to raise Sauocola's Christian population to 53. Many of the new converts were drawn from the Sauocola leadership class. They included Sauocola's principal cacique, two of his sons, his mother, and stepfather, the cacique governor and five of his family, the principal *eniha*, and his five sons, two other *enihas*, and other leading men with their wives and family. But beyond Sauocola, the atmosphere was not welcoming. The friar observed that the soldiers were sickly, attributing that in no small part to "the life that they have, sleeping with their clothes and shoes on and armed and all day long with their arms [in hand] and at night as sentinels and malnourished." The hostile attitude of the rest of the villages is indicated as well by the friar's suggestion that, if the governor were to visit and speak forcefully to them about conversion or to place another 12 soldiers in the northernmost village while retaining the existing dozen at Sauocola, the friars would be able to convert all the Indians. He felt that all that was lacking to achieve that was for someone to speak to them "with the power to produce the desired effect and that he had to be someone [like the governor] whose respect they fear to lose" (Gutiérrez de la Vera 1681; Márquez Cabrera 1680, 1681a, 1681b, 1682b).

Apalachicoli raiders' killing of two people in an Apalachee village brought an end to this second mission attempt only a few months later. The killings could have been contrived for that purpose, although there is no explicit evidence to suggest that. News of a Spanish-led Apalachee force dispatched toward Apalachicoli territory to apprehend the perpetrators created such an uproar among the Apalachicoli that the soldiers and friars at Sauocola found it advisable to withdraw. When the governor, chastened a bit, learned of that development early in September 1681, he offered a pardon to those responsible for the killings. But as a condition, he demanded that Apalachicoli's chiefs appear before him in St. Augustine to account for their behavior and to acknowledge again their obedience to him. If they did not, he threatened to go in search of them personally and to punish them as disobedient subjects.

Five Hitchiti-speaking chiefs, including their head chief from the town of Apalachicoli, responded to that ultimatum, arriving in St. Augustine on September 19, 1681. They denied responsibility for the killings, explaining that the perpetrators were bandits and fugitives who did not recognize or obey their chiefs. They denied ever having asked for friars or even having thought about doing so, informing the governor that they were not interested at the present in becoming Christians. They denied responsibility for the soldiers' and the friars' withdrawal, saying that the one responsible was "the cacique of Caueta, the most important one (*el mas principal*), and the one to whom they all render vassalage, and not the province of Apalachecole" (Márquez Cabrera 1681b).

In response to a request the governor made through those chiefs, Caueta's chief appeared in St. Augustine on January 2, 1682. The chief's meeting with the governor began on a very sour note when the governor read to Caueta's chief a very presumptuous letter that Bacuqua's Fray Rodrigo de la Barrera (1681) had asked the chief to deliver to the governor as the chief passed through that gateway village for travelers coming from the Apalachicoli country. Barrera's letter opened with the remark that "all the slander spoken about him [Caueta's chief] is false and that it is just the opposite. That he says that he will not refuse to admit a minister." The friar then qualified his remark by telling the governor, "it is in your lordship's hands whether or not he will admit one," implying that, if the governor were to apply a little pressure, the chief would admit them. The friar then went on to explain: "This will entail nothing less than the conversion of sixty-six places . . . not to mention other provinces such as that of Chiaha, the Chickasaw (*chicassa*), and many others who render homage to the said cacique of Caueta. And if this one should admit Christianity, I consider it to be without doubt that all of them will admit it" (Barrera 1681).

The governor interpreted Fray Barrera's opening statement literally, ignoring the friar's subsequent qualifications when he had the letter's contents explained to Caueta's chief and his party through Juan Sánchez, the governor's interpreter for the Apalachee language. As a consequence, the Indians became agitated, angrily informing the governor that they had not come to ask for priests. Caueta's chief explained that he had come only to make the peace agreements the governor had offered and to confirm those the governor had made with the Apalachicoli chiefs. The chief denied that the 66 villages that Barrera spoke of paid homage to him, noting that those provinces were "twelve days distant by trail" from his place "without there being any settlements in between." He affirmed that the only villages that paid homage to him were "the eleven which the province of Apalachecole has" (Barrera 1681; Márquez Cabrera 1682a).

The Creek Confederacy

Statements such as that one by Fray Barrera about the 66 villages have undoubtedly led authorities like Herbert E. Bolton (1925b:119) to speak of Caueta's chief in this era as "The Gran Cacique, or Emperor of the Cavetas (Cowetas), head tribe of the Confederacy," implying that the Creek Confederacy was already in existence at that time. While this and other documentation from the 1680s does not challenge Knight's (1994a:374–375) thesis that "There is no documentary evidence of any such political centralization prior to the eighteenth century," the evidence suggests that a prototype for the Confederacy was emerging among the Lower Creeks at that time. This is suggested in the power that Caueta and Casista's chiefs wielded over the rest of the Chattahoochee River towns; in the neutrality policy they were developing in the mid-1680s between rival European powers vying for their allegiance and trade; and in the feelers that they put out to Upper Creek leaders. Caueta's chief probably spoke the truth in denying that his power extended beyond the Apalachicoli towns. But, it is unlikely that Fray Barrera's statement about the chief's influence was entirely a fabrication. It is probable that it reflected a belief, at the very least, that Caueta's chief had great influence among the tribes that would later become known as Upper Creeks and among the other peoples whom Barrera mentioned. There probably was some foundation for the friar's belief, even though it may have been based as well on a degree of wishful thinking. In a report to the king, the governor said of Caueta's chief, "This is the cacique most feared in all these lands that share a border with the Chuchumecos and other provinces that render vassalage to the English of St. George [Charles Town], with whom they have wars" (Márquez Cabrera 1682b). Those remarks indicate that Brims' prestige was already impressive in the 1680s, even though it may not have matched that which he enjoyed by 1715 when Spaniards could refer to him as "emperor." The governor appears to have been confused in this reference to sharing a border with the Chuchumecos. By this time the Carolinians had destroyed the power of the Westo, something the governor should have been aware of. Fray Gutiérrez de la Vera had written to him on May 19, 1681, from Sauocola about the son of Caueta's chief having come to report to him that many refugee Chichimeco had come to live at Caueta (Gutiérrez de la Vera 1681).

As Corkran (1967:15, 78–79) noted: "The exact nature of the 'emperorship' of Coweta is difficult to define." Strong men arose by heredity and when one strong man of the four founding towns achieved ascendancy, "he was likely to be 'emperor' or supreme mico, having a voice of considerable dimension in regional and sometimes national affairs." It was thus that the Brims line achieved ascendancy. Although it was strongly influential, "it was not an absolute overlordship of the Creeks." Corkran concluded: "One must regard it as a 'first voice,' maintained through high hereditary prestige, which when wielded by a strong personality became as close to a true monarch as the Creek political organization was capable of sustaining." His having achieved such a status by the second decade of the eighteenth century is reflected in a reference to him as the "Great Chief of Caueta who represented one hundred and forty-nine settlements" (Ayala y Escobar 1717a).

Sauocola's Second Move Downriver

Caueta's chief remained firmly opposed to the presence of friars within his territory. However, he promised the governor that, if someone there wished to become a Christian, he would allow him to leave (Hann 1996a:72–73; Márquez Cabrera 1682a). That concession probably led to the Sauocola's second migration downriver between 1683 and 1685. Nothing appears to be known about the exact time or the circumstances of that move. The Sauocola mission does not appear on Solana's 1683 map but it was in existence by the fall of 1685 (Matheos 1685a). As a result of that lack of information and other factors, confusion, similar to that already noted relative to Bishop Calderón's Santa Cruz de Sabacola, mars some accounts of the second downriver mission bearing that name.

The confusion involves the exact location of the Sauocola mission during its second incarnation and its separateness from a nearby Chacato mission. Herbert E. Bolton (1925a:119) and Lanning (1935:173) located the Santa Cruz mission at the confluence of the Chattahoochee and Flint "not far from a new Franciscan mission among the Chatot." Their statements have been interpreted, at times, as meaning that the new Sauocola mission was located above the confluence of the Flint and the Chattahoochee when it was first mentioned. That does not seem to have been the case. Domingo de Leturiondo (1685b) warned the governor that if Spaniards obliterated the Apalachicoli villages as punishment for their hospitality toward English traders, the Apalachicoli could do the same in great security to the Spaniards' two places that "are on the River of Apalachicoli, Chacatos and Sauocolas, which are fourteen leagues from this province [Apalachee]." The two villages' closeness to one another is reflected in Matheos's (1686e:13) order to a Pansacola leader that he should go to the Chacato village to await Marcos Delgado's arrival, coupled with Delgado's report (Boyd 1937:14) that he set out from the Chacato village and Matheos's (1686g:17) remark a few weeks later that Delgado had left from the village of Sauocola. Delgado's description of the features of the trail he followed to reach the Chacato village "on the Apalachecolo River" match the descriptions of the trails taken in the 1677 and 1693 expeditions mentioned earlier (Boyd 1937:22). They give no indication that Delgado crossed the Flint at any point. The intermixing of the components of the two villages' names, as in Bishop Ebelino de Compostela's (1689) mission list in the hybridized form of San Carlos de Çabacola, also suggests a geographical closeness. But it could also simply be an indication that Chacato from the former San Carlos were living then at the Sabacola village. The Chacato village's name was given as San Nicolás de los Chacatos on the 1689 list, reflecting the return of many of the fugitive Chacato who had been living in Tawasa since 1675. On a 1690 listing of the convents, the one that served the two communities on the Apalachicola River was identified as the "*convento de Savacola Chuba*" (*Big Savacola*) (Luna 1690). The convent contained two friars, Pedro Hace and Matheo de Argüelles. In 1689 Sauocola had 30 families or about 150 individuals.

At some point this second Sauocola downriver village may have been moved to a site above the confluence of the Flint and Choctawhatchee. Diego Peña (1716) observed that the 1716-era village of Chislacaliche or Cherokeekiller, located to the west of the Flint River just above the confluence, was built on lands of the former Sauocola village. His remark is the only evidence for Sauocola's possibly having been located above the confluence at some time. That remark could be interpreted, of course, as meaning only that Sauocola's lands extended north of the confluence while the village itself remained below on the Apalachicola River.

Such a move was occasioned, possibly, by a falling out between the Sauocola and the Chacato, or between Sauocola and Spaniards. The Sauocola mission was not mentioned after 1690. Its demise occurred when Governor Diego de Quiroga y Losada's maintenance of a fort among the Apalachicoli in 1690–1691 pushed most of the upriver towns to move eastward and to launch hostilities against the Spaniards and their Indian allies. Fray Jacinto de Barrera (1692) stated that the Sauocola abandoned the mission, "solicited by the Apalachicoli, people of their same nation," because of the governor's "having placed the garrison of soldiers among them . . . against their will." By 1694 there was only one mission settlement on the Apalachicola River, the Chacato mission. When it was attacked, the survivors sought refuge at the Escambé mission. A force described as composed of 50 "Sabacola, Apalachicoli, and Tiquipache men" reportedly killed five Chacato men and carried off 42 men, women, and children as slaves. The first news was brought by an elderly Indian woman who escaped from her captors. Two other women who escaped, later identified four of the attackers as Sauocola, two as Chisca, and stated that the rest were "from the place of Cabeta, Apalachecolos."

Around that time Apalachee's lieutenant received word from the Aybama (Alabama) and Tawasa chiefs that they were sorely afflicted because the Indians of Tiquipache, Atasi, and other places were threatening them with death daily because they did not wish to follow the pro-English faction. They asked the lieutenant to send troops of his people so that they might move to Apalachee with security. Some of the Tawasa eventually came on their own. They also reported that Tiquipache had been responsible for the recent destruction of the crosses, church, and friary at "the old place of the Chacatos" (presumably one of those in the Marianna region) "because they did not find any people to kill" there "saying that they did it because the Spaniards greatly esteem those things" (A. Solana 1695b; Torres y Ayala 1695b).

Late in 1685 when Matheos was about to embark on his second foray to capture the English traders who had appeared in the Apalachicoli country a little earlier that year, Governor Márquez Cabrera (1685) sent his lieutenant instructions in anticipation of trouble. If Apalachicoli Province became disturbed, he was to propose to "the two villages of the crossing point (*passo*) of Santa Cruz that, if they feel insecure, they may withdraw to Apalache."

Beginning of the Troubles

In the wake of the Apalachicoli's rebuff of the friars who appeared in their midst uninvited late in 1679, the first act of British-inspired native hostility occurred that was perpetrated by peoples who had been on friendly terms with the Spaniards until then. The attack in 1680 involved assaults on San Simón on St. Simons Island and on Santa Catalina on St. Catherines Island by peoples identified as Chuchumecos, Uchizes (Vchizes), and Chiluques. These Chuchumeco, of course, were the Westo, and had always been enemies. As the governor remarked, "the Chichumeco [sic] alone were always enemies," while observing that "the Chiluques and Vchizes were sociable (*comunicables*), dealing and trading with these provinces [of Spanish Florida] in good friendship." But, "last year," he continued, "they all made peace and established friendship with the English, which they preserve. And this year these three nations have declared themselves enemies" (Hita Salazar 1680c). Later that same year the Carolina planters would destroy the power of the Westo despite the service they had rendered to the English.

Although Spaniards knew the identity of the peoples whom they referred to as Uchizes and Chiluques in 1680, their lineage remains uncertain for modern researchers. This is the Spaniards' first known use of the name Uchize, a name they applied regularly as the eighteenth century wore on to the Apalachicoli and other forebears of the Lower Creeks. In 1680 it designated people whom Spaniards seem to have viewed as distinct from the Apalachicoli of that era. Those

Uchisi probably were descendents of de Soto's Ichisi who had come to terms with their Westo tormentors. Spaniards used Chiluque over time to refer to several different peoples. Swanton (1922:90, 1946:46) identified Spaniards' Chiluque as Cherokee, suggesting that the name derived from a Muskogee word meaning "people of a different language." But Chalaque was the Spaniards' usual name for Cherokee. In the eighteenth century Spaniards used Chiluque or Chiluca to designate the Timucua-speaking Mocama (Hann 1996b:296). But the Chiluque of 1680 and other Spanish records going back to the early 1670s probably were Yamasee-speakers who were distinct enough from the Tama-Yamasee, to whom Spaniards usually applied the name Yamasee, for them to use this distinct name (Hann 1996b:293; Worth 1995:23, 24, 90, n. 47). Worth has established that they were living in the Santa Elena region in the 1670s and that Spaniards used the Guale language to communicate with them.

A crucial development in the early 1680s was the Carolina settlers' and Savannah Indians' campaign against the fearsome Westo, who had preyed on most of their neighbors at one time or another. The resulting virtual extermination of the Westo opened the way for English traders from Charles Town to go to the Apalachicoli country (Bolton 1925a:48; Crane 1981:19–21).

In February 1685 another group from the Santa Elena region whom Spaniards identified as Yamasee attacked and burned the Timucua mission of Santa Catalina de Ajoica instigated by Lord Cardross of Stuart's Town. The Yamasee in this case had previously lived on Amelia Island. About half the 60 Yamasee carried firearms and cutlasses, which they were to pay for by selling the mission Indians whom they captured as slaves. This attack is worthy of note here because of the influence it probably had on the nature of the Spanish response later that year to news of the arrival of the first British traders in the Apalachicoli country led by the already infamous Henry Woodward with whom Spaniards already were well acquainted (Hann 1996b:272–274; Worth 1998:II, 140–141).

Spanish Forays into the Apalachicoli Country 1685–1686

Reports that Caueta and the Apalachicoli were allowing English traders into their villages shattered the calm anew when Spaniards learned of the intercourse in the latter half of 1685. The governor and his new Apalachee lieutenant, Antonio Matheos, considered that a violation of the allegiance the chiefs had sworn to Spain's king. Matheos was as aggressive as the governor and without previous experience in Florida, having arrived with the governor at the end of 1680. Over the next four years or so, five Spanish-Apalachee military expeditions traveled through the Apalachicoli's territory in futile attempts to capture the Englishmen or stop the natives' contact with them. Spaniards established a fort in Apalachicoli territory in 1689, manning it with 21 soldiers and 20 Apalachee to permit a rapid response if the English reappeared.

Those moves resulted in pushing Caueta and the Apalachicoli into open hostilities with Spaniards and their native allies. This ended with the destruction of the missions and the decimation of their surviving native populations. That development may have been inevitable in the long run in view of English demand for native slaves, but some experienced Florida hands saw Caueta's contacts with the English as no more than pursuit of a policy of neutrality between the European rivals.

Documentation from the first two expeditions provides data on the identity and location of some of the towns and other useful information on Caueta and the Apalachicoli, and on relations between them. Matheos (1685a) placed the abandoned site of Big Sauocola one and one-half leagues south of a village he referred to simply (in a geographic sense) as "the first place of the province." Sauocola's *usinulo*, Juan Ysfane (1685), identified that first place as Talipasle. It was not among the towns the bishop mentioned, nor does it appear on other listings. It is likely that it was a satellite settlement whose chief was subject to the chief of a major town. There do not appear to have been any settlements in the valley south of the Sauocola site in this era.

The available documentation does not reveal how or exactly when Matheos first learned of the presence of the Englishmen. But it was probably very early in September, as he had already spent time at the Sauocola mission when he headed upriver from there on September 11, 1685. On arriving at the mission, Matheos sent two Sauocola northward to gather intelligence for him. One of them apparently returned to report to Matheos before he set out from the mission; after two and one-half days on the trail, he met the second spy. Following his arrival at the abandoned site of Sauocola, he consulted people knowledgeable about the region about the distance from there to Casista, where he expected to find one or more of the Englishmen. He also inquired about the time that his expedition could make on the trail. Matheos concluded that reaching Casista without his presence becoming known was impossible because Casista was nine leagues from Talipasle on a trail that passed through the middle of all the places in between. Matheos observed that these factors made it all but impossible to catch the Englishmen by surprise as long as the natives were disposed to protect them. He described the trail as troublesome in places even in daytime because of arroyos that were so deep they could only be crossed on a log, even though they contained no water. However, Fretwell (1980:106) shows paths to Coweta used by Spaniards on both sides of the river to a point just south of Sauocola el Grande where the east-bank trail ends.

Matheos identified Apalachicoli as the third town along the trail, failing to identify the second town where he stopped, which probably was Oconi. A young non-Christian Sauocola whom Matheos placed in the province earlier to gather intelligence met Matheos on the trail shortly after the expedition left Talipasle. The spy had slipped out of Oconi during the night, fearing that he might be killed if he were caught leaving, as the majority of the people were up in arms over the coming of Matheos and the Apalachee. Juan Ysfane (1685) confused the issue of Oconi's location somewhat in stating that he had passed on from Talipasle "to the second one, which is Apalachecole." But his remark could be interpreted as indicating that a trail went directly to Apalachicoli from Talipasle.

Talipasle was the only town for which Matheos maintained the element of surprise. Having set out at 3:00 a.m., he reached it by sunrise when all of its inhabitants were still sleeping. From there on he found all the towns virtually abandoned as word of his coming preceded him. Matheos found his talk with Talipasle's leaders unsatisfactory, presumably because they did not tell him where the Englishmen were. While there, he spotted an Indian "who seemed to be different from the rest." The Talipasle identified him as a Chickasaw (*Chicassa*) who had been there three days awaiting the return of companions from his nation who had gone out to hunt far from there. Matheos ordered them to detain the Chickasaw until the next day so that "as an outsider, he would not be able to stir up the other places." Shortly after Matheos left Talipasle, an Indian brought word that the Chickasaw had fled. Matheos (1685a) learned later that the Chickasaw was one of those who alerted the rest of the villages.

Initially Matheos had entertained some hope of keeping his arrival a surprise. This is indicated by his remark that, on writing to Apalachicoli's chief, apparently from the Sauocola mission, he had given that chief to understand that he had returned to San Luis until the chief responded to the queries he sent to him. But, because of the difficulties of the trail, his uncertainty about the attitude of the Apalachicoli toward his coming, and about the location and number of the Englishmen, he decided to enter during the daytime "as far as the place of Apalachicola or as far [at least]" as he should "encounter reliable reports about the state of affairs there."

When Matheos found the second village deserted, his concern over what the spy had told him about the people's anger prompted him to stop there and ask Apalachicoli's chief to meet with him there. He had apparently set out without a particularly large force, sending an appeal to St. Augustine for reinforcements. He received word later that the governor would send 16 Spaniards and 150 more Indians. Apalachicoli's Chief Pentecolo (written as Pontecolo by Matheos) came, accompanied by two men. He told Matheos that the people were abandoning their villages because of fear that he might kill them. Pentecolo professed not to know for certain where the Englishmen were, but said that common report had it that Casista, Tasquique, and Colone each had two and that Caueta had one. Pentecolo also stated that "they were saying that there was no reason for their fighting with me, nor I with them, because we were comrades (*camaradas*)." And that they were awaiting another 40 who would come very shortly. Pentecolo proved uncooperative when Matheos (1685a) sought to persuade him to use his influence to convince the other chiefs to agree to hand over the English traders or, at least, to provide definite information that would permit the Spaniards to capture them. Matheos was convinced that all of them were so attached to the English that "they would sooner deliver me to the English than the opposite."

Matheos went on to Apalachicoli the next morning accompanied by its chief and found it deserted despite his assurances sent through the chief that they had nothing to fear from him. While Matheos remained at Apalachicoli, many messengers came from the rest of the places, "sent," as he reported, "to advise me that the Englishmen were awaiting me without any apprehension about my coming and awaiting me . . . at Casista." To test that taunt, Matheos dispatched 10 men by a trail that went directly from Apalachicoli to Casista with a message for the caciques, telling them he was "coming only to see the Englishmen, for they wished to see him." But the 10 men found Casista deserted like the rest. Matheos described Casista as southernmost of the four northern towns.

Matheos continued on the regular trail, stopping for the night at Osuche, after passing through a number of unnamed towns. The 10 men he had sent to Casista met him at Osuche after doubling back on the regular trail on finding Casista deserted. Matheos reached Casista on the next day by or before nightfall, remaining there for three days. Knowing that there were three men at Caueta, Matheos sent for them to question them. They brought a white cross and a paper with writing on it that Matheos did not understand, which was Woodward's taunting letter in English. The three men, and two more who came along by chance, told contradictory tales and, among them, that the Englishmen had left with some Westo men and 20 Westo women. It was from the questioning of those men that Matheos learned that it was the Chickasaw who escaped from Talipasle who told the English of his coming. During this time he threatened to burn the villages and crops unless their people handed over the Englishmen or told him where he might find them. On receiving no response, Matheos set out for Caueta intent on burning it and doing the same to Casista on his return. But his uncertainty about how the governor would react, and warnings from the soldiers and Apalachee leaders that such action would surely provoke retaliation against the missions, dissuaded him from doing so.

Matheos then returned to Casista determined to depart for Apalachee, allegedly because he was achieving nothing other than annoying the Indians. The only Apalachicoli leaders who had come to see him were "the cacique of Apalachicole and an *ynixa* and a nephew who has come to see me from time to time." In a second reference to this trio, Matheos described them as "the cacique and his son and a nephew," indicating conclusively that they were three distinct individuals (Matheos 1685a). He suspected that the latter two's attendance on him served an intelligence purpose more than anything else.

One day after Matheos began his withdrawal southward on September 22, when he reached Ocmulque which was two leagues from Casista, he met the reinforcements sent to him. They had stopped there to wait for one of their snake-bit comrades to get better. In the wake of that encounter, Matheos decided to move northward again to re-provision his augmented forces for the return trip at the expense of the more recalcitrant northernmost towns. He was intent on annoying them, hoping they'd think about it for six or seven days and knowing that he took their provisions, so that they would be more cooperative in giving him information on the whereabouts of the Englishmen.

Departing from Ocmulque at sunrise, he reached Caueta at eight in the morning. He caught a woman there who told him the Englishmen and Indians were in a palisade. She did not know its exact location but stated that it was to the north. She explained that no one else had mentioned the palisade because the death penalty had been decreed for anyone who told Matheos about it. He set out the next day to search for it with three days' provisions, bringing along the woman and a son of Apalachicoli's chief. At an undisclosed time after his departure, he passed by Tasquique without stopping, describing it as "to one side." At about a league and one-half beyond Tasquique, on arriving at a place on the river known as "the waterfall," the woman told them the palisade had to be near according to what they had told her. They pushed on for another two leagues until two in the afternoon when they reached some cane thickets (*cañaverales*). They stopped there to refresh themselves because the heat was intense and they had not yet eaten on that day. From there Matheos (1685b) retraced his steps as far as Tasquique, reaching it at nightfall. There he hoped to acquire a more precise source of information on the palisade by sending out scouting parties to capture an Indian who might have the information needed.

One of Matheos's efforts located three men from the town of Apalachicoli who had been recruited to work on the palisade "because of the call and threats of the Chichimecos who were with the Englishmen." The three informants concurred in stating "that before making that palisade, they had begun another at the waterfall and that they had not completed either of the two because the Indians and English did not agree on this particular. And that they abandoned the first one before I came to Apalachicoli and that they had found the second one in the same shape two days ago, without knowing what trail the Englishmen had taken." The agent who had located the three men was from that province himself. He returned later that day to report that he had found a palisade and that there was no one in it.

That palisade was about six leagues north of Tasquique and two musket shots from the river's edge. Matheos was told that it was abandoned because the Apalachicoli did not wish to unite with the English and the Chichimecos to fight with the Spaniards and their native allies. The leader of the forces Matheos (1685b) sent to destroy that palisade reported that only the curtain that faced the river had been well completed. The other three sides were unfinished in the sense that "a man could almost fit between one post and another and none of the logs was any stouter than an arm." Although it was large enough to hold 2,000 people, its destroyers found no signs that many people had ever been at the site. They found remains of only two fires and the grass in the area very fresh and green. The ground between the palisade and the river consisted of slate or shale (*pizarras*) without a single plant growing through it. The river was so wide at that point that a musket shot would not carry across it. The site was surrounded by woods on the back and on its two sides. The Apalachee sent to destroy it saw a few Indians in that woods who fled at the sight of them.

Before heading back to Apalachee, Matheos, as a gesture of good will, returned 20 bundles of deerskins and dresses (*guaypiles*) to their owners. One of his scouting parties had taken them from a camp (*rancheria*) it had found in the woods. The owners of those goods had shown the only sign the expedition encountered of the Apalachicoli "wanting to put up resistance to them." But they took flight when the Apalachee fired some harquebus shots toward them, except for one woman whose injured foot prevented her from doing so. The Apalachee brought her back to Tasquique along with the booty.

Apalachicoli Neutrality

Natives of the Chattahoochee region whom Matheos (1685b) interviewed attributed the abandonment of both palisades to differences between the Apalachicoli and the English. Some indicated that the building of both was largely the inspiration of the English and the Westo who accompanied Henry Woodward upon his arrival. The informants maintained that Apalachicoli reluctance to provoke an open and complete breach with the Spaniards led to abandonment of both palisades before they were completed. The English reportedly expressed disgust with the Apalachicoli's refusal to stand and fight with the invaders, telling the Apalachicoli that they were not men like the Chichimeco and Chisca, who had the courage for fighting and dying and who were always singing.

Domingo de Leturiondo (1685b), whom the governor had commissioned to conduct a formal visitation of Apalachee and Timucua during this period, interviewed several of the Apalachicoli leaders. After talking with Pentecolo, Achito's Chief Acolaque, and Sauocola's Juan Ysfane shortly after Matheos returned from his first expedition, Leturiondo became convinced that neutrality was indeed the Apalachicoli's policy at this time. He advised the governor that additional expeditions to capture the English would be futile, warning "and if we are to break with them definitively, it will be necessary to go with forces of people and obliterate all of the villages. In this case they will withdraw toward the English and become declared enemies. And in great security they will be able to obliterate the two places that are on the River of Apalachicoli, Chacatos and Sauocolas, which are fourteen leagues distant from this province." He might have added that the rest of the missions faced the same danger. But that probably was not foreseen as clearly then except by the Apalachee leaders. Testimony by a soldier who served on this expedition indicates that the reason Matheos desisted from burning the villages at this time was remonstrations by Ivitachuco's chief and other Apalachee leaders present that their people would bear the cost of such action in the sense of being future targets for retaliatory attacks by Indians of Apalachicoli Province. The testimony was given during an investigation of complaints against Matheos that included Apalachee leaders' request for his removal and particularly leaders at San Luis (Hann 1988a:188). The warning apparently fell on deaf ears.

While Matheos was still in the Apalachicoli country, the governor ordered him to apprehend its caciques. As he was already well on his way back when he received those orders, and no chief made himself available for capture other than Apalachicoli's chief, Matheos (1685a) ignored the order. He explained to the governor that he did not apprehend Apalachicoli's chief, even though he had the opportunity to do so, because he had given him his word "not to do him any injury and also because the rest, after seeing such a thing, neither caciques nor vassals would return to their villages. And if, without my doing such a thing, they are so tied to the English, on seeing that I did them such an injury, it would have been impossible to reduce them again to their former state."

Matheos contented himself on his parting visit with Apalachicoli's chief with reminding him that he had been loyal to Spain's king for so many years and asking "how did he dare to consent that Englishmen should enter into that province," knowing that they were enemies of Spain's king? The chief reportedly replied that "all of this was true and that he had not brought them, nor was he at all pleased that the said Englishmen had come." Matheos closed with a threat that if they again introduced any Englishman, "they would all suffer blood and fire except for women and children." The chief promised to pass the word to the other leaders and to send his son with their reply. To monitor developments, Matheos left two Indians behind to function as undercover spies.

Interlude between Matheos' First Two Forays

When almost two weeks had passed since Matheos' return to San Luis without his having received any word from Apalachicoli's chief about the rest of the chiefs' reaction to the Spanish demand that the province sever all contact with the English, Matheos again headed for Santa Cruz de Sauocola on October 17, accompanied by the Visitor, Domingo de Leturiondo. There they ordered its chief to dispatch four messengers to Apalachicoli to repeat the Spaniards' demand. The chief's son, Juan Ysfane, headed the mission.

On reaching Talipasle after several days travel, the messengers found the atmosphere there sufficiently hostile to make them decide to advance no further for the present. Instead they sent local people on north to call on the caciques of Caueta, Casiste, Tasquique, and the rest of the places to come down to Talipasle so that they might deliver their message, although they eventually moved on to the next village, Apalachicoli. The caciques who replied insisted that the messengers should come on upriver to deliver their message, explaining that most of the chiefs were still out in the woods reassembling their people after the flight precipitated by Matheos' arrival with Apalachee warriors. While still in Talipasle, the messengers learned from an Indian who came from upriver that the English had indeed returned and were in Tasquique.

Their visit eventually prompted Chief Pentecolo and Achito's Chief Acolaque to journey downriver to Sauocola and on to San Luis, where they were formally questioned by Leturiondo. Pentecolo brought the message that the rest of the chiefs declined to come down at present and had, instead, delegated him to come in their name to test the water as it were. In the wake of their visit, when all of their people had been reassembled, the rest of the chiefs would come down (Hahn 2000:138; Leturiondo 1685a, 1685b; Matheos 1685c). But Indians serving as spies for the Spaniards brought details of a continued English presence by the latter part of November 1685 that soon led to a renewed Spanish and Apalachee invasion. Sauocola's Fray Juan Mercado (1685) reported that a Sauocolan had seen four Englishmen in Osuche assisting its inhabitants in the building of a council house, and that one among others at Caueta had married a niece of Juiaui, who was a kinsman of the caciques of San Luis (Matheos 1685c).

The Second Foray 1685–1686

When Márquez Cabrera (1685) learned of the Apalachicoli's continued dalliance with the English, he ordered Matheos to return to the Apalachicoli country with a large force of Spaniards and Indians. If he found solid evidence that its Indians were hiding the English, or if the Indians fled from their villages at his approach, he was to burn the villages and their provisions and capture the chiefs. The governor contrasted the Apalachicoli's warm reception of Spain's English enemies with the hostility with which they had greeted his friars and soldiers just four years earlier.

On this second foray, Matheos (1685c, 1685d) sought to maintain the element of surprise by proceeding overland to the Chattahoochee River. He crossed at the abandoned site of Big Sauocola and avoided the trails to circle around and approach Caueta by surprise. He avoided going near the Sauocola mission because of its proximity to the Chacatos mission, noting that it held many relatives and confidants of the Apalachicoli. He posted sentinels to prevent anyone from Apalachee from going to those two missions or to the Apalachicoli country. He also instructed the priests at Santa Cruz, Chacatos, and la Tama not to permit any person to leave those places who would be able to carry news of his coming. All his precautions were in vain. When he finally arrived at Caueta on January 8, 1686, he found it uninhabited "because as soon as they learned of our arrival in this province, in addition to there being many people in the woods [already] on their hunting expeditions, those who had remained behind, both in this place as in the rest of the places, loaded up their possessions and have gone to the woods."

Only Apalachicoli's chief and the chief of a small, unidentified place came to Caueta to see him in response to messages he sent them. Most of the rest of the villages temporized, saying that their leaders were out hunting in parts unknown. After waiting 22 days, Matheos (1686a, 1686b) summoned Chief Pentecolo to pass the word that he would destroy any villages whose leaders did not come to see him within seven days. Pentecolo returned by that deadline with the chiefs of Oconi, Achito, Alape, Tacussa, and Ocuti, and the leading men from Osuche and Ocmulque. Those leading men claimed that they had been unable to get word to their chiefs who were hunting deep in the woods. Matheos suspected that the two chiefs absented themselves because of their places having been the first into which the English had entered. Matheos recorded that the four northern towns had not even responded to the message he sent them, although he remarked cryptically, "the one [chief] of Casista and Colome agreed, while I was in sight of their villages."

Although Matheos (1685b) was skeptical about the excuses that submissive leaders gave for their tolerance of the English presence, he conceded that it proceeded for some of them more from duress than from their own free will. One of the justifications the Indians alleged was a hope of regaining freedom for five of their people whom the English were holding as slaves. The Apalachicoli's submissiveness had a limit, however. Matheos' threats to burn the villages of those who met with him unless they provided him with the information he needed to capture the Englishmen proved ineffectual. They replied that he should do what seemed best to him, as they had heard nothing about the four Englishmen since they left Osuche when the 10 Apalachee spies arrived.

The Apalachicoli Towns' Autonomy

This episode and others suggest that the southern Hitchiti-speaking towns enjoyed, or were purposefully allowed, considerable independence under the hegemony that Caueta's chief exercised. Before, during, and after this crisis, Chief Pentecolo served as point-man and spokesman as well for Caueta in most of the region's dealings with the Spanish authorities. Possibly his age, his position as head chief of the Hitchiti-speakers, and his role as Peace Chief gave him special stature. Spaniards estimated from his appearance that he was about 60 (Pontocolo 1685). Apalachicoli's chief still enjoyed such status a century later in Bartram's (1955:313) time.

The English Traders' Warehouse

Matheos' only success during his second expedition was his discovery of a warehouse in the woods, two leagues distant from Caueta, belonging to English traders. Its booty consisted of 506 deerskins, 23 beaver skins, eight pairs of homespun stockings—five were red, and three white—and a yard and one-half of "red scarlet basting with a trimming of false gold." He described the deerskins as not worth much because they looked more like cat skins than deerskins (Matheos 1686a).

Message from the Upper Creeks

Three days after Matheos' meeting with leaders from the eight southern villages, 26 Indians came to Caueta from Tallapoosa towns in response to messages that he had sent. Matheos (1686a) referred to the Tallapoosa towns as from the provinces of Atassi, Talissi, and Ticopache. The chiefs sent word that they were unable to come at that time but that they were pleased with his message, desirous to continue their relations with the Spaniards and the Apalachee, and not interested in contact with the English. They informed Matheos that they had rejected an invitation from Caueta and Casista's chiefs to come to meet the English when the latter first came to Apalachicoli Province. Matheos (1686a, 1686b) also reported that Tawasa's chief sent word of an invitation from the Chattahoochee River chiefs to join their league and then come to make war on Apalachee, which he had rejected. Matheos commented that he could find no trace of such a conspiracy, remarking that he reckoned "that they all entered into the league on an impulse and now each one is striving to separate himself from it and throw the blame on someone else." Early in 1687 Márques Cabrera noted in an *auto* for a proposed exploration westward that the provinces of Chicahiti, Tabasa, and La Mobila, neighbors of the Choctaw and Holy Spirit Bay, had offered obedience to the king (Márques Cabrera 1687). They had learned this from "a statement of the captain of the schooner from the squadron of Monsieur de Agramon . . . who said the bay was settled by Frenchmen." The governor decided to send Marcos Delgado with 12 soldiers and 40 Indian warriors to explore the lands that were unknown. This exploration was to have begun at the beginning of spring. This writer has seen no evidence of Delgado's departure. The governor's desertion of his post in April 1687 probably precluded it.

Those western territories attracted the governor's attention again in February 1687 as he convoked a tribunal (*acuerdo*) to consider dispatch of an exploratory expedition to search for the Bay of the Holy Spirit. Spaniards then believed that the Mississippi flowed into that mythical bay. The decision was prompted by a statement by a captured schooner captain from Monsieur de Grammont's squadron and papers taken in Spanish raids on Georgia's coast. The captain stated that the bay was settled by Frenchmen. The captured papers revealed that England's king had authorized settlement by his people southward to thirty-one degrees, just north of Cumberland Island, and westward to the South Sea. In support of his proposal, the governor noted that the western provinces of Chicahuti, Tawasa, and la Movila, neighbors of the Choctaw and Holy Spirit Bay, had offered obedience to the Spanish king.

Matheos's Destruction of the Four Northern Towns

On the day following the departure of the Tallapoosa, January 30, 1686, Matheos began his destruction of the four northern towns by setting fire to Tasquique and Casista. He found no one at Tasquique, but there were two women at Casista. He made them gather up their possessions and put them in another house that they had outside of the heart (*cohollo*) of the town. He burned Caueta and Colone on the next day. At Caueta he spared two houses belonging to people who had remained living in them during his stay there. As he passed through the southern towns on his withdrawal, he found many people in them who received him in a friendly fashion. He made no demands on them for food, having provisioned his forces for the entire journey from stocks he found at Caueta.

Matheos (1686b) expressed hope that his sparing of the southern towns might create sufficient discord in that province to rule out any retaliation because those whom he had spared would not want to risk losing their houses and conveniences by supporting the northern towns in that fashion. In a cryptic remark he noted that he based his expectation on the majority of the people of the four burned villages being "from other places and they will return to them." This suggests that they were relatively recent immigrants. But he expressed concern for the security of the two isolated mission settlements of the Chacatos and the Sauocola, observing that he had summoned the chiefs of the two villages "to see how things stand there." He felt, unless the governor thought otherwise, that those two peoples should "withdraw from their places at once so as not to give encouragement to the mischievous ones and so that they may understand that he has no fear for them." Then, in an obscurely worded passage, he seemed to recommend that ultimately they should reoccupy the old Sauocola site on the Chattahoochee River backed by four or six Spanish soldiers and 150 Apalachee families. With them he felt "it would be possible to build a place that would subject all those provinces, from whence it would be possible to assist this one in the time of needs with great ease, because the canoes can come from the place of Caueta to within three leagues of this one of San Luis."

The Aftermath

Not long after Matheos' return to Apalachee, Pentecolo came to San Luis, reportedly in the name of the four burned villages, to ask for mercy for them. The chief reported that they now renounced their intercourse with the English. The four chiefs promised to come to renew their obedience personally once they had completed their plantings and the rebuilding of their villages. For the present each town sent one deerskin as a token of their obedience and friendship. Matheos responded by sending each chief a knife and 20 strings of beads, apologizing that he had nothing better to send them at the moment and promising to regale them later in another manner (Matheos 1686c).

The prospect for better relations proved to be short lived as far as Casista and Caueta were concerned. Two Tama-Yamasee spies, whom Matheos (1686d) commissioned to visit all the towns of the region, reported in May 1686 that they had been welcomed everywhere except Casista and Caueta. Those two towns' chiefs sent word to them not to come to their villages because they would not be able to guarantee their safety because they were enemies from Apalachee. The two replied that they were not Apalachee but Tama, who were coming only to see relatives and to buy something. They arrived at a field between the two villages as they were playing the ball game. Although they had kin there, no one spoke to them during the game. When they headed toward Casista after the game, its chief confronted them, informing them that they would not enter his village. With that he gave them a canoe to cross the river. They found a warm welcome in Tasquique and Colone whose people told them that, "although the Christians had burned their towns, they had patience because they [themselves] had their guilt, although the ones fully responsible were the caciques of Casista and Cabeta, who had deceived and entangled all the rest in bringing the Englishmen and forcing them to receive them" (Matheos 1686d). Caueta gave the Tama the same reception as had Casista and intimated that they did not intend to remain there. The spies noted that no rebuilding had been done at Caueta or Casista in contrast to Tasquique and Colone, where many structures had been begun or finished. But subsequent documentation suggests that Caueta and Casista did not move to the Ocmulque River until 1690 when Spaniards placed a fort and garrison in their midst.

Two days later, on May 21st, one of another two spies Matheos (1686e) had left behind arrived at San Luis to report. He had been staying at a little Yamasee hamlet two leagues from Caueta. His colleague was based at Ocute, which suggests that its inhabitants also were Yamasee, like those of an Ocute near St. Augustine in the wake of the Yamasee War (Primo de Rivera 1717a:185). On hearing three shots from the direction of the town of Apalachicoli, which the Yamasee told him signaled the arrival of an Englishman and some other Yamasee, the spy headed for Apalachicoli. He hid his bow and quiver before doing so and put a deerskin over his shoulders to conform to the local fashion so that he would not stand out. The spy reported that, as he approached the town, "he encountered a young man who took the said spy for a native of that country because he saw nothing strange in his garb or in his speech because he understands the said province very well" (Matheos 1686e). As he and the young man came close to the houses, he saw that they were placing sentinels with muskets along the trails. The Yamasee who came with the Englishman told him that they were posting those sentinels in case people came from Apalachee. As he was going along with them as far as the council house (*bujio*) of Apalachicoli, he saw that all the chiefs and people, men, women, and youngsters, were coming to see the visitors. At that point the spy's cover failed to some extent when his colleague at Ocute, who was talking with the newly arrived Yamasee, beckoned him over. The visiting Yamasee then recognized that he, like his colleague who was a chief, had come from Apalachee's Tama-Yamasee community. The spy's explanation that he and the chief no longer wished to live in Apalachee seemed to satisfy his inquisitors, who then told him that another 45 Yamasee, whom the spy later saw, were coming with another Englishman.

The two groups of Yamasee together brought 27 muskets and 30 pistols. All had machetes and wore hats and waist-jackets. All the province's chiefs were in attendance except for Caueta's chief. Casista's chief distributed the Englishman's orders to the others. It is likely that the Yamasee who came with the Englishmen were among those who had migrated to Santa Elena from the Creek country in 1685. The spy's remark that he understood Apalachicoli Province very well suggests that Apalachee's Tama-Yamasee community may have tarried awhile in Apalachicoli territory before moving on to Apalachee.

Another Englishman came out at this point whom the young spy described as a lad (*mozo*) of the build and age of Diego de Florencia, a scion of San Luis's leading Spanish family at that period. The Englishman then asked the spy through a Yamasee interpreter why he had returned. When the spy gave the same reply as he had used earlier, the Englishman told him to be of good cheer, that he would do him no harm, having been sent by his governor only to see those lands and trade for their beaver and deerskins and that he would leave the rest for the Apalachee. Later the spy heard that the Yamasee, who was squad leader for this band, had participated in the 1685 attack on Santa Catalina de Ahoica.

After obtaining this intelligence, the two spies resolved to leave. But the chief was unable to get away. Because of his chiefly status, he was not permitted to go anywhere unaccompanied by a sentinel. On the other hand, the native authorities paid no attention to the second spy because of his being a very young man (*mosuelo*), thereby allowing him to return to Apalachee unobserved (Matheos 1686e).

Caueta and Casista did not retaliate at that time beyond severing trade contact between Apalachicoli Province and Apalachee. In June 1687 the king implicitly disapproved of Matheos's burning of the four towns in instructing his new governor of Florida to maintain friendly relations with the Apalachicoli, Movila, Chickasaw, and the rest, and to console the Indians whose villages Matheos had burned. Diego de Quiroga y Losada (1688b) carried out those orders entertaining envoys of the Apalachicoli and restoring communications. But, in a fruitless effort to capture the English traders whom the Apalachicoli continued to welcome, Quiroga sent two more armed expeditions to the Chattahoochee River towns before late 1689. Like the third expedition Matheos made, nothing is known about the nature of those last sallies. Quiroga's frustration over his two expeditions' failure to halt the Indians' trade with the English led him to adopt the strategy late in 1689 of building a palisaded blockhouse in Apalachicoli territory from which his forces could move expeditiously to capture any English traders who appeared. In response some of the river towns moved eastward to the Ocmulgee, Oconee, and Savannah rivers to continue their trade, becoming outright enemies of the Spaniards and their native allies, as Leturiondo had predicted they would if their neutrality were violated too flagrantly (Hann 1986a:175; Quiroga y Losada 1690a).

In an ironic serendipitous twist, four of the traders whom Matheos had labored so hard to capture perished at the hands of mission Indians the Englishmen had captured down on the coast as the Englishmen were returning to

Charles Town. Five Guale Indians who had sailed with the Havana privateer Captain Alejandro Thomás de León on an expedition to eliminate or harass English settlement south of Charles Town were stranded on that coast when their ship and captain perished in a hurricane. While they were making their way back to Spanish territory, they were captured and tied up by five English traders from Woodward's 1685 expedition to the Apalachicoli country whom they encountered at the mouth of a river. Later one of the Guale untied himself and freed his comrades. Catching their five captors by surprise, they killed four of them while the fifth escaped with two wounds. As a result the Indians gained considerable booty that included 180 deerskins, 200 beaver and otter pelts, and other skins from bear and buffalo (Baltasar et al. 1686; Worth 1995:146–151).

In late 1687 or early 1688, Fray Simón de Salas and a soldier journeyed to Charles Town to try to arrange for the return to Spanish territory of Christian and heathen Indians who had recently migrated to English territory after having been offended by Governor Márques Cabrera. Once they had arrived in Carolina, they had quickly become disenchanted with their treatment among the English. However, the English governor refused to allow the friar to talk to the Indians. But the latter sent word to the friar on the part of their cacique that, around July or August during the time when the figs were ripe, some among those Indians would, under the pretext of harvesting figs, journey to Guale's former Santa Catalina mission, to confer there with the friars to arrange for their passage to Spanish territory under the Spanish governor's full guarantee. This writer has seen no evidence indicating that these negotiations went forward (Quiroga y Losada 1688d).

6

A Hostile Apalachicoli, 1690–1715

Consequences of the Burnings

It is unlikely that Matheos or Márquez Cabrera saw the burning of the four Chattahoochee River settlements as the opening act of hostilities that would bring total destruction of the missions within two decades. But, viewed in hindsight, that is the role their action played. Márquez Cabrera's desertion of his post just over a year later and the consequent removal of Matheos delayed the reaction by easing tensions somewhat until the closing days of 1689. Although Spaniards' continued effort to prevent the river towns' ongoing trade with the English with three more armed forays between June 1686 and the latter part of 1689 remained an irritant, a quietus seems to have prevailed among the contenders. The only record of those efforts found to date is an offhand mention of them by the next proprietary governor, Diego de Quiroga y Losada (1690a). Such a conclusion seems justified by Governor Laureano de Torres y Ayala's (1695b) attribution of the beginning of hostilities by the Apalachicoli to Quiroga y Losada's having increased the pressure by building a fort in the heart of Apalachicoli territory. In his view, the Apalachicoli began hostilities with their 1691 attacks on the San Juan Guacara and Tarihica missions.

It is worthy of note that Governor Quiroga y Losada (1691a) identified the attackers who destroyed Guacara on August 30, 1691 as "Indians of Uchise, Yamasses, and Englishmen." That is the earliest use of the name Uchise to designate the Apalachicoli from the Chattahoochee River who had moved eastward into central Georgia. The Apalachicoli's involvement is confirmed by a petition from April 1692 in which Fray Jazinto de Barreda (1692) spoke of "the considerable damage that the heathen Indians from Apalachicoli have done to San Juan de Guacara ... on the thirtieth day of August ... of ninety-one." This early transference of the name Uchise to the Apalachicoli suggests that from the Spaniards' first recorded use of the name in 1680, they recognized that the Uchise of the Macon area were kin of the Apalachicoli-speakers of the Chattahoochee Valley. It also probably reflects the reality that by the 1680s, Macon-area Uchise were part of Apalachicoli Province's population.

Another factor, doubtless, in the Apalachicoli's growing antipathy toward the Spaniards was the presence among them in the late 1680s of a sizeable number of Apalachee disillusioned by the behavior of their province's growing Spanish population at Mission San Luis. The émigrés included members of the chiefly class. Conceivably, it was at this time that Emperor Brims' Apalachee wife, Qua, moved to the banks of the Chattahoochee. Although the next proprietary governor after Márques Cabrera induced many of the émigrés to return, it is likely that many among those who remained aligned themselves with the pro-English faction there (Hann 1988a:172, 288).

Building of the Fort on the Chattahoochee among the Apalachicoli

Surprisingly little documentation has surfaced to date from the almost two-year-long adventure that was the building, maintenance, and demolition of the Spanish fort on the Chattahoochee. There is even less detail on the Indians' reaction to it. A passing remark by Quiroga y Losada (1690b) in a letter to the king of August 31, 1690, that the garrison had been stationed at that fort "for eight months and more" places the fort's establishment at the end of 1689. He ordered the fort's demolition on September 18, 1691, just over two weeks after the attack on Guacara, although other considerations also brought about that decision (Quiroga y Losada 1691b).

In the absence of positive evidence to the contrary, it may be assumed that most or possibly all of the settlements of the mid-1680s remained on the Chattahoochee until some time after the building of the Spanish fort there. Quiroga y Losada (1690b) spoke on August 26, 1690, of the province of Apalachicoli being "composed of fourteen places and most of them very populous." The fort commander's instructions to Apalachicoli Indians who visited the fort in May 1690 that their leading men should assemble at Caueta a few days later so that he might address them indicates that even that settlement had been rebuilt and reoccupied in the wake of its destruction by Matheos at the beginning of 1686 (Angulo 1690b). Although the Scots trader, John Stewart, indicated that Caueta and Casista had moved to central Georgia early in 1690, only considerably later did additional towns follow their example.

The Apalachicoli had learned to cope with the passing Spanish forays, and there is no evidence that any violence was done during the third expedition that occurred while Márquez Cabrera still governed. Only the burning of the four towns appears to have been mentioned in the Apalachicoli's complaints to Governor Quiroga. The Apalachee émigrés provided the Apalachicoli a ready source of intelligence about such expeditions as some of the émigrés were from San Luis's leading families (Hann 1988a:227–228).

The Crown's instructions to Diego de Quiroga y Losada as successor to Márquez Cabrera in mid-1687 enjoined him specifically to maintain good relations with the "Apalachecolo, the Chickasaw (*Chicasa*), the Movila," and other such non-Christian peoples living beyond Apalachee. During a visitation of Apalachee early in 1688, Quiroga received the Apalachicoli leaders' complaints about Matheos' burning of four of their villages. He reported having consoled them and "helped them in their rebuilding (*reduccion*)" to the extent that he was able. He also restored trade between the Apalachee and the Apalachicoli, which had ceased in the wake of Matheos' second foray. Quiroga remarked with relief "that it was a Great Providence from God that, in revenge for their injury, they did not join together with the enemies from San Jorje and ruin the lands as the Yamas nation has done." He persuaded many of the émigré Apalachee to return to their homeland (Quiroga y Losada 1688b).

Nothing else seems to be known about Governor Quiroga's relations with the Apalachicoli prior to late 1689, beyond his dispatch of two expeditions in a futile effort to capture the English traders still operating on the Chattahoochee (Quiroga y Losada 1690a). It is unlikely that those expeditions did any violence against the Indians other than invading their territory. The orders that the Crown gave Quiroga when it appointed him cautioned expressly against any resort to force. When the Council of the Indies learned of his unauthorized building of the fort at the beginning of September 1691, it reproached him over that lack of authorization from either the king or his viceroy. It reminded him that the Crown's orders to him were that he should "avail himself of missionaries and use this gentle and secure means as the more proper one and [one] more in conformity with the king's intent than the resort to arms or military force" (Council of the Indies 1691). The Council's reflections and questions reveal that it was ignorant as to the location of Apalachicoli Province beyond a surmise that it must have been located somewhere on the Apalachicola River. They had seen that river's location indicated on a map made in 1687 by the pilot Juan Enríquez Barroto during his search for La Salle's settlement. They believed the settlement to be on the mythical bay of the Holy Spirit into which earlier Spaniards had believed the Mississippi emptied. Barroto's failure to find such a bay at the Mississippi's mouth led the Crown by 1691 to identify Mobile Bay by default as the old Holy Spirit Bay (Spain, Junta de Guerra, 1691).

Although the governor informed the king about his intention to build a fort in Apalachicoli Province about a week before his dispatch of soldiers and carpenters, he appears to have been tardy in sending word that he had done so. Only in mid-1690 did he report to the king that, because five successive expeditions had failed to capture the English traders, he had resolved to build a blockhouse in the Apalachicoli's midst and "place a garrison in it for defense and offense." To that end he dispatched Captain Enrique Primo de Rivera with 24 soldiers and 100 Apalachee Indians, most of whom were carpenters, with orders issued on October 6, 1689 to build the blockhouse. They completed it by

December 21st after about two months work. Rivera was to make it clear to the inhabitants that they could no longer permit the English to come among them and that they were to apprehend any Yamasee in the province. The latter would have been a tall order as the inhabitants of Ocuti and a small unnamed settlement were Yamasee, as probably were those of several other major settlements who had come from the Macon region. The lack of any indication of trouble during the initial months after Rivera's arrival suggests that he made no attempt to detain any Yamasee. Rivera served as the garrison's commander only until mid-April 1690 (Hahn 2000:167–168).

Description of the Fort

The governor appointed Favian de Angulo to replace him as the fort's commander with the title of Lieutenant of the Province of Apalachicoli. After arriving on Monday, April 11, Angulo took charge of the blockhouse on the 17th. Its 40-man garrison consisted of 20 Spanish soldiers (squad leader, two reservists, 17 simple soldiers) and 20 Apalachee warriors. Although they brought horses as well as cows with them, Angulo (1690a) referred to his men as foot soldiers (Quiroga y Losada 1690a).

Angulo (1690a) described the fort as being "twenty-two yards from north to south and nineteen from east to west. Its fence (*serco*) or wall (*muralla*) of props (*de muletteria*), closed (*serrada*). And for the outside part, a half-wall or parapet of a yard and a half of height and two thirds of thickness (*de gruesa*) in the same form as what [is] referred to, with its moat (*foso*) of four yards of mouth, and making the stockade for it that Your Lordship has ordered me to, taking out the clay (*sacando del barro*) in order to give more thickness to the parapet, which will render it sufficiently defended."

Late in May, Angulo (1690b) reported that more than 242 people, consisting of men, women, and youths (*muchachos*) from the province, had visited the fort to thank him for maize seed he had provided for their plantings, without which they would have had no recourse. Because of a drought, famine conditions prevailed in Tiquipache Province as well. He then ordered all the province's leading men to assemble at Caueta on Sunday, three days later, so that he might address them. His request that they foreswear contact with the English suggests the possibility that Rivera had not broached that subject, effectively at least. This is indicated by the Apalachicoli's reportedly assuring the new commander that they would no longer welcome the Yamasee and the English traders as they wanted friendship with the Spaniards and were appreciative of the food that they had supplied. Angulo did not identify the towns whose leaders attended the meeting or the ones represented by his 242-plus visitors.

In a third letter of June 28, Angulo (1690c) mentioned having gone out on the 25th to the place of Ocone (described as near the fort), where the leading men of the province were holding a customary yearly meeting. Only in that letter did he indicate that the province's welcome was something less than effusive. He noted, "with time it will be possible to hope for a happy outcome in your lordship's intention of attracting them to our holy law because they continue to visit a great deal." He went on to assure the governor that he had not strayed at all from his orders, remarking, "I am clothed with patience in order to tolerate their impertinences. That, although they have many reasons for their individual points, they lack justice and those of knowledge. But they do not surprise me; for their teaching (*doctrina*) is like that of their fathers; that they are all born of the woods." He closed with the wish: "May it please God that this calm may continue that they are manifesting to all appearances." There is no hint in that correspondence of the earlier defection of Coweta and Casista reported by Stewart.

Abandonment of the Chattahoochee by Some Apalachicoli

Exchanges between the Franciscans' provincial and the governor in August 1690 indicate that by then St. Augustine had become aware of the departure of some of the Indians from the Chattahoochee. But the allusions provide no clues about the identity of the émigrés or about the time of their departure. It is likely that those reports concerned the early departures of Caueta and Casista's people and that Primo de Rivera brought word of it when he returned from the Apalachicoli country on handing the fort over to Angulo.

Those first mentions were offhand in nature, incidental to the controversies between the governor and the Franciscan leadership clique. One involved the refusal from the beginning of the provincial and his council to assign any priests to serve in Apalachicoli Province even as chaplains to the soldiers and Apalachee warriors. It is difficult to gauge whether that refusal reflected a genuine fear of the possible danger, or simply a lack of zeal among the narrow clique known to have controlled the Franciscan administration in Florida in that era. Quiroga y Losada (1690c) touched on this issue himself, noting that Fray Pedro de Luna, the provincial, was falsely "giving the impression that the Indians have gone to other regions because of the fear of it [the garrison], when all of them are very pleased," and that it was those friars' opinion that he "had gone out too far ahead in placing the garrison in Apalachecolo." Early in March, Francisco Eslaque (1691), an Apalachee and interpreter for his language, cited the lack of a chaplain to say Mass as the principal reason the Apalachee did not wish to serve in the Apalachicoli garrison.

In May 1690 Tiquepache and Talisi's chiefs also visited the fort accompanied by their *enihas* and leading men. An advance party told Angulo (1690b) that more than 100 had died of hunger in Tiquepache Province.

Very little else is known about the Spaniards' relations with the Apalachicoli and Upper Creeks at the fort after late June 1690. The governor's enclosure of nothing later than Angulo's June letter in his report to the king at the end of August suggests that he had heard nothing pertinent from Angulo since June. While at Pensacola Bay, Governor-elect Laureano de Torres y Ayala (1693a:221–222), noted that the garrison had remained at Apalachicoli "nearly two years" for the purpose of controlling the Indians so that they could not trade with the English. That suggests that the general exodus probably did not occur until some time in 1691. He then remarked more delphically, "Like stupid fools, however, they revolted against the infantrymen so that they fled in great haste. Since then the Indians have withdrawn, and there have been wars which have been quite detrimental to the provinces." But, at the time Torres wrote this, the only experience he had had in Florida were the few days he had spent at San Luis readying his expedition to the bay. Two friars who accompanied him on that expedition were his most likely sources (Leonard 1939:230).

The evidence pertaining to the immediate consequences of the Apalachicoli's turning hostile is somewhat conflicting. Fray Jazinto de Barreda (1692), an adversary of Governor Quiroga, described the collapse of the Sauocola mission as an early consequence of the placing of the garrison in Apalachicoli Province against that people's will. Barreda chided the governor for attributing the Sauocola's depopulation of the mission to the absence of its friar, as he happened to be away when "the Sauocola Indians, solicited by the Apalachicolis, people of their same nation," left. At the same time, Fray Blas de Robles (1692) spoke of the "Sabacola" mission as still in existence. He was a severe critic of the clique of friars who were the governor's adversaries. It seems probable that both friars were correct to a degree. The mission may well have suffered defections, influenced by the Apalachicoli's break with the Spaniards. But others probably remained loyal to their new faith.

It is worthy of note that, among the English, Craven Palatine (1690), at least, deplored the enslavement of the Spanish Indians and, particularly, the shipment of them to the West Indies. He wrote to the governor: "We desire that you use your utmost diligence to prevent this pernicious inhumane barbarous practice." He was ready to change all the officers there, should that be required, to halt the practice.

Spaniards' Abandonment of Their Fort

When the governor ordered abandonment of the fort on September 18, 1691, Patricio de Florencia was its commander. Quiroga instructed him that, as soon as he received that order, he was to dispatch "a messenger to the Indians of Caueta, who are in the same province, so that they would advise the rest of them that they might return to settle in their places, provided that they did not permit Englishmen to trade among them." Florencia was to invite them to come to Apalachee to trade, promising a warm welcome. He was to threaten that, if they did not return, the governor would invite the Tiquepache and Tawasa to settle in that region. The need to send a messenger to Caueta with word of the Spaniards' imminent withdrawal from Apalachicoli Province indicates that by then all its settlements had been abandoned by their former inhabitants. However, the Spaniards' invitation to them to return leaves open the possibility that some may have done so not long after the Spaniards' retreat. Florencia was to advise the governor of Caueta's response as soon as he returned to Apalachee with his forces (Quiroga y Losada 1691b). Nothing is known of Caueta's response, if any.

Florencia was to set fire to the fort, removing its few nails, cutting down anything that remained standing, and filling in the ditches so that it offered no cover to enemy Indians. He did not expect the nails' removal to involve much work, noting that "the greater part of it is mortised with wooden pegs (*tarugos*)." In a meeting that Quiroga y Losada (1691a) convoked to endorse this order, he remarked that "it will be best to demolish the blockhouse [lest] the English who are on the River of Uchise [the Ocmulgee] attached to the Indian villages there strengthen their position by removing the nails that were used on it."

The fort's lieutenant and his 20 soldiers were to be withdrawn to St. Augustine to enhance its security. Its vulnerability was a consideration in the decision to abandon that outpost. Two French ships operating off Havana had recently captured the Florida supply frigate *Tiritera*. A Savoyard, whom the French had taken prisoner on that ship, had informed the French of Florida's shortage of soldiers, food, and other supplies, raising fears that the French might attempt to exploit those weaknesses (Fuente 1691; Quiroga y Losada 1691a, 1691b; Quiroga y Losada et al. 1691). In 1691, the fort built at such cost in 1689 was abandoned.

The governor was concerned as well for the security of the Chacato settlement on the Apalachicola River, suggesting that it should be on guard against attack as the mission closest to Apalachicoli Province. The junta that endorsed abandonment of the fort recommended that some soldiers be detached from Apalachee's garrison to strengthen the Chacato settlement's security (Quiroga y Losada et al. 1691).

Some such attacks may have occurred there by the following spring. Fray Jazinto de Barreda (1692), after speaking of the August 30, 1691, attack on Guacara and attacks on other places as having terrified the inhabitants "of the place of the Chacatos in particular," causing so many deaths that many of its Indians had abandoned the place. In response to the governor's critical remarks about the Chacato's friar going about heavily armed and thereby terrifying his people, Fray Barrera argued that the constant threat of attack was the reason its Fray Pedro de Haze went about armed. Torres y Ayala (1693a:221–222) observed from Pensacola Bay that the Apalachicoli had "had wars with all the Indians of San Luis de Apalache for two years now," noting that "though they are still engaged in hostilities, it is not with the same intensity as before." He went on to remark that those wars had been quite detrimental to the Spanish provinces.

One can only surmise about the depth of the new governor's knowledge of Florida affairs. After landing at St. Marks, he had spent only a few days organizing and provisioning his expedition to Pensacola Bay. But he was accompanied by friars with long experience in Apalachee. His remarks about the origin of that rift and the then current location of the Apalachicoli settlements suggest that his grasp of the situation was less than perfect. He reported that he had "learned that all of the Apalachicola Indians have withdrawn more than sixty leagues north on the Apalachicola River . . . carrying on a considerable trade with the English at San Jorge, and . . . living close to the latter settlement." He seems to have been unaware that their withdrawal had taken them away from the Apalachicola [Chattahoochee] River. [For details on the Apalachicoli attack on the Chacato settlement see chapter 2.] Sauocola and Tiquepache, as well as Apalachicoli, participated in that attack (Torres y Ayala 1695a). Another source identified the attackers as four Sauocola and two Chisca with the rest from Caueta and Apalachicoli (Torres y Ayala et al. 1694).

Governor Torres y Ayala's 1693 report on the Apalachicoli hostilities appears to have been reliable. About a year and a half later in the wake of the attack on the Chacato settlement, he informed the king that he had received detailed reports from the lieutenants of Apalachee and Timucua and from other residents about the great injuries the Apalachicoli had caused since their rebellion under Governor Quiroga. Quiroga is likely to have been one of the "other residents" whom he consulted as Quiroga remained in Florida after his term ended, serving on juntas the governor convoked to endorse major decisions as also did the 1670s-era governor, Pablo de Hita Salazar. Torres noted that the hostilities and deaths had continued since his assumption of the office in September 1693, citing the attack on San Carlos de los Chacatos in the fall of 1694 as the most recent such act.

Retaliation for the Apalachicoli Attack on the Chacatos

In response to October 25th and 26th letters from Apalachee's lieutenant, Jacinto Roque Pérez, requesting permission to retaliate for the attack on the Chacatos, the governor and his council acceded (Torres y Ayala et al., 1694). At their order, 400 Indians, led by the former acting chief of San Luis, Matheo Chuba, and seven Spaniards, set out from Apalachee to attack Apalachicoli settlements in central Georgia (Hann 1988a:190). Torres y Ayala (1695a, 1695b) identified those places as Caueta, Casista, Ocone, and Tiquepache. They caught only one of the villages by surprise, capturing about 50 people there and rescuing eight of the Chacato who had been carried off. They found the other three villages abandoned and burned. South Carolina's Governor, Joseph Blake, (1694) identified the towns the Apalachee had attacked as "Cauetta, Cassisto, Ocmulque, Tasquique, Vchichi, and the places of those of Ocone, protesting that they were places that were under his government and jurisdiction." Those six towns have been identified as the ones whose people moved to the Ocmulgee River (Hann 1988a:189–190, 1996a:77; Pluckhahn and Braley 1999:242). It is probable that Blake included Ocmulque, Tasquique and Vchichi because their inhabitants had burned them, but there is no ready explanation for his failure to mention Tiquepache. Because of the loss of the element of surprise after the attack on the first village, the expedition acquired only a scant booty of deer and buffalo hides and the 50 captives they took, whom the Indians were allowed to hold as slaves "in accord with their custom" as Torres y Ayala (1695b) phrased it.

This more hostile atmosphere stimulated the long-planned building of a new blockhouse at San Luis de Talimali in Apalachee. By April 1696 it was completed except for a third of the roof. That gap had been closed by mid-1697 (T. Menéndez Marqués and J. de Florencia 1697; Torres y Ayala 1696:21–23). The Crown noted that it would provide "a reasonable shelter or defense for the natives from the incursions that the neighboring Indians make at the instigation of the English" (Royal decree 1698:23–24). But, in the wake of that flare-up, there appears to have been an abatement of the hostilities. Relations were amicable enough during the winter of 1698–1699 for a group of Tiquepache to set out for Apalachee to trade their buffalo skins, leather shirts, and bezoar stones. On the way they were set upon treacherously by a party of 40 Chacato Indians led by a disreputable Spaniard named Francisco de Florencia, who were in west Florida buffalo hunting. They killed 16 of the sleeping Tiquepache and stole their trade goods (P. Hinachuba 1699:26–27; Zúñiga y Zerda 1700:30–32). The Chacato doubtless saw this encounter as an opportunity to avenge the 1694 attack on their village as Tiquepache were among its attackers.

Renewal of Peaceful Relations

Despite that incident, a delegation of Apalachicoli leaders went to Apalachee early in 1701 offering to renew peace and trade with the Apalachee and to reaffirm their former submission to Spain's king. The Apalachee and Apalachicoli soon worked out a peace treaty. But Florida's governor moved with equal speed to thwart it. He ordered his lieutenant in Apalachee to investigate the peace agreement carefully and in an order delivered there on February 22, 1701, he forbade Apalachee's Spanish and native inhabitants from traveling to Apalachicoli territory to consult or trade with its inhabitants without the express permission of the governor. Indians from Apalachicoli who came to Apalachee to trade were to be received "with all good will." But they were to be allowed to trade only in the usual native goods. Christians were prohibited from purchasing clothing, arms, or anything else of English origin from them. The governor forbade the Indians from giving the Apalachicoli traders "horses or silver or other thing which might be marketable among the said heathens and which the said natives formerly traded among themselves." A year and a half later in informing the king of the Apalachicoli's renewal of hostilities, the governor attributed the rupture to "his having been able to prevent the Apalachicolos from removing horses from Apalachee Province." He claimed as well that the peace agreement had been a subterfuge from its beginning designed only to obtain packhorses that they might trade to the English (Ayala y Escobar 1701:33–34; Zúñiga y Zerda 1702a:36–38).

The Return to Hostility

Two incidents signaled the Apalachicoli's renewed hostility: their 1701 killing of three Apalachee who had gone to the Apalachicoli country and their attack on the Timucua mission of Santa Fé on May 20, 1702. The party of 100 Apalachicoli that attacked Santa Fé had set out from Achito. It brought back many scalps, a chest of clothing, and silver (M. Solana 1702; Zúñiga y Zerda 1702a:36).

Fearful that more attacks would follow if Christians did not avenge the assault on Santa Fé, the Apalachee pressed the governor to permit a reprisal. Based on their familiarity with their neighbors' war practices, their fears were justified. In a general meeting of the Apalachicoli towns' leaders held at Achito in the fall of 1702, they resolved to make war on the Apalachee. They began at once with an attack on its two most exposed villages of Bacuqua and Escambé. They planned to descend on San Luis in the spring and occupy the province. Having received the governor's approval, the Apalachee simultaneously assembled a largely Apalachee force of 800 men. The Apalachicoli, forewarned of the Apalachee's plans by dissidents among the Apalachee, prepared an ambush for the Apalachee along the trail. Although the Apalachicoli mounted a force of only 400 Apalachicoli and Chisca men and 13 Westo (10 men and 3 women), their superior arms and the element of surprise enabled them to inflict a resounding defeat on the Apalachee in their well-known encounter on the Flint. More than half the Apalachee warriors were killed or captured. Many of the 300 or so who escaped left their arms behind. The severity of that blow, and the demoralization it induced, facilitated the Apalachicoli's final conquest of the Apalachee that began early in 1704 with James Moore's invasion of the province (Romo de Urisa 1702; M. Solana 1702:468–470; Zúñiga y Zerda 1702a:36–38, 1702c, 1702d).

The Apalachicoli's confidence prior to that victory had doubtless been bolstered as well by their awareness of the imminence of a planned English assault on the coastal missions and St. Augustine itself that began early in November 1702. This assault was designed to end the Spanish presence there and doom the Indians allied to the Spaniards. Carolina Governor James Moore's planned attack on St. Augustine had been among the topics discussed by the native leaders at Achito in October. Whether by design or not, the planned attack had been noised abroad in the village of Achito as destined to occur only in the spring of 1703. A Christian Chacato woman living at Achito hurried to Apalachee to alert Spanish authorities, arriving at San Luis during the afternoon of October 21, 1702, just after the disaster on the Flint. As news reached the governor early in November of the landing of the English enemy's forces on Amelia Island, he remarked that the rumored English attack must be imminent and "they are not waiting for the month of April to carry it out as an October 27th letter . . . [from San Luis] led us to believe" (Zúñiga y Zerda 1702c).

With Britain's launching of overt active hostilities against Florida's Spaniards and the Indians allied with them in what is known as the War of the Spanish Succession (or in America as Queen Anne's War), the Apalachicoli and the other Indians of the lower South who were allied with the English began a decade of unremitting warfare against the Spaniards and the Indians allied with them. From his vantage point at Pensacola, Francisco Martínez (1702) warned Mexico's viceroy of the need to do something promptly about the threat the Apalachicoli posed. He assured him that, unless the Apalachicoli were destroyed shortly, "they are going to destroy those among us who may [still] be around here." He remarked: "I have discovered that despite the fact that they are Indians, they are very brave people and the least among them have a musket (*escopeta*) and a pair of pistols and a machete," noting that he believed that they would attack any group the English persuaded them to (M. Solana 1702).

For Apalachee's missions and people, Indian and Spanish, the crisis Martínez foresaw began early in 1704 with James Moore and his Apalachicoli allies' assault on that province. A few months after Moore's withdrawal accompanied by a significant portion of Apalachee's population, a second Apalachicoli force moved into Apalachee in June 1704, destroying the remaining missions except San Luis and Ivitachuco. Aware that another Apalachicoli force would arrive shortly, the remaining Spaniards and Apalachee abandoned the province. Within weeks the Apalachicoli destroyed the two remaining Yustaga missions of western Timucua. In Florida's interior provinces that left only San Francisco Potano in the Gainesville area, the Apalachee migrants (largely from Ivitachuco) who moved to Abosaya near Payne's Prairie, and the Salamototo settlement at the St. Johns River crossing point.

In August and September 1705 three distinct troops of Indians allied to the English arrived in Florida. One passed by San Francisco Potano to put the Apalachee village under siege. A second force besieged Salamototo and a third one struck a native village three leagues south of St. Augustine (Hann 1996b:298–300). A new governor who assumed office early in 1706 reported at the beginning of May: "from the very day that I took possession, everything that has been done has been in attendance to the defense against the continuous hostilities, death, and destruction that the . . . Indians . . . have come to carry out in these surrounding regions, aided by the English, to such a degree that the provisions that were sent for the garrison of San Francisco, thirty leagues from this city were being held up at the Salamototo crossing." To resolve that impasse, on the second day after he took possession, he dispatched a force of soldiers "with the principal launch and a force of armed pirogues" (Córcoles y Martínez 1706b). Potano was abandoned finally at the beginning of May just prior to the arrival of another large enemy force of 300 men. At the governor's orders Indians and Spaniards soon abandoned Salamototo as well, reaching St. Augustine on May 23, 1706 (Hann 1996b:302). Governor Córcoles y Martínez (1706c) noted at the end of November that he had formed a cavalry company led by Captain Francisco Menéndez Marques to facilitate protection of the countryside around St. Augustine and, particularly, of the Indians living just outside the city (Primo de Rivera 1717a). In November of the following year the governor noted the enemies' persistence, observing that their attacks came "one on top of the other" (Córcoles y Martínez 1707b).

The impact of these recurring attacks was not confined to the native peoples of the former mission provinces. The governor remarked at the beginning of 1708 that the attacking Indians, urged on by the English, had "desolated the entire mainland and the coast of the south and of Carlos, and have carried off, as each day they are carrying [off], a growing number of these . . . Indians" so that there were no longer any of the Christians left who "were in Apalachee, Timuqua, Guale, and parts of Mayaca and Jororo." He estimated that those they carried off to be sold to the English as slaves "must number more than ten or twelve thousand persons" and that only about three hundred persons from those provinces survived in the vicinity of St. Augustine. He noted that "even of these they are carrying off and killing some each day" while they are out in search of firewood and food. That very day (January 14, 1708), out of a party of 28 Mayaca and Jororo, only four had escaped to report the capture of the rest (Boyd et al. 1951:90–91; Fairbanks 1957:94–96).

Nature itself added to St. Augustine's woes at the height of this crisis. On September 30, 1707, a hurricane began a 48-hour assault on the city, bringing down many of its houses and causing extensive flooding. Danger of attack outside the city discouraged most from venturing out to cut lumber for rebuilding the structures that had collapsed (Córcoles y Martínez 1707b).

A significant factor in the intensification of the Apalachicoli's attack on the Spaniards and their Indian allies was a formal alliance that the British extracted from a number of the Indians leaders, dated August 15 of 1705. A dozen chiefs, leading men, and warriors placed their marks on this agreement celebrated at Caueta. In it they acknowledged their alliance with and subjection to the Crown, pledging fidelity to "all her Majesties Governours of Carolina." By it they promised to assist the English against all declared enemies of the English, and specifically against the French and Spanish. The list of signees began with Caueta's chief and closed with a warrior from Caueta. Other signees represented Ocmulque, Casista, Tuckebatchee, the Uchises, Oakfuskees, the Alabama (Holbamah), Kealedji, and possibly the Okchai [*pooseatche*—Swanton's Potcas hatchee] (Crane 1956:82–83; Hahn 2000:208–212; Swanton 1922:276). Notably absent from the list of signees is the chief of the Apalachicoli, as Hahn noted. It is not known how much the interpreters told the signees about the obligations associated with the treaty in the minds of the English beyond the one of unrelenting hostility toward the Spaniards and French. Caueta's chief was the first of the signees, using his war title of *Hoboyetly*.

A possible indicator of the scope of the English-allied Indians' enslavement of "Spanish" Indians for sale to the English is a 1708 letter to the Carolina Lords Proprietors on South Carolina's total population of 9,580 people. Fourteen hundred out of that total were enslaved Indians, comprising 500 men, 600 women, and 300 children. Its writer reported that over the previous five years of warfare with the French and Spaniards and other Indian engagements, the number of Indians enslaved grew by 400 men, 450 women, and 500 Indian children (Snell 1972:60–61).

Both St. Augustine and its surrounding Indian settlements as well as Pensacola and its nearby Spanish allied Indians, while the latter survived, continued to suffer frequent attacks. The intensity of the harassment is reflected in the testimony of six Spaniards from Pansacola captured by Upper Creek raiding parties in 1706 and 1709. They were released early in December 1709 by South Carolina's governor after St. Augustine's governor sent him 17 Englishmen recently shipwrecked near that city. Most importantly, their testimony provides data on the Upper Creek Indians allied to the English pertaining to the numbers of villages in each province, the warriors they could muster, and their armament. Although four of the six were captured together, even their testimony differs, in part because they were separated after reaching Tiguale, the first of the Talapuze villages they encountered about 70 leagues from Pansacola. The other two, captured in distinct incidents, were brought to the Alabamas' country initially.

The principal provinces they mentioned included one (or possibly two) that they identified variously as Chalique, Chaliquele, Chalaqueles, and Chalaquizes, as well as the Abihkas, Alabamas, Talapuzes, Uchises, Chiscas, Tamahitas, Chickasaws, and Cosapuya for a total of nine or ten. One also mentioned four rebel Apalachee towns. Those peoples occupied lands belonging to or bordering on the Upper and Lower Creek territories through which the Spaniards passed from their capture just outside Pansacola and during their service to various Indians until their eventual arrival at Charles Town. Two witnesses, Juan Gabriel de Vargas and Joseph de Roxas, provided most of the more useful detailed information. The governor mentioned only six of the provinces in his cover letter, namely: Ayabamos, Chaliqui, Apicas [Abihkas of English sources], Talapuzes, Uchizes, and Chalaqueles. Thus he seemingly regarded Chalique and Chalaque as distinct peoples.

Roxas (1710) presented the most detailed listing:

Talapuzes—26 villages, 70 musketeers, 400 bowmen;
Apica—44 villages, 300 musketeers, 700 bowmen;
Ayabamos—4 villages, 400 musketeers;
Chalaquizes—14 villages;
Chicazaies (Chickasaws)—6 villages, 500 warriors;
Apalachecolos—11 villages;
Cosapuyas—3 villages;
Tamagitas—he does not know about them;
Rebel Christian Apalachee—He saw 4 villages: Thomole, Escambe, Patale, and Bacuqua.

Vargas (1710) gave 13 as the number of Talapuze towns while a third witness said 12. But as Vargas credited the Alabamas with 30 towns, those discrepancies may in part reflect differences among the witnesses as to the tribal affiliation of some of those towns. In his cover letter Governor Córcoles y Martínez (1710) echoed Vargas's figures for those two peoples, possibly because Vargas was the first to testify. The governor gave figures only for those two provinces. Vargas noted that the Talapuze towns averaged about 100 men each. He saw four or five of Apica's towns, but reported that the province was large and had many towns. He walked through three of Uchize's villages, observing that that province also was large and had many towns. His Uchizes probably were the Apalachecolos of the Roxas listing. Vargas did not see the province of his Chalaqueles but he knew that it was large and had many villages. He mentioned only those five provinces, describing Chalaque and Apica as "remaining to one side." In evaluating the testimony given by these formerly captive soldiers and its discrepancies, one should keep in mind that they were based on observations and remembrances from a rather traumatic experience and not on any sort of journal or notes.

Authorities have differed over the identity of the Chalaque who first appeared in the Elvas and Rangel accounts (Clayton, Knight, and Moore 1993: I, 86, 280) as located two-to-seven days beyond Cofitacheque. The Chalaque have been identified frequently as Cherokee, most recently by Patricia Galloway (1995:179). But Swanton (1946:46) challenged the traditional view of his time, suggesting that Chalaque was a variant of the Muscogee word Chilokee meaning "people of a different language" and "was most likely applied to people speaking an eastern Siouian language." Swanton (1922:319) had speculated that the Chalaque were Savanna and were represented in the Chalakagay of a 1750 French census. This was a Shawnee town among the Creeks, then located near the Coosa River in the country of the Abihka, with whom, interestingly, they are paired in this 1710 document.

Vargas rendered Tamagitas as Tamaxilas, mentioning it in a context that might be interpreted as indicating it was farther west with the Choctaws and Chiscas. The governor used the similar Tamajilas spelling.

The four Spanish soldiers who were captured together concurred in reporting that because of the Indians' hunting it took the prisoners a month (November 23–December 23, 1708) to cover the 70 leagues that separated Tiguale, the first of the Talapuze villages, from Pansacola. Their captors were a band of 300 Talapuzes, Apicas, and Alabamas. The other two were captured in distinct incidents by small bands of 20 Ayabamos all with firearms and 16 Talapuzes. It took the Alabamas about ten and one-half days to reach their province accompanied by only six of their captors. This witness, Antonio Monilla Hernández (1710), was employed to carry deer hides from the village of the Chiscas and other places. On a hunting expedition, six of the party were killed in a chance encounter with the Movila. Salvador Joseph de Aguado (1710), after his capture by the 16 Talapuze, traveled for a month to reach the Talapuze village of Ayubale. Ayubale's English lieutenant sent him to Charleston, a two-month-long trip in which he passed through more than 30 towns, each of which had an English lieutenant. Interestingly, Ayubale was also the name of the one of Apalachee Province's principal towns during the mission period; it was the one village that James Moore attacked and destroyed in January of 1704.

Even at this early date there was a hint of the Indians' growing dissatisfaction with their exclusive dependence on the English traders. In Charleston, Vargas (1710) was asked by Indians if they "might have peace with the Spaniards if they came with a white flag and whether they would sell them powder and balls as did the English." Vargas observed: "This because the English had ordered the Indians at San Jorge to retire to their village."

7

The Yamasee War and Its Aftermath

The Yamasee War

During the quarter century of conflict between Spaniards and the forebears of the Creeks and Seminoles that began in 1690, Spanish records have little to say about those native peoples beyond the mention of the hostilities. That dearth of information ended suddenly with the general uprising among Native Americans allied to the English of South Carolina known as the Yamasee War. The Carolinians' ultimate defeat of the revolt brought a wave of Indian refugees to St. Augustine. Later, there were visits by others involved in the revolt who were anxious to restore friendly relations with the Spaniards as a source for European goods. Spanish records indicate that some of these Indians visited for many months well before the beginning of the uprising (Córcoles y Martínez 1715a; Córcoles y Martínez, Menéndez Marques, and Garcia de Villegas 1715).

The Yamasee War involved far more than that one native nation. As Verner W. Crane (1981:162) noted, the war constituted a "far-reaching revolt against the Carolinian trading regime, involving the Creek, the Choctaw, and to a less extent the Cherokee, as well as the tribes of the piedmont and of the Savannah River and Port Royal districts." The Indians of the Savannah River district included Apalachicoli and Apalachee who had abandoned their homeland to go with Colonel James Moore in 1704. Although Yamasee played a leading role in the uprising, Crane rightly believed Creek were probable authors of the conspiracy, sharing with the Yamasee "and with other interior tribes a greater resentment of the tyrannies of the Charles Town traders." Spanish records indicate that Emperor Brims addressed the meeting at Pocotalaga in which plans for the revolt were made. He stressed the Carolinians' resort to enslaving their erstwhile Indian allies for unpaid debts as a motive. Brims participation was of particular importance. By 1715, if not earlier, his position as overall leader of both the Lower and Upper Creeks is signified by the title of "emperor" accorded to him. Pansacola's Spanish governor, Gregorio de Salinas Varona (1717b) spoke of a soldier from his garrison having been released around July 1715 by the "leaders of Talissi, Talespuches, and Tiquepaches" at the order of their emperor of Caueta reflecting their desire to give obedience to the king.

Corkran (1967:59) remarked that the extent of Creek participation in the fighting in Carolina is not clear except that "In August, 1715, in the last great push of the hostiles into Carolina, Chigelly, who was Brims' brother and the head warrior of Coweta, led several hundred Apalachees and Creeks almost to Charlestown, only to be thrown back." The Creeks strove also to draw in the Cherokees and put forces in the woods "outside the Lower Cherokee Towns awaiting the signal to strike" that never came, as the Cherokee chose to ally with the English. But the Yamasee deserve to have their name attached to the war because of the leading role they played in precipitating it and the steadfastness with which they pursued it. Their importance in this matter is reflected in the reciprocal steadfastness with which the English pursued a war of extermination against the Yamasee while coming to terms rather quickly with Brims once he showed a disposition to do so.

Crane concluded, relative to the consequences of this revolt, that "in its results, leading as it did to the awakening of the English colonial authorities to the danger of French encirclement, to a constitutional revolution in South Carolina, to far-reaching migrations of the southern tribes, and to a reorientation of wilderness diplomacy in the South which altered seriously the prospects of English, French, and Spanish rivalry, it takes rank with the more famous Indian conspiracies of colonial times."

An English source from South Carolina from early 1719 presented the following as an "exact account of ye number and strength of all the Indian nations that were subject to the governor of South Carolina . . . in ye beginning of ye year 1715" based on the Journals of Captain Nairn and John Wright and "compared and corrected by the Journals and observations" of John Barnwell.

Table 3. Village List for 1715

People (distance from Charleston)	Number of villages	Men	Women	Boys	Girls	Total
1. The Yamasee (90 m SW)	10	413	345	214	228	1,215*
2. The Apalachicoles (130 m SW)	2	64	71	42	37	214
3. The Apalatchee (140 m W)	4	275	248	65	55	638
The Savanas (150 m WNW)	3	67	116	20	30	283
The Euchees (180 m ?NW)	2	130	270	0	0	400
The Ocheesees or Creeks (250 m NW)	10	731	837	417	421	2,406
The Abikans (440 m W)	15	302	578	366	327	1,773
The Talleboosees (390 m WSW)	13	636	710	511	486	2,343
The Alabamas (430 m W)	4	214	276	161	119	770
Total		3,032	3,446	1,816	1,698	9,992

Source: Adapted from Johnson 1719.
* Mathematical error in original.

Interpretation of the second of those lists poses a problem in view of the great disproportion in the numbers under "Total" and the sum of the figures for boys and girls. The most likely explanation seems to be that the figures for boys and girls represent a narrow age range such as 12 to 16 or 18-year olds while totals include those from one day old to 12 years of age. Another possibility is that the "Total" includes adults as well. But in view of the lesser discrepancies manifested as well in the first list's totals for men and women, one might be justified also in concluding that the list's compiler was simply "mathematically challenged," as the modern euphemism would phrase it.

Crane (1981:164–167) and Corkran (1967:56–57) trace the unrest among the Indians at least as far back as 1711. They attribute it in part to the infiltration of whites into lands reserved for Indians. But they note that the "real mischief" arose from abuses perpetrated by the traders such as brutality, illegal enslavement of free Indians, "abuse of rum to facilitate sharp dealing," appropriating Indians' hogs, fowl, and crops, and the Indians' accumulation of huge debts and the adoption of force to collect them. [For a detailed account of those abuses and of the Indians' depredations and encounters with the Carolina forces during the war see Milling 1940:105–112, 135–151.] Based on remarks of the Yamasee War leaders who sought alliance with the Spaniards on May 27, 1715, Governor Córcoles y Martínez (1715a) traced the revolt's origins to 1712 when the English began to insist on Indian slaves as the principal means of paying off the large debts, and when they were overheard by Indians to say that they would begin to seize the women and children of such debtors.

Corkran saw a forecast of the storm in the Upper Creeks' celebration of peace with the French in 1711–1712 "on their own initiative." He observed that the Creeks' long wars with the Spaniards, French, and Indian allies of both of those European peoples "had given the Creeks fighting and scalp glory such as they had never known before." The Creeks had destroyed the Apalachee missions and many of their inhabitants, penned the French into Mobile and the Spaniards into St. Augustine and Pensacola, and given the Choctaws a severe thrashing. From "their own point of view they were a great success; from the English point of view they had formed a massive wall which dammed the French and Spanish advance into regions toward which England's rising empire was flowing." As a probable cause of this first crack in the dike, Corkran indicated "a Carolina trader's gross abuse of an Alabama headman," noting that, "combined with war weariness and heavy battle losses, this seemingly unimportant incident had the power to precipitate cessation of hostility toward an enemy as a rebuke to the ally."

Spanish records do not show any move by them to instigate the revolt. However the Spaniards welcomed it if only because it would alleviate the unremitting hostilities that the English and their Indian allies had waged since 1702. But St. Augustine had an inkling of the coming conflict between the Carolinians and their Indian allies at least as early as February 1715, and probably earlier in 1714. On February 22, 1715, the governor and treasury officials asked the king for an increase in the subsidy for the Indian gift fund. They also requested that he order Mexico's viceroy to pay the expenditures they were incurring in welcoming arriving heathen Indians who had come repeatedly (Córcoles y Martínez 1715a). Some of those visitors undoubtedly were Indians still nominally allied to the English.

On the evening of May 27, 1715, four Indian leaders formerly allied with the English came to St. Augustine asking for assistance, protection, and refuge for members of their families they brought with them. They formally alerted Spaniards to the outbreak of the Yamasee War at Pocotalago, Pocotaligo of English sources, early in the morning of April 15, 1715. The envoys were identified as the "principal *mico*, governor of the great village of La Tama,"[1] the cacique of Aligua, and two leading men from Nicunapa,[2] all heathens. La Tama is the Altamaha of English sources, principal town of the Lower Towns of the Yamasee in South Carolina at the end of the seventeenth century, referred to by Spaniards at times as La Tamaja. The Christian cacique, Antonio Perez Caniparia, served as interpreter in the contact with those envoys. The governor described him as governing the *Iguaja* (Guale) Indians living then in St. Augustine's vicinity. This is another indication that the Guale and the Yamasee's languages were closely related, if not identical. He was probably cacique of Tolomato or Santa Catharina de Guale.

The four leaders came as ambassadors in the name of all the provinces, heathen and Christian that were settled to the north and south of the Carolina English as their allies. They were ready now to give obedience to Spain's king. The governor remarked that they claimed to represent 161 villages, not counting the little places that the Indians call camps (*rancherias*) that had less than 200 persons "according to counts that they make after their fashion of explaining themselves and combination of figures (*guarismos*), which they delivered to me on eight strands of strips (*ramales de Correas*) of deerskins, with another equal number of 161 small knots (*nudos menudos*)." The Indians asked the governor to send those eight strands on to the monarch. Each one of those knots represented a village. Interim Governor Juan de Ayala y Escobar gave 149 places as the number of villages then subject to Caueta's chief. The visit of 157 Indians cost the king 12,101 pesos. The envoys explained that they had gone to war because Carolinians wanted to make slaves of their women and children when Indians could not make payment at once on large debts. The English had allowed the debts to accumulate during the war with Spain when their help was needed. The leaders of the villages involved in the conspiracy met at Pocotalago, the leader among the Yamasee Upper Towns, without the English being aware until almost the last minute.

Brims told the leaders assembled at Pocotalago that the English had begun to seize Indians and to ship them out to be sold as slaves to cover unpaid debts. The Indians' efforts to avoid that, such as handing over Indians they had captured from Spanish territory, were not adequate for solving the problem. He noted also that the English had killed Caueta's *usinulo*, heir to the chieftainship. The governor described the *usinulo* (beloved son) as being venerated by the Indians just as Spaniards venerated their crown prince. Spanish sources attributed Brims' hostility particularly to the killing of the *usinulo*.

Governor Córcoles y Martínez (1715a) reduced the envoys' lengthy explanations of the revolt's causes to English pressure since 1712 for the Indians' prompt payment of their large debts, and suspicions arising from those pressures as it became clear that the Indians' resources were not adequate for doing that. The suspicion turned to outright hostility when Indians who understood English heard their creditors remark among themselves on the need to kill the warriors to facilitate seizure of the women and children. The beginning of the killing at Pocotalago was touched off by the arrival there of an Indian woman married to an Englishman when she told chiefs of Salquicha and Pocotalago of the English plans. But, before going on the warpath, the Indians concealed their women and children in the interior on the Altamaha. Contemporaneously, Carolina's Governor Charles Craven charged the Spaniards with responsibility for the Yamasee War. He accused them of having encouraged it and of having provided powder and balls to the Indians, alleging that they thereby violated the 1714 peace treaty between the two Crowns.

Governor Córcoles y Martínez (1716) recorded that "the great cacique of Caueta" visited St. Augustine himself on July 27, 1715, to confirm the alliance forged in his name by the four leaders who had arrived on May 27th. Brims was accompanied by the chiefs of Casista and Tasquique and more than 50 vassals and other caciques and leading men. Boyd (1949:5, 8–9) gives a misleading view of Spanish contact with and awareness of Brims' importance in stating that Diego Peña's 1716 "expedition revealed the dominant position of the casique of Cavetta among the Chattahoochie bands." Seemingly, Boyd was not aware of Brims' 1715 visit to St. Augustine.

The New Migrants to the Vicinity of St. Augustine

Paradoxically, the Yamasee who, after the English rift with the Westo, had initially played the most predominant role in destroying Florida's missions, constituted far and away the largest element among those who sought refuge at St.

Augustine. The influx inspired a significant reorganization and expansion of the native settlements that had appeared in the city's vicinity in the period 1704–1711 to accommodate refugees from the destroyed missions and non-mission people of Florida such as the Ais (Córcoles y Martínez 1711). Prior to this time Spanish sources have little to say of a specific nature about the Yamasee such as the towns or provinces to which they belonged. English sources were not much more informative about those who moved into South Carolina in the 1680s beyond dividing the leaders assembled at Pocotalago into two distinct groups identified as the Upper Towns, of which Pocotalago was the principal town, and the Lower Towns (led by Altamaha as principal town, the Tamaja or Tama of the Spanish sources) with five towns in each group. Without specifying the group to which the other towns belonged, Swanton (1922:97) identified a few of the subordinate towns' leaders as "the Yewhaw king, the Huspaw king, the Chassee king, the Pocolabo king, the Ilcombe king, and the Dawfuskee king," commenting that the identity of the latter "is a little uncertain." Milling (1940:111), however, identified the Euhaw as originally a Guale tribe (the Yoa) who had joined the Yamasee, noting that even before that there were "the old Euhaw of Hoos Pau." But, beginning with the post-Yamasee War influx, Spanish sources become much more specific in identifying the various tribes or towns to which the newcomers belonged.

A prime source for the revolt's impact on St. Augustine and the native settlements girdling it is a detailed census taken by Joseph Primo de Rivera in April 1717 (Ayala y Escobar 1717a). Rivera listed each village by name, specified the language of the principal component of each and of attached chiefs, and the tribal identity of inhabitants belonging to other linguistic groups. He also recorded each head chief's name, the number of the chief's leading men and the number of ordinary Indians residing in the village. Rivera noted whether the leaders and the general population were heathen or Christian, whether the chief ruled de iure or de facto, and how many Indians were vassals of the ruling chief. He stated how many owed allegiance to other chiefs living in the village and how many lacked a chief. Rivera broke his tally into categories of men, women, and children. Children were listed by sex. He noted how many men were fit to be warriors. Those recently converted to Christianity were also specifically listed.

In a covering letter for the census, the governor, Juan de Ayala y Escobar (1717b), noted that the listings included "the number of heathen and Christian Indians of all the villages established in due form after I took possession." The governor's statement suggests that, in addition to authorizing or assigning settlement sites for the Yamasee War refugees, he had carried out a general reorganization of the pre-existing settlements inhabited by survivors from the missions destroyed in 1702, 1704, and 1705 who had sought refuge near St. Augustine. A census from early 1711 identified seven settlements whose 401 inhabitants were described as living in camps (*rancherias*) located within "a pistol shot" of the city's fort. It suggests impermanence because of the constant threat of attack by Indians allied with the English such as the Yamasee and Creek who had destroyed the earlier missions (Córcoles y Martínez 1711).

The Yamasee War removed that threat for a brief time. The Yamasee, one of the major predator peoples responsible for the constant harassment of "Spanish" Indians, now sought refuge from English vengeance among their former prey. Substantial elements among the various bodies that comprised the Creek, the other major predator, briefly moved toward a policy of neutrality and accommodation with the Spaniards, spearheaded by Lower Creek elements and a few Apalachee who urged Creek alignment with the Spaniards (Crane 1956:254–255; Hann 1988a:312–314). Those Lower Creek elements were largely Hitchiti-speakers, living along the lower to middle Chattahoochee once more.

That turnabout permitted a brief relaxation of the siege mentality that had held the settlements of 1711 to a narrow perimeter under the protection of the guns and forces at St. Augustine. The Rivera census and later documents indicate that some of the 1717 settlements were located three to five or more leagues from St. Augustine. Two of the ten settlements listed had a Spanish garrison and fort to assist the native warriors. The settlements' locations were doubtless chosen to suit Spanish interests as well as those of the natives (Ayala y Escobar 1717a; Bullones 1728). The disappearance or change of name of four of the 1711 settlements is also indicative of reorganization and relocation.

Three of the new villages were headed by Yamasee. They are:

1. Our Lady of Candelaria De La Tamaja (Yamasee language and nation);
Don Antonio de Ayala, principal cacique, and 8 leading men, 5 of them Christian and 3 heathen;
10 warriors, Christian; 10 men, heathen;
25 women, 16 heathen and 9 Christian;
18 boys, 15 heathen and 3 Christian;
18 girls, 13 heathen and 5 Christian;
Cacique Tospe (Yamasee language) attached to Candelaria;
23 warriors, 1 new Christian and 22 heathen;
23 heathen women;
14 heathen children, 7 boys and 7 girls;
Cacique Alonso Ocute, cacique of Ocute, Christian (Yamassee language); attached to Candelaria;

8 men, his vassals, 7 heathen and 1 Christian;
3 heathen children, 2 boys and 1 girl.
Total 162 persons.

2. Pocosapa (Yamasee language), heathens;
Cacique Langne Cap qui (or Chap), heathen;
7 leading men, 5 heathen and 2 Christian;
34 warriors, heathen;
11 Christian warriors, attached Apalachee and Timucua, who are under obedience to this cacique;
31 heathen women;
10 Christian women, Yamasee and Apalachee;
13 boys, 12 heathen and one new Christian;
19 girls, 14 heathen and 5 new Christians;
Attached Casapuya, heathen (Casapuya language);
Cacique (no name given), heathen;
14 warriors, 1 old man;
14 Casapuia women, heathen;
16 Casapuia children, 7 boys and 9 girls.
Total 172 persons.

3. Pocotalaca (Yamasee nation and tongue)
Don Francisco Ya (or La) Quisca
6 leading men, 2 of them Christian;
35 men, vassals, 2 of them old, 4 of them Christian of the Oapa nation;
31 women, 6 of them new Christians;
25 children, all heathen, 12 boys and 13 girls.
Total 96 persons.

Among the data provided for those three settlements, that for Candelaria de la Tamaja is perhaps the most significant. The name Candelaria and the presence of Christians links it with the earlier Yamasee mission of Tama in Apalachee. Equally significant is the presence of Ocute's chief and his identification as a Yamasee-speaker. The pairing of Tamaja and Ocute here in 1717 suggests that they were heirs of the Ocute and Tamaja of the de Soto era, who were neighbors in the upper Oconee River valley. In a recent study of de Soto's route through Georgia, Ocute was identified with the Shoulderbone site and Altamaha with the Shinholser site (Hudson et al. 1984:70). The absence of an Ocute among the villages that returned to the Chattahoochee in 1715 and the years immediately thereafter suggests that the Ocute living there in the 1680s belonged to this Yamasee Ocute.

Apart from the knowledge Rivera gained from his visitation to each of the settlements in 1717, he is likely to have been knowledgeable about the Yamasee already. He was at least a second-generation Floridian whose father had built the Spanish fort among the Apalachicoli. Rivera's identification of the Ocute as Yamasee-speakers provides a reinforcing resolution to the puzzle Swanton created by positing a linguistic dichotomy between de Soto's Ocute and Altamaha. The de Soto chroniclers' assertion that Altamaha then was subject to Ocute would seem to suggest that the two people were closely related linguistically in the absence of evidence to the contrary. Yet Swanton identified the Altamaha as Yamasee speakers and the Ocute as Hitchiti-speakers, revealing his own puzzlement over this conclusion in his statement that the Altamaha or Tama "were in some measure subordinate to the Hitchiti" (Swanton 1946:208). The remarks of the Yamasee spy of Chapter 6 support the conclusion that the two languages were very close, if not identical. Mark Williams (personal communication 1989), who has been studying the Hitchiti language more recently, concluded that the Yamasee's language was Hitchiti. Swanton (1922:107) himself fell only a little short of saying that in speaking of a nineteenth-century fusion of a Yamasee remnant "with the Mikasuki, whose language is supposed to have been nearest to their own." The Mikasuki speak Hitchiti.

The Cosapuya living with the Yamasee at Pocosapa, who were identified as having a language of their own, are likely to have been descendants of the Cosapue, known also as Cosahue or Cusabo according to Swanton 1922. The Casapuya were mentioned from the 1560s on as one of the peoples living in South Carolina just north of the Savannah River.

The identity of the people described as belonging to the Oapa nation remains a mystery. Although the presence of Christians among them suggests the possibility that they were Guale, such as the Yoa or people from other Guale towns who are known to have migrated to South Carolina along with or after the Yamasee, that possibility seems to have been ruled out by Rivera's identification of others known to have been Guale as Ibaja-speakers. I mentioned the Yoa in particular because the O of Oapa was open at the top and not very legible and, conceivably, meant to have been a Y. Yoa was identified early as a *visita* along the Georgia coast by Francisco Fernández de Ecija (Hann 1986c:46). Swanton (1946:209) identified Yoa as one of five Yamasee Upper Towns of which Pocotalaca was the head. Milling (1940:104, 111), identifying the Yoa as a Guale tribe, noted that the Yoa joined the Yamasee in 1703 and that there were a few living among them even prior to that.

Rivera identified two other new peoples by names that do not appear in any other sources. They were the Chachise and the Chasta, both described as heathen. He said nothing about the Chachise's nation or language, speaking of them as "attached" to the Mocaman mission of San Buena Bentura de Palica. The mission's Christian inhabitants were Timucua-speakers from the Georgian coast belonging to "the Mocama nation." The 41 Chachise people consisted of 19 men, 14 women, 5 boys and 3 girls. Two women of the "Chasta tongue and nation" were living "attached" to the Apalachee mission. Possibly, they had become associated with Apalachee who migrated to the Savannah River with Colonel Moore in 1704, some of whom migrated to St. Augustine in the wake of the Yamasee War. The Chasta's name does not appear on any of the subsequent lists. The Chachise's name also does not appear on lists from the 1720s and 1730s, but it reemerged in the form Chaschis in Fray Agustín Truixillo's 1759 census of the Guale's Tolomato mission. Bernardo Lachicha, owner of house number six on that census list, was identified as of the Chaschis nation. His wife was Guale (*Ibaja*).

Reestablishment of Relations with the Creeks

A more important consequence of the Yamasee War for the Spaniards than the influx of the Yamasee and other peoples to the vicinity of St. Augustine was reestablishment of friendly ties with the chief of Caueta and many of the other peoples who recognized his leadership or with whom he was allied. On severing ties with the English by their participation in the Yamasee War, those Indians needed another source for the guns, powder and balls, rum, and other trade goods that they were coming to regard as necessities. The primary go-betweens and advocates in this process were an Uchise chief named Chislacaliche and a Christian Apalachee chief named Adrian. They appear to have been intimates of Ysipacafi, *usinulo* and heir to Caueta's Chief Yslachamuque, better known as Emperor Brims. For a time, at least, Ysipacafi became the leader of the pro-Spanish faction among the Creeks. He is the Seecoffee or Seepeycoffee of English sources.

In mission times Adrian had been chief of Bacuqua, Apalachee's gateway to the Apalachicola country. It had always been among the least populous of Apalachee's mission centers. In 1716 Adrian was virtually a chief without followers. Ysipacafi's name has many variants in Spanish documents such as Chipacasi, Tsipacaya, and Sincapafi. His mother was an Apalachee named Qua who was a leader of the pro-English faction among the Creeks and appears to have maintained an abiding hatred for the Spaniards. Ysipacafi, like his father, married an Apalachee woman (Boyd 1952:115; Hann 1988a:288).

The Identity of Chislacaliche

Considerable confusion and lack of specificity has prevailed among scholars as to the tribal identity of Chislacaliche, known in English sources as Cherokeeleechee or Cherokee-killer. Corkran (1967:66–67, 70, 78), after identifying him initially as "the anti-English principal headman of the Apalachees" and referring to "Cherokeeleechee's marauding village of Apalachees," a few pages later spoke of the Englishman Charlesworth Glover having "persuaded the Apalachicolas to bring in Cherokeeleechee, one of their chiefs, who had participated in Yamasee raids on Carolina." Crane (1981:134, 247, 255), writing earlier, identified him variously as leader of "the pro-Spanish faction of the Apalachicola," "Lower Creek," and his people as "Creeks of Cherokeeleechee's town, migrants from the Palachacola Town of the old Carolina border." Swanton (1922:131, 1946:92) identified Cherokeeleechee as "chief of the Apalachicola" who in 1716 along with "part of the Yuchee and Shawnee, abandoned their settlements on the Savannah and moved over to the Chattahoochee." But in his 1946 work, he muddied the water somewhat by identifying Cherokeeleechee and his people with four towns mentioned in the suspect Lamhatty accounts. Swanton believed that those four towns, supposedly located on or near the Apalachicola River in the first years of the eighteenth century and constituting the Apalachicola nation at that time, were attacked in 1706 and 1707 by Indians allied to the English, probably Creeks or Yuchi. Refugees from those towns were then "settled on Savannah River below the Apalachee at a place known as the Palachocolas or Parachocolas Fort, nearly opposite Mount Pleasant" until 1716 when they moved back to their old country. Charles H. Fairbanks (1957:67, 105) in his "Ethnohistorical Report of the Florida Indians" for the United States Department of Justice identified "Chislascaliche" as Emperor Brims' brother, and as chief of the post-1715 town at the junction of the Flint and Chattahoochee known as the "Palachicolas Fort." But there is nothing in the Spanish records that I have seen, except possibly the reference to Chislacaliche as "chief of the Uchises," that identifies him specifically with the town of Apalachicoli. Most recently, Worth (2000:286) identified him as the leader of a splinter group from Apalachicola town. But the 1716 town of Apalachicoli's possession of far more warriors than any of the other Apalachicoli towns makes it unlikely that Chislacaliche's people represented a split-off faction from the late 1680s town of Apalachicoli. The documentation I have seen indicates that he was definitely a person of importance among the Lower Creeks, a chief, and a prominent leader of the pro-Spanish faction among the Apalachicoli in the years just after the Yamasee War.

The roster of the villages that returned to the Chattahoochee in 1716 in the wake of the Yamasee War contained only 10 names compared to the 13 and 14 on the earlier lists. The discrepancy was even greater as two of the 1716-era villages were not represented on the earlier lists. Among the earlier era's villages, one, Kolomi, moved farther west in 1716 to settle on the Tallapoosa. Eventually they migrated from there to Florida to escape contact with the English. After the war those who returned to the Chattahoochee included the Casista, Savocola, Caueta, Apalachicoli, Achito (Chiaha), and Taskiki. They remained there for more than a century until removal in the 1830s (Swanton 1946:92, 115–116, 127, 180, 200).

Chislacaliche was chief of a town bearing his name built in 1716. It was located just above the confluence of the Flint and Chattahoochee on lands that belonged earlier to a nearby Sauocola settlement. Spanish sources contain myriad renditions of his name such as Tascaliche, Chalquiliche, Talichasliche, Talischasliche, Chislacasliche, Chasliquasliche, and Chislacaliche. The notary Juan Solana (1717b) identified him as chief of the province "of the Uchises" (meaning Uchizes) referring probably to Hitchiti-speakers who were originally from the Ocmulgee River region of central Georgia rather than from the Chattahoochee River region of the Apalachicoli. But, considering that Spaniards by 1716 were applying the name Uchize to the Apalachicoli as well, and that so many modern authorities associate him with the Palachocola settlement on the Savannah River at the time of the Yamasee War, there is a possibility, however unlikely, that Chislacaliche's people represented a faction that developed among the original Apalachicoli inhabitants of the Chattahoochee Valley at the time that they moved eastward. Chislacaliche's people's decision to live so far south of the 1680s era Lower Creek homeland suggests that it was not his people's homeland in the 1680s unless they were Sauocola. In 1716 the reconstituted settlements of the Apalachicoli in the vicinity of present day Columbus included a town named Apalachicoli.

The trio of Chislacaliche, Adrian, and Ysipacafi formed the core of the leadership of the pro-Spanish element among the Lower Creeks in the years immediately following 1715. They seemingly assumed the role that Chief Pentecolo had played in the 1680s, although his advocacy appears to have been less exuberant toward the Spanish tie than that of this trio.

Chislacaliche seems to have taken the initiative in reestablishing the Lower Creeks' ties with Spaniards in visiting St. Augustine in 1715. Governor Córcoles y Martínez asked him to inform the other peoples who had returned to the Chattahoochee that the Spaniards desired to renew their former ties of friendship. Mark F. Boyd's (1949:9–10) account of Spanish acquaintance with the native peoples who returned to the Chattahoochee River at the time of the Yamasee War has to be read with caution in a place or two. That stricture applies particularly to Boyd's statement that Diego Peña's 1716 "expedition revealed the dominant position of the casique of Cavetta (Coweta) among the Chattahoochee bands." That was something that Spaniards had been well aware of from the mid-1680s at least. However it is likely that the extent of his preeminence had increased considerably over the two decades since 1685–1686 and that it was enhanced by those people's return to the compact settlement pattern of their earlier homeland.

Diego Peña's First Expedition to the Creek Country

Chislacaliche's second visit resulted in the new governor's dispatch of an expedition to the Chattahoochee River towns led by Diego Peña. His trek represents the first trip overland from St. Augustine by a Spaniard through the former inland mission provinces since the destruction of those missions in 1704–1705. Chislacaliche accompanied Peña on that trip.

Peña (1716) set out on August 4, 1716, and traveled about 45 leagues before crossing the Flint River just above its confluence with the Chattahoochee on September 13. Taking advantage of the complete elimination of the region's aboriginal population in 1704 and 1705, buffalo had spread eastward as far as Payne's Prairie in just over ten years. In mission times the Marianna region marked the eastern limit of buffalo in Florida. Peña noted that buffalo were particularly abundant on the abandoned mission sites, attracted by their stands of fruit trees in addition to their abundance of pasture lands.

Chislacaliche's village lay about half a league west of the Flint. Peña was taken at once to its council house, described as having benches covered with buffalo skins. The Indians there performed several kinds of dances in expression of their good faith. He remained there until September 20, no doubt in part to recover from the rigors of the journey, which was made more difficult in places by a recent hurricane's having flattened many stretches of forest along the trail.

He reached the village of Sauocola, rendered by Peña on this occasion as Savacola, on the seventh day after traveling about another 45 leagues. Peña had marched about two leagues from some prairies along the Chattahoochee, where he had crossed to that river's west bank in a canoe. He stayed that night with Christian Apalachee to whom the prairies belonged. Peña noted that they had a bountiful harvest of corn, beans, and pumpkin along with nuts and buffalo meat. Sauocola's cacique, leading men, and warriors received him initially on a bench near the council house. On learning of his mission, they fired a volley and cheered the king before leading his party into the council house, which he described as a gallery. He noted that "they had and were making very good houses, some covered with shingles, others with bark and, for them, the back parts (*culatas*) of clay and others of shingles, and they make strong houses with skill with small windows."

He spent the next night at a small farm belonging to Apalachicoli's cacique and some Apalachee. On reaching there, he sent a courier on to Apalachicoli so that the province's leaders would be there to meet him upon his arrival the next day. After covering the two leagues to the village, he found all the province's leading men and caciques waiting there to receive him. They fired many volleys with their guns after rendering obedience to the king. To communicate with them, he used the ensign Don Diego de Florencia, whom he described as an Apalachee interpreter. Florencia was from Apalachee's leading Spanish family in the last years of the Spanish missions there. The Apalachicoli leaders gave a favorable reception to his proposal that they move their villages southward to the provinces of Apalachee, promising to begin making canoes at once for the descent. He stated that Caueta's cacique agreed with the move, remarking that all the rest rendered submission to that chief. Caueta's cacique said that seven provinces that follow his orders would do the same.

Peña observed that both he and Caueta's chief had sent word at once of his arrival to the populous province of the Talapuses. Caueta's chief promised that all the chiefs under his jurisdiction would go to St. Augustine to render submission or send two warriors to do so in their place. He went on to Caueta on October 2, noting that it was six leagues distant from Apalachicoli. To reach it, one went through the villages of Achito, Ocmulque, Uchi, Tasquique, and Casista in that order. Only Chavajal lay beyond Caueta. Ten villages in all comprised the province, beginning in the south with Chislacaliche, rendered by Peña as Chilacaliche.

The following table presents Peña's (1716) listing of the warriors possessed by each of the valley's ten villages.

Village	Warriors	Village	Warriors
Chislacaliche	80	Sauocola	84
Apalachicoli	173	Achito	54
Ocmulque	58	Uchi	106
Tasquique	28	Casista	64
Caueta	62	Chavagal	46

Peña suggested that there was an imbalance between men and women with the women being considerably more numerous. Worth (2000:286) noted that the Kolomi of the 1680s moved farther west to the Tallapoosa River at this time rather than returning to the Chattahoochee as likewise did Atasi's inhabitants and those of Kealedji probably. But Eufala, which had been associated with Atasi, was listed later as among those on the Chattahoochee.

Languages

Some of Peña's remarks about the languages spoken in those ten places are puzzling, and at least one remark is clearly erroneous. He noted first of all that "the place of the Uchi had a distinct language and that there were no more than two or three interpreters for it." In his 1716 journal he described Tasquique as being of "the *diamaza* language." He then observed: "the rest of the villages is all one language except for Sauocola, which is distinct, but they speak Apalachino." Whatever was the origin of *diamaza* in this passage, it is at best a garbled form of "Yamasee." In a 1717 report Peña himself spoke clearly of the Tasquique as speaking Yamasee (Boyd 1952:113).

There is no question about the distinctness of the Uchi's language vis-á-vis the languages of the rest of the inhabitants of those villages. But authorities disagree about the identity of the people whom Peña, the English, and other Spaniards referred to as Uchi or Uchee. This writer believes that they were the people whom Spaniards referred to as Yuchi, Chisca or Ysicas. Although the Yuchi were a people distinct from the Westo, the Yuchi may have been related to them.

There is no good explanation for Peña's supposed use of the form *diamaza* in commenting on the Tasquique's language, except possibly an early eighteenth-century Spanish copyist's error. *Diamaza* is written clearly and Peña was familiar enough with the Yamasee to have used their proper name. Boyd (1949:26, note 37), based on a conversation he had with Swanton, speculated correctly that *diamaza* was "Perhaps intended for Yameza (Yamassee)."

Peña's final statement that the rest of the villages all spoke one language except for Sauocola is clearly erroneous. It is generally recognized today that Caueta and Casista's language, referred to usually as Muskogee, is the one from which modern Seminole speech is descended. The people of the town of Apalachicoli and the other towns of the province that gave allegiance to its chief spoke Hitchiti, known also as Uchise, from which the Mikasuki's speech is descended.

One of several possible explanations for Peña's confusion in 1716 on the distinction between Muskogee and Hitchiti is that he was deceived by Diego de Florencia's ability to communicate apparently with both Hitchiti and Muskogee-speakers by using Apalachee. Or he may have failed to note that the bilingual Chief Adrian translated Florencia's Apalachee into Hitchiti. In an account of the 1717 expedition, Peña recorded his use of two interpreters: "Joseph de Escobedo, who is qualified in the Apalachian idiom, and the chief of Bacuqua, qualified in the Uchise idiom," which all those in attendance were able to understand. Or, in a pinch, Apalachee may have been closely enough related to Hitchiti to be intelligible to Hitchiti-speakers. Another possibility is that the presence of many Apalachee had made their language a lingua franca there. Peña observed that there were many Apalachee living in the province at that time. Because of having an Apalachee wife, it is likely that Caueta's Chief Brims was bilingual. When Caueta's chief visited St. Augustine in the early 1680s, the governor used an Apalachee interpreter to converse with him. In view of Caueta's close association with the Hitchiti-speaking Apalachicoli, who constituted the majority of the valley-towns' population, Brims may well have been multi-lingual. That is the clear implication from the 1717 expedition's reliance on an Apalachee-speaking Spaniard and the Uchise-speaking Apalachee chief as their interpreting team (Boyd 1952:117).

As to the Sauocola's language, other sources disagree with Peña, affirming that the Sauocola spoke the same language as did the Apalachicoli. But it is not improbable that they spoke Apalachee as well.

In his 1716 linguistic comments, Peña also noted the presence in the Chattahoochee River towns of a few Costas Alafayes, originally from the Tampa Bay region, some regular Timucua, and some Mocama, who were Timucua-speakers who lived originally on the Atlantic coast from the mouth of the St. Johns River northward to St. Simons Island.

Peña headed back toward St. Augustine sometime after the beginning of October. He had reached the Suwannee River crossing point of Guacara by October 28 accompanied by 26 Indians, two of whom were chiefs, Adrian and Chislacaliche. At least two of the other 24 were Yamasee. Most of the rest appear to have been leading men and warriors who had come to represent their chiefs. In a letter to the governor written from Guacara, Peña spoke of his meeting with the Creek leaders assembled at the town of Apalachicoli. He remarked that Brims observed a policy of neutrality in that meeting vis-à-vis the competing interests of the Spanish and the English alliance. Boyd (1949:8–9) noted that "Peña states that Yslachamuque did not express his personal opinion or publicly, at least, attempt to influence the meeting." All the subordinate chiefs present at the meeting held in Apalachicoli indicated an intention to render submission to Florida's governor. Brims explained to Peña that, when he broke with the English, he had sent two of his leading men to St. Augustine to ask pardon and favor of the governor. But that they had returned without a reply from the governor, giving rise to his confusion over the Spaniards' attitude toward him that had prevailed until Peña arrived to dispel it. Brims reportedly said that he did not hold the governor responsible for the slight, attributing it to faulty interpretation or neglect by his emissaries. Brims regarded the new governor's dispatch of the Peña mission within ten days after that governor's arrival in Florida as ample expression of the Spanish Crown's goodwill. Brims promised to send an Apalachee chief to render submission in his name. Creek hostilities against the English were still occurring at that time. While Peña was at Caueta, a returning war party brought in four horses taken from four Englishmen whom it had killed.

Charles Fairbanks (1957:109) noted that six towns had promised to move to Apalachee. They were Tasquique, the three Uchise-speaking towns of Apalachicoli, Ocone, and Euchito and Yuchi and Sawokli (Savocola).

The Uchises' Visit to St. Augustine, November 1716

As Peña and his party entered St. Augustine on November 9, 1716, a military escort and salvo by the fort's artillery received them formally. The leading men and warriors in his party "came down the street dancing according to their custom, with the chiefs, who did not dance in advance," who would pause at intervals in their progress. A great concourse of people awaited them at the governor's palace and an infantry squad at its gate fired a volley while the treasury officials embraced the chiefs. The governor, who had been ill, waited inside to embrace the chiefs and leading men. In response to the governor's formal welcome, Chislacaliche stated that they came as envoys from Yslachamuque, "mico of the town of Cavetta," who had desired for many days "to come to render submission to the King of Spain," omitting to do so "because of ignorance of the reception accorded his earlier emissaries . . . as a consequence of which he was much vexed and displeased, without having that by which he could reassure his children and women." He went on to say that Peña's mission had remedied that and that the mico of Caueta was placing seven provinces at His Majesty's feet, "rendering vassalage for the seven which are subject to him, whose friendship and obedience will endure to the end of time" (Boyd 1949:10–12).

Provinces of the Creek Confederacy

The leaders of a much more numerous group of natives who visited St. Augustine the following spring seemingly reduced the number to six in response to a question from the governor, who asked them to identify the provinces that were rendering obedience to the king of Spain and "what were their languages." They identified those six provinces as the following.
1. "The province of Cauetta or Apalachicolo, in which the great *mico* resides with twelve places."
2. "The province of the Talapuses with twenty-six places."
3. "The province of the Chiscas with seventy places."
4. "The province of Ayabanos with twenty-nine places."
5. "The province of Apisca with twenty-nine places."

6. "The province of Cuasatte with six places, which amount to six provinces in all and in them, one hundred and forty-nine places."

There is a discrepancy between that total of 149 places and the sum of places given for the six individual provinces, which add up to 172 places. Back as early as the spring of 1715, shortly after the start of the Yamasee War, the total of the villages under the influence of Caueta's chief was given as 161, "the least of which," Andrés de Pez (1716) informed the Council of the Indies held more than 200 people. Ayabanos were the Alabamas, of course, and Apiscas were the Abihkas who "seem to have consisted primarily of remnants of the sixteenth-century chiefdom of Coosa" of northwestern Georgia (Waselkov and Smith 2000:244). The Cuasatte conceivably were the Koasati.

The visiting leaders went on to remark that, in addition to those that they had alluded to, "there are others that they do not remember." Their number was reduced to six here, it is likely, because of the omission of Chislacaliche's province of the Uchizes. It was mentioned earlier in this same document as a province distinct from that of Caueta (Ayala y Escobar 1717a). On this occasion, it may have been subsumed with the one of "Cauetta or Apalachicolo" in view of its contiguity with it or of the Uchizes' blood ties with the Apalachicoli or simply overlooked because of Chislacaliche's presence or his being so well known to the Spaniards.

Back in November 1716, Chiefs Chislacaliche and Adrian attributed the absence of the other chiefs of those provinces to great shortages prevailing in their villages, which caused them to send leading men instead. After the governor promised the visitors all possible aid and thanked them for the reception they had given to Peña's mission, he ordered that sweetmeats, wine, and rum be served. Afterward the Indians asked permission to retire to the patio to dance, which they did for half an hour. The governor provided another round of sweets and rum after that, and then the treasurer entertained them at his house while shelter was being found for the 24 visitors.

Boyd (1949:10–12) surmised that the "Indians appear to have remained . . . until about November 26th, as on that date Governor de Ayala" conferred "the title of *Generalissimo* on the mico . . . with a message that on request he would be glad to establish a garrison of infantry and supply arms and ammunition. These were accompanied by presents of . . . red cloth, a blanket," and 25 pounds each of powder and ball.

The governor who greeted Peña and the Indians who accompanied him was not the one who had given Peña his mission about three months earlier only shortly after having assumed the governorship. That governor, Pedro de Oliver, had died in the interim. He was succeeded by an acting governor, Juan de Ayala y Escobar, who held the post of sergeant-major and was a longtime resident. Ayala was still serving as interim governor, when the much larger delegation of 157 visitors from the Creek country arrived in St. Augustine on April 4, 1717, to pursue the development of an alliance with the Spaniards.

The visitors included 25 caciques and leading men. Ayala singled out four among them as the most important in his eyes. They were Ysipacafe, identified as "*usinjulo* and mico, heir to the great chiefdom of the province of Cabetta;" Chislacaliche, cacique of the province of the Uchises; Adrian, an Apalachee chief; and Tatepique, cacique of the province of the Talapuses. Talapuses was a general name Spaniards used at times to designate the Upper Creeks. The first three bore silver-headed canes the governor bestowed on them back in November, when he also sent one to Cauetta's chief along with the title of "Generalíssimo."

The Indians made a ceremonious entry into the city as they had in the previous November visit. They moved along "drawn up in formation . . . and two of them were coming along out in front in accord with their custom, which they call *Lelixen* . . . whooping as they were coming along, while others were playing some instruments they use, which they call *manuas*, and a bass drum. And they were coming along to the sound of these instruments with their knees almost against the ground making various gestures and ceremonies, which they use as a sign of a show of goodwill and submission" (J. Solana 1717a).

The two in the lead were noted warriors identified as *norocos* and *thascallos*, "who are strong and valiant men who have performed memorable deeds," especially chosen for that purpose. Among the Apalachee *tascaia* was the title given to a warrior who had killed one enemy. One achieved *noroco* status among the Apalachee by killing three enemies. The *manua* was probably a gourd rattle. What appears to be the same instrument was referred to as a *marua* in the Apalachee ball-game manuscript (Hann 1988a:341). One of the warriors carried a crown in his hand, "formed from various feathers, a creation of their forefathers." The other carried a pipe with a yard-long stem, "which they call *cachimbo*," used for smoking leaf tobacco. Whatever is the origin of the word *cachimbo*, it is worthy of note that the word appears in both modern Portuguese and Spanish as meaning "tobacco pipe."

Behind those two warriors came the four principal chiefs identified above. They were dressed in the Spanish fashion, wearing hats (*sombreros*) and carrying their silver-headed canes. The other 21 leaders followed them. They, like the rest of the Indians, were all clothed in animal skins. Some carried muskets and pistols; the rest, quivers, bows and arrows. Along the way they made various stops and pauses, with a show of solemnity.

When the visitors were within a pistol shot of government house, the governor and his party went out to receive them. When the governor gave the abrazo to Ysipacafi, the latter responded in kind, bending his knees. The soldiers then fired a volley and the Indians responded with another one. Once the mutual greetings had been completed, the 25 native leaders retreated to the governor's lower room, while the rest including the two "*tascallos norocos*," remained outside in the patio. The governor gave the leaders a welcoming speech through the soldier-interpreter, Antonio Pérez, who had a native's grasp of the Iguaja or Guale language from his mother. Ysipacafe responded in kind, promising that the obedience they had come to pledge "would be stable and permanent forever." The governor then served a drink to all, inside and out. Ysipacafe, the first to be served, on taking the vessel, explained that he was toasting the king of Spain's health. On standing up, he drank it, but left a portion, which he tossed up against the ceiling, making the toast customary in those parts while bowing at the same time. Then, after kissing the vessel, he placed it on the tray and sat down. The other three caciques then did the same with their drink.

After the rest, inside and out, had been served and made their toasts, Ysipacafe asked the governor's permission to perform their customary demonstration of goodwill and obedience. To the accompaniment of their musical instruments, they began a sonorous chant "from their ancient times and in their languages, with great pauses and ceremony, prostrate on the ground." The two *tascayas* then entered and went around the room in separate directions to sit down at the governor's feet. "After being there quite a while with their chants and ceremonies," one of the warriors removed the governor's hat and the other placed the crown of feathers on the governor's head, saying through the interpreter that it represented the crown of the king of Spain and that his placing it on the governor's head at the behest of "the great Cacique of Cavetta" was to demonstrate that chief's submission and obedience, which they had come to give in his name. They explained that the rest of their demonstration, done according to their custom, signified permanent and perpetual friendship until the end of the world. After the governor assured them that he liked "their very endearing demonstrations very much," the caciques expressed their gratitude for his hospitality stating "that later in the days ahead they would speak the rest that the Great Cacique of Cavetta had charged them to" (J. Solana 1717a).

On April 6th the governor met again formally with the Creek delegation to discuss the portent of their obedience to the king. He began by asking the four principal leaders to state their names and positions. The governor recorded that:

> the most important one (*el mas principal*) replied that he was called Isipacafi, *Usinjulo* and mico, and that he was the son, legitimate heir of the great cacique of the province of Cauetta, and the one of highest esteem

among the rest of the caciques. . . .; The second one replied that he was called Chislacaliche, cacique of the province of the Vchizes. . . . The third one said that he was called Adrian, Cacique of the Apalache, of the same nation, . . . Christian, and what he referred to [was] his Christian name. The fourth one said that he was Tactipique, cacique of the province of the Talapuses. (Ayala y Escobar 1717a)

Isipacafi went on to explain that his father had not come in person because of his great age and preoccupation with protecting his places from any threat by enemies, but had sent him to represent him as his beloved son and as mico. He observed that "mico in his nation was the same as Governor." In his father's name he promised "perpetual friendship and union" and that in defense of the Spaniards, "both he and his vassals and the rest of his confederated provinces would give their lives."

The Pro-Spanish Trio's Return to St. Augustine July 1717 and October 16, 1717

Caueta's *usinulo* and Chiefs Chislacaliche and Adrian returned to St. Augustine on July 10, 1717, and October 16, 1717, to ratify the obedience given in April, and to ask for more arms and munitions for their people. Governor Ayala y Escobar (1717f), in reporting the July visit rendered Chislacaliche's name as Talichasliche, identifying him as "the great general and major war chief." They came with an entourage of 57 of their subjects and made another ceremonious entry. On reaching the governor's house they performed singing and dancing to which the Indians gave the name *La Paloma* or The Dove. They remained there for 16 days during which the governor wined and dined the caciques so that they might return to their lands content. For Emperor Brims, the governor prepared a suit of great splendor along with a cane and fine feathered hat decorated with gold lace (Ayala y Escobar 1717d).

Chislacaliche brought up an offer made by Governor Ayala's predecessor to place a Spanish garrison in Creek territory, informing Ayala that Caueta's great cacique and his faction had been pleased by the offer. Chislacaliche then formally asked for such a garrison. When Ayala asked what site would be suitable, Ysipacafe and the rest of the caciques suggested that the Guacara River, the modern Wakulla, site of the earlier fort about two leagues from the port of St. Marks in Apalachee Province seemed to be the best one because of its closeness to the Gulf and suitability for trade with vessels from Havana. They left that matter to be settled through an envoy whom the Spaniards were to send to the Creek country.

After a break for lunch, the Indians requested the firearms and munitions they needed for their defense: 199 muskets (*escopetas*), represented by 199 little sticks tied into bundles, which was their method for showing the numbers desired. When Ayala countered by offering them 150, they asked that he add four more and that he supply two pounds of powder and three pounds of ball for each gun to enable them to hunt for game on their long trek home. Additionally they requested a small allowance of powder and the balls for the forts that they had built to shelter their women and children during possible enemy attacks. Ayala's offer of 100 pounds of powder and balls to match it left them content, after which they took their leave to prepare for their return home (Ayala y Escobar 1717f).

The governor lost no time in laying the groundwork for fulfilling his pledge to place a garrison in Apalachee, informing the king on April 21, 1717, that he would dispatch 25 soldiers and a lieutenant, hopefully by the beginning of September. They would leave once he had assembled the iron tools, cannon, munitions, provisions and other supplies needed for the enterprise. For the long run, he suggested that the garrison's provisions be shipped from Havana to the port of St. Marks, which was only two leagues south of the site where the garrison was to be housed (Ayala y Escobar 1717b). But not until February 6, 1718, would José Primo de Rivera set out with 70 foot and mounted soldiers, carpenters, and the rest needed to build the blockhouse, accompanied by Chislacaliche, Chief Adrian, and other Apalachee. A sloop would set out four days later with provisions and other necessities.

Developments at Pensacola

Even before the contacts assumed importance at St. Augustine between the Spaniards and the Indians formerly allied with the British, Pensacola's governor moved to try to end the British-allied Indians' steady harassment of his garrison by a direct approach to the British, unaware of the native uprising in Carolina. He dispatched a peace mission overland toward Charles Town on April 8, 1715, as soon as he learned that Spain, France, and England had signed peace treaties with each other in Europe. He hoped to convince Carolina's governor that its terms should be observed in the New World, and therefore the governor would persuade his native allies to cease their harassment of Pensacola's garrison. When his emissaries reached the Talipuses' head place on May 25, 1715, they learned of the Yamasee War's having turned many of Britain's erstwhile native allies into enemies of the British. The Talipuse leaders refused to let them pass on, detaining them there while they informed Caueta's cacique of this turn of events. Caueta's cacique ordered the Spaniards to return to Pensacola, informing them that the Indians that acknowledged Caueta's leadership now wished to have good relations with the Spaniards and that their caciques would hold assemblies shortly to discuss the establishing of good relations with the Spaniards. In reporting this, Pensacola's Governor Salinas Varona (1717b) highlighted Caueta's chief's preeminence among the Creeks in general, noting that in July 1715 "leading Indians of Talessi, Talepuches, and Taquipuches (sic) came ordered by their Emperor of Cauetta to give obedience to Spain's king." As an earnest of their goodwill, they sent along three Spaniards whom they had held as prisoners. The governor reciprocated with gifts of powder, balls, shirts, cloth, and hats.

On the last day of September 1715, the principal chief of the Tiquepache and Talipuse arrived to work out the formal agreement, accompanied by over 50 caciques and captains and more than 300 Indians with arms, who all gave obedience to the king. As in these Indians' first such visits to St. Augustine, the negotiations were preceded by the Indians' performance of a number of ceremonies spelling out their peaceful intentions, including presentation of a highly ornamented ceremonial pipe, the calumet. Seven of the chiefs were sent on to New Spain to impress them with the grandeur of the vice-regal court and to some degree to lessen the drain they represented on Pensacola's scarce rations (González Barcía Carballido y Zúñiga 1951:359). The governor drew up a list of the native towns and nations that were parties to that agreement, forwarding copies to the viceroy and to the king (Salinas Varona 1717a, 1717b).

The most important among the native visitors sent to Mexico City were Tixjana, warrior captain of the Talisi village of the Talapuse, and the Apalachee cacique Juan Marcos. Tixjana was baptized not long after his arrival in Mexico taking the Christian name Baltasar José Antonio. The viceroy gave him the title of campmaster general of the Talapuse Indians. Florida Spaniards' efforts to secure Caueta authorities' recognition of Tixjana's new stature seems to have generated some friction. Juan Marcos was given the title of governor of the Apalachee (González Barcía Carballido y Zúñiga 1951:361–362).

Creek Overtures to the English

As Crane (1981:255) noted, "the eclipse of English prestige, for the moment complete" in the wake of the Yamasee War "was reflected in the enhanced influence of the Spanish and French." The first moves among the Creeks to reverse this came "from an Anglophile faction . . . in the spring of 1717" and were ineffectual. But later an English mission made progress among Upper Creeks and Caueta's chief received the English while making Peña, who was then on his second mission for the governor, cool his heels for a time. When the *usinulo* (or *osinulo*) and Chislacaliche returned to the Chattahoochee at the end of July, they found those Englishmen there. This led to a momentary schism between the *usinulo* and his father, Brims, when the *usinulo* called for a rupture with the English (Ayala y Escobar 1717f). In November 1717 agents for the Creeks formalized that rapprochement by signing a treaty with the English in Charles Town (Crane 1981:257–259). The Creeks made several important concessions in the treaty. One, as Hahn (2000:273) observed, "made the Creek nation 'an English trading fief.'" The treaty also empowered Carolina authorities exclusively "to punish both English and Indian miscreants." At the Indians' insistence Carolina's Governor Robert Johnson promised that the English "would not settle south of the Savannah River." But that proviso remained only a verbal commitment that was not incorporated into the treaty.

Diego Peña's 1717 Expedition

When the July visitors from the Chattahoochee were ready to depart, Governor Ayala commissioned Diego Peña to escort them back to their homeland with a squad of 12 soldiers.[3] Peña himself spoke of having only eight soldiers. Peña was to convince at least some of the Lower Creek leaders to move their villages into the former Apalachee territory ostensibly to facilitate their protection by the Spanish garrison to be established there. He was also to purchase horses in the Apalachicoli country to mount a cavalry unit at St. Augustine and to assess the sincerity of those Indians' recent alliance with the Spaniards and the open-handedness of the hospitality they offered (Ayala y Escobar 1717d; Boyd 1952:111–113).

Having set out on July 26, Peña and his party reached Chislacaliche's place just above the junction of the Flint and Chattahoochee on August 24. On August 28th the *usinulo* set out from there in great haste on a good horse. Peña and the rest followed on August 30th. The next day a Sauocola Indian, whom they met on the trail, told them the province was stirred up over the arrival of a dozen Englishmen and a black. As the English approached Casista bearing a white flag, the Indians there responded with a red one, indicating that they would not be admitted. However, they were allowed to enter Caueta and housed in a structure relatively close to the emperor's house and the goods they brought were placed in his storage building.

At a farm of a Tama who had lived earlier in Apalachee where Peña stopped on September 4th, he was told not to go any further north for the present until the Indians determined what to do about the English visitors. While he was detained there, a steady stream of Indian leaders and warriors came from all the villages except Caueta, Casista, and Chavagale to visit and hold meetings. The *usinulo* from Caueta arrived on the third day with two warriors. The chiefs who met there resolved that the Englishmen should be imprisoned and sent to St. Augustine. But the emperor's influence was such that when Peña reached

Caueta, the English were still moving about freely and Peña had doubts about the sincerity of some of those professions of adherence to the Spaniards.

When Peña's party reached Tasquique, a short league from Caueta, the *usinulo* told him to stay there for the night while he went on to see how they were to receive Peña. Caueta received him with a white flag "with the *usinjulo* captaining." He found the emperor in bed with a swollen foot from a bamboo that had pierced it. Yslachamuque convoked a meeting of all the leaders for the next day to hear Peña's message from the governor delivered by an Apalachee-speaking Spaniard and then translated into Uchise by Bacuqua's Chief Adrian. Through spies placed by Adrian, Peña learned that the Englishmen had been there since the end of July and that the emperor's wife, the Apalachee chieftainess, Qua, and the pro-English faction had welcomed them. Ten had gone on with the black to the Talapuses' province to reestablish friendship there.

Peña's reproaches to the emperor about the liberty the English enjoyed initially brought denials from him that he was aware of it. When Peña contrasted that freedom with the detention to which he had been subjected, the emperor was stunned to silence and then tears. Only after a little while did the emperor suggest that, as Peña was white like the English, he and the Englishmen should work out an agreement (Peña 1717a).

An assembly held the next day voted to give obedience to Spain's king and for friendship with the French. Afterward the *usinulo* and Chief Adrian held a long debate with the emperor over the killing or imprisonment of the Englishmen and the taking of their horses for Spain's king. Before Peña left, the *usinulo* assured him that "if no accommodation is to be had [to resolve the impasse], he will know how to make war on his father." To forestall such an outcome, some of the pro-English faction at Caueta, influenced by the Englishmen, were thought to have contemplated eliminating Peña and his party. Peña reported that, after leaving Caueta, he had learned that fear of such a development had prompted the *usinulo* to tell him that he should leave Caueta as soon as possible. As a precaution against that, Chislacaliche had accompanied Peña and secured 14 warriors from Achito (Ayala y Escobar 1717d; Peña 1717a).

Shortly thereafter, the Indians allied to the Spaniards, expressed concern over their own safety, fearing that they might become targets of an English-inspired attack from the pro-English faction among the Lower Creeks. They suspected that Emperor Brims may have been a party to the conspiracy or that he was tolerating it because of the gifts the Englishmen had brought him. Once Peña and his party arrived at Chislacaliche's village, Achito's chief asked for the prompt return of his warriors to provide security for his village against such an English-instigated attack. When Peña asked Chislacaliche for two men to carry a letter to St. Augustine, Chislacaliche demurred, alleging that there was too great a danger they would come to grief because of their tie to the Spaniards. Peña's identification of the place where he wrote his diary as Sabacola indicates that it was the location of Chislacaliche's place.

That concern probably was responsible for two pledges given by various Lower Creek towns' leaders to move their communities to the vicinity of the fort Spaniards had promised to build a little north of St. Marks. On the first occasion Chislacaliche had promised that he would move to Apalachee shortly upon the expected arrival of 100 families from another province who were his vassals. The other villages or leaders identified at that time as ready to move southward were Tasquique, Apalachicolo (Abalachicolo), Sauocola, and Bacuqua's chief along with other Apalachee. In the wake of the panic over possible attack, Peña included among those ready to move: Euchitto (Achito), the village of Uchi (Yuchi), and Ocone. He again mentioned Tasquique, Apalachicolo, and Sauocola (Sabacola) as making up the rest of the six villages that planned to move down during the coming winter, making no mention of Chislacaliche's readiness to move at this time. On this second listing he identified Achito (Euchito), Apalachicolo, and Ocone as all Uchise-speakers and the Tasquique as Yamasee-speakers. He remarked that there were only two interpreters for the Uchi's language and that they were a very warlike people and as "very loyal on this occasion," as though their friendship with the Spaniards was unusual. None of the six nor Chislacaliche followed through on their promise (Peña 1717a:123, 1717b:134). The only apparent consequence was the impulse it gave the Spaniards to end their temporizing and establish their presence at St. Marks.

A census of the Indian villages in Spanish territory reported in 1726 that the settlement of San Juan adjacent to the Fort at St. Marks of Apalachee contained 46 persons, consisting of 16 men, 17 women, and 13 children. All but one were Christian (Hann 1991b:367). But only two years later, Cuba's bishop indicated that the native population in the vicinity of that fort was considerably larger, based on the testimony of soldiers from the St. Marks fort. One soldier testified that he had seen there a village of about 200 persons. In 1724 and 1725 other soldiers indicated that there were two separate Indian villages. One of them contained 80 warriors, Christian and pagan, but it lacked women and children. The other had only between 30 and 40 people among men, women, and children.

Peña and his soldiers returned to St. Augustine on October 16, 1717 accompanied by a large number of Indians led by Chislacaliche, the Apalachee's Chief Adrian, described then as "cacique and war captain," and the cacique of the Yuchi nation, who had come to renew the peace agreements. As they were setting out from Chislacaliche's place, Caueta's *usinulo* headed for Pansacola, according to Governor Ayala y Escobar (1717c) "to search for arms, munitions, and people in order to expel the English" and to punish the discontented Lower Creeks "who were united with his father." The visiting Indians received a salute from the fort's artillery as they entered singing the dance called "the Dove (*la Paloma*)" (J. Solana 1717b).

The governor received them formally at the entrance to his residence, accompanied by a squad of soldiers, their leader, the active reservists, and the governor's ministers, who formed a court for the governor, who was ill at the time. Despite his illness, he received them personally, after which the Indians carried out various ceremonies and dances and presented their requests. These presentations were accompanied by a liberal distribution of alcoholic beverages.

Two days later the governor convened a formal *auto* to take statements from Peña and the soldier-interpreter who had served him on the mission to the Apalachicoli country on the reception that they had received. Peña (1717c) reported that at the entrance to Apalachicoli the Indians came out to receive him with a white flag and a cross that they gave him to kiss, resurrecting an earlier practice and explaining that it meant that "they wanted union and peace with the Christians." Peña stated that the Indians very much wanted the Spaniards to establish a garrison in Apalachee at St. Marks and that on its establishment, many of them would move their villages to be close to them to avoid having to worry about the English. He reported the incident that had occurred at Casista when 11 Englishmen and a black approached with a white flag. The Casistans put out a red flag to indicate that they were not welcome. Peña attributed the friendlier reception the English received at Caueta to the intervention of Cacique Brims's wife rather than to the will of Brims himself.

Peña spoke in a delphic way of a people whom he identified as Natuaques, who had sent messengers saying they wanted to give obedience to the king. He described their province as having been "extensive," with many places, noting that they were greatly feared "because they were very tall and fierce" and cannibals. The interpreter Joseph Escobedo (1717) gave their name as Naturaques, observing additionally that they did not come from Caueta to give their obedience to the king "because most of them died from an epidemic." He added that it had been the Naturaques' intention, when the winter came, to incorporate themselves with the Apalachicoli so that they might make war on the Chalaques. The latter were first mentioned in the de Soto narratives as living "beyond Cofitachequi." Elvas (Clayton, Knight, and Moore 1993:I, 86) placed them seven days beyond that center while Rangel (Clayton, Knight, and Moore 1993:I, 280) reduced that distance to two days, noting that de Soto never found Chalaque. It is likely those Chalaque were Cherokee.

Escobedo also identified another people, the Yllache, who do not seem to have been mentioned by any other source. He affirmed that they favored the Spaniards, saying they were ready to die at the Spaniards' side in defense of the lands of Spain's king. Yllache's old cacique, who had remained in Apalachicoli, accompanied Peña on his return to St. Augustine in order to ratify the obedience he had given to Spain's king. The old chief also, no doubt, hoped to receive some of the largess that Spanish officials in this era bestowed on such visitors to cultivate their good will. Pansacola's Governor Gregorio de Salinas Varona (1717a) spoke of its importance frankly to his counterpart in St. Augustine, observing, "although it is at the cost of a great deal of wealth because of their being children of interest who find and receive." He went on to note: "Here they do the same and everything appears to them [to be] little."

The ceremonies that marked this October visit are described in greater detail than those of earlier visits. On October 16th, between 8:00 and 9:00 in the morning, 50 fifty Indians, led by General Chislacaliche, Chief Adrian of Bacuqua, and the chief of the Yuchi nation, entered the city again singing and dancing the Paloma. As they entered, the fort's artillery fired a volley in salute. At the entrance to the governor's houses, a squad of soldiers fired more volleys. Within the house toasts were exchanged and the Indians performed various ceremonies and dances in the presence of the governor who served sweet cakes, chocolate and other sweets and liberal amounts of firewater. Two days later, Peña made a formal statement about the events that had transpired during his July trip to the Creek country. He highlighted the Indians' revival of a ceremony from earlier times. It consisted of receiving the visitor with a cross as he approached the village council house. The governor responded to the Indians by promising that, as soon as possible, he would satisfy their request to place a Spanish garrison in Apalachee near the port of St. Marks. He hoped that the garrison would serve as an incentive for some of the Indians to move down from the Chattahoochee and thereby lessen the English influence among them (Ayala y Escobar 1717d; Peña 1717c; J. Solana 1717b).

When Peña and the soldiers who accompanied him made formal statements on their return, the soldier-interpreter, Joseph Escobedo (1717) mentioned that he knew that unidentified "native Indians were coming" to St. Augustine "to give obedience who did not pass beyond Cauetta because the most of them died from an epidemic." He described these migrants as "the most feared among the rest of the natives because they eat people." They allegedly had come with the intention of joining forces with the Apalachicoli at the beginning of winter to make war against the Chalaques (the Cherokees). From there they would go down to attack Charleston. He went on to identify a cacique of Yllache whose "nation and villages" strongly favored the Spaniards whose "old cacique remained in Apalachecolo," and then accompanied Peña when he returned to

St. Augustine to ratify the obedience he had given to Spain's king. But he was unable to communicate with the Spaniards for the lack of an interpreter for his language among the Apalachicoli as well as at St. Augustine.

Whatever threat, if any, that English mission represented to the Creeks' renewed alliance with the Spaniards appears to have evaporated quickly. Peña returned to St. Augustine accompanied by the *usinulo* and Chislacaliche. Chief Adrian was already there with a party of Apalachee. In Pensacola in the name of his father, the *usinulo* reaffirmed Caueta's decision to maintain good relations with the Spaniards. A delegation of Talipuses returning to Pensacola from Mexico City at the beginning of 1718 prevailed on its governor to send a deputy with them to Teguala in Talipuse territory to ratify the peace treaty and so that they might reaffirm the loyalty they had sworn to Spain's king. In response, Juan Fernández de Orta arrived at Teguala with them on February 26, 1718 for a meeting with Brims and the other Creek leaders (González Barcía Carballido y Zúñiga 1951:360).

Chipacafi Assumes the Chieftainship at Caueta

The *usinulo* set the tone more or less on the second day in asking Orta why the Spaniards, who were such good Christians remained at peace with the English, who were such bad actors, explaining that he did not ask the question idly. He wanted to know the answer before taking over as cacique from his father on the following day, February 28th. Brims retained his position as chief-over-all. When Tixjana was formally installed in the campmastership the viceroy had bestowed on him as lord of the Talipuses, Chipacafi made it clear that as cacique and *usinulo* he was second in command after the emperor. Chipacafi also made it clear that he wished it understood that he did not consider himself an infidel inasmuch as his mother had been a Christian Apalachee and he was married to a Christian Apalachee. He mentioned this so that the governor might know that he took pride in being a good subject of the king (González Barcía Carballido y Zúñiga 1951:362).

The question of relations took on new urgency when news reached the assembled Indians that a new party of 30 Englishmen had arrived at Casista. Against the Indians' expressed desire to strip the English of their possessions and to expel or harm them, Orta felt compelled to prevent that. These English brought captive Creek whom the Cherokee had enslaved, whose release the English had secured. Peace was established with the English and Chipacafi set prices for the Indians' purchase of the merchandise they brought with them. The ultimate result was that the Indians resolved to remain at peace and maintain friendly relations with all three of their European neighbors, the Spanish, French, and English garrisons, something they had contemplated from the beginning (Primo de Rivera 1718a; González Barcía Carballido y Zúñiga 1951:362–366).

Later in 1718 Peña made a third trip to the Apalachicoli country. The emperor received him warmly at Caueta, suggesting that it would be important for Peña to accompany his son and heir, Sincapafi (Chipacafi) who was about to visit the province of the Talipuses. A two-day march brought them to its first village, Talasi, one of 12 in that province which gave obedience to Spain's king. At Talasi, Peña met "the great cacique of the Apiscas," who also pledged obedience (Benavides 1718b).

At the insistence of the Talapuse, Peña accompanied them on a visit to the French fort in Alabama territory. On his arrival he received a friendly reception from a Viscayan officer who was then in charge. But a new commander, who arrived a few days later, was less friendly, warning Peña that if he returned, he would detain him and send him to France.

Benavides was skeptical of the worth of those Indians' pledges of friendship. He remarked that "there is little [reason] for trusting in their friendship and that they must keep very much in mind the extortion that Spaniards had inflicted on them of having burned their villages and killed some," realizing that only the Indians' break with the English made them give obedience to Spain's king.

Spanish Fort at St. Marks, Apalachee

Spaniards had been contemplating a return to Apalachee for some time. But the move was given urgency by developments in Europe. The Quadruple Alliance brought England, Holland, France, and Austria together in 1718 to check the ambitions of Spain's Philip V (Coker 1996:123). When the 50 soldiers who were to build the new fort finally set out early in 1718, they were accompanied by some caciques from the interior who had been awaiting that event since October 16, 1717 in order to avail themselves of the security the soldiers would provide (Ayala y Escobar 1718a). Among those Indians were Caueta's *usinulo*, who made the request in the name of his father and of "the great general Chislacasliche" in particular, and in the name of all the other caciques and leaders of Apalachicola Province (Ayala y Escobar 1718a). The soldiers' commander, José Primo de Rivera (1718a), had reached an old site of the Tomole mission just above the trail to the coast by March 15th. He paused there for two days to hunt for meat to bring down to the fort site. Such old missions' open grazing land and orchards attracted wild cattle as well as deer.

While he was still there, 20 men arrived at the fort, accompanied by 150 caciques, leading men, and warriors. Rivera was unimpressed by all of them except Bacuqua's Chief Adrian, describing the rest as "all talk and no action." Adrian won his approval by promising to settle near the St. Marks fort. People from seven Talapusa settlements also visited the fort. Oconi's cacique informed him of ten Tocopacas encamped at Wacissa, revealing that they had pledged allegiance to Caueta's chief. Rivera, fearing that Brims might enslave or kill them, had the Tocopacas brought to the vicinity of his fort. Conceivably his suspicions were aroused by his talks with some Yamasee who asserted that they were being persecuted by the Uchisi and were at odds with Chislacaliche. They told Rivera that, once they had harvested their corn at the site of a former Chacato village, they would come down to the coast to settle in Sartouche forest only one and one-half leagues from St. Marks.

While Orta had been proceeding from Pensacola to Teguala with the Indians returning from Mexico, Joseph Primo de Rivera set out from St. Augustine on February 6, 1718, with 70 soldiers to begin the building of a blockhouse at St. Marks. He was accompanied by Chislacaliche, Chief Adrian, and other Apalachee. A few days later a sloop sailed from St. Augustine with supplies for Rivera's enterprise. By March 15th he was encamped at the remains (*chiquassa*) of the Tomoli mission, located in the southern quadrant of present-day Tallahassee probably in the vicinity of the fairgrounds (Jones 1987). He encamped there on the 16th and 17th "to kill some meat to bring with" him to the port of San Marcos as his provisions were running low. During that interval 20 men arrived "from the place of Chaliquasliche . . . with a letter for him." Orta informed him that on his "arrival at Teguale he met the great cacique of Caueta there" and that 30 Englishmen were headed for it. The Indian leaders had urged Orta to inform Primo de Rivera of this development. Orta also informed Primo that the Indian leaders had convoked a general junta to be held shortly at Caueta.

In the light of this development, Primo headed west toward Sauocola on March 18th to attend the junta at Caueta, placing ensign Francisco de Fuentes in charge of his remaining forces, who were to continue on to San Marcos. On reaching Sauocola on the 21st, Primo decided to rest the horses there for six days before pushing on. A leading man brought word two days later that the junta had already completed its work and adjourned after deciding that its Indians would live "in friendship with us, Pansocola (sic), Movila, and the said English." But if anyone deceitfully took this decision amiss, they would go to war with him. Faced with this *fait accompli*, Primo departed Sauocola on April 1st, headed anew for San Marcos, reaching it on the 4th.

On April 20th Caueta's "great Cacique" visited San Marcos with 150 men, consuming, as Primo reported with regret, the contents of thirty palm-mat bags (*petates*). To guarantee Brims's continued goodwill, Primo used some of the cloth he had brought to purchase horses to make gifts to Caueta's and Casista's chiefs and to the "little *Usinjulo*." Among the gifts were eight muskets belonging to the garrison's soldiers for which Primo had to request replacements.

When Primo pressed the Indians for a commitment for some of them to settle in Apalachee, they demurred that it was not the proper "time for that but that when the time of their fasts arrived in order to eat the fruit, then he would see whether the people would be pleased" to do so. Primo correctly interpreted the response as reflecting "their scant will to do so" while trying not to displease anyone and extract as much as they could in the way of gifts. Primo de Rivera (1718a) noted also that "the *Usinjulo* of Caueta, who is already governing the province, was called from La Mobila with great urgency by its governor."

Spaniards continued to press the Lower Creeks and the Apalachee living among them to move down into Apalachee as a way of "removing them from communication with the English." The governor pressed that point particularly in a March 30th letter that he had sent to Primo with the Apalachee's chief of Ocone. After reestablishment of a Spanish presence in Apalachee, some of the Apalachee living along the Chattahoochee who had moved to Pensacola soon moved back east to the vicinity of the St. Marks fort (González Barcía Carballido y Zúñiga 1951:378). Authorities made repeated efforts to induce the remaining Apalachee living among the Apalachicoli, as well as some of the Creek themselves, to resettle Apalachee, particularly in the area of the abandoned missions (Ayala y Escobar 1718a, 1718b; Boyd 1952:199; Primo de Rivera 1718a). Chief Adrian promised to round up all the Apalachee he could to establish a new settlement near the fort (Primo de Rivera 1718a), but there is no evidence that he did so except possibly a 1719 statement by Juan Marcos, head chief of the Apalachee. While he was recruiting settlers among the Apalachee at Pensacola, he mentioned that some Apalachee had established a settlement near St. Marks. As Juan Marcos had just come from St. Augustine, he may have recruited settlers there among the refugee population or from the considerable number of Apalachee from the Chattahoochee River settlements who were in St. Augustine as visitors in September and October 1718. A 1723 listing of the missions did not mention an Apalachee presence there but they do appear in a 1726 mission list as sharing the village of San Juan near the fort with the Yamasee. That 45 of its 46 inhabitants were Christians suggests that most may have been Apalachee. A second all-Yamasee mission of San Antonio contained 146 residents, described as 48 recently converted Christians and 98 heathens (Hann 1991b:366–367).

The cacique of Ocone brought to Primo's attention the presence of about ten Tocopacas who were settled at Basisa, the modern Wacissa. The chief observed that the Tocopaca were being ordered to give obedience to the cacique of Caueta. Their number evidently was larger (Primo de Rivera 1718a). In August, Primo de Rivera (1718b) reported that there were two caciques and that on the 29th of July a band of Pojoy, who had come in from the sea, had killed eight of the Tocopacas at Basisa and carried off three. By then there was a second Tocopaca settlement close to the San Marcos fort on Casina Point. Primo hoped to enlist Chalisquasliche into avenging this attack, promising that Spaniards would provide them with the canoes to do so.

Governor Benavides (1718a) reported on August 2, 1718, that Rivera had been well received by Caueta's chief and the other leading men. On his arrival Brims told him it was important that Rivera accompany his son and heir, the *osinjulo* (*usinulo*), Sincapafi, to the province of the Talapuses. They reached its first place called Talasi after a two-day march. Its people gave them a great welcome, telling Rivera that its twelve places of the Apiscas were under obedience to the king. The Talapuse chiefs allegedly made a gift to the king of mines that were close to Talasi, giving Rivera stones (*piedras*) that appeared to Rivera to contain silver. They also persuaded Rivera to accompany them on a visit to the Aiabamos (Alabamos) province where the French had a garrisoned wooden fort along the banks of the Mobila River.

The officer in charge of it, who was about to be relieved, appears to have received them civilly. But shortly after his replacement arrived, the latter warned Lieutenant Diego Peña that if he returned, he would be shipped off to France. Upon that party's return to Talasi, some of its leaders accompanied Rivera to St. Marks and then went on to St. Augustine with the Spanish expedition, which apparently was accompanied by Apalachicoli chiefs who had joined them at St. Marks. Concerning the latter, Benavides (1718a) commented that they should not place much trust in their friendship, mindful of their long hostility in the wake of the Spaniards' burning of some of their villages in the late 1680s until the Indians' 1715 attack on the British made them renew their Spanish ties. Nonetheless, he pledged to continue regaling them when they came, "dedicating his full vigilance to their preservation" (Benavides 1718a).

Among the Indians, the Yamasee showed the greatest interest at that time in relocating to Apalachee. They wanted to escape incessant attacks from Uchise bands who were partial to the English or attracted by English offers of prizes for Yamasee scalps. In mid-1718, the fort's commander, Rivera, spoke of the intent once the crops were in of a Yamasee group who had settled at the site of the Chacato village of San Carlos on the Apalachicola River to move to the forest of Sarturcha in the fort's vicinity (González Barcía Carballido y Zúñiga 1951:378; Primo de Rivera 1718a, 1718b). Primo de Rivera (1718a) identified them as the people of Tamasle, noting that following Brims departure on April 25, Tamasle's chief remained until the next day with a hangover, confiding to Primo that he and all his people "found themselves with a bad heart toward the Chaliquasliche" because of their harassment by the Uchise people. Their new settlement was about a league and a half distant from the San Marcos fort.

The English themselves, and Indians allied to them, continued to wage an unrelenting war against the Yamasee. Adopting the spirit enshrined in the maxim delenda est Carthago, the English made that war's goal the extermination of the Yamasee people. Despite the formal cessation by agreement of the armed conflict between Britain and Spain early in 1721, English authorities at Charleston continued to encourage and reward Indians allied to them to carry out attacks in East Florida against the Indians allied to the Spaniards (Benavides 1722a). Late in 1723 Governor Benavides (1723b, 1723c) complained that he had appealed in vain to the viceroy for arms that would allow the Spanish-allied Yamasee to defend themselves against such attacks (Peña 1723). The English promised a considerable reward for Yamasee and Apalachee scalps that were brought in. The Talapusa and the Apisca in particular responded strongly. Peña reported that the Uchise "resisted greatly," but that the "ones of Caveta and Chavagale and the common people of Casista, Ocmulgue, Osuche and the Yuchi yielded to their suggestion." In anticipation of attack, Chislacaliche and the Yamasee of Tamasle abandoned their settlements. The villages of Latama and Guacara apparently were considered more secure because of their proximity to the fort.

The governor learned of a new British genocidal plan from Diego Peña, then the officer in charge of the St. Marks fort. On August 4, 1723, an Indian spy, whom Tamasle's chief maintained in the Chattahoochee River towns, reported on a sizeable group of warriors. Originating from seven Talapuse towns and one Apisca town, the warriors accompanied by four Englishmen and bringing considerable armament, had come to Caueta Province with the object of exterminating the Yamasee living there by offering rewards for their scalps. The spy reported that they had already killed two Christian Yamasee males in "Palachicolo" and one woman each in Ocone and Yufala. But Peña (1723) reported that these warriors met considerable resistance to their plans in what he referred to as the province of the Uchises. Peña noted: "the one of Caveta, Chavagale, the common people of Casista, Ocumulque, Osuche, and of the Yuches yielded to their suggestion. He does not know whether the remaining villages did not wish to agree. They said only that they did not want war with the ones from these nations alluded to. And that they consider it as very certain that they will soon be coming down to . . . Tamasle and the one of Chislacaliche." Tamasle's inhabitants abandoned their village at this time as did the people of Chislacaliche's settlement. Peña identified two other pro-Spanish villages in the area as Lactama, and later as Lacma, and Guacara. He remarked, in concluding, that he had invited Lactama's chief to visit him "in order to see whether he wishes to maintain himself in the said Lacma with the three villages." At that time, Lactama's chief had not come to see him.

In a postscript he reported that 15 days earlier a Frenchman and two Chacato women had disappeared in the vicinity of Chislacaliche's place, noting "it is thought they have killed them" and in closing remarked, "everything is going badly."

That last remark probably also reflects a deterioration in Chislacaliche's alliance with the Spaniards. When Peña acquainted Chislacaliche with the Talapuse threat, he pledged initially that he would not abandon his village but rather die in its defense. But within half an hour Chislacaliche returned to say he would leave the village but go to St. Marks to support the Spaniards. He suggested that Peña should give him the clothing for gifts that remained in his possession. When Peña demurred, Chislacaliche repeated the request, threatening that, if he did not, he would take it from him on the trail. Before daylight Chislacaliche and his people had abandoned their village as had those of Tamasle. At this time of stress there was tension as well between Indian groups allied to the Spaniards. Primo de Rivera (1718a) reported hearing from the Yamasee that they were being persecuted by Chislacaliche's Uchises. The Yamasee, who were then at a former Chacato site, informed the Spaniards that, because of that persecution, they intended to abandon the site once they had harvested their corn there. They planned to resettle in the Sartouche forest within a league and one-half of the St. Marks fort. When Peña caught up with them on the trail of Lactama, the fugitives amounted to more than 100 people. Peña advised realistically that they should count no longer on any support from the upriver Indian provinces in view of their perception of Spain's weakness reflected in their abandonment of their garrison at St. Joseph, the loss of Pensacola, and their failure to settle Apalachee. He remarked that fear alone kept Tamasle, Lactama, Guacara, and Chislacaliche loyal. To strengthen Spain's hand in the interior, a new proprietary governor spoke in 1718 of bringing families from Spain to settle in Apalachee. But nothing resulted from that suggestion (Benavides 1718a).

The Rising French Threat

Back in 1718 the French seemed to represent more of a threat to Spanish interests on the Gulf of Mexico than did the English. Pensacola's new governor, Juan Pedro Matamoros, found its defenses in a perilous state, while the French were speedily developing their forces and settlement at Mobile and establishing extensive contacts with the natives living inland from it. When tardy arrival of Rivera's sea-borne supplies led him to appeal to Pensacola for relief, Captain Juan Roldán, who brought it, discovered a new French establishment being erected on St. Josephs Bay as his pirogue was returning westward. Spanish concern was soon heightened when 15 deserters from the French enterprise on St. Joseph's Bay reached St. Augustine. They reported that the French had built "a wooden redoubt with five cannon [and] a warehouse with munitions and provisions for fifty men . . . and that they were awaiting another fifty soldiers as reinforcements" (Benavides 1718a). In the face of French rejection of Spanish Florida authorities' demand for their withdrawal from that bay, which Spanish forces had once occupied, they lacked the means to compel them to leave. When Chipacafi visited Mobile, Bienville entertained him and presented gifts to him with such generosity that the Caueta cacique's attachment to the Spaniards began to wane. The effect was felt almost at once at Pensacola. Only a few days after Chipacafi's arrival at Mobile, the Caueta, Talipuses, and other Indians ceased to frequent Pensacola. Well prior to this, Spanish efforts to persuade Chipacafi to release Christian Indians whom the Creeks held as slaves proved fruitless (González Barcía Carballido y Zúñiga 1951:366–372, 375). Although Bienville withdrew his force from St. Josephs Bay early in the second half of 1718 because he had taken that step without authorization, Spaniards had good reason to be concerned about the intentions of the French (González Barcía Carballido y Zúñiga 1951:376).

On learning of the French intrusion at St. Joseph's Bay, the Council of the Indies approved of what St. Marks' fort's commander had done there in its wake. As to future policy, it simply restated its position that the Gulf Coast should remain a Spanish preserve. To Florida's governor it wrote that it was "trusting in his zeal that he will maintain the appropriate vigilance so that no posts at all on that coast and frontier may be occupied by other nations." The Council assured the governor that precise orders were to be sent to New Spain's viceroy to assist him promptly with people, arms, munitions, and foodstuffs so that its people "will be able to maintain themselves and so that posts so important may be defended" (Council of the Indies 1719).

A 600-man French force on ships, supported on land by more than 700 Indians, attacked Pensacola on May 14, 1719. The Spaniards, with only 160 men capable of bearing arms, accepted generous surrender terms that allowed the Spanish families to leave with all but their chased silver, coins, and cloth. The village of La Soledad's Apalachee inhabitants were to be left unmolested as vassals of Spain's king and be allowed to go where they chose. A Spanish force recaptured Pensacola in August and turned away a French relief force that had come overland after the French defenders' surrender. But later, when another French force attacked, the Spanish surrendered eventually on September 18th after putting up a heroic defense and having been ground down. Fearing the arrival of another Spanish expedition, the French destroyed everything and withdrew most of their force on October 21st, leaving only a rear guard of 25 men with four cannon and a few Indians. Because of being becalmed, they remained until October 24th. After the Spaniards' recapture of Pensacola two months earlier, the Apalachee chief, Juan Marcos, brought word from Chipacafi that his people were willing to help the Spaniards against the French. When Juan Marcos returned with 60 Indians, the Spaniards' second surrender had already occurred. On seeing the destruction, he dismissed his force (González Barcía Carballido y Zúñiga 1951:379, 385–388, 391–393).

The ongoing game of musical chairs for control of Pensacola was ended by a treaty signed on March 27, 1721, by the participants in the War of the Quadruple Alliance (1719–1721) that had pitted Austria, Holland, and England as well as France against Spain (Tebeau and Marina 1999:57–58). But well over a year and a half was to pass before a Spanish force under Alejandro Wauchope arrived from Mexico to assume control from the small French force (Ford 1939:130–131). All that remained of the earlier presidio was a dilapidated hut. One of Wauchope's first tasks was to bring in a Spanish force that had been holding the French-built fort on St. Joseph's Bay.

Ford (1939:148) estimated that during this unsettled time "by 1720 half the lucrative trade in skins and furs which the English had enjoyed with the Creeks and other Indian tribes north of Pensacola had fallen to England's rivals." The new Carolina governor who took over in May 1721 had been instructed to regain the friendship of those Indians. He soon had trading posts among the Alabamas within three leagues of the French fort. He sought to prevent the traders' abuse of the Indians that had motivated the Indians' desertion to Mobile and Pensacola. He hoped to drive a wedge between the Creeks and the Spaniards and he even tried to win back the Yamasee's loyalty. But only the perennially anglophile Casista would listen to his agent, Theophilus Hastings. And among the Upper Creeks only the Talapusa were actively hostile to Spaniards and Yamasee. Benavides accordingly asked Madrid to reverse its hostility to providing arms and ammunition to the Indians. The Council of the Indies opposed that governor's proposal to buy 600 guns from the French and sent only 200, resorting instead to appealing to London to abstain from agitating the Indians on Florida's borders (Ford 1939:149–151). In view of the French intrusion in waters Spaniards regarded as mare nostrum, Madrid remained more concerned with the French threat there than with the English one, even though the English represented a greater menace.

8

The Final Years, 1718 to the Mid-1740s

Restoration of Ties with Upper and Lower Creeks

A chronic shortage of supplies was the major problem the Spaniards faced in the wake of their restoration of ties with the forebears of the Upper and Lower Creeks in the period beginning around 1718 and the reestablishment of a Spanish presence in the hinterland in Apalachee. Tepaske (1964:205–206) observed that "no single factor weakened the Spanish position among the Indians more than the shortage of supplies . . . Without bountiful supplies of arms and food, the governor's Indian policy lost its effectiveness . . . and the Indians turned more and more to English and French traders who were more generous and more opulent." And the Spaniards' firm alliance with the Yamasee proved to be a potent source of friction as well when English traders pressed their crusade among the Creeks for the extermination of the Yamasee, who had been among the Spaniards' most trustworthy allies since 1715.

On learning of the suspension of arms in Europe between Spain and Britain, Florida's Governor Benavides (1722a) hastened to dispatch the royal accountant, Francisco Menéndes, to secure a punctual observance of the treaty so that they might "cease to incite the spirits of the Indians" responsible for the frequent attacks on the Spaniards and the Indians living in the vicinity of St. Augustine. The Carolina government claimed not to have heard of that agreement but promised, nonetheless, to maintain good correspondence with St. Augustine during the suspension of hostilities.

At this time the English were moving southward aggressively by constructing a wooden fort on the Altamaha River and in "the mouths of Talasje" Swanton (1922:243) in former Guale territory (Benavides 1722b). In October 1723, based on a report from Peña in early August, Benavides observed that "Englishmen from Carolina with their greediness . . . were trampling underfoot the good correspondence they were supposed to have under the treaty for the suspension of arms." He noted that in the interior they strove to win over heathen Indians who had given obedience to Spain and to win them as allies for a campaign to wipe out the Yamasee who had established themselves in Apalachee "and ten [villages] that there are belonging to the same nation and to others" in the vicinity of St. Augustine. That threat had inspired the governor's request for 600 light rifles mentioned earlier along with 6,000 gun-flints to enable those Indians to defend themselves better. The viceroy did not supply them. The governor described the villages in Apalachee as "two populous villages of the Iamasee Indians" (Benavides 1723b). In this era those two villages soon became the target of English intrigues among the Indians living along the Chattahoochee to bring about the extinction of those two villages' inhabitants. Peña (1723) learned from the Yamasee village of Tamasle's chief that four Englishmen from Carolina were then agitating for an Indian expedition to eliminate the two Yamasee villages of Tamasle and Guacara, located in the vicinity of St. Marks. The Tamasle chief's spy in the Chattahoochee River towns reported that four Englishmen had enlisted a sizeable troop of Talapuses drawn from seven places, along with some Apiscas, for that purpose. The spy reported that already in "Palachecolo they have killed two Christian Yamasee men and in Eufala and Ocone two women," delivering their scalps to the Englishmen. Influenced by the English, the Talapuse also planned to kill any Apalachee whom they encountered.

But when the Talapuse sought to enlist the province of the Uchise in this enterprise, they met great resistance from the Uchise proper, who said, in response, that they did not want war with the Yamasee. However, the chiefs of Caueta and Chavagale and the "common people (*la pleve*) of Casista, Ocumulque, Osuche" responded favorably to the Englishmen. Peña did not know what the Yuches' response had been. Peña expected that the ones allied to the English would be coming down to attack Tamasle and Chislacaliche's town. Peña reported that the people of those two towns abandoned their settlements to seek refuge at the Spanish fort or at the village of Lactama. Peña also mentioned the presence of a fourth village named Guacara in the general area of the fort. With English encouragement, the Talapuse had attacked the pro-Spanish Yamasee in 1723.

Statistics on the Indians Just Outside St. Augustine and St. Marks

Among those Indians, 465 adults and 193 children had become Catholics since Benavides assumed the governorship in August 1718 (see table 4).

Earlier in 1723, Governor Benavides (1723a) identified some of the Yamasee living at St. Marks in Apalachee as Amapejas. Those Amapejas consisted of 79 adults but only 12 children. They were, undoubtedly, the same people whose name was rendered as Amapiras in another 1723 document, a register of Indians who had been baptized between 1718 and early 1723. All 91 of the Amapiras had been baptized (Hann 1991b:362). Late in 1725 Uchises, Yuches, and Apriscas launched attacks that destroyed the Christian settlements of the Jororos, Timucua, and Tama (*La Ottama*) (Fuentes y Herrera 1734). The identity of the

Table 4. Statistics on the Indians Just Outside St. Augustine and St. Marks, 1723

Children	Adults	
7	23	baptized at St. Augustine's convento
7	18	Yamasee boys at St. Marks
15	39	from the Costa nation Guasacara [Ais]
21	26	Yamasee at Nombre de Dios Chiquito
7	8	Casipuias
15	—	in the village of Palica
28	134	Alafaes in a Timuqua village
4	13	Yamasee at Poco Talaqua
4	26	Hororo at the Hororo village
18	4	Timucua at Nombre de Dios Amacarise
6	—	Apalache at Moze

Source: (Benavides 1723b).

Apriscas is uncertain. The native name that resembles it most closely is Abihkas or Apicas, the name of an Upper Creek group.

It is not clear what had become of the Amapiras by the time of the visitation in 1726 of the native settlements at St. Augustine and St. Marks. The group among those mentioned in 1726 whose name most closely resembles Amapiras was identified as "Indians of the *rinconada* of the Macapiras nation who were attached to the church of San Buena Bentura." That church, located in the vicinity of St. Augustine, belonged to the "old Christian Chiluca." Those Macapiras consisted of only seventeen men, six women, and one child, eighteen of whom were recently converted Christians, while the other six remained heathens. Consequently, it is unlikely that these Macapiras were drawn from the Amapiras of the 1723 document. In the same 1726 visitation record two settlements were described for Apalachee Province. The first was inhabited solely by Yamasee, 48 of whom were recent converts and 98, heathens (66 men, 51 women, and 29 children). The second one, named San Juan, held Apalachee and Yamasee, who were "attached to the church of St. Marks," and consisted of 45 Christians and one heathen (16 men, 17 women, and 13 children) (Hann 1991b:365–367).

But only two years later Cuba's bishop indicated that the native population in the vicinity of the St. Marks fort was considerably larger, based on testimony of soldiers from that fort. One soldier testified that he had seen a village of about 200 persons there. In 1724 and 1725 other soldiers indicated that there were two separate Indian villages at St. Marks. One village contained 80 warriors, Christian and pagan, but lacked women and children. The other one had only between 30 and 40 people including men, women, and children.

Little is known about the few Casipuias mentioned here by Governor Benavides. When they were first mentioned by Spaniards in the sixteenth century, their name was rendered as Cosapuya. In the time of Menéndez de Aviles they had a fortified town 20 leagues from St. Augustine. Swanton's (1946:128–129) identification of them with the Cusabo of southern South Carolina is very questionable in this writer's opinion.

English Aggressiveness

With English encouragement, the Talapuse had attacked the pro-Spanish Yamasee in 1723. When the Talapuse attacked Pensacola in 1727, the settlement was hard pressed until Louisiana's Governor Perier came to its rescue—that despite the hostility between the two nations that led to war between them in Europe in the latter part of 1727. As Ford (1939:152–153) noted, even then Perier saw Spanish Pensacola "as a useful buffer between Carolina and Louisiana."

In that same year of 1727, the English took a harder line, planning two expeditions to enhance their position vis-à-vis Spanish Florida. In the first of those expeditions Colonel John Palmer wreaked havoc in the eastern Yamasee country, driving those who survived to seek refuge at St. Augustine. Colonel Charlesworth Glover was to have led a second expedition against the Lower Creeks. But at the last moment, it was converted to a diplomatic mission to try to persuade them to abandon Brims' policy of neutrality between the three European powers to one of exclusive reliance on English traders. Ford (1939:153–155) maintained that "the tidings of Palmer's victory over the Yamasees proved to be the deciding factor in the contest," noting, "Even Brims appeared to be convinced and again opened up his towns to the English traders."

Peña (1723) reported, on the basis of intelligence from a Yamasee spy whom Tamasle's cacique maintained in the Lower Creek country, the arrival in Caueta of Talapuse and Apisca forces, accompanied by four Englishmen, whose goal was to exterminate any Yamasee or Apalachee whom they encountered. Peña recorded that they killed two Christian Yamasee in "Palachicolo," and one woman each in Ocone and Eufala. They also pressed the Lower Creeks to join their campaign against the Yamasee. According to Peña, the Uchise "resisted greatly," while the "one of Caveta, Chavagale, and the common people (*la pleve*) of Casista, Ocumulque, Osuche, and of the Yuches yielded to their suggestion." The remaining villages declined to participate, saying that they did not want war with those nations. The intelligence that Peña reported came from a spy whom Tamasle's chief maintained in the Lower Creek villages in the vicinity of Columbus. The spy went downriver to Chislacaliche's village on August 4, 1723.

Peña by then felt that Spaniards could no longer count on any support from the upriver Lower Creek villages. As to the one of Chislacaliche and those in the vicinity of the fort, fear of the English kept them loyal for the present. But he went on to note that, even among Spain's Indian allies, English propaganda was making inroads in convincing them that the days of Spanish control were numbered. They stressed the Spaniards' loss of Pensacola and withdrawal from St. Joseph and that the Spaniards' could not assure the Indians of a reliably steady supply of the trade goods they desired.

This campaign to exterminate the Yamasee was still in process late in 1725. At that time, Governor Benavides (1725) received a report from his lieutenant in Apalachee that he had encountered a strong detachment of "heathen Indians of the partiality of the English." Those Indians assured him that they had no quarrel with the Spaniards and that they were very grateful to the governor and that they had come only to fight the Yamasee. The lieutenant hastened at once to inform the "nine neutral villages," and even the heathen ones aligned with the English, that Spanish forces were still firmly allied with the Yamasee and would fight to the death to defend their allies. Peña was confident that word of that commitment would suffice to deter the anti-Yamasee force from carrying out their threat and discourage the neutrals from joining them.

Indian Populations in the Vicinity of St. Marks

During the era of the mid-1720s various Spanish sources gave diverse accounts of the Indian populations in the vicinity of St. Marks in Apalachee. What is probably the most trustworthy one appears in Governor Benavides's 1726 census of the Indian villages in the territory under Spanish control. The census reported that late in 1726 there was a village named "San Juan, settlement of the Apalache and Yamasee nation established in the province of Apalachee." It had "forty-eight recently converted Christians, ninety-eight heathens" who were made up of sixty-six men, fifty one women and twenty-nine children (Hann 1991b:366–367).

Those figures are corroborated roughly by a report about 20 months later by the Bishop of Cuba on September 1, 1728 that, among other things, contains testimony by a number of soldiers on the status of the Indian villages at St. Augustine and in the vicinity of the fort of St. Marks in Apalachee. Concerning the latter one soldier testified that there are "many heathens in those of Apalache and among them is a village of Indians, of about 200 persons that set itself up more or less as it saw fit" during the time that this witness was there. The soldier seemed to insinuate that the friar then stationed at St. Marks showed no interest in that largely heathen nearby Indian village. Other soldiers added details such as that of the existence in 1724 and 1725 of two distinct Indian villages in the vicinity of St. Marks. One about two leagues from the fort was composed of 80 warriors, Christian and heathen, but without women or children. The other village was one league from the fort and contained between 30 and 40 people, Christian and heathen, including men, women, and children. Both lacked a priest (Bishop of Cuba 1728). It is not clear whether these two villages were affected at all by the epidemic of 1727 that severely reduced the population of the villages in the vicinity of St. Augustine (Hann 1991b:370).

The village composed of men only had lost all its women and children in 1728 after it was forced to surrender to Uchise attackers when its defenders exhausted their ammunition. The 80 surviving warriors had been able to escape to the Spanish fort two leagues away. At that time and earlier the village bore the name of Tamasle (Bishop of Cuba 1728; Hann 1988a:291–292; Montiano 1745).

Franciscan Mission Activity

Franciscan mission activity appears to have been at a low ebb in Florida during this period, even though substantial numbers of friars were still being sent from Spain. Many of those sent to Florida appear to have migrated quickly to Cuba. Early in 1730, the Council of the Indies, fearful that the lack of religious to preach the Gospel would have an adverse effect on the continued loyalty of the heathen Indians who had renewed their obedience to Spain, ordered the return to Florida of some of the friars who had gone to Havana to work on strictly Franciscan projects there, especially those with experience in the Indians' languages. Fray Domingo Losada (1730), in response to those fears, argued that the nine friars left at St. Augustine and two at St. Marks were adequate for work with the Indians living in the vicinity of those two Spanish establishments. He stressed that because of the heathen Indians' aversion to being Christianized and their ties with the English who armed them, it was not safe to stray far from the fort in search of new Indians to evangelize. In mid-1736 Florida's auxiliary bishop, Francisco de San Buenaventura y Tejada expressed his belief that the heathen Indians' occasional pledges of obedience were a fraud and made only to obtain a handout, after which they returned to their ties with the British.

Relations with the Lower Creeks and Yamasee

In the midst of the Yamasee War and in its immediate wake, with the restoration of settlement on the Chattahoochee, the Creek and Yamasee turned to St. Augustine and Pensacola for trade goods and ammunition. Even after peace had been restored between the Creek and the English, the Apalachee and Yamasee were able to play a role in Brims' policy of maintaining peace with all his European neighbors and not tying himself too closely to any of them, in order to preserve a balance of power in the region that served the Indians' interests.

Thus, while Governor Ayala y Escobar was entertaining the Apalachee's Chief Adrian of Bacuqua and a number of Lower Creek chieftains in St. Augustine, Don Gregorio de Salinas was hosting a large group of Talapuse and Apalachee at Pensacola. In order to strengthen the renewed ties, and also, probably, to relieve the pressure on his chronically short food supplies, Salinas dispatched a number of the Apalachee and some of the Upper Creek headmen to Mexico in 1717. He hoped to impress them with the grandeur of the vice-regal capital and to give more solemnity to their renewal of their profession of allegiance to the king of Spain. In Mexico the viceroy named the Apalachee cacique, Juan Marcos, as governor of all the Apalachee in the hope that it would enable him to promote the resettlement of the province. To Texjana, the warrior captain of the Talisi village of the Tallapoosa, he gave the title of "Campmaster General" among the Creek (Crane 1956:255; González Barcía Carballido y Zuñiga 1951).

Spanish soldiers returned to Apalachee in 1718, building a fort and settlement at St. Marks rather than inland. Apalachee Indians from an undetermined location, along with some from Pensacola, established a settlement near the new fort at St. Marks. Yamasee, who had been living on the Apalachicola River at the site of the former Chacato village, also established a village named Tamasle in the new fort's vicinity. A few Tocobaga were reported to be living at Wacissa and on an island at the mouth of the Aucilla. The Apalachee's continued presence there was last mentioned in 1728 (Hann 1988a:326–327).

Upon their return from Mexico, Juan Marcos and Texjana hastened to the Creek country to meet with Brims and to try to persuade some of the Upper Creek to settle near Pensacola. Diego Peña, at the same time, sought to persuade Chief Adrian and the Apalachee among the Lower Creek as well as some of the Lower Creek themselves to repopulate Apalachee.

Spaniards' relations with the Lower Creeks appear to have been cool at best through the mid 1730s. As early as April 1738, Cuba's Governor Juan Francisco de Güemes y Horcasitas spoke of using St. Marks to establish relations with the Lower Creeks. At the end of May he mentioned that Marques de Toros was in contact with the Apalachicoli and Talapuses. On August 8, 1738, Governor Montiano (1738) chose Tama as the site for a new settlement near the fort of St. Marks. By March 1739, he was providing military supplies to the Uchise for their war against the Chickasaw. A heightening of tensions with the English beginning in 1738 had been a factor behind these moves designed to improve the Spaniards' situation vis-à-vis the Indians. Among the first fruits of that effort was a listing of the Lower Creek villages that had received gifts in the King's name, along with the names of four of the leaders and the number of warriors they commanded. See Table 5 for that list.

By the beginning of March 1739, Governor Montiano (1739) reported hopefully of the development of hostilities between the Uchises and the Chickasaw in the expectation that this might lead the Yuches and others of Apalachicola Province to align with Spain and thereby thwart English plans of having the Chickasaw and others establish themselves in Apalachee.

Table 5. List of the Lower Creek Villages, 1738

Village Name	Chief or Leading Man	Warriors
Tamaxle the Old	Paal Juuchufca, leading man	12
Chaschdue (new village)		
Chalaquiliche	Chalaquiliche, chief;	10
	Yafcuimarla, governor	47
Jufala	Atasimico, chief	111
Sabacola		
Ocone		
Ayfichiti (possibly a synonym for Hitchiti) (Swanton 1922:175, 465)		
Apalachicole		
Ocmulgee		
Osuchi		
Chioga?		
Casista		
Cabeta		
Tamaxle New (Marques del Toro 1738)		

Prior to Oglethorpe's attack in 1740 there had been eight small villages of Indians near St. Augustine allied to the Spaniards. In the wake of that attack the villages were reduced to four by early 1743 because many withdrew during the English siege. Some did so in order to look for sustenance in the woods. Others moved to Pensacola to escape the danger. Later at St. Augustine, enemy Indians killed those who ventured out in search of firewood. As a result there remained only 39 men and 71 women, all very much frightened and given to drunkenness, with 93 children to protect. Four friars served them, but only one made the effort to learn the Indians' languages. However, the Indians understood Spanish.

The Uchise remained the major threat for the Spaniards. Their 14 villages in Apalachee in relative proximity to St. Augustine had from 600 to 1,000 warriors who were armed superbly by the English. When Uchise leaders came to St. Augustine to be regaled, they responded to Spanish complaints by attributing the raids to "some wayward ones who are not subject to the government of their villages." These unruly ones, referred to in Spanish sources as *cimarrones* or wild ones were the immediate ancestors of the Seminoles, whose name developed from *simarrones*. As a remedy, Florida's governor proposed in 1743 that the Royal Company of Havana be ordered to maintain a store in Apalachee supplied with the same goods the Indians bought from the English. His list included muskets, belt pistols, light sabers, powder, balls, flint stones, small and medium cauldrons, brass, razors, scissors, needles, awls, combs, hawks bells, glass beads, finger rings (or possibly buckles), buttons of linen and metal, red dye and ash from England (the colors they painted themselves with), blue and red cloth with white edges, striped shirts of semi-fine cotton or linen stuff (*crea*), or of fine Brittany linen (*Bretaña*), painted linen cloths and light fabrics (*telas ligeras*) like chintz (*Zarazas*) for skirts, belts, ribbons (*colonias*), firewater, honey, sugar, tobacco, and pipes for smoking it. These, he indicated, were the goods the Indians consumed, noting that the English and French had them in abundance and exchanged them for the Indians' deerskins and skins of other animals. He noted in conclusion that the presence of many Christian Apalachee and Yamasee among the Uchise might be used as a lever, if the Indians' trade with the English could be supplanted, suggesting that it might be possible to induce those peoples to friendship with the Spaniards again (Montiano 1743).

During the latter part of the 1730s tensions mounted once more with the ever closer British in the wake of the formal establishment of the Georgia colony in 1733 under James Edward Oglethorpe. Although Oglethorpe's initial claim on the Atlantic coast reached southward only to the Altamaha River in mid-Georgia, the Englishman soon extended his claim as far south as the St. Johns River. In 1737, Florida's Governor Francisco del Moral Sanchez reached an accord with Oglethorpe under which the Englishman withdrew northward from the St. Johns River's mouth but maintained his rights as far south as the Altamaha. Madrid recalled Moral Sánchez to Spain, court-martialed him, rejected the agreement he had signed, and began preparations for war to defend its claims in Georgia until March of 1738 when it suspended its bellicose stand.

Oglethorpe's continued aggressive stance led to hostilities by October 1739 in what became known as the War of Jenkins Ear, which was sparked by trade controversies in the Caribbean. In May 1740 Oglethorpe attacked Florida by land and sea. His forces soon captured the small outlying forts north of St. Augustine and occupied the north end of Anastasia Island in order to besiege the town and its major fort. But the Spaniards maintained firm control of St. Augustine's castillo and repelled all Oglethorpe's overland assaults aimed at approaching the castillo. In mid-July the British ordered the ending of the siege, but remained on Anastasia Island into early August (Arnade 1996:110–114).

Early in 1745, Montiano (1745) suggested that the best way to end hostilities by the Uchises and to win their friendship was to establish a store at St. Marks. Alvares de Toledo, a Spanish soldier who had traveled with the Uchises attributed their hostility to Spaniards' failure to keep their repeated promises to settle people at San Luis. Other soldiers attributed it to Uchise dissatisfaction with the store's failure to stock many of the things they wanted. One soldier said Uchise leaders attributed the hostilities to lawless elements not subject to the leaders. One portrayed the Yamasee in particular along with the Uchise as preferring to sell skins to Spaniards at St. Marks because they detested the English and that Uchises would probably follow their example because most of the Uchise troops had Yamasee captains because of the Yamasees' reputation as superior warriors.

Governor Likened to Viracocha

In a curious document written in 1722 by Florida's interpreter for the Indian tongues, allegedly in the name of "all the most remote caciques of the provinces of Florida, as are those of Caveta, Casista, Thamasle, Chilacasliche, Huacara, Vchichicas, Niquilache" as well as those of the villages in the vicinity of St. Augustine, Florida's incumbent Governor Benavides is referred to "as son of the Sun (*Sol*)" and "this singular Viracocha." Viracocha was the "Supreme Being, the Creator and Ruler of the Universe" for the natives of Peru (Péres de Ecompano 1722; Prescott 1961:86). They refer to "his valor (*fortalesa*) as son of the Sun in order to defend them. We the most remote caciques set out together with the principal men to see this singular Viracocha." The caciques allegedly were asking that Benavides be kept on as governor. Their request was granted as Benavides has the distinction of being Spanish Florida's longest-serving governor, ruling from 1718 to 1734 (Tepaske 1964:Appendix 1).

Peña (1723) observed that he had a report that the Frenchmen also were proceeding in war, "having finished off one or two villages of Apalachees who were attached to the Movila and a bunch of Chickasaws." Peña spoke murkily about the seeming existence of four villages in the vicinity of Apalachee at the time, mentioning having given some clothing to the "Villages Tamasle and Chilacoleche, and the rest, to give it to these villages Lactama and Guacara." He had sent to call the cacique of Lactama to learn whether he wishes to maintain himself in "Lacma" (sic) with the three villages.

In his summary Charles Fairbanks (1957:126, 135–136) remarked that "in the period after 1708 the destruction of all organized tribal life in Florida was continued by Yamasee, Creek, and Carolinians." By the mid-1740s, Apalachee had been settled largely by migrant Creeks who had come initially as visiting hunters. Lower Creek elements, and particularly the Ocone, settled on the Alachua prairie in the time of Oglethorpe, attracted by that area's wild cattle. There Cowkeeper's band was consistently pro-British, while Brims' son and heir, Secoffee, leader of the Apalachee, was consistently anti-British. But that did not prevent him from making war on the anti-British Yamasee. Chislacaliche also continued to raid the Yamasee even though he remained friendly toward the Spaniards (Fairbanks 1957:113).

Even well after the end of the war, St. Augustine's residents remained under a virtual state of siege for much of the year, fearful of venturing into the countryside to gather firewood, lest they be attacked by Indians allied to the English.

Offshore, corsair privateers remained a problem. One such vessel that Spaniards captured late in 1743 or early 1744 provided intelligence that the English were awaiting a transport with 300 men from Europe and six half-galleys. To gather more information on this, Governor Montiano (1744) dispatched Cacique Pedro Chislala with 40 warriors to capture Englishmen who might provide more intelligence on this matter. In the vicinity of St. Simons Island, where the English had a wooden fort on the mainland on the bank of a river, they captured five men from a lumber-cutting detail. But they were ambushed in turn at the St. Johns River crossing by 40 or 50 Englishmen and more than 30 Indian allies. In the ensuing confusion their five prisoners were able to escape.

But by mid-1747 at least, and probably earlier, the threat to the city's residents had lessened considerably. In August 1747 the governor advised the king of word he had received from Captain Juan Isidoro de León at Apalachee's Fort St. Marks that their former enemies, the Uchises, had become friendly and were interested in trade. That change of heart was verified during the ensuing winter by their not having experienced the attacks that were usual at that time of year and by the arrival during that interval of four distinct troops amounting to about 30 persons to test the Spaniards' hospitality. In the second group, which arrived on January 24, 1748, came a nephew of Chiquile, sent by that leader. Montiano (1748) described Chiquile as "one of the most principal governors of the Uchise nation," saying they were inclined to live in peace with the Spaniards. As a sign of this they sent a feather or wing of a white heron, asking whether the Spaniards would forget past injuries to establish good relations and to provide them with arms, munitions, clothing, and the rest in exchange for deerskins and other pelts, and to make peace.

A probable factor in this change of heart was their being short of food as a result of two years of no maize harvest because of drought and their fears of a shortage of guns for their ongoing war with the Cherokees, partisans of the English.

The Indians asked the governor to make the trade items they had requested available to them in Apalachee. In response the governor made the Royal Company of Havana aware of all these circumstances, asking that it see to it that the stock of the existing store at St. Marks be upgraded to meet the Indians' demands in conformity with royal orders.

Another Spaniard, who had been St. Marks' commandant in 1741 and 1742, corroborated that statement, observing that the Uchise nation as a whole did not participate in such attacks, even though they were not well disposed toward the Spaniards.

One of the most voluble and believable witnesses was a Guale Indian named Francisco Luis de Caracas, who gave his age as about 35. He served as an interpreter for Spanish contact with the Uchise. It was his opinion that the Uchise leaders as a group "were in friendship with the Spaniards and that this was the reason that the Uchise, as a nation, did not make war against the Spaniards, but only some unruly ones influenced by the English. A girl from that Guale's village, who had been prisoner of the Uchise for a long time, had assured him that when such a war-party returned with the scalp of a Spaniard or of a Christian Indian, "the more mature among the Indians and the women reproached the young warriors over their having killed someone who has done us no harm and someone who gives us food, clothing, and ammunition without any ulterior motive when we go to see them." That man went on to remark on the culpability of the caciques and leaders who failed to apprehend and punish such delinquents and thereby hinder their raids. He felt that, in not doing so, they were giving tacit permission to them for such conduct. He observed also that during the 1740 English war against St. Augustine only one troop of Uchise showed up outside the city and that before long "they had withdrawn to their province with some horses they had taken from other Indians who were on the English side. They had also killed some Englishmen before withdrawing after the Uchise troops' captain had spoken with a Spaniard captured by the English."

The same Guale interpreter remarked that, because the same Uchise caciques allowed the scalps taken to be danced in the council house, it could be concluded that, even though the caciques "do not order them to harm the Spaniards," their not having impeded them indicated that their friendship is insincere. This Guale witness concluded that, if such caciques chose to block such actions by the lawless ones, they could do so. He cited as evidence of this, the Uchises' recent war with the Chalaques (Cherokees), noting that since they had made peace with them, they were no longer offending one another. From this he concluded that the Uchise chiefs could do the same vis-à-vis the Spaniards if they chose to do so.

The Guale interpreter went on to note that he had heard one of the Uchise leaders named Chacate speaking to the effect that they should not ally themselves with any of the European powers. But, rather, that they should live in peace with Spaniard, Englishman, and French, considering that they were surrounded by all three. For, if they drew close to one and declared war on the other two, they would then be at the mercy of their ally who might do with them what he would with the assurances that they would not find favor with either of the others whom they had offended in this manner. Chacate concluded that, by themselves, they were not capable of defending themselves because of their lack of guns, balls, and powder. And that, between the English and the Spaniards, the Englishmen were far better at providing the goods that they needed and on following through on the establishment of the settlements that they promised than were the Spaniards. The interpreter went on to observe that since 1739 Chacate had died along with many other leaders among those partial to the Spaniards. Out of that group, Quilate alone was left and the other present Uchise leaders "have taken no steps in this direction because the present Spanish governor has had little to do with them."

As a result of these developments, the governor remarked that "from now on the Spaniards would be able to go to their villages with pirogues by way of the river named Chacatos." This would seem to be the origin of the name Chattahoochee presently used for that river because Spaniards, at times, rendered the name Chacatos as Chattos.

Despite Governor Montiano's (1748:10–11) continued suspicions about the fickleness of the Uchises, and their realization that he saw through their behavior, he was impressed by an offer they had made. In the course of the negotiation, some among the Uchise told the interpreter confidentially that they had something special to tell the governor. But others involved in that parley gave them no opportunity to do so before they left. However, those pledged to do so returned to St. Augustine from the trail six days after their departure. The returnees declared that their leading men genuinely wanted to be at peace with the Spaniards and that, to secure their steadfastness, the governor should deputize them to go on a mission to the Chickasaws to enlist their support in this issue. They described the Chickasaw as "a people of regular behavior, obedient to their caciques and leading men, warlike and valiant, not so fickle like the Uchises" and that the Uchise "had a certain respect for and fear of the Chickasaw." They pledged that if they were able to win the Chickasaw over to friendship with the Spaniards, that would rule out any Uchise retreat from their pledge to the Spaniards, inasmuch as the Uchises would then not venture to "move against us in order not to displease the Chickasaws who knew how to maintain their word: and would take umbrage at such dishonesty once they had become involved. To that end they volunteered to serve the Spaniards so that they might become acquainted with the Spaniards "and put aside the horror that they had of us and come to be our friends." The governor accepted their offer and dispatched them, remarking that he was waiting to hear the results—this despite his having heard that the Chickasaws had been largely exterminated in a war with the French not many years earlier (Montiano 1748).

Governor Montiano (1748) went on to warn the Crown that keeping these Indians would be expensive, costing much more than it had up to now. In addition to feeding them "while it suits their fancy to stay here," he felt it would be necessary to regale the leaders with "a coat decorated with silver and gold, a shirt, hat, shoes, a yard and a third of cloth for pants and laced boots, a silk cloth for the throat, a musket, ammunition in abundance, vermilion, cauldrons, and many other little things." He recommended almost the same for the individual Indians except for the coat. Clothing and gold beads would be needed for the women "because the English and the French have accustomed them to all of this and much more."

He commented nonetheless that the Indians were anxious for a good Spanish store in Apalachee. Because they did much of their hunting in the environs of the Alachua (Gainesville) area, they passed the St. Marks fort coming and going on those expeditions. Thus, it would be advantageous for them to be able to unload their skins halfway on the trail so that they would not have to carry them all the way back to their villages on the Chattahoochee River. And some, after unloading them at the store in Apalachee, might well return to the hunt without ever going home.

This in turn would lessen their inclination toward ties with the English. They [the Yamasee] still remembered those carried off from Tamasle a generation earlier when the warriors of that settlement, two leagues distant from the St. Marks fort, exhausted their ammunition and had to surrender except for the 80 warriors who were able to escape to the St. Marks fort.

The Guale, Francisco Luis de Caracas, believed if the Spaniards kept a well stocked store in St. Marks or at the San Luis site, most of the Yamasee "would come to the Spaniards except for a few who have an interest in dealing with the English." He thought that "a major part of the Uchise" would then follow the Yamasees' example. His reason for that conclusion was that, inasmuch as the Yamasee were very good warriors, they were the captains of the major part of the Uchise bands. Once the Yamasee allied with the Spaniards, many of the Uchise would follow suit. He based that judgment on the experience and judgment of an Apalachee warrior who had served with an Uchise band but who was then living in the Guale witness's home village. While coming from New Georgia in an Uchise troop, the Apalachee had deserted from it when the troop reached St. Augustine. Francisco Luis believed that the Uchises allied to the English "went about the business of killing and capturing Spaniards very lazily and lukewarmly, doing just enough to satisfy the English who rewarded them for scalps presented." He stated that the Uchise even occasionally brought in an English scalp, passing it off as Spanish to collect the reward. This witness also suggested that, in addition to maintaining the store well stocked, there should be provision made for gifts to the caciques and leaders of the 14 Uchise villages.

When the Spaniards installed a store at St. Marks, they failed to heed those soldiers' advice. When the Indians came to see the long-sought-for store installed by the Havana Company, the Indians objected that it was nothing more than a tavern and not what they had requested from the officials from Havana.

They found it lacking in some of the most important items such as clothing and arms and the trifles that they prized. And the articles that they saw, which they were interested in, did not match in quality their English counterparts that they were accustomed to. Nonetheless, those first supplies did sell well, consisting mainly of firewater (*aguardiente*), tobacco, molasses, and sugar. And although the profits were good, the merchants' loss of the return cargo of skins in a shipwreck very much dampened the interest of those merchants. As a result, they did not exert themselves much to supply goods desired by the Indians other than aguardiente and even that was lacking at times. The Havana Company's officials complained to the governor and the king that the Indians' skins were not as marketable in Cuba or elsewhere in Spanish territory as they were in the North (Montiano 1746). The governor noted as well that, except for their leader Quilate, the Uchises were becoming more hostile and no longer visiting St. Augustine. But, that hostility does not seem to have been manifest at St. Marks except on the part of the Eufalans. There that seems to have been a result, in part, of discontent among the Uchise leaders over the fort that the English desired to place in Caueta.

A later witness identified those 14 villages as follows:

1. Zalacaxliches
2. Yufala
3. Savacola
4. The other Savacola
5. Ocone
6. Apalachicola
7. Ajachito
8. Chaquitpe
9. Chiaja
10. Ocomulgee
11. Osuchi
12. Yuches
13. Casista
14. Caveta

Another witness, Clemente Ytorio, a pilot for the coast, had been stationed at St. Marks for four years. His wife apparently was Uchise. As she, the children, and a sister-in-law were living with him, he was required to build a house and live separately from the troops. Since his wife and sister-in-law spoke Uchise, all the Indians stopped at this house. Ytorio described the 14 Uchise villages as "situated on the bank of a river southwest northwest in the order in which they are listed above." He observed that only Ocone, Chiaja, and Ocomulgee had enmity toward the Spaniards. The rest, in his opinion, maintained a friendly disposition and contacts. He mentioned that Chiaja's cacique also governed Ocomulgee. On one occasion when Chiaja's cacique was at his house, Ytorio took him to task for permitting his people to wage hostilities against the Spaniards. The chief replied that he was unable to remedy the situation as those who engaged in such roguery were unruly types (*zimarrones*) and social misfits, similar to those to be found among the whites as well. Their captains were unable to control them and that he faced the same problem because he was only one person and the disobedient ones were many. He observed that the Indians were disappointed above all with the Spaniards over their lack of firewater in the store. This witness identified Chiquile as "devoted to the Spaniards."

Another witness indicated that at St. Marks there was considerable fraternization between the visiting Indians and the soldiers. The Indians supplied the soldiers with fresh meat while the soldiers reciprocated with fresh bread, as both groups often dined together. This witness, another former commandant, asserted that the Uchise desired to see Spanish settlers in Apalachee once again. He noted that a few days before he left St. Marks three canoes of Indians had arrived, saying they intended to plant that year at the Tamasle site two leagues from the fort. His dealings with them led him to believe that they would be friendly neighbors (Montiano 1745).

That move by the Uchise may well have been influenced by the outbreak of a war between the Uchise and the Cherokees (*Chaleques*) and Talapuses. The Uchise may well have felt vulnerable. On May 2, a Yamasee named Pancho brought word that a horseman sent to arrange support was refused help by the then small Yamasee community. They were ready to come down to St. Marks with their families if the Uchise pressed the matter.

Compared to the later English accounts by people such as Benjamin Hawkins, the Spanish accounts do not seem to have much information on vessels and weapons and utensils that the Indians used in their daily lives and peregrinations. A good example is Hawkins' (1982:89) mention of the construction quality of many native canoes. The ones he described had been made of rotten red oaks that retained the bark. As he observed, the making of such canoes did not require much labor beyond the chipping out of the rotten interior of the log. Such canoes were easily concealed, as once the canoe was turned over it had the appearance of an old log.

Of particular value are Hawkins' comments on various Indian foods and the manner in which they were produced. Although they date from the late nineteenth century, they relate specifically to the Creeks and describe practices that probably had not yet changed substantially from what they had been a century earlier. This is true particularly of his description of the products they extracted from acorns and hickory nuts.

He noted that the women gathered red oak acorns for the purpose of making oil for cooking. They dried them on reed mats before hulling them and beating them into a fine powder. On mixing the powder with water, they let it stand overnight. The oil that rose to the top was then skimmed off with a feather and used as food. A bushel of acorns yielded about a pint of oil. Other sources reveal that the powder residue could be used as flour.

Hickory nuts were more highly valued as they were the source of a particularly tasteful oil and, additionally, of a milk-like liquid and a useful flour. But the oil turned rancid quickly.

China briar or zamia was also the source of flour that was baked into cakes or made into a honey-sweetened gruel. Bread made out of that flour, known as coonte, was an important food among hunters in the woods.

Hawkins also described techniques the Indians used to gather large numbers of fish that were stunned or poisoned by chemicals from buckeye roots and from ground horse chestnuts "steeped awhile in a trough" and then scattered "over the surface of a middle-sized pond" and then stirred into the water with poles.

Governor Montiano's successor, Melchor de Navarette (1749 to 1751) followed Montiano's policy in putting considerable emphasis on attracting Indians to Christianity through the gifts he bestowed on them. Among his first targets were four Uchise and a Cherokee who were living with a village of Christian Indians. In the month he wrote the letter, 24 more Uchise men, women, and children arrived from Caueta Province. He pressed them to leave two or three of their young sons under his power so that he might provide for their support with decency and so that he might have them educated in preparation for being baptized and later adopt them, giving them his name. After considering it, they replied that they would not dare to enter such an agreement because of the respect that they owed their chiefs. Three of the twenty-four were *tascayas* (warriors with a scalp to their credit), which gave them the status of leading men and one was a *Genifa*, the equivalent of a Spanish captain. But they promised to present the matter to their cacique for his resolution, reminding the governor that the sons of caciques were usually the first in line in the Indians' scheme of things to receive such honors and advantages.

Origins and Emergence of the Names "Seminole" and "Creek"

These people allied to the English were then on their way to becoming the forebears of the people we know as the Seminole in its more inclusive sense, meaning Mikasuki as well as Muscogee-speakers. But as Brent R. Weisman (1999:5) remarked: "Documentary accounts before the third quarter of the 1700s do not call the Indians then living in Florida 'Seminole.'" He noted that "the blanket term Seminole" was not widely used even in the 1800s, observing, "Chroniclers were more likely to write about bands of Tallasses, Mikasukis, Tohopekaligas, or simply the 'enemy.'" In the Spanish documentation from the 1730s and 1740s that I have seen, authorities continued to refer to the Lower and Upper Creek forebears of the Seminoles as Apalachicolas, Cauetas, Yamasees, and Talapuses and to the non-Muskogean peoples among them by using names such as Yuchi.

But Weisman (1999:14) concluded: "As the Lower Creeks in Florida moved farther away from the Creek sphere of influence they began to take on an identity as 'Seminoles.'" Their settlements on the margin of the Creek heartland reflected the sense of the Spaniards' term *cimarron* that was the origin of the name Seminole. Initially the term designated a wild or unruly domesticated animal such as a horse or a steer. But it was applied later to runaway slaves. Weisman (1999:5–6) concluded that "If the birth of the Seminole can be traced to a specific time and place, that date is November 18, 1765, the place, Picolata, on the banks of the St. Johns River." But he then cautioned that extensive research in the 1950s "only weakly supported the conclusion that by the early 1800s the Florida Indians were operating independently of their Creek relatives and had some degree of political autonomy under the rubric Seminole."

The first documented use of the British form of the term "Seminole" occurred "in 1771 during the British era" of Florida's history. J. Leitch Wright (1986:104) observed: "The term, an anglicized corruption of the Spanish *cimarron* was first applied to Musgogulges who had migrated to Alachua, and later to those who settled in Apalachee." That early usage, however, appears to have been exceptional. Most recently Brent Weisman (1999:5) remarked: "Documentary accounts before the third quarter of the 1700s do not call the Indians then living in Florida 'Seminole.' . . . Even in the 1800s . . . chroniclers were most likely to write about bands of Tallasses, Mikasukis . . ., Tohepekaligas, or simply the 'enemy' rather than the blanket term *Seminole*." But the transformation of the Spaniards *cimarron* into Seminole does indeed indicate that the term was being used by Indians. The change was made necessary by the Indians' languages' lack of the letter "r." For that reason the "rr" of the Spaniards' *cimarron* became an "l" in the Native Americans' tongue.

Similarly, as Wright (1986:2) observed: "The term Creek is of English origin, and Englishmen in the southern colonies began to use it in the late seventeenth and early eighteenth centuries." But he offers no documentation to support that statement. When the term *cimarron* appears in Spanish documentation for the late seventeenth and full first half of the eighteenth century, it is not used as a tribal name. It indicates rather their status of breakaways or wild stallions who have effectively thrown off their allegiance to the chiefs of the mother towns of which their forebears had once been a part. And Wright, in his explanation of the names' emergence, cites only "Minutes taken from General McGillivray respecting the Creeks, Aug. 1790" and the modern article by Verner Crane on the "Origin of the Name of Creek Indians." Wright, following McGillivray's suggestion on that occasion, attributes the name to a reflection of the geographical reality that the southeastern Indians were living "in a fertile region watered by many rivers and streams." But Crane (1956:36) offers a seemingly more plausible explanation for the origin of the name "Creeks" being attached to the Lower Creeks. According to Crane the name may have begun to be used for them in the 1690s when the Lower Creeks migrated eastward from the Chattahoochee, and the fort they had established on that river, to escape Spanish interdiction of their trade with the English. Most of the new towns were placed along the upper Ocmulgee known to the English as Ochese Creek. Not long thereafter they began to be referred to as "Ochese Creeks," which was soon abbreviated to "Creeks."

Notes

Chapter 3. The Chisca and Chichimeco-Westo

1. There are variant versions of this document. In preparing my initial typescript draft of this chapter, I used a Connor Collection transcription of the document that I now suspect contains errors of transcription. Rendered literally, the Connor manuscript runs as follows: "In the midst of others [causes] that I do not allude to [is] the fear and terror which the English and the heathen instilled in them with the burning alive of the Indians; roasting others and eating them. The Chichimeca and Chisca and Enbateguela Indians caught the blood that ran from the wounds." On seeing my translation, Ronald Wayne Childers informed me that, in the original Spanish text in AGI, SD 858, the text runs as follows: "the fear and terror that the English and heathens instilled in them with burning the Indians alive, roasting others, and with the Chichumecos and Chisca Indians eating them and catching in small wooden bowls (*basequelas*) the blood that ran." Childers' rendition makes more sense. The modern form of *basequelas* is *batehuelas*, which means "small wooden tray or bowl." In no other document that I am aware of is there any reference to "Enbateguela Indians." It should be noted, however, that the Connor transcript may be the more reliable of the two versions in rendering the word as "*bateguela*," inasmuch as it is closer to the modern form.

Chapter 4. The Pansacola

1. For lack of access to Sigüenza's Spanish text, I have chosen Barcia's version of this passage because I suspect that Leonard (1939:160–161) translated it poorly. I am particularly suspicious of Leonard's reference to "stewed entrails" where I have "lungs." Even though Indians of the far north of Canada consumed the entrails of ruminants as recently as the 1930s for the vitamins provided by the digested or semi-digested greenery they contained, that practice would not seem to have been necessary in Florida. Barcia's text struck me as being possibly a literal copy of Sigüenza's original. Anthony Kerrigan rendered Barcia's "Peces como Chucos" as "Some fish resembling herring" (González de Barcia Carballido y Zúñiga 1951:336). Leonard (1939:161) rendered the baskets passage as "In several baskets made of *otate* (a hard solid reed)."

Chapter 7. The Yamasee War and Its Aftermath

1. Hahn (2000:239) identified him further as "the mico and governor of the town of Ocuti of Tama."

2. Hahn (2000:239) identified one of the Nicunapas as that town's chief, Istopoyole, and the other as "Yfallaquisca or 'Brave Dog,' the war captain of Satiquicha."

3. Hahn (2000:246) dated Brim's visit as occurring on September 26, 1715, citing Córcoles y Martínez to Charles Craven (the Carolina governor) from the AGI, SD 853 from the John Worth Collection. Mark Boyd (1949:8–9) gave a misleading view of Spanish contact with and awareness of Brim's importance. Boyd described Diego Peña's 1716 expedition as having revealed the dominant position of Caueta's chief among the Indians living along the Chattahoochee River.

Bibliography

Aguado, Salvador Joseph de
1710 [Statement, January 10, 1710.] In Córcoles y Martínez 1710.
Alvarez de Toledo, Fray Lucar
1705 [*Auto* of Inquiry, June 9, 1705.] AGI, SD 863.
Anderson, David G.
1994 *The Savannah River Chiefdoms: Political Change in the Late Prehistoric Southeast*. Tuscaloosa: University of Alabama Press.
Angulo, Favian de
1690a [Letter to Diego de Quiroga y Losada, Abalachecolo, April 14, 1690.] AGI, SD 227, SC.
1690b [Letter to Diego de Quiroga y Losada, Abalachecolo, May 24, 1690.] AGI, SD 227, SC. Enclosure in Quiroga y Losada to the King, June 8, 1690.
1690c [Letter to Diego de Quiroga y Losada, Abalachecolo, June 28, 1690.] AGI, SD 228, SC. Enclosure in Quiroga y Losada to King, August 31, 1690.
Arana, Luis Rafael, and Albert Manucy
1977 *The Building of the Castillo de San Marcos*. Eastern National Park and Monument Association for Castillo de San Marcos National Monument.
Aranguíz y Cotes, Alonso de
1662 [Letter to the King, September 8, 1662.] AGI, SD 225, WLC, reel 3 of the copy of the Strozier Library, Florida State University.
Arnade, Charles W.
1996 "Raids, Sieges, and International Wars." In Gannon 1996:100–116.
Ayala y Escobar, Juan de
1701 *Auto*, San Luis de Talimali, February 22, 1701. AGI, SD 858. In Boyd, Smith, and Griffin 1951:33–34.
1717a [Letter to King, April 18, 1717.] AGI, SD 843, SC.
1717b [Letter to King, April 21, 1717.] AGI, SD 843.
1717c [*Autos* concerning the coming of the son of the emperor of Caueta, July 10, 1717.] AGI, SD 843, SC.
1717d *Auto*, October 18, 1717. AGI, SD 843. In Benavides 1718a.
1717e Orders to Diego Peña, July 20, 1717. Abstract in Boyd 1952:111–113.
1717f [Letter to King, November 19, 1717.] AGI, SD 848, SC, reel 37.
1718a [Letter to the King, January 28, 1718.] AGI, SD 843, SC.
1718b [Letter to the King, February 28, 1718.] AGI, SD 843, SC.
Baltasar, Augustín Domingo, Bernave Matheo Ventura, and Tunaque Alonso
1686 [Petition to the governor of Florida, September 1686.] AGI, SD 839, JTCC, reel 5, or SD 227, JTLC, vol. 5.
Barreda, Fray Jazinto de
1692 [Petition to Diego de Quiroga y Losada, April 1692.] AGI, SD 228, doc. no 42,

JTLC, vol. 4 of "Misiones Guale." Enclosure in Quiroga y Losada, April 30, 1692.

Barrera, Fray Rodrigo de la
- 1675 Letter to Andrés Pérez, Santa Cruz (de Sauocola). AGI, Escribanía de Cámara, Leg. 156, ZZ Coyer, fol. 119–142, SC. Translation by Hann in *Florida Archaeology* (1993) 7:40.
- 1681 [Letter to Juan Márquez Cabrera, San Antonio de YbaCuqua, December 8, 1681.] AGI, SD 226, JTCC, reel 3.
- 1693 Journal of Friar Rodrigo de la Barreda, Great Bay of Pensacola, August 3, 1693. Translation by Irving Leonard 1939:265–282.

Barrientos, Bartolomé
- 1965 *Pedro Menéndez de Avilés, Founder of Florida*. Translation by Anthony Kerrigan. Gainesville: University of Florida Press.

Bartram, William
- 1955 *Travels of William Bartram*. Edited by Mark Van Doren New York: Dover Publications.

Benavides, Antonio de
- 1718a [Letter to the King, August 12, 1718.] AGI, SD 843, SC. (unsigned)
- 1718b [Letter to the King, September 28, 1718.] AGI, SD 843, SC and in Boyd 1952, 136–139
- 1718c [Letter to the King, September 30, 1718.] AGI, SD 843, SC.
- 1722a [Letter to the Governor of Carolina, February 11, 1722.] Enclosure in Benavides 1722b.
- 1722b [Letter to the King, April 21, 1722.] AGI, 58-1-9 32, SC, reel 38.
- 1723a [Letter to the King, March 8, 1723.] AGI, SD 865.
- 1723b [Letter to the King, October 5, 1723.] AGI, SD 842, JTCC, reel 5.
- 1723c [Letter to the King, October 15, 1723.] AGI, SD 842, JTCC, reel 5.
- 1724 [Letter to the King, February 6, 1724.] AGI, SD 842, JTCC, reel 5.
- 1725 [Letter to the King, November 20, 1725.] AGI, SD 842, JTCC, reel 5.
- 1726 Visitation of Settlements near St. Augustine and San Marcos de Apalachee, December 1–11, 1726. In Hann 1991:363–368.
- 1727 [Letter to the King, September 23, 1727.] AGI, SD 844, SC.

Bienville, Jean Baptiste Le Moyne de
- 1704 Letter to Phelypeaux de Maurepas de Pontchartrain, September 6, 1704. In Rowland and Sanders, 1932, 3:27.
- 1726 Memoir in Louisiana. In Rowland and Sanders, 1932, 3:499–539.

Bishop of Cuba
- 1728 [Letter to the King, Havana, September 1, 1728.] AGI, SD 865, SC.

Blake, Joseph
- 1694 [Letter to Laureano de Torres y Ayala, Carolina January 24, 1694 [sic—probably should be 1695].] Enclosure in Torres y Ayala* to the King, March 11, 1695.

Bolton, Herbert E.
- 1925a *Arredondo's Historical Proof of Spain's Title to Georgia*. Berkeley: University of California Press.

Bolton, Herbert E., editor
1925b "Spanish Resistance to the Carolina Traders in Western Georgia (1680–1704)," *Georgia Historical Quarterly* 9:115–130.

Bowne, Eric E.
2005 *The Westo Indians: Slave Traders of the Early Colonial South*. Tuscaloosa: University of Alabama Press.

Boyd, Mark F.
1937 "The Expedition of Marcos Delgado to the Upper Creek Country in 1686." Translation and notes by Boyd, *Florida Historical Quarterly* 16:2–32.
1949 "Diego Peña's Expedition to Apalachee and Apalachecolo in 1716." *Florida Historical Quarterly* 28:1–27.
1952 "Documents Describing the Second and Third Expeditions of Lieutenant Diego Peña to Apalachee and Apalachecolo in 1717 and 1718." *Florida Historical Quarterly* 31:109–140.
1953 "Documents: Further Considerations of the Apalachee Missions." *The Americas* 9:459–479.
1958 "Historic Sites in and around the Jim Woodruff Reservoir Area, Florida-Georgia." In Frank H.H. Roberts Jr., editor, *River Basin Surveys Papers. Inter-Agency Archeological Salvage Program*, Numbers 9–14. Smithsonian Institution, Bureau of American Ethnology, Bulletin 169. Paper no. 13, pp. 199–314. Washington, D.C.: United States Government Printing Office.

Boyd, Mark F., Hale G. Smith, and John W. Griffin
1951 *Here They Once Stood: The Tragic End of the Apalachee Missions*. Gainesville: University of Florida Press.

Braley, Chad O.
1998 Yuchi Town (1Ru63) Revisited: Analysis of the 1958–1962 Excavations. Report submitted to Environmental Management Division, Directorate of Public Works, U. S. Army Infantry Center, Fort Benning, Ga., by Southeastern Archeological Services, Athens, Ga.

Bullones, Fray Joseph de
1728 Letter to the King. Report on the native villages, October 5, 1728. AGI, SD 865, SC. Translation in Hann 1991a:371–380.

Bushnell, David I., Jr.
1908 "The Account of Lamhatty." *American Anthropologist* n.s., 10:568–574.

Callendar, Charles
1994 "Central Algonkian Moieties." In Raymond J. DeMallie and Alfonso Ortiz, eds., *North American Indian Anthropology: Essays on Society and Culture*. Norman: University of Oklahoma Press.

Carlos, Cacique of San Carlos
1675 Statement, Place of San Carlos, October 5, 1675. AGI, Contratacion 3309. Translation by Hann in *Florida Archaeology* (1993) 7:49–50.

Castilla, Juan de, Scribe
1740 [Letter to Joseph de la Quintana, January 6, 1740.] AGI, SD 265, SC.

Castro, Pedro de (soldier)
1740 [Statement before Governor Manuel de Montiano.] Enclosure in Montiano 1740.

Caueta, Chief of
1682 [Statement, January 2, 1682.] AGI, SD 226, JTCC, reel 3. In Márquez Cabrera 1682b.

Chacato Indian, unidentified
1676 Testimony, November 3, 1676. AGI, Escribania de Camara, leg. 156A tomo ZZ, fol. 143–157, microfilm roll 27-I of the *Residencia* series of the P. K. Yonge Library. Translation by Hann in *Florida Archaeology* (1993) 7:62–63.

Charles II
1682 [Order to Juan Márques Cabrera. Madrid, August 31, 1682.] AGI, SD 834, SC.

Childers, Ronald Wayne
1998 Personal communication by letter, St. Joe, December 3, 1998.

Clayton, Lawrence A., Vernon James Knight Jr., and Edward C. Moore, editors
1993 *The De Soto Chronicles: The Expedition of Hernanddo de Soto to North America in 1539–1543*. 2 vols. Tuscaloosa: University of Alabama Press.

Coker, William S.
1996 "Pensacola, 1686–1763." In Michael Gannon, editor, *The New History of Florida*, 117–133. Gainesville: University Press of Florida.

Córcoles y Martínez, Francisco de
1706a [Letter to the King, May 3, 1706.] AGI, SD 840, JTCC, reel 5.
1706b [Letter to the King, May 31, 1706.] AGI, SD 840, JTCC, reel 5.
1706c [Letter to the King, November 30, 1706.] Enclosure in "Explanation of what is evident in the S^{ria} pertaining to the first formation of the Cavalry Company of the Presidio of St. Augustine of Florida." Enclosure in Joseph Primo de Rivera 1717a.
1707a [Letter to the King, November 12, 1707.] AGI, SD 840, JTCC, reel 5.
1707b [Letter to the Viceroy, Duque de Albuquerque, November 12, 1707.] AGI, SD 840, JTCC, reel 5.
1709 [Letter to the King, July 20, 1709.] AGI, SD 843, SC.
1710 [Letter to the King, January 22, 1710.] Translation by R. Wayne Childers. AGI, SD 841, NCC, reel 2-15.
1711 [Letter to the King, April 9, 1711.] AGI, SD 843.
1715a [Letter to the King, Florida, July 5, 1715.] AGI, SD 743, SC.
1715b [Letter to the King, Florida, November 28, 1715.] AGI, SD 843, SC.
1716 [Letter to the King, January 25, 1716.] AGI, SD.

Córcoles y Martínez, Francisco de, Franciso Menéndez Marques, and Salvador Garcia de Villegas
1715 Letter to the King, December 3, 1715. AGI source not indicated. John Worth Collection.

Cordell, Ann S.
2001 *Continuity and Change in Apalachee Pottery Manufacture: A Technological Comparison of Apalachee-Style and Colono Ware Pottery from French Colonial Old*

Mobile and Mission San Luis de Talimali. Mobile: University of South Alabama Center for Archaeological Studies.

Corkran, David H.
1967 The Creek Frontier, 1540–1783. Norman: University of Oklahoma Press.

Council of the Indies
1691 Junta, Madrid, September 6, 1691. In Quiroga y Losada 1690a.
1719 [Madrid, January 18, 1719.] AGI, SD 837, SC.

Crane, Verner W.
1918 "The Origin of the Name of the Creek Indians." Journal of American History 5:339–342.
1956 The Southern Frontier 1670–1732. Ann Arbor: University of Michigan Press.
1981 The Southern Frontier 1670–1732. New York: W. W. Norton.

Craven Palatine
1690 [Letter to Governor of Carolina, London, October 18, 1690.] B.P.R.O. Col Entry Book, vol. 22, p. 168, reel 1, vol. 11, pp. 292–293. South Carolina Archives.

Crawford, James M., editor
1975 Studies in Southeastern Indian Languages. Athens: University of Georgia Press.

Cumming, William P.
1998 The Southeast in Early Maps, 3rd ed., revised and enlarged by Louis de Vorsey Jr. Chapel Hill: University of North Carolina Press.

Cutca Martín
1676 Statement, November 16, 1676. AGI, Escribanía de Cámara, leg. 156A, tomo ZZ, fol. 143–157, microfilm roll 27-I of the P. K. Yonge Library, Translation by Hann in Florida Archaeology (1993) 7:66–68.

Davis, Dave D., editor
1984 Perspectives on Gulf Coast Prehistory. Gainesville: University Presses of Florida.

DePratter, Chester B.
1994 "The Chiefdom of Cofitachequi." In Hudson and Tesser, eds., The Forgotten Centuries: Indians and Europeans in the American South, 1521–1704, 197–226. Athens: University of Georgia Press.

Descovedo, Andrés, Pedro Florencia, Joseph de Salinas, and Diego Salvador
1675 [Statement, May 23, 1675.] Enclosure in Hita Salazar 1675c.

Díaz Vara Calderón, Bishop Gabriel
1675 [Letter to the Queen, Havana, 1675.] AGI, SD 151. [Microfilm copy furnished to W. H. Marquardt by Victoria Stapells-Johnson.]

Diocsali [Diocsale], Juan Fernández de (former chief of San Carlos de los Chacatos)
1675 Confession, San Luis de Talimali, October 20, 1675. Translation by Hann in Florida Archaeology (1993) 7:54.

Diosale, Juan Fernández de
1676 Confession, November 3, 1676. AGI, Escribanía de Cámara, Leg. 156A, Tomo ZZ, fol. 143–157. Microfilm roll 27I of the Residencia series of the P. K. Yonge Library of Florida History. Translation by Hann in Florida Archaeology (1993) 7:64–65.

Dunn, William Edward
1971   *Spanish and French Rivalry in the Gulf Region of the United States 1678-1702: The Beginning of Texas and Pensacola.* Freeport, N.Y.: Originally published by the University of Texas in 1917 as No. 1705 of the University of Texas *Bulletin*.

Ebanjelista, Juan (interpreter for the Chacato language)
1675   Testimony, San Carlos de los Chacatos, October 3, 1675. AGI, Escribanía de Cámara, leg. 156, Coyer ZZ, fol. 119-142, SC. Translation by Hann in *Florida Archaeology* (1993) 7:44-46.

Ebelino de Compostela, Bishop Diego de
1689   [Letter to the King, Havana, September 28, 1689.] AGI, SD 151, SC.

Elena, wife of Cacique Carlos
1675   Testimony, San Carlos de los Chacatos, October 5, 1675. AGI, Escribanía de Cámara, leg. 156, Coyer ZZ, fol. 119-142, SC. Translation by Hann in *Florida Archaeology* (1993) 7:50-51.

Escobedo, Joseph de
1717   [Statement, October 18, 1717.] Enclosure in Benavides 1718a.

Eslaque, Francisco
1691   [Statement, March 7, 1691.] Enclosure in Quiroga y Losada 1691a.

Ewen, Charles R. and John H. Hann
1998   *Hernando de Soto among the Apalachee: the Archaeology of the First Winter Encampment.* Gainesville: University Press of Florida.

Fairbanks, Charles H.
1957   "Ethnohistorical Report of the Florida Indians before the Indian Claims Commission." Dockets No. 73 and 151. Florida State University Library.

Fernández de Ecija, Francisco
1609   Report of His 1609 Voyage to the Bay of Jacan, June 19th-September 24th 1609. AGI, Patronato, WLC. Translation by Hann in *Florida Archaeology* (1986) 2:24-46.

Fernández de Florencia, Juan (rendered by him at times as Hz. [Hernández])
1674   Certification, April 28, 1674. AGI, SD 235. Translation by Hann in *Florida Archaeology* (1993) 7:74-75.
1675a   [Letter to Pablo de Hita Salazar, San Luis de Apalache, July 15, 1676, in Hita Salazar 1675b.] AGI, SD 839, SC.
1675b   [Report to the Governor of the villages of Apalachee and Timuqua, July 15, 1675.] AGI, SD 839, SC, reel 14.
1675c   *Autos* Concerning the Tumult of the Chacatos, 1675, San Carlos de los Chacatos and San Luis de Talimali. AGI, Escribanía de Cámara, leg. 156, Coyer ZZ, fol. 119-142, SC. Translation by Hann in *Florida Archaeology* (1993) 7:35-57.
1675d   Address, San Carlos de los Chacatos, October 3, 1675, in Fernández de Florencia, 1675c.
1675e   Address to all the people, San Carlos, October 12, 1675, in Fernández de Florencia, 1675c.
1675f   Confession of Juan Diozali, San Luis de Talimali, October 20, 1675 in Fernández de Florencia 1675c.

1675g Sentence of Diocsali, San Luis, October 25, 1675 in Fernández de Florencia 1675c.
1678 [Report which the principal leaders who went to make war on the Chiscas . . . made in the presence of Captain Juan Fernandez de Florencia (who took it down in the Apalachee language at San Luis de Talimali, 1677) (Translated by him into Spanish), San Luis de Talimali, August 30, 1678.] AGI, SD 226.

Florencia, Joachin de
1694–1695 Visitation of Apalachee 1694–1695. AGI, Escribania de Camara, leg. 157A, cuaderno I, fol. 44–205, SC. Translation by Hann in *Florida Archaeology* (1993) 7:147–219.

Ford, Lawrence Carroll
1939 *The Triangular Struggle for Spanish Pensacola 1689–1739*. Studies in Hispanic-American History, vol. II. Washington, D.C.: Catholic University of America Press.

Fretwell, Mark E.
1980 *This So Remote Frontier: The Chattahoochee Country of Alabama and Georgia*. Historic Chattahoochee Commission.

Fuente, Juan de la
1691 [Testimony, Havana, July 12, 1691.] AGI, SD 228, doc. no. 32, JTLC, vol. 4. Enclosure in Quiroga y Losada 1692a.

Fuentes y Herrera, Augustín Guillermo
1734 [Letter to the King, April 29, 1734.] AGI, 86-7-2/6, SC.

Galloway, Patricia
1995 *Choctaw Genesis 1500–1700*. Lincoln: University of Nebraska Press.

Gannon, Michael, editor
1996 *The New History of Florida*. Gainesville: University Press of Florida.

Gardiner, William R.
1966 "The Waddells Mill Pond Site," *The Florida Anthropologist* 19:43–61.
1969 "An Example of the Association of Archaeological Complexes with Tribal and Linguistic Grouping: The Fort Walton Complex of Northwest Florida." *The Florida Anthropologist* 22:1–11.

Gatschet, Albert S.
1969 *A Migration Legend of the Creek Indians*. New York: Krause Reprint.

González Barcía Carballido y Zúñiga, Andrés
1723 *Ensayo Cronológico para la Historia general de la Florida 1512–1722* por Gabriel de Cardenas Z. Cano (pseud.). Madrid: in the Oficina Real.
1951 *Barcia's Chronological History of the Continent of Florida*. Translation by Anthony Kerrigan. Gainesville: University of Florida Press.

Green, Michael D.
1979 *The Creeks: A Critical Bibliography*. Bloomington: Indiana University Press for the Newberry Library.
1998 "The Erie/Westo Connection: Possible Evidence of Long Distance Migration in the Eastern Woodlands during the 16th and 17th Centuries." Paper presented

at the Southeastern Archaeological Conference, Greenville, S.C., November 1998.

Gutiérrez de la Vera, Fray Francisco
1681   [Letter to Juan Márquez Cabrera, Sabacola, May 19, 1681.] WLC, reel 4.

Haas, Mary R.
1978   *Language, Culture, and History: Essays by Mary R. Haas.* Stanford: Stanford University Press.

Hahn, Steven C.
2000   "The Invention of the Creek Nation: A Political History of the Creek Indians in the South's Imperial Era, 1540–1763." Unpublished Ph.D. dissertation, Emory University.

Hally, David J.
1994   *Ocmulgee Archaeology, 1936–1986.* Athens: University of Georgia Press.
1996   "Platform Mound Construction and the Instability of Mississippian Chiefdoms." In John F. Scarry, editor, *Political Structure and Change in the Prehistoric Southeastern United States*, 92–127. Gainesville: University Press of Florida.

Hann, John H.
1986a Translation of Alonso de Leturiono's Memorial to the King of Spain. AGI, SD 853, SC and positive photostat in the library of the St. Augustine Historical Society. *Florida Archaeology* 2:165–225.
1986b "Translation of Governor Rebolledo's 1657 Visitation of Three Florida Provinces and Related Documents." *Florida Archaeology* 2:81–146.
1986c Translation of the Ecija Voyages of 1605 and 1609 and the González Derrotero of 1609. Woodbury Lowery Collection, reels 2–3. *Florida Archaeology* 2:1–80.
1988a *Apalachee: The Land Between the Rivers.* Gainesville: University Presses of Florida/Florida State Museum.
1988b "Florida's Terra Incognita: West Florida's Natives in the Sixteenth and Seventeenth Century." *Florida Anthropologist* 41:61–107.
1989   "St. Augustine's Fallout from the Yamasee War." *Florida Historical Quarterly* 68:180–200.
1991a "San Pedro y San Pablo de Patale: A Seventeenth-Century Spanish Mission in Leon County, Florida." In Jones, Hann, and Scarry, *Florida Archaeology* 5:149–170.
1991b *Missions to the Calusa.* Gainesville: University Press of Florida.
1993   "The Chacato Revolt Inquiry." *Florida Archaeology* 7:31–76.
1995a "The Indian Village on Apalachee Bay's Rio Chachave on the Solana Map of 1683." *Florida Anthropologist* 48:61–66.
1995b "Demise of the Pojoy and Bomto." *Florida Historical Quarterly* 74:184–200.
1996a "Late Seventeenth-Century Forebears of the Lower Creeks and Seminoles." *Southeastern Archaeology* 15:66–80.
1996b *A History of the Timucua Indians and Missions.* Gainesville: University Press of Florida.
1999   "Cloak and Dagger in Apalachicola Province in Early 1686." *Florida Historical Quarterly* 78:74–93.

Hann, John H, and Bonnie G. McEwan
1998   *The Apalachee Indians and Mission San Luis.* Gainesville: University Press of Florida.

Hawkins, Benjamin
1982   *A Sketch of the Creek Country, in the Years 1798 and 1799.* Spartanburg, S.C.: Reprint Company Publishers.

Hernandez de Florencia, Juan
1675   [Same person as Juan Fernandez de Florencia; see entries].

Herrera, Antonio Francisco de
1675   Letter to Andrés Pérez, deputy-governor of Apalachee, Santa Cruz [de Sauocola], July 31, 1675. AGI, Escribanía de Cámara, leg. 156ZZ, Coyer, fol. 119–142, SC. Translation by Hann in *Florida Archaeology* (1993) 7:40–41.

Higginbotham, Jay
1977   *Old Mobile, Fort Louis de Louisiane.* Mobile: Museum of the City of Mobile.
n.d.   Personal communication.

Hinachuba, Patricio
1699   Letter to Antonio Ponce de Leon, Ivitachuco, April 10, 1699. AGI, SD 863. Translation in Boyd, Smith, and Griffin 1951:26–27.

Hita Salazar, Pablo de
1675a   [Statement, May 1675.] AGI, SD 839, SC, reel 14.
1675b   [Letter to the King, June 11, 1675.] AGI, SD 839, JTCC, reel 6.
1675c   Instruction to Pedro de Florencia, August 15, 1675. Escribanía de Cámara, leg. 156A Tomo ZZ, fol. 142–157, microfilm roll 27I of the Residencia series of the P. K. Yonge Library of Florida History. Translation by Hann in *Florida Archaeology* (1993) 7:41–44.
1675d   Letter to the Queen, August 24, 1675. Escribanía de Cámara, leg. 156A Tomo ZZ, fol. 142–157, microfilm roll 27I of the Residencia series of the P. K. Yonge Library of Florida History. Translation by Hann in *Florida Archaeology* (1993) 7:42–43.
1675e   Letter to Fray Juan de Paiva, September 5, 1675. Escribanía de Cámara, leg. 156A Tomo ZZ, fol. 142–157, microfilm roll 27I of the Residencia series of the P. K. Yonge Library of Florida History. Translation by Hann in *Florida Archaeology* (1993) 7:51.
1676a   Naming and swearing in of an interpreter, October 31, 1676. Escribanía de Cámara, leg. 156A Tomo ZZ, fol. 142–157, microfilm roll 27I of the Residencia series of the P. K. Yonge Library of Florida History. Translation by Hann in *Florida Archaeology* (1993) 7:59–60.
1676b   Order, November 14, 1676. Escribanía de Cámara, leg. 156A Tomo ZZ, fol. 142–157, microfilm roll 27I of the Residencia series of the P. K. Yonge Library of Florida History. Translation by Hann in *Florida Archaeology* (1993) 7:65–66.
1677a   Sentences pronounced, January 3, 1677. Escribanía de Cámara, leg. 156A Tomo ZZ, fol. 142–157, microfilm roll 27I of the Residencia series of the P. K. Yonge Library of Florida History. Translation by Hann in *Florida Archaeology* (1993) 7:68.

1677b Notification of sentences, January 4, 1677. Escribanía de Cámara, leg. 156A Tomo ZZ, fol. 142–157, microfilm roll 27I of the Residencia series of the P. K. Yonge Library of Florida History. Translation by Hann in *Florida Archaeology* (1993) 7:68–69.

1677c *Auto* for Resentencing of Diocsale, July 5, 1677. Escribanía de Cámara, leg. 156A Tomo ZZ, fol. 142–157, microfilm roll 27I of the Residencia series of the P. K. Yonge Library of Florida History. Translation by Hann in *Florida Archaeology* (1993) 7:69–70.

1677d [Order, July 20, 1677.] In Quiroga y Losada 1688.

1679 [Letter to Fray Jazinto de Barreda,] October 31, 1679. AGI, SD 226, JTCC, reel 3.

1680a [Letter to Fray Jazinto de Barreda, January 26, 1680.] AGI, SD 226, JTCC, reel 3.

1680b [Letter to the King, March 8, 1680.] AGI, SD 226, reel 3.

1680c [Letter to the King, March 14, 1680.] AGI, SD 226, JTCC, reel 3.

1680d [Letter to the King, May 14, 1680.] AGI, SD 839.

Hita Salazar, Pablo de, Francisco de la Rocha, and Salvador de Zigarroa

1680 [Record of a Junta with treasury officials and others, January 29, 1680.] AGI, SD 226, JTCC, reel 3. Enclosure in Hita Salazar to King, March 14, 1680.

Hoffman, Paul E.

1990 *A New Andalucia and a Way to the Orient: The American Southeast during the Sixteenth Century.* Baton Rouge: Louisiana State University Press.

Horruytiner, Luis

1633 [Letter to the King, November 15, 1633.] AGI, SD 233, SC.

1640 [Relation of services, March 12, 1640 (Council).] AGI, IG 111, no. 239.

Hudson, Charles

1990 *The Juan Pardo Expeditions: Exploration of the Carolinas and Tennessee, 1566–1568.* Washington, D.C.: Smithsonian Institution Press.

1994 "The Social Context of the Chiefdom of Ichisi." In David J. Hally, editor, *Ocmulgee Archaeology 1936–1986*, 1994:92–126, 175–180.

1997 *Knights of Spain, Warriors of the Sun: Hernando de Soto and the South's Ancient Chiefdoms.* Athens: University of Georgia Press.

Hudson, Charles, and Carmen Chaves Tesser, editors

1994 *The Forgotten Centuries: Indians and Europeans in the American South 1521–1704.* Athens: University of Georgia Press.

Hudson, Charles, Marvin T. Smith, and Chester B. DePratter

1984 "The Hernando de Soto Expedition: from Apalachee to Chiaha." *Southeastern Archaeology* 3:65–77.

1990 Refinements in Hernando de Soto's Route through Georgia and South Carolina. In Thomas (1990) 2:107–119.

Jackson, Jason Baird

1996 "Everybody has a part; Even the Little Bitty ones: Notes on the Social Organization of Yuchi Ceremonialism." *Florida Anthropologist* 49:121–130.

1998   "Dressing for the Dance: Yuchi Ceremonial Clothing." *American Indian Art Magazine* 23:32–41.
2000   "Signaling the Creator: Indian Football as Ritual Performance among the Yuchi and Their Neighbors." *Southern Folklore* 57:33–64.

Jackson, Jason Baird, and Mary S. Linn
2000   "Calling in Members: Linguistic Form and Cultural Context in a Yuchi Ritual Speech Genre." *Anthropological Linguistics* 42:61–80.

Johnson, Robert
1719   Village List and Census, January 12, 1719. *South Carolina Archives* 7:237.

Jones, B. Calvin
1972   "Colonel James Moore and the Destruction of the Apalachee Missions in 1704." Florida Bureau of Historic Sites and Properties *Bulletin* 2:25–33.
1973   "Ceremonial Complex." Florida Department of State, *Archives and History News* 4.
1975   "Waddell's Mill Pond Site Artifacts Being Analyzed." *Archives and History News* 6, no. 5:3.
1987   Personal communication, June 1987.

Juachín (the fiscal)
1675   Statement, San Luis de Talimali, October 20, 1675. AGI, Contratación of Seville. Asientos de Armada. Contratación 3309. Translation by Hann in *Florida Archaeology* (1993) 7:55–56.

Junta de Guerra
1673   [Letter to Viceroy, Madrid, February 27, 1673.] AGI, SD 848, SC, reel 13.
1705   [Report to the King, Madrid, May 26, 1705.] AGI, 61-6-22 (Document from Pensacola).

Knight, Vernon J., Jr.
1984   Late Prehistoric Adaptation in the Mobile Bay Region. In Dave D. Davis, editor, *Perspectives on Gulf Coast History*, 198–215. Gainesville: University Presses of Florida.
1986   "The Institutional Organization of Mississippian Religion." *American Antiquity* 51:675–687.
1994a   "The Formation of the Creeks." In Charles Hudson and Carmen Chaves Tesser, eds., *The Forgotten Centuries: Indians and Europeans in the American South, 1521–1724*, 373–392. Athens: University of Georgia Press.
1994b   "Ocmulgee Fields Culture and the Historic Development of Creek Ceramics." In David J. Hally, editor, *Ocmulgee Archaeology 1936–1986*, 181–189. Athens: University of Georgia Press.

Knight, Vernon James, Jr., and Tim S. Mistovich
1984   *Walter F. George Lake: Archaeological Survey of Fee Owned Lands, Alabama and Georgia*. Office of Archaeological Research, Report of Investigations no. 42.
1986   "The Institutional Organization of Mississippian Religion." *American Antiquity* 51:675–687.

Lanning, John Tate
1935 *The Spanish Missions of Georgia*. Chapel Hill: University of North Carolina Press.

Leonard, Irving, translator
1939 *Spanish Approach to Pensacola, 1689-1693*. Albuquerque: Quivira Society, 1939; reprint by Arno Press, New York, 1967.

Leturiondo, Domingo de
1672 [Report to Don Francisco de Madrigal, Madrid, December 30, 1672.] AGI, SD 148, JTCC, reel 6.
1685a [*Auto*, Santa Cruz de Sauocola, October 17, 1685.] AGI, SD 639, JTLC, vol. 3, of "Misiones Guale."
1685b [Letter to Juan Márquez Cabrera, San Luis, November 5, 1685.] AGI, SD 639, JTLC, vol. 3 of "Misiones Guale."
1685c [Letter to Márquez Cabrera, San Pedro (de Potohiriba), November 28, 1685.] AGI, SD 639, JTLC, vol. 3 of "Misiones Guale."

Lopez de Toledo, Alvaro
1734 [Letter to the Governor, San Marcos de Abalache, June 29, 1734.] Enclosure in Moral Sanchez to Patino 1734.

Losada, Fray Domingo
1730 [Letter to the King, Madrid December 2, 1730.] AGI, SD 865, SC.

Luna, Fray Pedro de
1690 [Memorial of the Distribution and Assignment of the Religious, August 15, 1690.] AGI, SD 228, SC. An enclosure in Quiroga y Losada 1690c.

McCartney, Martha W.
1989 Cockacoeske, Queen of Pamunkey: Diplomat and Suzeraine. In Peter H. Wood, Gregory A. Waselkov, and M. Thomas Hatley, editors, *Powhatan's Mantle: Indians in the Colonial Southeast*, 173-195. Lincoln: University of Nebraska Press.

McEwan, Bonnie G., editor
2000 *Indians of the Greater Southeast: Historical Archaeology and Ethnohistory*. Gainesville: University Press of Florida.

Marques del Toro, Alonso
1738 [Letter to Governor of Florida, San Marcos de Apalache, April 18, 1738.] AGI, SD 2593, SC.

Márquez Cabrera, Juan
1680 [Letter to the King, December 8, 1680.] AGI, SD 226.
1681a [Letter to the King, June 14, 1681.] AGI, SD 839, JTCC, reel 5.
1681b [*Auto*, September 20, 1681.] AGI, SD 226. In Márquez Cabrera 1682b.
1682a [Letter to the King, January 25, 1682.] AGI, SD 226, JTCC.
1682b [Letter to the King, October 7, 1682.] AGI, SD 226, JTCC, reel 3.
1685 [Letter to Antonio Matheos, December 5, 1685.] AGI, SD 639, JTLC, vol. 3 of "Misiones Guale," doc. dd., no. 5.
1686a [Letter to the King, March 20, 1686.] AGI, SD 227, SC.
1686b [Letter to the King, November 8, 1686.] AGI, SD 227, JTLC, vol. 5 of "Misiones Guale," doc. no. 5.

1687 [*Auto* convoking an *Acuerdo* for exploration for the Bay of the Holy Spirit, February 18, 1687.] [The AGI source of this document was not indicated.]

Martín, Teresa
1600 Testimony, February 4, 1600. AGI, SD 224. In Serrano y Sanz, 1912.

Martínez, Francisco
1566 "The Martínez Relation." In Charles Hudson 1990:317–321.

Martínez, Francisco
1702 [Letter to Andrés de Arriola, Santa María de Galve, December 3, 1702.] AGI, Mexico 618, Coker Collection, reel 28, University of West Florida Library, translation furnished by R. Wayne Childers.

Martínez, Thomás (cattle hunter)
1740 [Statement before Governor Manuel de Montiano, March 10, 1740.] Enclosure in Montiano 1740.

Matheos, Antonio
1685a [Letter to Juan Márquez Cabrera, Casista, September 21, 1685.] AGI, SD 639, JTLC, vol. 3 of "Misiones Guale," doc. dd.
1685b [Letter to Márquez Cabrera, San Luis, October 4, 1685.] AGI, SD 639, JTLC, vol. 3 of "Misiones Guale," doc. dd.
1685c [*Auto*, Savocola, October 17, 1685.] AGI, SD 839, Mary Ross Papers, F 88, no. 27.
1685d [Letter to Márquez Cabrera, San Luis, November 27, 1685.] AGI, SD 639, JTLC, vol. 3 of "Misiones Guale," doc. dd.
1685e [Letter to Márquez Cabrera, Bacucua, December 26, 1685.] AGI, SD 639, JTLC, vol. 3 of "Misiones Guale," doc. dd.
1686a [Letter to Márquez Cabrera, Caueta, January 12, 1686.] AGI, SD 639, JTLC, vol. 3 of "Misiones Guale."
1686b [Letter to Márquez Cabrera, San Luis, February 8, 1686.] AGI, SD 639, JTLC, vol. 3 of "Misiones Guale."
1686c [Letter to Márquez Cabrera, San Luis, March 14, 1686.] AGI, SD 639, JTLC, vol. 3 of "Misiones Guale."
1686d [Letter to Márquez Cabrera, San Luis, May 19, 1686.] AGI, SD 639, JTLC, vol. 3 of "Misiones Guale."
1686e [Letter to Márquez Cabrera, San Luis, May 21, 1686.] AGI, SD 639, JTLC, vol. 3 of "Misiones Guale."
1686f [Letter to Márquez Cabrera, San Luis, August 21, 1686.] In Boyd 1937:12–13.
1686g [Letter to Márquez Cabrera, San Luis, September 29, 1686.] In Boyd 1937:16–17.

Melgar, Manuel de
1673 [Report to the Council of the Indies, Madrid, in Juan Moreno, Petition concerning the religious for Florida, February 27, 1673, Madrid.] AGI, SD 848, SC.

Méndez de Canzo, Gonzalo
1598 [Letter to the King, February 24, 1598.] AGI, SD 224.
1600 ["Report Concerning La Tama and Its Land and of the Settlement of the English." February 1600.] AGI, SD 224.

Menendez, Luisa
1600   Testimony, February 6, 1600. AGI, SD 224. In Serrano y Sanz, 1912.
Menéndez Marqués, Francisco, and Pedro Benedit Horruytiner
1646   [Letter to the King, April 11, 1646.] AGI, Escribanía de Cámara, leg. 155B, fol. 322. P. K. Yonge Library of Florida History, microfilm 27F, reel 5.
Menéndez Marqués, Thomás, and Joachín de Florencia
1697   "Certification by Officials of the Royal Hacienda of the Construction Costs of the [Block] house in Apalachee." July 3, 1697. In Boyd, Smith, and Griffin 1951:22-23.
Mercado, Fray Juan de
1685   [Letter to Antonio Matheos, Today Sunday (ca. November 1685), Santa Cruz (de Sauocola).] AGI, SD 639, JTLC, vol. 3 of Colección "Misiones Guale," doc. dd.
Miguel, Cacique of San Nicolás (of the Chacatos)
1676   Testimony, November 3, 1676. AGI, Escribanía de Cámara, Leg. 156A, Tomo ZZ, fol. 143–157. Microfilm roll 27I of the Residencia series of the P. K. Yonge Library of Florida History. Translation by Hann in *Florida Archaeology* (1993) 7:63–64.
Milán Tapia, Francisco
1693   Journal of, Pensacola Bay, August 1, 1693. In Leonard 1939:283-305.
Milanich, Jerald T.
1994   *Archaeology of Precolumbian Florida*. Gainesville: University Press of Florida.
1995   *Florida Indians and the Invasion from Europe*. Gainesville: University Press of Florida.
Milanich, Jerald T., and Charles Hudson
1993   *Hernando de Soto and the Indians of Florida*. Gainesville: University Press of Florida.
Milling, Chapman J.
1940   *Red Carolinians*. Chapel Hill: University of North Carolina Press.
Monilla Hernández, Antonio
1710   [Statement, January 10, 1710.] In Córcoles y Martínez 1710.
Montiano, Manuel de
1738   [Letter to the King, July 16, 1738.] AGI, SD 865.
1739   Letter to Governor Juan Francisco de Guemes y Horcasitas, March 2, 1739. M167 Montiano. Papers of the East Florida Collection, No. 124, pp. 149–150.
1740a [Letter to Don Joseph de la Quintana, March 10, 1740.] AGI, 86-6-5, JTCC, reel 7.
1740b [Letter to Don Joseph de la Quintana, March 10, 1740.] AGI, 86-6-5, JTCC, reel 7.
1743   [Letter to the King, March 15, 1743.] AGI, SD 848, JTCC, reel 6, part 1.
1744   [Letter to the Marquis de la Ensenada, February 8, 1744.] AGI, 86-6-5. [Paul Hoffman's conversion table has no modern SD equivalent—probably because it is not strictly "Santo Domingo," but rather "Sto. Domingo, Luisiana, and Florida,"] JTCC, reel 7.

1745 [Letter to the King, February 17, 1745.] AGI, SD 862, SC.
1746 [Letter to the King, March 6, 1746.] AGI, SD 228, SC.
1748 [Letter to the King, March 15, 1748.] AGI, 86-6-5, [Not in the Hoffman table], doc. no. 81, JTCC, reel 7.

Moral, Alonso del, Sebastian Martínez, Martín Lasso, Roque Domínguez, Francisco de San Joseph, Juan Bauptistia Campaña, and Juan de Paiva [iHaest (?) and an indecipherable signature]
1673 Authentic Record of the Religious Who Have Been Provincial Ministers in the Province of Santa Elena of Florida during the Last Forty Years, August 30, 1673, St. Augustine. Buckingham Smith Collection of the New York Historical Society.

Moral Sanchez, Francisco del
1734 [Letter to Don Joseph Patino, July 29, 1734.] AGI, Audiencia of Santo Domingo—Luisiana and Florida. Stand 66, Box 7, bundle 219. [It has no equivalent in Hoffman's table].

Moreno, Juan
1673 [Petition, Madrid, February 27, 1673.] AGI, SD 848, SC.

Nicolás (fiscal)
1675 Testimony, San Carlos de los Chacatos, October 4, 1675. Translation by Hann in *Florida Archaeology* (1993) 7:47–49.

Nuñez Cabeza de Vaca, Alvar
1964 *The Journey of Alvar Nuñez Cabeza de Vaca.* Translated by Fanny Bandelier. Chicago: Rio Grande Press.

Pedro, son of Diocsale
1676 Testimony, October 31, 1676. Translation by Hann in *Florida Archaeology* (1993) 7:60–62.

Peña, Diego
1716 [Diary of This Trip, of Apalache and of the province of Apalachecole ordered to be made by the Señor Governor and Captain General Don Pedro de Oliver y Fullana.] AGI, SD 843, SC.
1717a Diary of the Trip that the Lieutenant Diego Peña Made to Apalachicolo. Sabacola, September 20, 1717, to Juan de Ayala Escobar. AGI, SD 843. In Serrano y Sanz, 1912:227–237. [A manuscript copy appears as an enclosure in Benavides 1718a:42–80. Mark F. Boyd published a not very satisfactory translation of it in 1952 in the *Florida Historical Quarterly.*]
1717b Letter to Juan de Ayala Escobar, Santa Fé, October 8, 1717. In Peña 1717d:132–135.
1717c [Statement before Governor Juan de Ayala y Escobar, October 18, 1717, enclosure in Benavides 1718c:103–116.] AGI, SD 843, SC.
1717d "Documents Describing the Second and Third Expeditions of Lt. Diego Peña to Apalachee and Apalachicolo in 1717 and 1718." *Florida Historical Quarterly* (1952) 31:109–140.
1723 [Letter to Antonio de Benavides, San Marcos (Apalache), August 6, 1723.] Enclosure in Benavides 1723b.

Péres, Andrés
1674   Certification, province of Chacatos, June 23, 1674. AGI, SD 235. Translation by Hann in *Florida Archaeology* (1993) 7:75.
1675a   [Letter to Pablo de Hita Salazar, San Luis, August 2, 1675.] AGI, Escribanía de Cámara, Leg. 1566ZZ Coyer, fol. 119–142, SC. Translation by Hann in *Florida Archaeology* (1993) 7:39.
1675b   Letter to Hita Salazar, San Luis, July 29, 1675. Translation by Hann in *Florida Archaeology* (1993) 7:37–38.
Péres de Ecompaño, Antonio (general interpreter)
1722   [Letter to the King, October 23, 1722.] AGI, SD 849, JTCC, reel 6.
Pez, Andrés de
1716   Letter to the Council of the Indies, Madrid, January 18, 1716. AGI, SD 837, SC.
Pez, Andrés Matias de
1689   Memorial, Mexico City, June 2, 1689. In Leonard 1939:77–98.
Phelipe, *usinulo*
1675   Testimony, San Carlos de los Chacatos, October 4, 1675. AGI, Contratación of Seville. Asientos de Armada. Contratación 3309. Translation by Hann in *Florida Archaeology* (1993) 7:46–47.
Pluckhahn, Thomas J., and Chad O. Braley
1999   "Connections across the Southern Frontier. Spanish Artifacts from Creek Contexts at the Tarver Sites (9Jo6 and 9Jo198)." *The Florida Anthropologist* 52:241–253.
Ponce de León, Nicolás
1651   [Order to Antonio de Argüelles, May 17, 1651.] AGI, SD 23. Translation furnished by Eugene Lyon.
Pontocolo, Chief of Apalachicoli
1685   [Statement, November 6, 1685, San Luis.] AGI, SD 639, JTLC, vol. 3 of Colección "Misiones Guale," doc. dd.
Prescott, William H.
1961   *The Conquest of Peru*. Partly abridged and revised by Victor W. von Hagen. New York: New American Library Mentor Edition.
Primo de Rivera, Joseph [José]
1717a   [The memoria of, January 12, 1717 Madrid? (sic)]. AGI, SD 848, SC.
1717b   [Census of Native Villages in the Vicinity of St. Augustine, April 1717.] In Juan de Ayala y Escobar to the King, April 18, 1717. AGI, SD 843, SC.
1718a   Letter to Juan de Ayala y Escobar, San Marcos de Apalache, April 28–August 3, 1718. AGI, SD 843, SC. See Hann 1991b:355–356.
1718b   Letter to Juan de Ayala y Escobar, San Marcos de Apalache, August 3, 1718. AGI, SD 843, NCC 14–25. See Hann 1991b:356–357.
Quiñones, Fray Bartolomé de
1682   [Report on Mayaca, March 11, 1681.] AGI, SD 839, JTCC, reel 5.
Quintana, Don Joseph de la
1740   [Letter to Manuel de Montiano, March 10, 1740.] AGI, 86-6-5, JTCC, reel 7.

Quiroga y Losada, Diego de
- 1688a [Letter to the King, April 1. 1688.] AGI, SD 234, NCC.
- 1688b [Letter to the King, April 1, 1688.] AGI, SD 839. Microfilm 28B, reel 9, fol. 743-744, *Residencia* series of the P. K. Yonge Library of Florida History.
- 1688c [Letter to the King, April 1, 1688.] AGI, SD 838, JTCC, reel 5.
- 1688d [Letter to the King, April 1, 1688.] AGI, SD 838, JTCC, reel 5.
- 1690a [Letter to the King, June 8, 1690.] AGI, SD 227, SC.
- 1690b [*Auto* (sent to Fray Pedro de Luna and to the King), August 26, 1690.] AGI, SD 228, no. 13, JTLC, vol. 4 of "Misiones Guale."
- 1690c [Letter to the King, August 31, 1690.] AGI, SD 228, SC and JTLC, vol. 4 of "Misiones Guale."
- 1691a [*Auto*, September 18, 1691.] AGI, SD 228, doc. no. 32, JTLC, vol. 4. Enclosure in Quiroga y Losada, 1692a.
- 1691b [Order to Patrizio de Florencia, September 18, 1691.] AGI, SD 228, doc. no. 32, JTLC, vol. 4. Enclosure in Quiroga y Losada 1692a.
- 1692a [Letter to the King, April 10, 1692.] AGI, SD 228, JTLC, vol. 4 of "Misiones Guale."
- 1692b [Letter to the King, April 30, 1692.] AGI, SD 228, doc. no. 42, JTLC, vol. 4, "Misiones Guale."

Quiroga y Losada, Diego de, Pablo de Yta Salazar, Joachin de Florencia, Juan de Pueyo, Antonio de Argüelles, Juan Sánchez de Uriza, and Juan de Ayala Escovar.
- 1691 [Junta, September 18, 1691.] AGI, SD 228, doc. no. 32, JTLC, vol. 4. Enclosure in Quiroga y Losada 1692a.

Ramírez, Nicolás
- 1687 [Testimony, December 10, 1688.] AGI, Escribanía de Cámara, leg. 156, pieza 25 (E. 20), fol. 108-110, SC.

Rebolledo, Diego de
- 1657 Reply to the Franciscans, August 5, 1657. AGI, Escribanía de Cámara, leg. 155b. Translation by Hann in *Florida Archaeology* (1986) 2:109-115.

Reding, Katherine, translator and editor
- 1925 "Notes and Document. Plans for Colonization and Defense of Apalachee, 1675." *Georgia Historical Quarterly* 9:169-175.

Reina, Juan Jordan de
- 1686 Report, Pensacola Bay, February 6, 1686. In Leonard 1939:13-14.

Reyna, Francisco de (bondsman for Governor Benito Ruiz de Salazar Vallecilla)
- 1656? [Testimony (1656?) for Benito Ruiz de Salazar Vallecilla's posthumous *residencia*.] AGI, Escribanía de Cámara, leg. 155b. P. K. Yonge Library of Florida History, microfilm 27F, reel 5, fol. 428-431.

Ribas, Juan de
- 1600 Testimony, February 4, 1600. AGI, SD 224. In Serrano y Sanz, 1912.

Robles, Fray Blas de
- 1692 [Letter to Diego de Quiroga y Losada, April 29, 1692.] Enclosure in Quiroga y Losada 1692. AGI, SD 228, JTLC, vol. 4 of "Misiones Guale."

Rogel, Father Juan
1570   Letter to Pedro Menéndez, Havana, December 9, 1570. In Zubillaga 1946:471–479.

Romero, Fray Julian
1745   [Petition to authorities in Mexico City, August 27, 1745.] AGI, Audiencia of Mexico, 61-3-1, Papaleta 185 JTCC, reel 1 [Mexico 61-3-1 does not appear on Hoffman's index.]

Romo de Urisa, Francisco
1702   [Letter to Joseph de Zúñiga y Zerda, San Luis, October 22, 1702.] AGI, SD 258, JTCC, reel 6.

Rowland, Jerome Dunbar, and A. G. Sanders, editors and translators
1932   *Mississipi Provincial Archives, 1704–1743, French Dominion*, vol. 3. Jackson: Mississippi Department of Archives and History.

Roxas, Joseph de
1710   [Statement, January 10, 1710. Enclosure in Córcoles y Martínez 1710.] AGI, SD 841, NCC.

Royal decree
1698   Letter to Laureano de Torres y Ayala, Madrid, March 1698. AGI, SD 835. In Boyd 1951:23–24.

Royal Officials
1647   [Letter to the King, March 18, 1647.] AGI, SD 229, SC.

Ruiz de Salazar Vallecilla, Benito de
1645   [Letter to the King, April 16, 1645.] WLC, vol. 7.
1647   [Letter to the King, May 22, 1647.] AGI, SD 229, JTCC, reel 3.
1650   [*Auto*, August 5, 1650.] AGI, Escribanía de Cámara, leg. 155b, fol. 448, SC, P. K. Yonge Library of Florida History, microfilm 27F, reel 5.

Salinas Varona, Gregorio de
1717a   Letter to Juan de Ayala y Escobar, Santa María de Galves, July 24, 1717. Enclosure in Benavides 1718a. In Serrano y Sanz 1912.
1717b   Letter to Juan de Ayala y Escobar, Santa María de Galves, September 9, 1717. Enclosure in Benavides 1718a. In Serrano y Sanz 1912.

Salley, Alexander S., Jr., editor
1911   *Narratives of Early Carolina, 1650–1708*. New York: Charles Scribner's Sons.

Sánchez Grinan, Pedro
1756   [Letter to the King, Madrid, July 7, 1756.] JTCC, reel 7.

Santiago, principal *enija* of San Nicolás (de los Chacatos)
1675   Testimony, San Carlos de Yatcatani, October 11, 1675. AGI, Contratación 3309. Translation by Hann in *Florida Archaeology* (1993) 7:52–53.

Santos Cazares, Juan de los (cattle hunter)
1740   [Statement before Governor Manuel de Montiano.] Enclosure in Montiano 1740a.

Scarry, John F.
1984   "Fort Walton Development. Mississippian Chiefdoms in the Lower Southeast."

Unpublished Ph.D. Dissertation, Department of Anthropology, Case Western Reserve University.

1990a "Mississippian Emergence in the Fort Walton Area: The Evolution of the Cayson and Lake Jackson Phases." In Bruce D. Smith, editor, *The Mississippi Emergence*. Washington, D.C.: Smithsonian Institution Press.

1990b "Regional Chronologies." In Mark Williams and Gary Shapiro, eds., *Lamar Archaeology: Mississippian Chiefdoms in the Deep South*. Tuscaloosa: University of Alabama Press, 37.

1990c "Phase Characteristics of the Middle Chattahoochee River." In Mark Williams and Gary Shapiro, editors, *Lamar Archaeology: Mississippian Chiefdoms in the Deep South*, 67-69. Tuscaloosa: University of Alabama Press.

Scarry, John F., editor

1996 *Political Structure and Change in the Prehistoric Southeastern United States*. Gainesville: University Press of Florida.

Schnell, Frank T.

1989 "The Beginnings of the Creeks: Where Did They Sit Down?" *Early Georgia* 17:24-29.

1990 "Phase Characteristics of the Middle Chattahoochee River." In Mark Williams and Gary Shapiro, editors, *Lamar Archaeology: Mississippian Chiefdoms in the Deep South*, 67-69. Tuscaloosa: University of Alabama Press.

Schnell, Frank T., Vernon J. Knight Jr., Gail S. Schnell

1981 *Cemochechobee: Archaeology of a Mississippian Ceremonial Center on the Chattahoochee River*. Gainesville: University Presses of Florida.

Segura, Father Juan Baptista de

1568 Letter to Father Francisco Borgia, July 9, 1568. In Zubillaga 1946:314-317.

Serrano y Sanz, Manuel

1912 *Documentos Históricos de la Florida y Luisiana, Siglos XVI al XVIII*. Madrid: Libreria General de Victoriano Suarez.

Smith, Marvin T.

1987 *Archaeology of Aboriginal Culture Change in the Interior Southeast: Depopulation during the Early Historic Period*. Gainesville: University Presses of Florida.

Snell, William R.

1972 "Indian Slavery in Colonial South Carolina, 1671-1795." Unpublished Ph.D. dissertation, University of Alabama.

Solana, Alonso

1695a [Record Concerning the Junta Held in St. Augustine on November 3, 1694. In Lauereano de Torres y Ayala 1695b.] AGI, SD 839, JTCC, reel 5.

1695b [Certification, March 9, 1695. In Torres y Ayala, 1695b]. AGI, SD 839, JTCC, reel 5.

Solana, Juan (notary)

1717a [Certification, April 4, 1717. In Juan de Ayala y Escobar to the King, April 18, 1717.] AGI, SD 843, SC.

1717b [Certification, October 18, 1717.] Enclosure in Benavides 1718a.

Solana, Manuel
1702 [Letter to Joseph de Zúñiga y Zerda, San Luis, October 22, 1702.] In Joseph de Zúñiga y Zerda to the King, November 1, 1702. AGI, SD 858, JTCC, reel 6.
1705 [Testimony, June 9, 1705. Enclosure in Fray Lucar Alvarez de Toledo, *Auto* of Inquiry, June 9. 1705.] AGI, SD 863.
Somoza, Fray Antonio de
1673 [Letter to Francisco Fernández de Madrigal, San Francisco de Madrid, January 7, 1673.] AGI, SD 848, SC, reel 13.
Spain, Junta de Guerra
1691 [September 6, 1691, "Description of the Location, region, latitude and Longitude in which the River of Apalachecole is Located," in which Province the Governor of Florida says he has had a blockhouse built and garrison. Enclosure in Quiroga y Losada 1690a.] AGI, SD 227, SC.
Swanton, John R.
1922 *Early History of the Creek Indians and Their Neighbors*. Smithsonian Institution, Bureau of American Ethnology, Bulletin 73. New York: Johnson Reprint Corporation, 1970.
1929 "The Tawasa Language." *American Anthropologist*, n.s., 31 (1929), 435–453.
1946 *The Indians of the Southeastern United States*. Washington, D.C.: Smithsonian Institution Press.
1985 *Final Report of the United States De Soto Expedition Commission*. Washington, D.C.: Smithsonian Institution Press.
2000 *Creek Religion and Medicine*. Lincoln: University of Nebraska Press.
Tebeau, Charlton W., and William Marina
1999 *A History of Florida*, 3rd edition. Coral Gables, Florida: University of Miami Press.
TePaske, John Jay
1964 *The Governorship of Spanish Florida, 1700–1763*. Durham, N.C.: Duke University Press.
Terrazes, Juan Bauptista
1678 [Memorial. October 20, 1678.] AGI, SD 234, SC.
Thomas, David Hurst, editor
1990 *Columbian Consequences: 2, Archaeological and Historical Perspectives on the Spanish Borderlands East*. Washington, D.C.: Smithsonian Institution Press.
Toro, Alonso Marqués del
1738 [Letter, San Marcos de Apalache, April 18, 1718.] AGI, SD 2593, SC.
Torres y Ayala, Laureano de
1693a Letter to the Conde de Galve, Great Bay of Pensacola, August 5, 1693. In Leonard 1939:218–227.
1693b Journal of Governor Torres y Ayala, Great Bay of Pensacola, August 5, 1693. In Leonard 1939:228–255.
1694 [Letter to Don Thomas Shimth (sic), August 5, 1694. Enclosure in Torres y Ayala 1695b.] AGI, SD 839, JTCC, reel 5.

1695a   [Letter to Joseph Blake, March 3, 1695. Enclosure in Torres y Ayala, 1695b.] AGI, SD 839, JTCC, reel 5.
1695b   [Letter to the King, March 11, 1695.] AGI, SD 839, JTCC, reel 5.
1696   Letter to the King, Florida, April 15, 1696. AGI, SD 228. In Boyd, Smith, and Griffin 1951:21–22.

Torres y Ayala, Laureano de, Thomas Menéndez Marquez, and Joaquin de Florencia
1694   [Record of Junta, November 3, 1694. Enclosure in Torres y Ayala 1695b.] AGI, SD 839, JTCC, reel 5.
1697   [Letter to the King, April 20, 1697.] AGI, SD 230, JTCC, reel 4.

Truxillo, Fray Agustín
1759   [Census of the village of Our Lady of Guadalupe of Tolomato, February 3, 1759.] AGI, SD 2604.

Valdés, Bishop Gerónimo
1728   [Letter to the King, Havana, September 1, 1728.] AGI, SD 865, SC.

Valverde, Fray Miguel de, and Fray Rodrigo de la Barrera
1674   Certification, San Nicolás de Tolentino, September 10, 1674. AGI, SD 234. Translation by Hann in *Florida Archaeology* (1993) 7:34–35.

Van Doren, Mark, editor
1955   *Travels of William Bartram*. New York: Dover Publications.

Vargas, Juan Gabriel de
1710   [Statement, January 9, 1710. Enclosure in Córcoles y Martínez 1710.] AGI, SD 841, NCC.

Vega, Dionisio de la
1732   [Letter to the King, Havana, July 7, 1732.] AGI, SD 860.

Vega Castro y Pardo, Damián de
1639   [Letter to the King, August 22, 1639.] AGI, SD 225, SC.
1643   [Letter to the King, July 9, 1643.] AGI, SD 224.

Villareal, Brother Francisco
1570   Letter to Father Francisco Borgia, Tupiqui, March 3, 1570. In Zubillaga 1946:413–421.

Villareal, Fray Juan Miguel de
1682   [Report on San Antonio de Anacape, April 12, 1682.] AGI, SD 839, JTCC, reel 5.

Waselkov, Gregory A., and Bonnie L. Gums
2000   *Plantation Archaeology at Riviere aux Chien, ca. 1725–1848*. Prepared for the Alabama Department of Transportation. Mobile: University of South Alabama Center for Archaeological Studies.

Waselkov, Gregory A., and Marvin T. Smith
2000   Upper Creek Archaeology. In Bonnie G. McEwan, editor, *Indians of the Greater Southeast: Historical Archaeology and Ethnohistory*, 242–264. Gainesville: University Press of Florida.

Weddle, Robert S.
1973   *Wilderness Manhunt: The Spanish Search for La Salle*. Austin: University of Texas Press.

Weisman, Brent Richards
1989   *Like Beads on a String: A Culture History of the Seminole Indians in North Peninsular Florida.* Tuscaloosa: University of Alabama Press.
1999   *Unconquered People: Florida's Seminole and Micosukee Indians.* Gainesville: University Press of Florida.

Westbrooke, Caleb
1684/1685 [Letter to the Governor of Carolina, St. Helena, February 21, 1684–1685.] In Alexander S. Salley, editor, *Records in the British Public Records Office Relating to South Carolina.* 5 vols. Columbia: Historical Commission of South Carolina.

White, Nancy M.
2003   "Unknown and Known Historic Indians of the Apalachicola Valley, Northwest Florida." Paper presented at the annual meeting of the Florida Anthropological Society, May, 10 2003, Tallahassee.

Williams, Mark
[1984?] Personal communication, 1984.
1996   "Mississippian Political Dynamics in the Oconee Valley." In John Scarry 1996:128–149.

Williams, Mark, editor
1992   *Hitchiti: An Early Georgia Language.* Athens: Lamar Institute.

Williams, Mark, and Gary Shapiro, editors
1990   *Lamar Archaeology: Mississippian Chiefdoms in the Deep South.* Tuscaloosa: University of Alabama Press.

Wood, Peter H., Gregory A. Waselkov, and M. Thomas Hatley, editors
1989   *Powhatan's Mantle: Indians in the Colonial Southeast.* Lincoln: University of Nebraska Press.

Woodward, Henry
1674   "A faithful Relation of my westoe voiage." Transcribed in Salley 1911:130–134.

Worth, John E.
1995   *The Struggle for the Georgia Coast: An 18th-Century Spanish Retrospective on Guale and Mocama.* Anthropological Papers of the American Museum of Natural History, no. 75.
1998   *Timucuan Chiefdoms of Spanish Florida,* 2 vols. Gainesville: University Press of Florida.
2000   The Lower Creeks: Origin and Early History. In Bonnie G. McEwan, editor, *Indians of the Greater Southeast: Historical Archaeology and Ethnohistory,* 265–298. Gainesville: University Press of Florida.

Wright, J. Leitch, Jr.
1986   *Creeks and Seminoles: Destruction and Regeneration of the Muscogulge People.* Lincoln: University of Nebraska Press.

Ygnacio, Juan (Guale Indian)
1740   [Statement before Governor Manuel de Montiano.] Enclosure in Montiano 1740a.

Ysfane, Juan, *osinulo* of Sauocola
1685   [Statement, San Luis, November 5, 1685. In inquiry conducted by Domingo de Leturiondo as Visitor.] AGI, SD 639, doc. no. 82, JTLC, vol. 3 of "Misiones Guale," doc. dd.

Zubillaga, S. J., Felix, editor
1946   *Monumenta Antiquae Floridae (1566-1572)*. Vol. 69 of Monumenta Historica Societatis Iesu, Rome.

Zúñiga y Zerda, Joseph de
1700   [Order to Jacinto Roque Pérez, deputy-governor of Apalachee, November 5, 1700.] AGI, SD 858, JTCC, reel 6.
1701   [Letter to the King, November 1, 1702.] AGI, SD 858, JTCC, reel 6.
1702a   Letter to the King, September 30, 1702. In Boyd, Smith, and Griffin 1951:36–38.
1702b   [Letter to the King, November 1, 1702.] AGI, SD 858, JTCC, reel 6.
1702c   [*Auto*, November 5, 1702.] AGI, SD 858, JTCC, reel 6.
1702d   [*Auto*, November 5, 1702.] AGI, SD 858, JTCC, reel 6.
1704   [Letter to the King, October 6, 1704.] AGI, SD 858, JTCC, reel 6.
1705   [Letter to the Viceroy, October 26, 1705.] AGI, SD 857, SC.

Index

Abercrombie phase, 17, 20, 79
Abihka Indians, 4–5, 81–82, 154, 176
Abihka Province, 92, 134, 135
Abikan Indians, 138
Abosaya (settlement), 132
Achercatane (settlement), 29
Achese Indians, 8–9
Achito (settlement): archaeology of, 93; and attacks on Christian provinces, 65, 130; Chacato Indians and, 50, 65, 131; English names for, 9; gatherings at, 130, 131; languages in, 90, 162; location of, 7, 87, 93; maps of, 88; and Matheos expeditions, 114; and Peña expeditions, 150, 162; population of, 150
Achito Indians, 112, 148, 161
Achuse (settlement), 13, 69
Acolaque (Achito chief), 112
Acuera. *See* Santa Lucia de Acuera (mission)
Adair, James, 8, 77
Adrian (Apalachee chief): and delegations to St. Augustine, 155, 157, 162, 164, 165, 179; and English, 161; and expedition to St. Marks, 158, 167; languages of, 151; as leader, 146, 148, 166; and Peña, 151, 152, 154, 161, 180; and resettlement of Apalachee Province, 166, 168, 180; spies of, 161; and Ysipacafi, 166
Adrian, Savacola, 11
Agna. *See* Ochlockonee River
Agramon, Monsieur de (Frenchman), 116
Agriculture: Apalachee Indians and, 35; Chacato Indians and, 21, 48, 63; Chisca Indians and, 62; hoeings for, 35; Lower Creeks and, 94; during Middle Woodland period, 18–19; during Mississippian period, 16; Pansacola Indians and, 63, 77; along Pensacola Bay, 73; and population, 16; Uchise Indians and, 84, 94, 184, 189; Upper Creeks and, 94; and weather, 35, 124, 184; Yamasee Indians and, 167, 169, 171. *See also* Crops; Plants
Aguado, Salvador Joseph, 135–136
Ahachito (settlement), 87
Ahachito (settlement), 92

Ais Indians, 142, 176
Ajachito (settlement), 188
Alabama (language), 7
Alabama (state), 1, 4, 18, 93
Alabama Indians: and Atasi Indians, 105; and English, 133, 139, 173; and firearms, 135; languages of, 4–5; leaders of, 139; population of, 138–139; settlements of, 5, 138, 154; and Spanish captives, 135; and Tiquipache Indians, 105; and Upper Creek Indians, 4–5
Alabama-Kosati (language), 11, 12
Alabama Province, 134–135, 153, 166, 169
Alabama River, 2, 5, 88
Alabama River culture, 18
Alabama River Valley, 1
Alachua (location), 187, 191
Alachua prairie, 183
Alafae Indians, 176
Alape (settlement), 13, 87, 88, 91, 93, 114
Albemarle Sound, 54
Algonkian Indians, Central, 66
Algonquian (language), 8, 91
Algonquian Indians, 10
Aligua (settlement), 140
Alonso, Chacato or Chacta, 6, 36, 43
Alonso, Juan, 44
Altamaha (settlement), 15, 90, 140, 142, 144. *See also* La Tama (settlement)
Altamaha Indians, 15, 145
Altamaha River, 43, 58, 91, 141, 174, 182
Amacano Indians: in Apalachee, 27; and Apalachee Indians, 20, 23, 81; archaeology of, 22; and Chacato Indians, 22; and Chine Indians, 20, 22, 23, 25; and Christianity, 20, 23, 27; forebears of, 11; and Fort Walton culture, 20; homeland of, 22; and Lamar culture, 43; languages of, 11, 20, 22, 23, 24, 25, 42, 43; mentioned, 1; and migration, 85; and Pacara Indians, 20, 22, 23; and Pojoy Indians, 22; scholarship on, 24; settlements of, 20, 22; and Spaniards, 20, 23

Amapeja or Amapira Indians, 175, 176. *See also* Yamasee Indians
Amelia Island, 106, 131
Anastasia Island, 182
Anderson, David G., 18
Angulo, Favian de, 124–125, 126
Animals: bears, 47, 94; birds, 47, 48, 74; bones of, 75; buffalo, 49, 63, 73, 74, 94, 129, 149; cardinals, 74; cattle, 28, 49, 124, 166, 183; deer, 48, 74, 94, 129, 166; English traders and, 139; fish scales, 75, 193n1 (chap. 4); fowl, 139; foxes, 74; game, 158; herons, 184; herrings, 193n1 (chap. 4); hogs, 139; horses, 48, 75, 124, 130, 153, 160, 161, 167, 185, 191; martens, 74; mules, 75; otters, 74; panthers, 47; steers, 191; turkeys, 74
Antonio, Baltasar José, 159
Apalachecole (settlement), 90
Apalachee (language): and Alabama-Koasati language, 12; and Alabama language, 7; and Creek language, 12; French on, 51; and Hitchiti language, 7, 12, 151; interpreters and, 11, 25, 36, 44, 101, 151; and Koasati language, 7; as Muskogean language, 11; places spoken, 150, 151–152, 161; Sabacola Indians and, 90, 91; Sauocola Indians and, 10; scholarship on, 11–12; Spaniards and, 10, 12, 44, 65, 101
Apalachee Ball Game manuscript, 38, 155
Apalachee Indians: and agriculture, 21, 35; and Amacano Indians, 20, 23, 81; and Apalachicoli Indians, 23, 24, 81, 100, 122, 168; in Apalachicoli Province, 91–92, 121–122; and Apisca Indians, 170, 177; attacks by, 172; attacks on, 38, 53; Cacique Miguel and, 37; as carpenters, 123; and Caueta Indians, 92, 146, 165; and ceramics, 14, 21, 51; and Chacato Indians, 23, 28, 34–35, 38, 39, 47–48, 50–51, 61, 81; in Chattahoochee Valley, 80, 151–152; and Chichimeco Indians, 58; and Chickasaw Indians, 183; and Chine Indians, 25; and Chisca Indians, 38, 39, 41, 43, 53, 55, 59, 61, 63, 70; and Christianity, 53, 101, 125, 144, 146, 149, 157, 165, 168, 176, 182; and Claudio de Florencia, 43; and construction of Spanish settlements, 49; descendants of, 15; and English, 147, 168, 170, 177; at Escambé, 35, 50; expeditions of, 49, 130–131; farms of, 150; and fishing, 30; and forts and palisades, 48, 60, 67, 123–124; and French, 50–51, 183; and gathering, 47; and Guale Indians, 187; hairstyles of, 77–78; and horses, 48; housing of, 14; and hunting, 21, 30, 47; immolation of, 49; as interpreters, 44, 125; 151, 152; languages of, 43, 91, 151; leaders of, 41–42, 147, 157, 159, 168, 172, 173, 180, 183; and literacy, 42; and Lower Creek Indians, 4, 168; maps of, 2; and Matheos, 109, 113; and matrilineal succession, 42; mentioned, 14, 117; in Mexico, 180; and migration, 50–51, 80, 91, 137, 146, 168, 180; and missions, 30, 168; and Mississippian period, 16; and Movila Indians, 183; murders of, 130; and neutrality, 143, 179; and Peña, 150, 162; in Pensacola, 179; at Pocosapa, 144; political organization of, 41–42; population of, 50–51, 138–139; and resettlement of Apalachee Province, 168; revolts by, 33, 55, 63; at San Luis, 35, 50, 51; and Sauocola Indians, 11, 91, 104; and seasons, 30; settlement patterns of, 14, 44; settlements of, 138, 168, 172, 176, 178, 180, 183; Spaniards on, 41; Spanish names for, 105; as spies, 115; and St. Augustine, 168; and St. Marks, 167; and Talapusa Indians, 170; and Talapuse Indians, 175, 177; and Tallapoosa Indians, 115; and term "Pansacola," 69; and trade goods, 119; as traders, 49; and Uchise Indians, 170, 182, 187; warriors of, 155; and Yamasee Indians, 168, 178, 182; and Yamasee War, 137, 138, 146; and Yuchi Indians, 170
Apalachee Province: Amacano Indians and, 27; Apalachee Indians and, 178; Apalachicoli Indians and, 130; areas west of, 24; attacks on, 33, 38, 67, 86, 128, 130, 131–132, 133; Barroto and, 72; borders of, 96; as boundary, 42; Cacique Miguel and, 36; Catase Indians and, 27; cattle in, 49; Caueta Indians and, 92; censuses of, 176; Chacato Indians and, 27, 32, 49, 50; Chine Indians and, 77; Chisca Indians and, 33, 56, 57, 58, 80; and Christianity, 23, 38, 83, 132, 162, 178; Creek Indians and, 183; de Soto and, 13, 20; Díaz Vara Calderón and, 26; Diocsale in, 36; Echagaray in, 71; English and, 167, 180; expeditions from, 61, 75; forts and garrisons in, 86, 129,

Index / 221

157, 158, 160, 163, 166–169, 184; Fray Barreda and, 31; friars in, 83, 99; Gov. Torres y Ayala and, 96; horses in, 48, 130; Indians near, 20–21; interpreters in, 43; Juaquín in, 36; Leturiondo in, 46; Lower Creek Indians and, 183; maps of, 88; Matheos and, 71, 111, 117, 119; mentioned, 1, 98, 118; and migration, 85, 93, 132, 191; and missions, 20, 23, 24, 26, 95, 98–99, 103, 139, 146; murders in, 100; Pacara Indians and, 27; Pansacola Indians and, 72; Peña and, 160; population in, 18, 31, 121–122; priests in, 179; raiding parties from, 23; resettlement of, 168, 171, 180, 189; Sauocola Indians and, 27, 96, 100; settlements in, 38, 176, 178, 183; Spaniards in, 4, 20, 49, 58, 67, 132, 168, 174, 180; Spanish allies in, 178; Tama Indians and, 15, 160; Tama-Yamasee Indians and, 85, 98, 118, 119; Tawasa Indians and, 27, 46; Tocopaca Indians and, 168–169; trade with, 28, 119; Uchise Indians and, 181; visitations to, 44, 46, 79, 81; Westo Indians and, 86; Yamasee Indians and, 169, 174, 176, 178

Apalachee River, 84, 98

Apalachicholi (settlement), 82, 87, 100, 113

Apalachicola (settlement), 80, 147, 188

Apalachicola River: convents on, 104; languages along, 80; maps of, 56, 86, 123; mentioned, 1, 21, 38, 59, 73; and migration, 82, 128; missions along, 41, 44, 68, 92, 93, 96, 103, 104, 112, 127; and Sauocola River, 45; settlements along, 5–6, 19, 33, 46, 49, 56, 59, 72, 85, 147, 169, 180; Spanish definition of, 5, 89

Apalachicola River Valley, 21

Apalachicoli (language), 10, 12, 121, 151

Apalachicoli (settlement): council house at, 118; and Creek origins, 17; dominance of, 8; English in, 118, 119; forts near, 93; languages in, 91, 151; leaders of, 6, 8; location of, 93, 148; maps of, 88; Matheos and, 108, 109, 118, 119; mentioned, 7; Peña and, 150, 152; population of, 150; relocation of, 153; spies in, 118, 119; Yamasee Indians in, 118

Apalachicoli (Spanish term), 6

Apalachicoli Indians: and Apalachee Indians, 23, 81, 121–122, 123, 168; attacks by, 48, 49, 50, 65, 68, 104, 107, 121, 128, 130, 131–132; burning of settlements of, 122, 123; and Chalaque Indians, 163, 164; characteristics of, 84, 95, 131; and Chattahoochee Valley, 82, 83, 85, 148; and Cherokee Indians, 164; and Chichimeco Indians, 12; and Chisca Indians, 12, 67; and Christianity, 23, 28, 83–84, 95, 98, 99; delegations of, 130; and Diocsale, 33; and English, 23–24, 48, 50, 67, 103, 106, 111, 114, 124, 128, 131, 133, 147, 160; expeditions against, 49, 130–131; factions of, 147, 148; and famine, 124; farms of, 150; and Favian de Angulo, 124; first contacts with, 80, 83; forebears of, 82; and forts, 121, 122, 126; and friars, 83, 101; in Georgia, 82, 129; and Gov. Márquez Cabrera, 101; and Gov. Quiroga y Losada, 119, 122, 123; and Gov. Torres y Ayala, 128; and horses, 130; killings by, 49, 100, 130; languages of, 7, 9, 10, 43, 101, 152; leaders of, 10, 11, 12, 101, 108, 112, 115, 133, 147, 150; and Matheos, 108–109, 110, 112, 114–115; and migration, 84, 98, 121, 137, 148; and missions, 23–24, 99–100, 105, 114, 121, 128; and Natuaques/Nauraques Indians, 163; neutrality of, 112; and Pansacola Indians, 48, 75; and Peña, 150, 169; population of, 84, 138–139; and San Luis, 48; and Sauocola Indians, 126; as Seminole forebears, 190; settlement patterns of, 84; settlements of, 11, 67, 83, 96, 138; and Spaniards, 11, 12, 20, 28, 46, 67, 81, 83, 84, 96, 100, 119, 122, 135, 180; Spanish terms for, 148; and trade, 28, 48, 81, 103, 128, 130; and Uchee Indians, 64; and Uchise Indians, 121; and Uchize Indians, 135, 154; and War of the Spanish Succession, 131; and weapons, 131; and Yamasee Indians, 124; and Yamasee War, 137, 148; and Yuchi Indians, 64

Apalachicoli Province: Apalachee Indians in, 91–92, 121–122; armaments in, 134; borders of, 96; burning of villages in, 71; Chichimeco Indians and, 54, 58; Chisca Indians and, 80; and Choctaw territory, 29; Christianity in, 83–84, 89, 97; Council of the Indies on, 123; definitions of, 6, 8; English and, 89, 97, 99, 106, 112, 113, 114–115, 122, 126; famine in, 124; and forts and palisades, 48, 67, 106–107, 110–111, 119, 121, 145, 166; Franciscans and, 125; friars and, 82; Henry

Apalachicoli Province—*continued*
  Woodward and, 106, 120; horses in, 160; languages in, 6, 7, 17, 81, 90, 98, 115; leaders in, 166; location of, 4; maps of, 26; Márquez Cabrera on, 105; and migration, 82, 85, 86, 127; and missions, 95–97, 99, 127; Peña and, 150, 163; political organization in, 115; population of, 94, 122, 154; settlement patterns in, 98; settlements in, 8, 10, 17, 71, 87–89, 91, 122, 134, 150, 153; shortages in, 154; Spaniards and, 79; Spanish allies in, 180; Spanish-Apalachee expeditions in, 106; Spanish names for, 8; spies in, 7; Tama-Yamasee Indians and, 119; trade with, 83, 119, 130; and Uchize Province, 154; visitations to, 79, 81, 83; warriors in, 134; Yamasee Indians and, 86; Yllache Indians and, 164
Apalachicolo (settlement), 87, 162
Apalachôcoli (settlement), 87, 92, 181
Apica Indians, 134, 135, 176
Apisca Indians, 154, 166, 170, 175, 177
Apisca Province, 153
Appalchian Mountains, 52, 53
Aprisca Indians, 175–176
Arana, Luis, 60
Architecture: bark-covered, 74, 149; bastions, 60; blockhouses, 119, 123, 124, 127, 129, 158, 167; buffalo skin–covered, 149; central roof supports in, 19; charnel houses, 74–75; clay, 149; of convents, 44; corncribs, 62; council houses, 44, 47, 113, 118, 149, 164, 185; Creeks and, 44; emperor's house, 160; fishermen's huts, 73; of forts, 169, 171, 173, 174; Fort Walton culture, 14; glacis, 60; government house, 155; governor's residence, 153, 157, 163, 164; granaries, elevated, 44; guard posts, 44; hay-covered houses, 14; houses, 62, 116, 118, 133, 149, 188; huts, 73, 74; materials for, 14, 49, 133; palm-leaf covered, 74; patios, 156; plazas, 44; post houses, 19; rectangular, 19; reed-covered houses, Elvas on, 14; and seasons, 14, 44; shingle-covered, 149; sizes of, 44; square grounds, 44; Stewart period, 19; storehouses, 62, 160; two-story, 44; underground, 14; warehouses, 115, 171; wattle and daub, 14, 19; windows in, 149
Argüelles, Matheo de, 104

Armas, Andrés de, 83
Asile Indians and settlement, 28
Assumpción de Nuestra Señora or del Puerto (mission), 25, 26
Atanchia (settlement), 29
Atasi Indians, 13, 66, 105
Atasimico (Indian), 181
Atasi Province, 115, 150
Aucilla River, 2, 30, 88, 180
Austria, 166, 173
Aute (settlement), 27
Ayabanos. *See* Alabama Indians; Alabama Province
Ayala y Escobar, Juan (acting governor, 1717–1718): and Apalachee Province fort, 158, 164; assumption of office by, 154–155; background of, 155; on Emperor Brims, 140–141; illness of, 163; and Indian delegations, 153, 154–158, 164, 179; mentioned, 165; and Peña expeditions, 160, 161, 162–163; on resettlement of Apalachee Province, 168; Salinas Varona and, 164; on St. Augustine-area settlements, 142–143
Ayfichiti (settlement), 181
Ayjichito Province, 60
Ayubale (mission), 50
Ayubale (settlement), 11, 26, 38, 59
Ayubale (Talapuze village), 135–136

Bacuqua (settlement): Apalachee Indians and, 38, 134; attacks on, 38, 59, 130; friars at, 92; languages at, 151; leaders of, 146, 162, 164, 166, 179; maps of, 88; population of, 146; as "Rebel Christian" settlement, 134
Bahama Channel, 84
Ballgames, 65–66, 117
Baltasar or Balthasar (Sauocola Indian chief), 41, 96
Barcia. *See* González Barcia Carballido y Zúñiga, Andrés
Barnwell, John, 138
Barreda, Jazinto de, 121, 126, 128
Barreda, Rodrigo de la: on Caueta Indians, 92, 101, 102; and Chacato Indians, 24, 29–30; and Chief Chine, 24, 42; on Chine languages, 11; conspiracy against, 27, 31–34, 36–37, 40, 44, 45; expeditions by, 31, 96; on Gov. Torres y Ayala expedition, 24; journals

of, 24, 25, 31; and missions, 26, 47, 99; on Pansacola Indian settlements, 48; on San Nicolás mission, 31
Barroto, Juan Enríquez, 72–73, 123
Bartram, William: on Apalachicoli village, 82, 93; on Hilibi Indians, 13; on languages, 7; mentioned, 12, 115; and variations of "Sauocola," 10
Basisa (settlement), 168. *See also* Wacissa (settlement)
Baskets, 73, 74, 75, 193n1 (chap. 4)
Benavides, Antonio de (governor, 1718–1734): on Apalachee Province settlements, 175; assumption of office by, 175; on Brims and Joseph Primo de Rivera, 169; on Casipuia Indians, 176–177; censuses by, 178; Council of the Indies and, 172, 173; on Indian allies, 166, 169, 178; and Indian delegations, 169; requests for arms by, 170, 173, 175; on resettling Apalachee Province, 171; and South Carolinia, 174; term of, 183; as "Viracocha," 183; on Yamasee Indians, 175
Bentura, Bip, 61
Bernardo (chief), 61
Beverly, Robert, 10, 86
Biedma, Luys Hernández de, 13, 14
Bienville, Jean Baptiste Le Moyne de, 50–51, 76, 172
Big Bend, 21, 22
Big Sabacola (settlement), 97
Big Sauocola: abandonment of settlement, 95; and Christianity, 97; leaders of, 11, 97; location of, 10, 93, 95, 107; Matheos and, 114
Big Savacola. *See* San Carlos de Çabacola (Sauocola mission)
Big Town, 82
Biloxi Indians, 76
Bishops, 176, 178, 179. *See also* Díaz Vara Calderón, Gabriel
Blackmon phase, 17, 18, 20, 79; and site, 95
Blacks, 160, 161, 163
Blake, Joseph, 129
Bolton, Herbert E., 9, 102, 103
Bowne, Eric E., 54–55
Boyd, Mark F.: on 1717 Indian delegation, 154; on Apalachicoli Province population, 94; on Caueta leaders' dominance, 148; on Chaugale, 93–94; on Chisca Indians, 64–65;

on "diamaza," 151; on Emperor Brims, 141, 152, 194n3; on Peña's 1716 expedition, 194n3; on San Nicolás mission, 31; on Sauocola mission, 96; translations by, 49–50; on Yuchi Indians, 64–65
Braley, Chad O., 18, 19–20, 80
Brims (Caueta chief): authority of, 101–102, 103, 115, 137, 141, 150, 153, 154, 159, 160, 165, 194n3; brother of, 82, 138; and Caueta primacy, 82; and Chief Adrian, 161; and English, 138, 152, 159–161, 177; and forts, 157; on friars in Caueta territory, 103; gifts to, 155, 157, 161; grandsons of, 82; heir to, 146; and Indian delegations, 152, 153, 156; Juan Marcos and, 180; languages of, 152; as leader, 80, 103; and Lower Creek Indians, 163; and neutrality, 152, 177, 179; and Orta, 165; and Peña expeditions, 141, 150, 152, 153, 159, 161, 166; prestige of, 102; and Primo de Rivera, 169; residence of, 160; scholarship on, 141; and slaves, 167; sons of, 82, 92, 146, 148, 155, 156–157, 159–160, 165, 166, 169, 183; Spaniards on, 103, 141; and Spanish mission to Charles Town, 158–159; in St. Augustine, 80, 141, 152, 194n3; at St. Marks, 167–168, 169; storehouse of, 160; at Teguale, 167; Tixjana and, 180; and Tocopaca Indians, 167, 168; wife of, 11, 92, 122, 146, 152, 161, 163; and Yamasee War, 137, 141
Buffalo, 149
Bull Creek phase, 17, 19
Bushnell, David I., Jr., 10, 86
Bussell Island, 52

Çabacola Chuba. *See* San Carlos de Çabacola (Sauocola mission)
Cabeta (Spanish term), 6, 8
Cabeta or Cabita (settlement), 87, 92, 104, 181
Cabeza de Vaca. *See* Nuñez Cabeza de Vaca, Alvar
Camuñas, Diego, 12
Candelaria de la Tamaja. *See* Our Lady of Candelaria De La Tamaja (settlement)
Caniparia, Antonio Perez, 140
Capacheque or Capachequi Indians, 14, 43
Capara. *See* Pacara Indians
Capoli (settlement), 26
Cap qui, Langne (cacique), 144

Captives: from Apalachee raids, 23; Chacato Indians as, 129; Chichimeco Indians as, 12, 54, 58; Creek Indians as, 165; and de Soto's Gulf coast expedition, 14; English as, 184; Guale Indians as, 185; Spaniards as, 50, 134, 135–136, 137, 159, 185
Caribbean, 41, 182
Carib Indians, 64
Carlos (Chacato cacique), 34, 36, 37, 40, 42, 45
Carolina Lords Proprietors, 133
Carpenters, 123, 158
Casapuya (language), 144
Casipuia Indians, 176–177
Casista (settlement): and Apalachee Indians, 170; archaeology of, 93; and ballgames, 117; burning of, 71, 81, 86, 116, 117, 121; in de Soto chronicles, 90; English and, 92, 109, 117, 118, 165, 170, 175, 177; and Gov. Benavides, 183; houses at, 116; languages in, 7, 91, 151; leaders of, 102, 167; location of, 81, 87, 89, 93, 107, 109, 129, 181, 188; Lower Creeks and, 90; map of, 88; and Matheos expeditions, 71, 81, 86, 109, 110, 114, 116, 117, 119, 121; and migration, 117, 125; and Peña expeditions, 150, 160, 163; population of, 150; predecessors of, 82; rebuilding of, 117, 118; relocation of, 87, 118, 122; Spanish officials in, 29; spies in, 117, 118; towns south of, 89; and Yamasee Indians, 170
Casista Indians: and Abihka Indians, 81–82; and Caueta Indians, 82; and English, 115, 125, 133, 173; languages of, 81; and migration, 81, 82, 148; and mounds, 82; neutrality of, 102; origins of, 81; settlements of, 81–82; and Tallapoosa Indians, 115; and Yamasee War, 148
Casista Province, 60, 141
Casista or Casiste (settlement), 13, 82, 90, 113
Casista or Casiste Indians, 6, 15
Catase Indians, 27
Catufa Province, 58
Caueta (settlement): Angula and, 124; and attack on Chacato mission, 128; and ballgames, 117; burning of, 71, 81, 86, 116, 117, 121, 122; Chichimeco Indians at, 102; and Christianity, 99; dominance of, 8; and English, 92, 109, 110, 113, 115, 117, 118, 161, 163, 175, 177, 188; forts and palisades near, 110, 188; and Gov. Benavides, 183; houses at, 116, 160; languages in, 7, 11, 91, 151; leaders of, 11, 87, 97, 99, 101–102, 167; location of, 93, 129, 150, 188; maps of, 88; and Matheos expeditions, 71, 81, 86, 109, 110, 113, 114, 116, 117, 119, 121, 122; and migration, 117, 125; and Peña expeditions, 150, 153, 160–161; population of, 150; rebuilding of, 117, 118, 122; relocation of, 118, 122; scholarship on, 92; Spaniards and, 129; and Spanish mission to Charles Town, 158; spies in, 117, 118; storehouse at, 160; treaty ceremony at, 133; vessels at, 117; warehouse near, 115
Caueta Indians: and Abihka Indians, 82; and Apalachee Indians, 146, 165; and Casista Indians, 82; in Chattahoochee Valley, 80, 82; and Christianity, 101; and English, 106, 107, 115, 133, 146; and friars, 46; in Georgia, 82; and Gov. Márquez Cabrera, 101–102; and Gov. Quiroga y Losado, 127; leaders of, 46, 82, 92, 101–103, 133, 137, 146, 148; and migration, 82, 148; neutrality of, 102; at Pensacola, 172; and prototypes of Creek Confederacy, 102; and Sauocola Indians, 46; as Seminole forebears, 190; and Spaniards, 107, 146; and Tallapoosa Indians, 115; and trade goods, 146; and Yamasee War, 148
Caueta Province: Chuchumeco Indians in, 67; delegation from, 190; dominance of, 7; English in, 170; languages in, 7; leaders of, 67, 87, 140, 141, 155, 190; location of, 7; Spaniards and, 165; Spanish names for, 7; and Uchize Province, 154
Cauetta (settlement), 6, 87
Caurenti, Savocola, 11
Caveta (Spanish term). *See* Caueta Province
Cazîtho (settlement), 87, 92
Cemochechobee (settlement), 11
Censuses: of 1675, 25; of 1681, 27; of 1711, 143; of 1717, 142, 143–144, 146; of 1723, 175, 176; of 1726, 162, 178; of 1750, 135; of 1759, 146; French, 135; of missions, 27
Ceramics: Abercrombie phase, 17–18; Alabama River, 18; Apalachee Indians and, 21, 51; black-burnished, 18; Blackmon phase, 20; brushed, 18; Bull Creek, 19; burnished, 20; Chacato Indians and, 21, 51; Chattahoochee Brushed, 20; complicated stamped, 19, 20; Creeks, 5; curvilinear complicated stamping on, 19; Dallas, 18; Fort Walton, 14, 19, 21;

Fort Walton Incised, 19; incised, 18, 19, 20, 21; jars, 19; Lamar, 5, 19–20; Lamar Complicated Stamped, 19; Lawson Field phase, 20; McKee Island, 18; and migration, 19, 79; Mississippian, 20; Moundville type, 19; new forms of, 19, 79; pans, 73, 74; Pansacola culture, 76, 77; plain, 18, 19, 20; polished, 20; pots, 74; punctated, 20, 21; rims of, 19; Rood, 19–20, 79; Sigüenza on, 74; Singer-Moye, 20; smoothed, 20; Stewart, 19; and Stewart phase, 17–18; tempers of, 18, 19, 20, 21, 51, 77, 79; Weeden Island, 19

Chacate (Uchise leader), 185

Chacato (Indian man), 10

Chacato (mission): and Apalachicoli Indians, 114; and attack on Guacara mission, 128; attacks on, 104, 105; dangers to, 112; Delagado and, 103–104; friars at, 47; Gov. Quiroga y Losada and, 127; location of, 47, 112, 127; Matheos and, 114, 117; and migration, 128; and Sauocola mission, 103; Spanish soldiers at, 127. *See also* San Carlos de los Chacatos (mission)

Chacato (settlement), 2, 46

Chacato Indians: ages of, 45; and agriculture, 21, 48, 63; and Apalachee Indians, 23, 28, 38, 39, 50–51, 61, 81; in Apalachee Province, 27, 72; and Apalachicoli Indians, 49; archaeology of, 21, 22, 30, 51; architecture of, 44; attacks by, 41, 49–50, 65, 129; attacks on, 44, 49, 170–171; as captives, 129; and cattle drives, 49; and ceramics, 21, 51; and "Chacato contract," 47–48; and Chine Indians, 20, 25; and Chisca Indians, 25, 30, 32–33, 39, 41, 43, 45, 60, 61, 63; and Christianity, 23, 28, 29–30, 31, 32, 46–47, 48, 49, 51, 131; and construction of Spanish settlements, 49; and English, 30, 48; as envoys, 45; and epidemics, 45, 49; forebears of, 11, 21, 30, 31; and Fray Barreda, 24; and Fray Paiva, 45; and French, 50–51; and friars, 86; and gathering, 47–48; as guides, 38, 43, 61; and horses, 48; and hunting, 21, 47, 49, 63; as interpreters, 6, 25, 43; killings by, 49; languages of, 11, 20, 22, 36, 42, 43, 44, 51, 77; leaders of, 22, 29, 41–42, 45; maps of, 2, 51; and matrilineal succession, 42; mentioned, 1; and migration, 27–28, 38, 44, 45–46, 50–51; and military expeditions, 25; and missions, 25, 29, 44, 46–47, 61, 87, 95, 104; and mounds, 21; and Movila Indians, 46; nineteenth-century references to, 51; and Pansacola Indians, 30, 45, 70, 72, 75, 77; and patrilineality, 42; political organization of, 21, 41–42; and polygamy, 32; population of, 50–51; and priests, 47; protests and rebellions by, 27, 30, 31–39, 44, 57, 66, 95; religious organization of, 21; and Sauocola Indians, 50, 104; scholarship on, 6, 24, 28; settlement patterns of, 21, 44, 51; settlements of, 5–6, 20, 21, 22, 25, 27–28, 29, 35, 38, 39, 40, 41, 44, 45, 46, 47, 48, 49, 50–51, 59, 60, 61, 67, 72, 86, 104, 167, 169, 171, 180; as slaves, 48, 104; and Spaniards, 11, 20, 28, 45, 46, 75; Spanish terms for, 6, 65; at St. Josephs Bay, 51; strife among, 10; and Tasquique Indians, 49, 50; and Tawasa Indians, 27–28; territory of, 21; in Tiquepache Province, 46

Chacato Province, 21, 58, 85, 88

Chacatos River, 186. *See also* Chattahoochee River

Chaccabi (mission), 22, 23, 24, 26, 27, 29

Chachise Indians, 146

Chacta or Chactos (Spanish term), 6

Chalakagay Indians, 135. *See also* Savannah Indians

Chalaque Indians, 106, 135, 163, 164, 185. *See also* Cherokee Indians

Chalaque Province, 134, 135

Chalaquiliche (Indian). *See* Chislacaliche (Uchise chief)

Chalaquiliche (settlement), 181

Chaliquasliche Indians, 169

Chalique Province, 134, 135

Chalqiliche. *See* Chislacaliche (Uchise chief)

Chaoakle (variation of "Sauocola"), 10

Chaouakle (settlement), 94

Chaquitpe (settlement), 188

Charles Town (Charleston), S.C.: and Apalachicoli Province, 97, 99; and attacks on East Florida, 170; Chisca slaves at, 58; English expeditions from, 67, 86; English traders in, 106; Gov. Quiroga y Losada on, 123; Indian plans to attack, 164; Indians loyal to, 102; Spanish captives in, 134, 135–136; Spanish delegations to, 120, 158; and trade, 128; traders and, 4, 89, 120, 137; treaty signing at, 160; and Yamasee War, 137, 138

Chaschdue (settlement), 181
Chasliquasliche. *See* Chislacaliche (Uchise chief)
Chasta Indians and language, 146
Chata Indians, 65, 78
Chata or Chato (Spanish term), 6
Chatauchi River, 7
Chatot (English term for the Chacato), 6, 24
Chattahoochee River: Apalachee Indians and, 168; and Apalachicola River, 5; Apalachicoli Indians and, 83, 121; Chisca Indians and, 80; cultures along, 15; English and, 121, 123, 124, 159; and Flint River, 93, 96, 103, 104, 148, 149, 160; forts and palisades near, 67, 111, 122, 123–124, 125–126, 127, 145, 192; Indians along, 1, 9; landscape along, 149; languages along, 143; leaders along, 115, 141, 194n3; maps of, 86, 88; Matheos and, 114, 121; and migration, 98, 122, 125, 128, 147–148; missions on, 96, 103, 117; Ocute Indians and, 15, 144; polities along, 92; population along, 18; settlement patterns along, 98; settlements on, 67, 81, 87, 89, 91, 93, 95, 119, 143, 147–148, 149, 152, 168, 175, 179, 187, 192; Shawnee Indians and, 147; Spanish expeditions along, 121; Spanish names for, 5, 89; spies along, 170; Uchee Indians and, 64; Uchize Indians and, 148; Yuchee Indians and, 147
Chattahoochee Valley: Abercrombie phase in, 79–80; agriculture in, 18; Apalachee Indians in, 80, 151–152; Apalachicoli Indians in, 43, 82, 85, 148; archaeology of, 79, 86, 98; Blackmon phase in, 79; Casista Indians in, 82; Caueta Indians in, 80, 82; ceramics in, 19–20; Chisca Indians in, 80, 86; Creek forebears in, 5; cultural traditions in, 5; delegations from, 160; de Soto in, 86; English and, 8, 164; Indians in, 4, 8, 13; Lamar culture in, 19; Lamar occupation in, 79; languages in, 4, 8, 86, 121; late Middle Woodland period in, 79; Middle and Late Woodland periods in, 19; and migration, 4, 8, 82, 98, 126; Mississippian period in, 19; mounds in, 82; Ocute Indians in, 90; origins of peoples of, 80; political organization in, 19; population of, 86, 98, 149; prehistoric occupants of, 18, 79; settlement patterns in, 19; settlements in, 86, 87; Spaniards and, 16; Stewart phase in, 79; Weeden Island cultures in, 19; Yuchi Indians in, 80

Chaugale or Chavagale (settlement), 87, 88, 93–94, 150, 160, 170, 175, 177
Chavagale Indians, 91
Chavagal (settlement), 150
Cheeauhau (settlement), 93
Cherokee Indians: and Apalachicoli Indians, 164; and Chalaque Indians, 163; and Chiluque Indians, 106; and Christianity, 190; and Creek Indians, 138, 165; and English, 138, 184; and slaves, 165; Spanish names for, 106, 135; and Talapuse Indians, 189; and Uchise Indians, 184, 185, 189; and Yamasee War, 137, 138
Cherokee-killer (English term), 6. *See also* Chislacaliche (settlement); Chislacaliche (Uchise chief)
Cherokeeleechee (settlement), 96. *See also* Chislacaliche (settlement)
Chiaha Indians, 15, 148
Chiaha Province, 92, 101
Chiaja (settlement), 188
Chicahiti Province, 116
Chicahûti (settlement), 87, 89–90, 91, 92, 93
Chicases. *See* Chickasaw Indians
Chichimeco (Spanish term), 6, 12
Chichimeco Indians: and Apalachee Indians, 58; and Apalachicoli Indians, 12; in Apalachicoli Province, 54; attacks by, 49, 53, 54, 56, 57, 58, 63, 65; and cannibalism, 54–55, 64, 67, 68; as captives, 12, 54, 58; Chacato Indians on, 65; Chisca Indians on, 58; and English, 53, 58, 59, 110, 111; and Erie Indians, 54; and Guale Indians, 12; languages of, 12, 63, 64; and migration, 58, 102; and non-Christian Indians and provinces, 60, 99; and Oconee River, 85; origins of, 12; origins of name of, 53; in Savannah River valley, 58; scholarship on, 12; and slaves, 58; Spaniards on, 12, 53–54, 56–57; and Spanish withdrawal from Apalachee Province, 67; in Tama, 57; and Tama-Yamasee Indians, 85; and Timucua Indians, 58; and weapons, 55, 58–59, 61
Chichumeco Indians, 193n1 (chap. 3)
Chickasawhatchee Swamp, 14
Chickasaw Indians: and Apalachee Indians, 183; characteristics of, 186; and Christian-

ity, 101, 122–123; and English, 109, 180; and French, 186; Gov. Quiroga y Losada and, 122; and Matheos, 108, 109; origins of, 81; raids by, 95; and Spaniards, 63, 95, 119; and Uchise Indians, 180, 186
Chickasaw Province, 92, 134
Chigelly. *See* Chiquile (Caueta Indian)
Chilacaliche (settlement), 87, 93
Chilacasliche (settlement), 183
Chilacoleche (settlement), 183
Childers, Ronald Wayne, 68, 193n1 (chap. 3)
Chiliquile (chief), 188–189
Chiluca or Chiluque Indians, 105, 106, 176
Chine (Chacato chief), 11, 22, 24–25, 42
Chine (mission), 26–27
Chine (settlement), 88
Chine Indians: and Amacano Indians, 20, 22, 23, 25; and Apalachee Indians, 25; archaeology of, 22; and Chacato Indians, 20, 22, 25; and Chisca Indians, 59; forebears of, 11; and Fort Walton culture, 20; as guides, 24, 77; and Gulf coast, 69, 77; as interpreters, 72; and Lamar culture, 43; languages of, 11, 20, 22, 23, 24, 25, 42, 43, 77; mentioned, 1; and migration, 85; and missions, 24, 25, 26–27, 29, 95; origins of name of, 24; and Pacara Indians, 22, 23, 25; and Pansacola Indians, 69, 72; as pilots, 24, 71, 72; settlements of, 23, 26, 44, 72; Spaniards on, 11; and Spanish expeditions and visitations, 24–25, 44
Chioga (settlement), 181
Chipacafi. *See* Ysipacafi (Caueta Indian)
Chipola Cutoff mound, 21
Chiquile (Caueta Indian), 82, 138, 184
Chisca (Chisca chief), 52
Chisca (on maps), 2, 88
Chisca (Spanish term), 6
Chisca Indians: and agriculture, 62; in Apalachee, 58, 80; and Apalachee Indians, 55; and Apalachicoli Indians, 12, 67; in Apalachicoli Province, 80; attacks by, 33, 37, 41, 46, 49, 53, 55, 56, 59, 65, 67, 68, 104, 128, 131; attacks on, 52, 86; ballgames of, 65; Cacique Miguel on, 40; and cannibalism, 67, 68, 193n1 (chap. 3); and Chacato Indians, 25, 30, 32–33, 34, 41, 45, 57, 60, 63, 65, 66; characteristics of, 53, 55, 63, 64; and Chichimeco Indians, 58; and copper, 52;

culture of, 57; delegations of, 63; descendants of, 15, 64; diet of, 57; and Diocsale, 32, 39–40, 45, 59; and English, 111; expeditions against, 24, 41, 43, 44, 56, 61–62, 63, 66, 70, 96; and firearms, 60; first contacts with, 52, 53, 63; foods of, 63; forebears of, 53; foundaries of, 52; and gathering, 63; and gold, 53; and Gov. Hita de Salazar, 86; and Guale Indians, 56; houses of, 62; and hunting, 57, 63; as interpreters, 12, 54, 56, 58, 63; languages of, 11, 12, 39, 42, 54, 63, 64, 68; leaders of, 57, 86; and Lower Creek Indians, 68; and magic, 61; mentioned, 1, 3, 135; and migration, 33, 52, 80; and missions, 68; and Movila Indians, 66–67; names for, 68; palisades of, 59–60, 62; and Pansacola Indians, 30, 45; population of, 57, 66; revolts by, 33, 55, 63, 80; at San Carlos, 30; at San Nicolás, 30; at San Nicolás mission, 32, 33; and Sauocola Indians, 67; scholarship on, 10, 12, 64–65; as sentries, 61; settlements of, 24, 25, 30, 39, 41, 45, 55, 56, 57, 59–60, 61, 62, 63, 66, 68, 80, 86; as slaves, 58; and Spaniards, 12, 32, 33, 54, 55–57, 63, 64, 67; Spanish terms for, 68; territories of, 52; and trade, 53, 54; and trade goods, 135; and Uchee Indians, 64; and Uchi Indians, 151; and wealth, 52; and weapons, 62, 131; and Yamasee Indians, 86; and Yamasee War, 80; and Yuchi Indians, 68
Chisca Province, 88, 134, 153
Chislacaliche (settlement): attacks on, 167, 170–171, 175; council house at, 149; and English, 177; establishment of, 148; location of, 93, 104, 148, 149, 160, 161; loyalty of, 177; Peña and, 93, 104, 149, 150, 160, 161, 162, 175; Yamasee spies at, 177
Chislacaliche (Uchise chief): and Emperor Brims, 153; and English, 159; and English allies, 170; as leader, 148, 157, 181; and migration, 170; and Peña, 149, 152, 153, 159, 160, 161–162, 165, 171; and Primo de Rivera, 169; and resettlement in Apalachee Province, 162; and Spaniards, 146, 148, 149, 152, 153, 154, 155, 157, 162, 164, 165, 167, 171, 183; and St. Marks, 157, 158, 167; synonyms for, 6, 147, 148, 157; tribal identity of, 147, 148; and Yamasee Indians, 167, 183; and Ysipacafi, 146, 148, 155, 157, 159, 165

228 / Index

Chislacasliche. *See* Chislacaliche (Uchise chief)
Chislala, Pedro, 184
Choctawhatchee Bay, 2, 21, 45, 76, 77
Choctawhatchee River, 30, 59, 62–63, 66, 72, 88
Choctaw Indians: British and, 30; and Christian provinces, 50; and Creek Indians, 139; Díaz Vara Calderón on, 69; hairstyles of, 77, 78; languages of, 21, 77; mentioned, 116, 135; and Pensacola Indians, 21; scholarship on, 6, 22, 24, 50; Spanish terms for, 6, 65; territories of, 28, 29, 81; and Yamasee War, 137
Christianity: Alafae Indians and, 176; Amacano Indians and, 20, 23, 27; Amapira Indians and, 175; Apalachee Indians and, 53, 125, 144, 146, 149, 157, 165, 168, 178, 182; in Apalachee Province, 132, 162; Apalachicoli Indians and, 23, 28, 83, 95, 98, 99, 101; in Apalachicoli Province, 89, 97; Casipuias Indians and, 176; Chacato Indians and, 23, 28, 29–30, 31, 32, 46–47, 48, 49, 51, 131; Chachise Indians and, 146; Chasta Indians and, 146; Cherokee Indians and, 190; Chiaha Indians and, 101; Chichimeco Indians and, 99; Chickasaw Indians and, 101, 122–123; Chiluca Indians and, 176; Diocsale's son and, 39; and gift-giving, 95, 190; Guale Indians and, 140, 145; Guasacara Indians and, 176; Hororo Indians and, 176; Macapiras Indians and, 176; Movila Indians and, 122–123; Oapa Indians and, 145; Pacara Indians and, 27; resistance to, 179; Sabacola Indians and, 89; Sauocola Indians and, 10, 99, 100; St. Augustine–area Indians and, 142; Talapuse Indians and, 159; Tama Indians and, 175; Timucua Indians and, 53, 175, 176; Uchise Indians and, 190; Yamasee Indians and, 143–144, 170, 175, 176, 177, 178; Yoa Indians and, 145
Chuba, Matheo, 129
Chuchiguale Indians, 91
Chuchumeco Indians, 12, 67, 99, 102, 105. *See also* Chichimeco Indians
Churches: and 1647 revolt, 55; at Achercatane, 29; Amacano Indians and, 20, 23; at Atanchia, 29; at Chaccabi, 26; destruction of, 105; at la Encarnación a la Santa Cruz de Sabacola, 89, 97; at San Buena Bentura, 176;
at San Carlos, 29, 30, 44; at San Nicolás, 29, 30, 44; at Santo Domingo de Talaje, 58; at St. Augustine, 176; at St. Marks, 176
Claraquachine. *See* Ochlockonee River
Clothing and accessories: animal skins, 94, 118, 155; belts, 182; boots, 94, 186; buckles, 181; buttons, 181; canes, 155, 157; coats, 186; dresses, 111; English, 130; as gifts, 171, 183, 185, 186; gold on, 157, 186; hats, 118, 155, 156, 157, 159, 186; jackets, 94; leather, 94, 129; Lower Creeks and, 94; neckcloths, 186; pants, 186; ribbons, 182; sandals, 94; sashes, 74–75; shirts, 129, 159, 182, 186; shoes, 74, 186; silver on, 186; skirts, 182; at St. Marks store, 188; stockings, 115; suits, 157; as trade goods, 115, 129, 130, 182; Uchise Indian requests for, 184; Upper Creeks and, 94; waist-jackets, 118; for women, 187. *See also* Trade goods
Cofitacheque (legendary land), 14, 90, 135, 163
Cofitachequi (settlement), 81
Colômme (settlement), 87, 92
Colone (settlement): archaeology of, 93; burning of, 71, 81, 86, 116, 117, 121; on Delagado list, 87; English and, 109, 117; languages in, 7, 91; location of, 7, 93; maps of, 88; Matheos and, 71, 81, 86, 114, 116, 117–118, 121; and migration, 117; rebuilding of, 117, 118; Spaniards and, 119; spies in, 118
Columbus, Ga.: Abercrombie phase near, 79; ceramics in, 19; Indians near, 6, 13, 17, 20, 148, 177; mounds near, 79; and Weeden Island cultures, 19
Connor Collection, 193n1 (chap. 3)
Continuity and Change in Apalachee Pottery Manufacture (Cordell), 51
Convents: Amacano Indians and, 20, 23; architecture of, 44; destruction of, 105; in Havana, 83; listings of, 47, 104; locations of, 44, 58, 104, 176
Coosa (region), 79, 80
Coosa Indians, 13, 15, 16, 154
Coosa River, 2, 15, 81, 88, 90, 135
Coosa River Valley, 1, 5
Coosa-Tallapoosa River country, 15
Copper, 52
Córcoles y Martínez, Francisco de (governor, 1706–1717): assumption of office by, 132; on attacks by English allies, 132–133; and

Chattahoochee Valley émigrés, 148; and Creek Indians, 159; and defenses, 132; and English, 134; and Gov. Craven, 194n3; illness of, 153; and Indian delegations, 153; and Indian gift fund, 140; on Indian settlements, 134–135; and Peña, 152; and Yamasee War, 139, 141
Cordell, Ann S., 51
Corkran, David H., 8, 102–103, 138, 139, 147
Coronado, Francisco de, 70
Cosahue or Cosapue Indians, 145
Cosapuya Indians, 145, 177
Cosapuya Province, 134
Cossate Province, 66
Costa nation Guasacara, 176
Costas Alafaye Indians, 152
Council of the Indies, 123, 154, 172, 173, 179
Coweta (English term), 6, 8
Coweta (settlement), 4, 80, 93, 107, 138
Coweta Indians: and English, 92, 125; languages of, 4, 81; leaders of, 102–103, 148–149; origins of, 81; Spanish policies toward, 46; and Yamasee Indians, 15, 86
Cowkeeper (Indian), 183
Crane, Verner W.: on Casista (settlement), 92; on Caueta (settlement), 92; on Chief Chislacaliche, 147; on English, 159; on French, 159; on origins of "Creek" as tribe name, 8, 191–192; on Spaniards after Yamasee War, 159; on Yamasee War, 137, 138, 139, 159
Craven, Charles, 141, 158, 194n3
Crawford, James M., 7, 76
Creek (language), 7, 11, 12
Creek Confederacy, 1, 3, 80, 92, 102
Creek Indians: in Apalachee Province, 183; archaeology of, 16; architecture of, 44; ballgames of, 65, 66; Benjamin Hawkins on, 64; as captives, 165; and Cherokee Indians, 138, 165; and Choctaw Indians, 139; culture of, 57; delegations of, 155–158, 167–168; and English, 92, 143, 146, 147, 152–153, 159–160, 161, 165–166, 167, 173, 174, 179; English names for, 8; and food preparation, 189–190; forebears of, 13, 15, 94, 137; and forts, 157; and French, 139, 165–166; gatherings of, 167; and hunting, 183; Indian allies of, 139; leaders of, 42, 44, 159; Lower Creek Indians and, 191; and migration, 81, 147, 183; and missions, 139, 143; and neutrality, 143, 165–166, 167; origins of, 17, 81; origins of name of, 191–192; and Peña, 164; political organization of, 42, 103; population of, 138–139; and resettlement of Apalachee Province, 168; scholarship on, 16; and seasons, 44; settlements of, 138, 191; and Shawnee Indians, 135; and slaves, 165, 172; and Spaniards, 139, 143, 146, 159, 165–166; Spanish names for, 6, 8; territories of, 118; and trade, 8, 173, 179; and Uchee Indians, 64; and warfare, 139; and Yamasee Indians, 174; and Yamasee War, 137–138, 179
Crops: beans, 73, 149; of Chacato Indians, 35; chilis, 73; corn, 73, 84, 90, 98, 149, 167; English traders and, 139; figs, 120; maize, 19, 63, 73, 94, 124, 184; pumpkin, 149; squash, 18, 73; tobacco, 57; tomatoes, 73; vegetables, 94; wheat, 28, 84, 98. *See also* Agriculture; Foods and beverages
Cuba: bishop of, 162, 176, 178; friars enroute to, 98–99; friars in, 85, 179; governors of, 180; trade in, 188
Cuchiguâli (settlement), 87, 89, 92, 93
Cummings, Lederer, 54
Cupaica (settlement), 59, 61
Cusabo Indians, 145, 177
Cusseta or Cussita (English term), 6, 8
Cussetuh (settlement), 93

Dallas culture, 5, 18
Debt, 137, 139, 140, 141
DeCrenay, 10, 94
Delaware Indians, 66
Delgado, Marcos: expeditions of, 46, 66, 71, 72, 87, 103–104, 116; as interpreter, 44; and Pansacola Indians, 72
De Soto, Hernando: in Apalachee, 13, 20; and Casiste village, 82; and Chalaque, 163; in Chattahoochee Valley, 86; and Chattahoochee Valley natives, 13; and Chisca Indians, 52; and Cofitachequi, 90; and Coosa Indians, 16; at Coste, 52; expeditions of, 13, 14–15, 69, 98; in Georgia, 144; and Ichisi Indians, 9, 106; in Lower Chattahoochee Valley, 17; and Lower Creek settlements, 90; mentioned, 1, 3, 9, 16, 19, 27, 43, 98; in Oconee Valley, 7; and Ocute Indians, 7, 90; on Tampa Bay, 70; in Upper Creek territory, 17

Díaz Vara Calderón, Gabriel: in Apalachee, 26; on Apalachicoli Province towns, 87, 89, 92, 96, 107; on Chichimeco Indians, 64; on Chisca Indians, 57, 66; and Choctaw Indians, 69; on migration, 85; and Movila Indians, 69; and Pansacola Indians, 69; and Sabacola mission, 89, 93, 96–97; on San Carlos population, 30; at Santa Cruz de Sabacola el Menor, 96; and Sauocola Indians, 95; and Tawasa Indians, 69; visitations by, 95

Diego, Bacta, 36, 37, 45

Diocsale, Juan Fernández de: age of, 42, 45; and Apalachicoli Indians, 33; and Atasi Indians, 66; birthplace of, 53; and Cacique Carlos, 42; and Cacique Miguel, 39; Chacato identity of, 42; and Chacato rebellion, 31–33, 34, 36–37, 39–40, 59, 66; and Chisca Indians, 32, 33, 37, 38–40, 42, 45, 59, 66; and Christianity, 32; as exile, 37, 40; father of, 32; godfather of, 32; as leader, 32, 42; in Mexico, 40; mother of, 32, 33, 53; predecessor of, 42; sons of, 39–40; at St. Augustine, 37, 38, 40; at Tawasa, 36, 37, 45; and Tawasa Indians, 66; wives of, 32, 37, 40

Dog River, 51

Early History of the Creek Indians and Their Neighbors (Swanton), 3

East Florida, 170

Ebanjelista, Juan, 36

Ebelino de Compostela, Diego de, 104

Echagaray, Martín de, 71

Echete (English term), 6

Echete (settlement), 9

Elena (wife of Cacique Carlos), 34, 36

Elvas (de Soto chronicler), 13, 14, 91, 135, 163

Emperor Brims. *See* Brims (Caueta chief)

Enbateguela Indians, 193n1 (chap. 3)

Encarnación a la Santa Cruz de Sabacola (settlement), 89

England, 76, 158, 166, 170, 173, 181–182

English: and Alabama Indians, 173; and Apalachee Indians, 147, 168, 170; and Apalachee Province, 127, 167, 180; and Apalachicoli Indians, 23–24, 48, 50, 67, 103, 106, 111, 124, 131; and Apalachicoli Province, 89, 97, 99, 106–107, 112, 113, 114–115, 117, 118, 119, 126, 165; and Apisca Indians, 170, 175, 177; and Atasi Indians, 105; attacks and seiges by, 65, 121, 131, 132, 177, 183, 185; and cannibalism, 193n1 (chap. 3); as captives, 184; and Casista Indians, 115, 125, 173; and Caueta Indians, 92, 106, 115, 141, 163, 175; and Chattahoochee River Valley, 111, 124; and Cherokee Indians, 138, 184; and Chichimeco Indians, 58, 59, 110, 111; and Chickasaw Indians, 109; and Chiluque Indians, 105; and Chisca Indians, 111; and Chuchumeco Indians, 67, 105; and Coweta Indians, 92, 125; and Creek Indians, 92, 139, 143, 147, 152–153, 160, 165–166, 167, 173, 174, 179; deaths of, 119–120; and Emperor Brims, 138; encroachment by, 139, 182; and forts and palisades, 111, 127, 174, 184, 188; and French, 138; in Georgia, 86; and Gulf of Mexico, 171; and horses, 130, 161; Indian allies of, 76, 102, 129, 139–140, 158, 175, 177–178, 183, 185; and Indian debts, 137, 139, 140, 141; in Indian towns, 135–136; and Indian women, 113, 141, 187; and Lower Creek Indians, 92, 168, 192; names used by, 4, 5, 8, 10; and Pamunkey Indians, 54; and Peña expeditions, 160; reinforcements for, 184; and Ricahecrian Indians, 57; and royal settlement decrees, 116; and Seminole forebears, 190; settlement boundaries of, 160; settlements of, 185; ships of, 86; and slaves, 48, 76, 107, 114, 126, 132–133, 137, 140, 141, 165; and Spaniards, 138–140, 185; Spanish expeditions against, 105, 106–111, 112, 114–115, 119, 121, 123; and Spanish missions, 23–24; spies of, 86; and Talapuse Indians, 170, 175, 177; and Tallapoosa Indians, 115; and Tiquipache Indians, 105; and trade, 8, 48, 126, 173, 181–182; as traders, 15, 59, 86, 89, 103, 105, 115, 121, 128, 139, 173, 174, 177; treaties with, 133, 160, 173, 174; and Uchise Indians, 170, 181, 182–183, 185–186; and Uchize Indians, 105; and Upper Creek Indians, 4, 134; and War of the Spanish Succession, 131; and Westo Indians, 57, 64, 86, 102, 105, 106, 109, 141; and Yamasee Indians, 86, 118, 138, 143, 169–170, 173, 174–175, 177, 182–183, 187; and Yamasee War, 137, 138; and Yuchi Indians, 147

Epidemics: of 1702, 49; and 1717 Peña expedition, 164; of 1729, 179; Chacato Indians and, 45, 49; of the mid-seventeenth century, 45; Natuaques/Naturaques Indians and, 163; and population, 17; Spaniards and, 28. *See also* Illnesses and injuries
Erie Indians, 54, 57, 58
Escambé (mission): Apalachee Indians at, 35, 38, 50; attacks on, 38, 130; Chacato Indians at, 25; Chisca Indians and, 41; leaders at, 41, 48; location of, 47; refugees at, 104; visitation to, 47, 48
Escambe (settlement), 134
Escambia River, 2, 69, 88
Escobedo, Joseph, 151, 163-165
Esfan (Apalachee men's name), 11. *See also* Ysfane, Juan
Eslaque, Francisco, 125
Estanani (settlement), 71
Estanani Indians, 78
Etowa (settlement), 2
Euchee (English term), 6
Euchee Indians, 138-139
Euchito (settlement), 153
Euchitto (settlement). *See* Achito (settlement)
Euchitto Indians, 9
Eufala (settlement), 93, 150, 175, 177
Eufalan Indians, 188
Euhaw Indians, 142
Europeans, 3, 21, 70, 77
Ewches (settlement), 91

Fairbanks, Charles, 153, 183
Felipe (Chacato Indian), 45
Fernández de Ecija, Francisco, 145
Firewood, 133, 181, 183
Fishermen, 73
Fishing, 30, 73, 190
Flint River: ambushes along, 24, 49, 50, 65, 130-131; and Chattahoochee River, 93, 96, 103, 104, 148, 149, 160; cultures along, 15; Delgado and, 104; de Soto and, 14, 17; languages along, 43; maps of, 2, 86, 88; missions on, 96, 103; settlements on, 93, 104, 148; Spanish names for, 96; Toa Indians and, 14
Florencia, Claudio de, 43
Florencia, Diego de, 119, 150, 151
Florencia, Francisco de, 129
Florencia, Joaquín, 47
Florencia, Juan Fernández de: in Apalachee, 22; brother of, 35, 36, 43; on Cacique Miguel, 40, 41; and Chacato rebellion, 33, 36, 37, 44; on Chaccabi (settlement), 22; and Chine Indians, 24; and Chisca Indians, 39, 41; and Diocsale, 33; father of, 43; informants for, 41; languages of, 36, 43; and missions, 23, 26, 30; on Pacara Indians, 27; on population, 25; at San Carlos, 35; and son of Gov. Hita Salazar, 60
Florencia, Matheo Luis de, 56
Florencia, Patricio de, 127
Florencia, Pedro de, 35, 36, 43
Florida: architecture in, 14; communication with, 84, 85; in early 1680s, 70; epidemics in, 45; food shortages in, 127; Indians in, 9, 28; languages in, 7, 11, 21, 42; maps of, 2; Pansacola culture in, 76-77; Pansacola Indians in, 73; post-1708, 183; scholarship on, 3, 28; settlement patterns in, 14; ships in, 84; shortages in, 127; Tawasa Indians in, 27; town size in, 14; west coast of, 11
Florida Caverns State Park, 31
Florida Master Site File, 21
Foods and beverages: acorns, 189; alcoholic beverages, 163; at battle scenes, 50; bear meat, 47, 94; beef, 49; breads, 189, 190; buffalo lungs, 73, 193n1 (chap. 4); buffalo meat, 73, 74, 94, 149; cakes, 190; China briar (zamia), 190; chocolate, 164; coonte (bread), 190; deer meat, 94; entrails, 193n1 (chap. 4); firewater, 164, 182, 188, 189; fish, 73; flours, 189, 190; French and, 76; fruits, 48, 168; as gifts, 185; ginger, 74; grapes, 47; gruel, 190; hickory nuts, 189, 190; honey, 182, 190; maize cakes, 94; maize tortillas, 72; meats, 63, 76, 166, 167, 189; mentioned, 133; military expeditions and, 61, 62; molasses, 188; mussels, 74; nuts, 47, 57, 149; oils, 189, 190; oysters, 48, 73; palm hearts, 94; pemmican, 74; preparation of, 73, 74, 189-190; pumpkin seeds, 73; roots, 94; rum, 139, 146; shortages of, 174, 184; smoked, 63; sugar, 182, 188; sweet cakes, 164; sweetmeats, 154; as trade goods, 139, 146, 174, 188, 189; tree roots, 57; vegetables, 94; wine, 154. *See also* Crops

Ford, Lawrence Carroll, 173, 177
Forts and palisades: abandonment of, 127, 171; in Alabama Province, 169; in Alabama territory, 166; on Altamaha River, 174; among Apalachicoli Indians, 104; Apalachee Indians at, 48; in Apalachee Province, 86, 106–107, 129, 157, 158, 160, 162, 163, 164, 166–169; in Apalachicoli Province, 48, 67, 93, 119, 145; architecture of, 119, 124, 129, 171, 173; at Caueta, 188; on Chattahoochee River, 122, 123–124, 125–126, 127, 145; construction of, 127, 166, 167, 180; Creek, 158; destruction of, 127, 172; English and, 111, 174, 184; French fort, 166, 169, 171–172, 173; locations of English forts, 110–111; Matheos and, 110–111; at Mobile, 173; at or near St. Augustine, 39, 84, 143, 153, 163, 182; at San Luis, 50; at San Luis de Talimali, 129; settlements near, 162, 168–169, 170, 171, 176, 178–179, 180, 187, 189; sizes of, 111; Spanish fort and migration, 104, 119, 122, 163, 164, 166–168, 175; on St. Josephs Bay, 171–172; at St. Simons Island, 184; stores at, 187–188, 189; supplies for, 158, 166, 167, 171–172, 189. *See also* St. Marks, Fla.: forts at and near
Fort Walton (place), 21
Fort Walton Complex, 21
Fort Walton culture: archaeological sites associated with, 21; ceramics from, 14, 19, 21; housing from, 14; Indians and, 11; locations of, 20–21, 76; and Pansacola culture, 76, 77; specific tribes and, 14, 20, 30, 43
Foundries, 52
France: and England, 158; La Salle's departure from, 71; mentioned, 169; and Quadruple Alliance, 166, 173; and Spain, 158, 173, 177; treaties with, 173
Franciscans: in 1730s, 179; in Apalachee, 20, 22; at Chaccabi, 26; commissaries general of, 83–84, 85; council of, 125; and Gov. Quiroga y Losada, 125, 126, 128; in Guale, 57; leaders of, 125; in Madrid, 83–84; provincials of, 26, 29, 33, 83, 95, 97–98, 99, 125
French: in Alabama Province, 169; and Apalachee Indians, 50–51; attacks by, 172–173, 183; censuses by, 135; and Chacato Indians, 50–51; and Chickasaw Indians, 186;

and Creek Indians, 165–166; diet of, 76; and English, 133, 138; forts of, 166, 169, 171–172, 173; on Gulf coast, 24; and Gulf of Mexico, 171; at Havana, 127; Indian contacts of, 171; and Indian women, 187; killing of, 170–171; military forces of, 171; and Mississippi River, 70; at Mobile, 50–51, 76, 171; names used by, 10; and Pansacola Indians, 76; and Ricahecrian Indians, 57; and Spaniards, 24, 138; at St. Augustine, 171; and St. Josephs Bay, 171–172; at Tampa ("Holy Spirit") Bay, 116; and trade, 76; and trade goods, 182; as traders, 174; and Uchise Indians, 185; and Upper Creek Indians, 139; weapons of, 173; and Yamasee War, 159
Fretwell, Mark E., 93–94, 96, 107
Friars: and Amacano Indians, 20; in Apalachee Province, 23; and Apalachicoli Indians, 12; in Apalachicoli Province, 82, 99, 105; arrivals of, 97; attacks on, 26; and Chacato Indians, 86; at Chacato mission, 47; on Chichimeco refugees, 102; and Council of the Indies, 179; in Cuba, 83, 85; on English activities, 86–87; expulsions of, 92; and forts, 125; and gift-giving, 99; and Gov. Torres y Ayala, 126, 128; in Havana, 179; and Indian languages, 181; as liaisons, 23; losses at sea of, 98–99; in Marianna region, 86–87; recruitment of, 84, 98; requests for, 82, 85, 95, 96, 98, 101; and revolts and uprisings, 55, 98–99; at Sauocola, 35, 67, 95; and Sauocola Indians, 97; from Spain, 179; at St. Augustine, 179, 181; at St. Marks, 178, 179; and Tama-Yamasee Indians, 85–86; and weapons, 128
Fuentes, Francisco de, 167

Gainesville, Fla., 132, 187
Galloway, Patricia, 135
Garcilaso de la Vega (the Inca), 13, 14, 27, 52, 90
Gardiner, William R., 21, 31
Gaspar, Ubapt, 25
Gaspar, Hubabaq, 44
Gathering, 47–48, 63
Gatschet, Albert, 7, 9
Georgia: Apalachee Indians in, 187; Apalachicoli Indians in, 82, 129; archaeological

sites in, 93; boundaries of, 182; Casista Indians in, 82; Casista (settlement) in, 93; Caueta Indians in, 82; Coosa Indians in, 154; de Soto in, 144; English in, 86; establishment of, as colony, 182; Guale Indians in, 56; Indians in, 4; languages in, 148; Middle Woodland settlements in, 79; and migration, 121; Mocama Indians in, 146; relocated settlements in, 122; and Spanish-Indian contact, 1; Spanish raids on, 116; Tama Indians in, 15; Tama-Yamasee Indians in, 98; Tama-Yamasee territory in, 86; Uchise Indians in, 187; Weeden Island period in, 79; Westo Indians in, 15, 86, 98; Yamasee Indians in, 89; Yoa Indians in, 145
Glover, Charlesworth, 147, 177
Gold, 53
González Barcia Carballido y Zúñiga, Andrés, 73–74, 193n1 (chap. 4)
Governorship of Spanish Florida, 1700–1763, The (TePaske), 3
Grammont, Monsieur de (French schooner captain), 116
Green, William, 54
Guacara (mission). *See* San Juan de Guacara (mission)
Guacara (settlement), 152, 170, 175, 183
Guacara Indians, 171
Guacara River, 157
Guale (language), 106, 156
Guale Indians: Apalachee Indians and, 187; attacks on, 12, 58; as captives, 185; and Chaschi Indians, 146; and Chichimeco Indians, 12; and Chisca Indians, 56; and Christianity, 145; and English, 120; as interpreters, 140, 184–186; languages of, 145; leader of, 140; mentioned, 1, 12; and migration, 145; and missions, 8, 146; and privateers, 120; settlements of, 187; sexual mores of, 32; at St. Augustine, 140; on St. Marks store, 187; territories of, 174; tribes of, 142; and Uchise Indians, 185; and Yamasee Indians, 142, 187
Guale Province, 32, 56, 57, 58
Guanaytique (settlement), 53
Guasacara Indians, 176
Güemes y Horcasitas, Juan Francisco de, 180

Guides, 9, 24, 38, 43, 61, 77
Gulf coast: Amacano Indians and, 22; Chine Indians and, 69, 77; Council of the Indies on, 172; de Soto expedition and, 13; English ships and, 86; Fort Walton culture along, 21; French and, 24; Indian cultures along, 76; late-seventeenth-century Spaniards and, 70; prehistoric Indians and, 30; Weeden Island culture along, 19
Gulf of Mexico: English and, 171; forts near, 157; French and, 171; maps of, 2; and Mississippi River, 70; navigation in, 84; pirates in, 70; ports near, 157; river system reaching, 16
Gums, Bonnie L., 51
Gutiérrez de la Vera, Francisco, 102

Haas, Mary R., 7
Hace, Pedro, 104
Hahn, Steven C.: on 1705 British-Indian treaty, 133; on 1715 Indian delegation, 193n1 (chap. 7), 193n2 (chap. 7); on 1717 English-Creek treaty, 160; on Apalachicoli Indians, 67, 85; on Chicahuti (settlement), 87; on Emperor Brims, 194n3; on friars, 85; on Hillabee (settlement), 91; on Ilapi (settlement), 91; on Tama leader, 193n1 (chap. 7); on Westo Indians, 57
Halley, David J., 3
Hastings, Theophilus, 173
Havana, Cuba: Barroto expedition in, 72; French and, 127; friars in, 83, 179; military shipments from, 158; and pirates, 84; privateer from, 120; trade with, 157
Havana Company. *See* Royal Company of Havana
Hawkins, Benjamin: on Big Sauocola, 93; on Creek Indians, 42, 64; on fishing, 190; on Indians' daily lives, 189; on Sauocola Indians, 10; on Uchee Indians, 12, 64
Haze, Pedro de, 128
Hernández, Antonio Monilla, 135
Herrera, Antonio, 34–35
Herrera López y Mesa, Antonio de, 20, 28, 81
Higginbotham, Jay, 75
Hilibi (English term), 13
Hilibi Indians, 13
Hillabee (settlement), 91

Hita Salazar, Pablo de (governor, 1675–1680): on Apalachicoli Indians, 44, 95; on Cacique Miguel, 41; and Chacato rebellion, 35, 39, 44; on Chiluque Indians, 105; and Chisca Indians, 41, 57, 60, 86; on Chisca settlements, 66; on Chuchumeco Indians, 105; and Diocsale, 38; and English, 97; and friar, 86; and Gulf coast exploration, 70; on Indians and Christianity, 97–98; on missions, 99–100, 105; and Pansacola Indians, 69; son of, 60; and successors, 128; on Uchize Indians, 105

Hitchetee (settlement), 93

Hitchiti (English term), 6, 9

Hitchiti (language): and Apalachee language, 7, 12, 151; Apalachicoli Indians and, 101; English names for, 9; Lower Creeks and, 6; and Mikasuki language, 7, 151; as Muskogean tongue, 11; and Muskogee, 7; Peña on, 8; places spoken, 4, 7, 9, 17, 43, 80, 81, 86, 90, 91, 98, 115, 143, 145, 148, 151, 152; scholarship on, 7, 8; Spanish names for, 8, 9; speakers of, 143, 148; and Yamasee language, 7, 9, 91

Hitchiti (settlement), 9, 93, 181

Hitchiti Indians, 8, 92

Hoffman, Paul E., 3

Hogtown Bayou-Point Washington (variant of Pansacola culture), 77

Holiwahali Indians, 13

Holland, 166, 173

Holy Gospel Province, Mexico, 84

Holy Spirit Bay, 70, 71, 116, 123. *See also* Mobile Bay; Tampa Bay

Hooseche (English term), 6

Hororo Indians, 176

Huacara (settlement), 183

Hudson, Charles: on Capachequi chiefdom, 14; on Chisca territory, 52; on Creek forebears, 3; on de Soto expeditions, 13–15; on Indian languages, 9; on Ocute (settlement), 90; on settlement patterns, 14; on Toa chiefdom, 14–15; on town size, 14; on Ylapi (settlement), 90

Hunting: and ambushes, 135; Apalachee Indians and, 30; Biloxi Indians and, 76; Chacato Indians and, 47, 49, 63, 129; Chisca Indians and, 57, 63; Creek Indians and, 183; Indian delegations and, 158; on land, 21; locations for, 187; Lower Creeks and, 94; Pansacola Indians and, 76; and seasons, 30; Spaniards and, 166, 167; and Spanish captives, 135; supplies for, 190; Uchee Indians and, 64; Upper Creeks and, 94

Huron territory, 54

Hurricanes, 16, 120, 133, 149

Ibaja (language), 145

Ibiniute Province, 55

Ibiniuti, 36, 43

Ichisi (language), 9

Ichisi (Spanish term), 6

Ichisi Indians, 8–9, 15, 106

Ichisi Province and settlement, 15

Ilapi (settlement), 90

Ilcombe mission. *See* Escambé (mission)

Illnesses and injuries, 94, 100, 110, 111. *See also* Epidemics

Inca. *See* Garcilaso de la Vega (the Inca)

Indians of the Greater Southeast: Historical Archaeology and Ethnohistory (McEwan), 4

Inquiries, Spanish: into 1675 Chacato rebellion, 32, 33, 36–38, 39–40, 43, 44; into 1676 Chisca attacks, 38, 39–41, 44; on 1704 Spanish withdrawal from Apalachee Province, 67–68; into lands and natives of Tama region, 52

Interpreters: Apalachee Indians as, 44, 125, 151, 152, 161; and Apalachee language, 11; Apalachee speakers as, 25; at British-Indian treaty ceremony, 133; Chacato Indians as, 25, 36, 43; and Chacato rebellion inquiries, 36, 43; Chine Indians as, 72; Chisca Indians and, 33; Chisca Indians as, 12, 54, 58, 63; documents by, 183; Guale Indians as, 140, 184–186; Ichisi Indians as, 9; Indians as, 53; as messengers, 33; Sauocola Indians as, 10; Spaniards and, 11, 43; Spaniards as, 10, 36, 43, 44, 101, 150, 151, 152, 156, 161, 163–165; Timucua Indians as, 36, 43; and Uchi language, 9, 151, 162; Yamasee Indians as, 119

Iroquois (language), 55

Iroquois Indians, 54

Isfane (Apalachee girl), 11

Isidoro de León, Juan, 184

Istopoyole (Nicunapa Indian), 193n2

Itaba Indians, 15

Itoyatin (Virginia Indian), 54
Ivitachuco (mission), 38, 59, 112, 132

Jacan. *See* Virginia
Jackson, Jason Baird, 65, 66, 68
James River, 54
Joara (location), 52, 53
Johnson, Robert, 160
John Worth Collection, 194n3
Jones, B. Calvin, 26, 31
Jororo Indians, 133, 175
Jororo Province, 132
Juaquín (Chacato Indian), 31–32, 33, 36, 37–38, 45
Jufala (settlement), 181
Juiaui (Indian), 113
Juuchufca, Paal, 181

Kaeledji Indians, 133
Kasihta (English term), 6, 8
Kasihta (settlement), 80
Kasihta Indians and settlement, 4
Kealedji Province, 150
Kerrigan, Anthony, 193n1 (chap. 4)
Knight, Vernon James, Jr.: on annexation of Indian refugees, 92; on archaeological phases and cultures, 17, 18, 76; on Casiste (settlement), 91; on ceramics, 18; on Chattahoochee Valley sites, 17, 79–80; cited by Braley, 19; on Creek and Seminole forebears, 3; on Creek archaeology, 5, 16; on Creek Confederacy, 80, 92, 102; on Ichisi Indians, 9; on origins of Chattahoochee Valley peoples, 80; on Pansacola culture, 77; on population, 17
Koasati (language), 7, 91. *See also* Alabama-Kosati (language)
Koasati Indians, 154
Kolomoki (settlement), 11, 19, 79
Kuseetaw Indians, 15, 86

Lactama (settlement), 171, 175, 183
Lamar culture, 5, 14–15, 17, 19, 43, 79
Lamar Mound site. *See* Ichisi Province and settlement
Lamhatty (Indian), 86, 147
Lamhatty manuscript, 86
La Mobila Province, 116, 168

La Movila, 116
Lanning, John Tate, 103
La Salle, René-Robert Cavalier de, 70–71, 72, 123
La Tama (settlement), 114, 140. *See also* Altamaha (settlement)
Latama (settlement), 170
La Tamaja (settlement), 140. *See also* Altamaha (settlement)
Late Woodland period, 19
Lawson Field phase, 20
León, Alejandro Thomás de, 120
Leonard, Irving: on Chacato Indians, 6, 24; on Chief Chine, 22; on Choctaw Indians, 24; and Milán Tapia account, 62; on Pansacola charnal house, 75; on Pansacola Indians, 73, 75; translation of Sigüenza y Góngora by, 193n1 (chap. 4)
Le Soledad (settlement), 172
Leturiondo, Domingo de: and Apalachicoli Indians, 10, 83, 84, 103, 112, 119; on Big Sauocola (settlement), 95; as deputy-governor, 85; and English, 112; on languages, 12; in Madrid, 83, 85; and Sauocola Indians, 10, 11; visitations and expeditions by, 46, 85, 113
Levasseur, Charles, 75–76
Literacy, 42
Little Sauocola (settlement), 93, 95
Little Sawokli (English term), 6
Little Tennessee River, 52
London, England, 173
Losada, Domingo, 179
Louisiana, 76, 177
Lower Chattahoochee River, 20. *See also* Chattahoochee River
Lower Chattahoochee Valley, 4, 9, 16, 17, 18. *See also* Chattahoochee Valley
Lower Cherokee Towns, 138
Lower Creek country, 15
Lower Creek Indians: and agriculture, 94; and Apalachee Indians, 168; and Apisca Indians, 177; archaeology of, 16, 17; characteristics of, 94; and Chisca Indians, 68; clothing of, 94; cultural assemblages of, 5; descendants of, 190, 191; and Emperor Brims, 137, 163; and English, 168, 177, 183, 192; forebears of, 1, 15, 105, 174; and gifts, 180; and Green Corn Ceremony, 94; and hunting, 94; languages of,

Lower Creek Indians—*continued*
6, 18, 143; leaders of, 80, 147; and medicinal herbs, 94; and migration, 18, 192; and neutrality, 143; origins of name of, 6, 8, 192; and Peña, 160, 161–162, 180; population of, 17, 18; and prototypes of Creek Confederacy, 102; and resettlement of Apalachee Province, 168, 180; scholarship on, 1, 3, 16; settlements of, 4, 6, 9, 17, 68, 80, 90, 91, 143, 148, 177, 180, 181, 183, 191; and Spaniards, 6, 147, 148, 180, 183, 192; Spanish names for, 8, 80; in St. Augustine, 179; and Talapuse Indians, 177; and trade, 192; and Uchee Indians, 12; and Upper Creek Indians, 102; and warfare, 94, 161; and Yamasee Indians, 177; and Yuchi Indians, 68. *See also* Creek Confederacy; Creek Indians; Upper Creek Indians

Lower Creek Province, 134

Lower Towns (of Yamasee), 140, 142

Lower Yamasee Indians, 15

Luis, Coquita, 37

Luis de Caracas, Francisco, 184–186, 187

Luna, Pedro de, 125

Luna, Tristán de, 16, 69

Mabila Indians, 15

Macapiras Indians, 176

Macon, Ga., 1, 8–9, 15, 121, 124

Madrid, Spain, 70, 83, 173, 182

Magnolia Plantation, 14

Malatchi (Caueta Indian), 82

Manaytique (settlement), 53

Mandeville (settlement), 19

Manucy, Albert, 60

Maps: by Alonso Solana, 38, 103; anonymous, 91; of Apalachee Province, 26; Apalachicola River on, 56, 86, 123; Chacato settlements on, 38, 51; Chattahoochee River and settlements on, 86, 88; Chisca villages on, 45; by DeCrenay, 10, 94; Flint River on, 86; by John White, 54; by Juan Enríquez Barroto, 123; by Lamhatty, 86; by Lederer Cummings, 54; missions on, 27, 46, 103; by Pineda, 70; Rickohockan Indians on, 54; rivers on, 26; Spanish, 45, 56; of Virginia, 54

Marcos, Juan, 159, 168, 172, 173, 180

Mariana, Chuguta, 48

Marianna, Fla.: archaeology near, 21; buffalo in, 149; Chacato forebears and, 30; Chacato Indians and, 5, 20, 21, 22, 38, 44, 45, 86, 95; Diocsale in, 53; friars at, 86–87; missions near, 30, 38, 61, 105; population density at, 31; prehistoric sites in, 31; Spanish expeditions at, 96

Marianna Lowlands, 21

Marine ecology, 21

Márquez Cabrera, Juan (governor, 1680–1687): and Apalachee Province, 100; and Apalachicoli Indians, 100–101, 122; and Apalachicoli Province, 100, 105, 112; and Caueta Indians, 92, 102; and Chicahiti Province, 116; desertion of post by, 116, 121; and Emperor Brims, 101–102, 152; Fray Barreda and, 92; on geography west of Apalachee, 71; and Holy Spirit Bay, 71; and interpreters, 12; and La Mobila Province, 116; and Matheos, 113–114, 117, 121; mentioned, 10, 120; and missions, 100; and Sauocola Indians, 100; successor to, 122; on Tabasa Province, 116; and westward territories, 116

Martín, Cutca: on Cacique Carlos, 42; and Chacato rebellion, 32, 34, 35, 36, 37, 40; children of, 35; and Chisca Indians, 37, 39, 45; on Diocsale, 40, 42; escape by, 39; in Florida, 35; as leader, 32, 34, 35, 39; pardoning of, 39; Pedro (son of Diocsale) on, 39; sentencing of, 40–41; at St. Augustine, 39; at Tawasa, 37, 39; wife of, 35

Martín, Teresa, 53

Martínez, Francisco, 52

Matamoros, Juan Pedro, 171

Matheos, Antonio: and Apalachee Indians, 112; and Apalachicoli Indians, 67; background of, 106; on Big Sauocola, 10, 95, 107; burning of Apalachicoli villages by, 71, 81, 86, 121, 123; characteristics of, 106; on Chata Indians, 78; and Chief Pentecolo, 108–109, 112–113; on Chine Indians, 77; and Delgado expeditions, 103; on Estanani Indians, 78; expeditions of, 71–72, 105, 107–111, 112, 113–120, 119, 121, 123; on geography west of Apalachee by, 71; and Pansacola Indians, 72, 78, 103; removal of, 121; and Woodward, 109

Mavilla (settlement), 69

Mayaca Province, 132, 133

McGillivray, Alexander, 4, 191

McKee Island culture, 18
Medicines, 94
Medina, Juan de, 83
Memorial (Pez), 73
Memphis, Tenn., 52
Menéndez, Luisa, 53
Menéndez de Aviles, Pedro, 177
Menéndez Marques, Francisco, 132
Messengers, 10, 11
Mexico: communication with, 84, 85, 131; Diocsale in, 40; La Salle and, 70; nomads in, 53; northern, 53; ports in, 70; provinces in, 84; Spaniards in, 53; Spanish forces from, 173; trips to, 159, 167, 180; vice-regal court in, 159; viceroys of, 70, 71, 72, 84, 123, 131, 140, 159, 165, 170, 172, 175
Mexico City, Mexico, 159, 165
Middle Woodland period, 18–19, 79
Migration: during 1690s, 9; Achito Indians and, 148; Amacano Indians and, 85; Apalachee Indians and, 50–51, 80, 91, 137, 146, 168, 180; and Apalachee Province, 85, 132, 191; Apalachicoli Indians and, 84, 98, 121, 137, 148; and Apalachicoli Province, 82, 85, 86; archaeology of, 98; and Atasi Province, 150; and attacks on missions, 38, 45, 142, 143; Casista Indians and, 81, 82, 125, 148; Caueta Indians and, 82, 148; and ceramic styles, 19; Chacato Indians and, 27–28, 38, 44, 45–46, 50–51; and Chacato Province, 85; and Chacato rebellion, 10, 45; and Chattahoochee River, 98, 122, 125, 128; and Chattahoochee Valley, 8, 82, 98, 126; Chiaha Indians and, 148; Chichimeco Indians and, 58, 102; Chickasaw Indians and, 81; Chine Indians and, 85; Chisca Indians and, 33, 52, 80; Chuchumeco Indians and, 67; Costa Alafaye Indians and, 152; Coweta Indians and, 81; Creek Indians and, 81, 147; and cultural change, 79; eastward, 8; Erie Indians and, 54; Eufala (settlement) and, 150; and European settlement, 1; and forts, 104, 119, 122, 163, 164, 166–168, 175; Fray Moreno on, 86; Guale Indians and, 145; and Kealedji, 150; Kolomi Indians and, 150; Lower Creek Indians and, 192; and missions, 97, 128; and Mobile, 173; Musgogulges and, 191; and Ocmulgee River, 8; Oconi Indians and, 9; Ocute Indians and, 90; Pacara Indians and, 85; Pansacola Indians and, 76; and Pensacola, 173, 181; and population, 18; Sauocola Indians and, 11, 46, 85, 95, 103, 126; Savacola Indians and, 148; Shawnee Indians and, 147; Spaniards and, 49, 171; and St. Augustine, 137, 141–143, 146, 181; Tama Indians and, 15; Tama-Yamasee Indians and, 85, 86, 98; Taskiki Indians and, 148; Tasquique Indians and, 89; Tawasa Indians and, 27–28, 50, 105; Tocobaga Indians and, 85; Uchise Indians and, 121; and Virginia, 12, 54; and warfare, 170; warriors and, 85; Westo Indians and, 57, 64, 86; Yamasee Indians and, 15, 89, 118, 124, 141–142, 145, 171, 189; and Yamasee War, 4, 7, 8, 80, 82, 87, 137, 138, 142, 146, 147–148, 179; Ysica Indians and, 80; Yuchi Indians and, 80
Miguel (Chacato cacique): age of, 45; and Chacato rebellion, 34, 36, 37; and Chisca Indians, 37, 41; detention of, 39; Fernández de Florencia on, 40; and Fray Paiva, 37, 39; as leader, 34, 37, 41; and Pedro (son of Diocsale), 39; release of, 37, 39; at royal works, 37, 40; and Spanish investigations, 39; at St. Augustine, 39, 40, 41; at Tawasa, 36, 37, 45
Mikasuki (language), 7, 151
Mikasuki Indians, 9, 145, 151, 190, 191
Milanich, Jerald T., 76, 77
Milán Tapia, Francisco, 62–63
Milling, Chapman J., 139, 142, 145
Mines, 169
Missions: agriculture at, 149; Apalachee Indians and, 146, 168; archaeology of, 30; attacks on, 8, 49, 54, 55, 58, 59, 105, 106, 119, 128, 130, 131–132; censuses and lists of, 25, 27, 104, 168; Chacato, 87; Chacato Indians and, 25, 29, 46–47, 61; Chine, 25, 26–27; Chisca Indians and, 68; Col. James Moore and, 50; Creeks and, 139; destruction of, 26, 49, 106, 121, 136, 139, 141, 142, 143, 149; Franciscan, 20; Guale Indians and, 120, 146; locations of, 8, 24, 25, 26, 27, 56, 58, 61, 68, 92, 93, 95–97, 99–100, 127, 139, 149, 150, 166, 167, 168; maps of, 88, 103; populations of, 25, 56, 146, 168; relocations of, 24, 26, 27; as response to English contacts, 97; threats to, 23–24, 112; Yamasee Indians and, 141, 168

Mission San Luis, 92, 121–122
Mission San Nicolas, 10
Mississippian cultures, 5, 15, 20, 79, 92
Mississippian period, 16, 19
Mississippi (state), 4, 24
Mississippi River, 70, 71, 72, 116, 123
Mistovich, Tim S., 17, 18, 19
Mobila River, 169
Mobile, Ala.: Apalachee Indians and, 50–51; ceramics in, 51; Chacato Indians and, 50–51; Chine Indians and, 69; Creek Indians and, 139; English and, 76; forts at, 173; French and, 50–51, 76, 139, 171; and Gulf of Mexico, 16; and migration, 173; newspapers in, 51; Pansacola Indians and, 76; population of, 50–51; and Spanish-Indian contact, 1; Ysipacafi at, 172
Mobile Bay: ceramics from, 21; de Soto and, 69; harbors in, 13; and Holy Spirit Bay, 123; Indian cultures along, 76; Indians along, 72; map of, 2; Pansacola Indians on, 75; settlements on, 71; Spanish expeditions to, 24
Mocama Indians, 106, 146, 152
Moloa (settlement), 56
Montgomery, Ala., 1, 27, 72
Montiano, Manuel de (governor, 1737–1749), 180, 181–182, 184, 186–187, 188, 190
Moore, James: Apalachee Indians and, 137, 146; and Apalachee Province, 50; Apalachicoli Indians and, 137; attacks by, 131–132, 136; and fort at San Luis, 50; Indian captives of, 50, 68; and missions, 26, 50; as South Carolina governor, 131; Spanish captives of, 50
Moral, Alonso del, 26, 29
Moral Sánchez, Francisco del (governor, 1734–1737), 182
Moreno, Juan, 83, 84, 85, 86, 95, 98
Moscoso (settlement), 43
Mounds: Abercrombie phase, 18, 79; archaeology of, 31; Casista Indians and, 82; centers for, 21; Chacato Indians and, 21; in Chattahoochee Valley, 82; functions of, 31; locations of, 90; in Lower Chattahoochee Valley, 17, 18; platform, 17, 79; and political organization, 18, 21; as population centers, 18; sizes of, 79, 90
Moundville, Ala., 19
Mount Pleasant, 147
Movila (settlement), 2, 77

Movila Bay, 71
Movila Indians: and Apalachee Indians, 183; attacks by, 46, 135; and Chacato Indians, 46; and Chisca Indians, 66–67; and Christianity, 122–123; Delagado and, 66; descendants of, 15; Díaz Vara Calderón on, 69; and English allies, 76; Gov. Quiroga y Losada and, 122; Matheos on, 71–72; and Pansacola Indians, 48, 72, 75, 76; and Spaniards, 119
Moyano, Hernando, 52, 53
Moze (location), 176
Muscogee (language), 4–5, 7, 8, 11, 91, 135, 190
Muscogee (word), 8
Musgogulge Indians, 191
Muskogee (language): and Apalachee language, 11; Hilibi Indians and, 13; and Hitchiti language, 7; and Koasati language, 7; places spoken, 13, 80, 81, 151; scholarship on, 7; terms from, 106
Muskogee Indians, 8, 68, 80, 92
Myths and legends, 80, 81, 82

Nahuatl (language), 53
Narváez, Panfilo de, 27, 69
Natuaques/Naturaques Indians, 163
Navarette, Melchor de, 190
Navia, Alvaro de, 83
New Georgia, 187
New Spain, 40, 159, 172
Nicolás (Chacato Indian), 36, 45
Nicunapa (settlement), 140
Nicunapa Indians, 193n2
Niquilache (settlement), 183
Nolichuky River, 52
Nombre de Dios Amacarise (location), 176
Nombre de Dios Chiquito (location), 176
Nuñez Cabeza de Vaca, Alvar, 77

Oakfuskee Indians, 133
Oapa Indians, 144, 145
Ocaña, Francisco de, 23
Ocatase Indians. See Catase Indians
Ocatoses (settlement), 26
Ocheese (settlement), 9
Ocheesee (English term), 6, 8
Ocheesee Indians, 138–139
Ocheesee River. See Ocmulgee River
Ocheesehatche. See Ocmulgee River

Ochese Creek, 192. *See also* Chattahoochee River
Ochesee Creeks (English term), 6
Ochesee or Ochise Creek. *See* Ocmulgee River
Ochise Creek, 8
Ochlockonee River, 25, 47, 97
Ochus or Ochuse (settlement), 13, 69
Ocmulgee (settlement), 90, 181, 188
Ocmulgee National Monument. *See* Ichisi Province and settlement
Ocmulgee River: Apalachicoli Indians and, 82, 129; Casista Indians and, 82; Caueta Indians and, 82; Creek Indians and, 15; cultures along, 15; de Soto and, 15; English and, 8, 127; Indians along, 8–9; languages along, 43, 148; location of, 8–9; Lower Creeks and, 91; maps of, 2; and migration, 8, 119; names for, 4, 15; settlements along, 15, 127, 192
Ocmûlgui (settlement), 87, 92
Ocmulque (settlement): Apalachee Indians and, 170; burning of, 129; English and, 114, 170; languages in, 91; location of, 87, 110, 129; maps of, 88; and Matheos expeditions, 110, 114; and Peña, 150; population of, 150; and Spanish retaliatory expedition, 129; Yamasee Indians and, 170
Ocmulque Indians, 133
Ocomulgee (settlement), 188
Ocone (settlements): Angulo at, 125; attacks on, 170, 175, 177; and forts, 125; gatherings at, 125; languages in, 91, 162; leaders of, 168; locations of, 90, 129, 188; as Lower Creek village, 181; and Peña expedition, 162; and relocation, 153; Spaniards and, 129, 188
Ocone (Spanish term), 9
Oconee River: Apalachicoli Indians and, 82; Casista Indians and, 82; Caueta Indians and, 82; Chichimeco Indians and, 85; cultures along, 15; Indians along, 12; Indians near, 9; Indian territory near, 1; languages along, 43; Lower Creeks and, 91; and migration, 119; Ricahecrian Indians and, 85; Westo Indians and, 85
Oconee River Valley, 1, 7, 144
Ocone Indians, 9, 183
Oconi Indians, 9
Oconi or Ocôni (settlement): leaders of, 167; location of, 87, 89, 108; maps of, 88; and Matheos expeditions, 108, 114; mentioned, 7; Peña on, 92–93; relocation of, 93; towns north of, 89
Oconi Province, 60
Ocuia (chiefdom), 10, 11
Ocumulque (settlement), 175, 177
Ocute, Alonso (Yamasee cacique), 143
Ocute Indians: chiefs of, 7–8; descendants of, 15; forebears of, 7, 144; languages of, 9, 145; and migration, 90; settlements of, 15, 90
Ocute or Ocuti (settlement), 8, 87, 89, 90, 91, 114, 118, 124, 143–144, 193n1 (chap. 7)
Ocute Province, 15
Ogchay (settlement), 46
Ogechee (location), 12
Oglethorp, James Edward, 181, 182, 183
Oigonets (settlement), 51
Okchai (settlement), 46
Okchai Indians, 133
Okfuskee Indians, 4–5
Oklahoma, 66, 68
Oliver, Pedro de (governor, 1717), 154
Onondaga Indians, 57
Ooseeochee (settlement), 93
Orchards, 149, 166
Orta, Juan Fernández de, 165, 167
Ortes, Pedro de, 28–29, 81
Osuche (settlement): and Apalachee Indians, 170; council house at, 113; English and, 113, 114, 170, 175, 177; languages in, 90, 91; location of, 91; and Matheos expeditions, 109, 114, 115; and Yamasee Indians, 170
Osuchi (settlement), 7, 87, 88, 92–93, 181, 188
Our Lady of Candelaria De La Tamaja (settlement), 143, 144

Pacara Indians: and Amacano Indians, 20, 22, 23; in Apalachee, 27; archaeology of, 22; and Chacato Indians, 22; and Chine Indians, 22, 23, 25; and Christianity, 27; first contacts with, 22, 23–24; forebears of, 11; and Fort Walton culture, 20; and Lamar culture, 43; languages of, 11, 20, 22, 23, 25, 42, 43; mentioned, 1; and migration, 85
Paiva, Jaun de: and Cacique Miguel, 37, 39; and Chacato rebellion, 35, 36, 45; documentation by, 38; at San Carlos, 35; and son of Gov. Hita Salazar, 60
Palachacola or Palachocola (settlement), 147, 148

Palachecolo or Palachicolo (settlement), 175, 177
Palachocolas Fort (location), 147
Palachoocle (settlement), 93
Palatine, Craven, 126
Palica (settlement), 176
Palmer, John, 177
Pamunkey Indians, 54, 58
Pancho (Yamasee Indian), 189
Panhandle (Fla.), 1, 4, 19, 86
Pansacola (meaning of), 78
Pansacola (settlement), 2, 10–11, 69
Pansacola culture, 76–77
Pansacola Indians: and agriculture, 63, 77; and Apalachicoli Indians, 48, 75; archaeology of, 76; attacks by, 41, 75; attacks on, 72; and canoes, 72; and Chacato Indians, 30, 45, 70, 77; and Chine Indians, 69; and Chisca Indians, 30, 41, 45, 70; and English allies, 76; first contacts with, 69; as fishermen, 73; in Florida, 73; food supplies of, 72; forebears of, 11; and French, 75–76; hairstyles of, 77; and hunting, 76; languages of, 77; maps of, 2; mentioned, 1; and migration, 76; and Movila Indians, 48, 72, 75, 76; population of, 76; separate identity of, 76; settlements of, 48, 61, 72, 75–76, 77; and Spaniards, 11, 41, 60, 69–70, 72–73, 75, 77, 103; and trade, 76; and weapons, 72; and white refugees, 73
Pansacola Province: Apalachee Indians and, 50; Chacato Indians and, 50; governor of, 137, 164; Matheos and, 71; mentioned, 24; raids in, 133–134; Spanish captives in, 135; Tawasa Indians and, 50; Ysipacafi in, 162–163
Parachocolas Fort (location), 147
Pardo, Juan, 52, 53
Patale (settlement), 38, 59, 134
Payne's Prairie, 132, 149
Pedro (son of Diocsale), 39–40, 59–61, 62
Peña, Diego: on Achito (settlement), 9; and Apalachee Province, 180, 183; and Apalachicoli Province, 92–93, 94; and Chief Chislacaliche, 171; on Chislacaliche (settlement), 104; on Emperor Brims, 141; and English, 174; on English allies, 170–171, 177–178; expeditions of, 148, 149–153, 159, 160–165, 166, 169, 194n3; on French, 183; on languages, 7, 8, 9, 10, 91, 151–152; on Oconi, 93; on plans to attack Chattahoochee Valley settlements, 175; and Sabacola (settlement), 96; as St. Marks commander, 170; in Tasquique, 7; on Tasquique Indians, 89; on Uchee or Uchi Indians, 9, 64; use of "Uchisi" by, 8; and Yamasee Indians, 151, 171
Pensacola, Fla.: Apalachee Indians and, 168; attacks and sieges at, 133–134, 139, 172–173, 177; Caueta Indians and, 172; Chacato Indians and, 51; Chisca Indians and, 68; communication with, 131; Creek Indians and, 139, 167; defenses at, 171, 173; as English-French buffer, 177; European settlement at, 16; expeditions to, 62–63; Gov. Córcoles y Martínez at, 131; governors of, 158, 159, 171; Indian delegations at, 179; Joseph Primo de Rivera and, 171; loss of, 171, 178; and migration, 173, 180, 181; missions at, 68; Orta at, 167; scarcity at, 159; settlements at, 180; Talipuse Indians and, 165, 172; trade with, 179; Ysipacafi at, 165
Pensacola Bay: accounts of, 73; agriculture along, 73; as boundary, 42; Cabeza de Vaca at, 77; ceramics from, 21; Chacato Indians at, 48; expeditions to, 24, 47, 48, 67; Fray Barreda at, 31; Gov. Torres y Ayala at, 96, 126, 128; harbors in, 13; Indian settlements along, 16, 69, 72, 73, 75; maps of, 2; Pansacola culture along, 77; Spanish settlements on, 49, 69
Pentecolo (Apalachicoli chief): age of, 115; on English, 109; languages of, 115; and Leturiondo, 112; as liaison with Spaniards, 100, 108–109, 113, 115, 148; and Matheos, 108–109, 112–113, 114, 117; nephew of, 110; as Peace Chief, 115; son of, 110, 113
Péres, Andrés, 29, 30, 33, 34–35, 57, 66
Pérez, Antonio (soldier-interpreter), 156
Pérez, Jacinto Roque (lieutenant in Apalachee), 129
Perier, Etienne, 177
Pez, Andrés Matías, 73, 75, 154
Phelipe (Chacato Indian), 36
Picolata (location), 191
Pilots, 24, 25, 71, 72, 123, 188–189
Pineda, Alonso Álvarez de, 70

Pirates and privateers, 70, 71, 84, 120, 184
Plants, 16, 110, 149, 161, 190. *See also* Agriculture; Crops; Trees
Pocosapa (settlement), 144, 145
Pocotalaca or Pocotalaga or Pocotalago (settlement), 137, 140, 141, 142, 144, 145
Poco Talaqua (settlement), 176
Pocotaligo (settlement), 140
Pojoy Indians, 9, 22, 168
Priests, 32, 47, 101, 114, 125, 178–179
Primo de Rivera, Enrique, 123, 124, 125, 145
Primo de Rivera, Joseph (José): appeal for supplies by, 171; and attacks on Spanish allies, 168–169; background of, 145; census by, 142, 143, 145, 146; and Emperor Brims, 167, 169; expeditions by, 158, 166–167, 169; and Indian delegations, 166–168; and Indian gathering at Caueta, 167; on languages, 145; on Ocute Indians, 145; and resettlement of Apalachee Province, 167–168, 169; as St. Marks fort commander, 166, 169; and Tocopacas Indians, 167; and Yamasee Indians, 145, 171

Qua (Apalachee woman): and Emperor Brims, 11, 92, 146, 152, 161, 165; and English, 146, 161, 163; and migration, 122; sons of, 11, 146, 165; and Spaniards, 146
Queen Anne's War, 131
Quilate (Uchise leader), 186, 188
Quiroga y Losada, Diego de (governor, 1697–1693): and Apalachee Indians, 123; and Apalachee Province émigrés, 122, 123, 127; and Apalachicoli Indians, 119, 122, 123; and Apalachicoli Province, 122; and Caueta Indians, 127; and Chattahoochee River fort, 104, 119, 121, 122, 123, 124, 127; and Council of the Indies, 123; Crown's instructions to, 119, 122–123; and English, 119, 123, 126; and Franciscians, 125, 126, 128; and missions, 127, 128; and rebuilding of burnt villages, 123; reports of, 126; and Spanish expeditions, 119, 121, 123; and successors, 128; and Tawasa Indians, 127; and Tiquepache Indians, 127; and Yamasee Indians, 123
Quisca, Francisco Ya (or La), 144
Quizquiz (location), 52

Rangel, Rodrigo, 13, 52, 90, 135, 163
Rebolledo, Diego de, 57
Red River, 81
Ricahecrian Indians, 12, 53–54, 56, 57, 85. *See also* Chichimeco Indians
Ricahokene (settlement), 54
Rickohockan Indians, 54, 58
Riguj (settlement), 57, 58
Rio Chachave, 26, 27
Rio Lagna. *See* Ochlockonee River
Rio Pansacola, 60, 66
Riqueherron Indians. *See* Ricahecrian Indians
Riquehronnon Indians. *See* Erie Indians
Rituals and ceremonies: adoption, 190; Apalachicoli Indians and, 84; ballgames as, 65, 66; baptism, 29, 95, 100, 159, 175, 176, 190; body painting, 74; bowing, 155, 156; calumet ceremony, 159; cannibalism, 54–55, 64, 164, 193n1 (chap. 3); chanting, 156; for chiefs' visits, 15; cremation, 74–75; dancing, 53, 149, 153, 154, 157, 163, 164; fasts, 168; feasting, 154, 157, 163, 164, 167, 186; firing volleys, 149, 150, 153, 156, 163, 164; gestures during, 155; gift-giving, 9, 15, 72, 99, 154, 159, 164, 167, 171, 172, 180, 185, 186–187, 190; Green or Great Corn Ceremony, 66, 94; La Paloma, 157, 163, 164; locations for, 65–66, 149; mourning-war, 55; objects for, 61, 72, 74, 75, 105, 155, 156, 159, 163, 164, 193n1 (chap. 3); regaling, 181; singing, 157, 163, 164; sympathetic magic, 61; toasts, 156; Yuchi and, 65–66
River Agna. *See* Ochlockonee River
River of the Chacatos, 5. *See also* Apalachicola River; Chattahoochee River
River of Uchise. *See* Ocmulgee River
Robles, Blas de, 126
Rock Arch Cave, 31
Rojas y Borja, Luis de (governor, 1624–1630), 22
Roldán, Juan, 171
Romo de Urisa, Francisco, 49, 50, 65
Rood phase, 17, 19–20, 79
Roxas, Joseph de, 134, 135
Royal Company of Havana, 181, 184, 187, 188
Royal works, 37, 40
Ruíz de Salazar Vallecilla, Benito (governor, 1645–1646, 1647–1650), 28, 79, 81, 83

Sabacola (mission), 93, 96–97
Sabacola El Menor (mission), 96. *See also* Sauocola (mission)
Sabacola Indians, 89, 90, 91, 96
Sabacola or Sabacôla (settlement): 87, 92; Chacato Indians and, 40, 104; Chisca Indians and, 96; languages in, 90, 91; locations of, 90; as Lower Creek village, 181; mentioned, 59; and Ocuia chiefdom, 10–11; Peña on, 96
Sabacola or Sabocola (Spanish term), 6, 10–11
Sabacola the greater (settlement), 92
Sabacola the lesser (settlement), 92
Sabocola River, 45, 59
Salamototo (settlement), 132
Salas, Simón de, 120
Salinas, Joseph de (interpreter), 36
Salinas, Juan de, 53
Salinas Varona, Gregorio de, 137, 158, 159, 164, 179–180
Salquicha (settlement), 141
Saltketchers (location), 12
Salvador, Diego, 36, 43, 44
San Antonio (mission), 168
San Antonio de los Chines (mission): and Chacato rebellion, 33; leaders of, 32, 37, 39, 40; location of, 27; and migration, 45
San Buena Bentura (church), 176
San Buena Bentura de Palica (mission), 146
San Buenaventura y Tejada, Francisco de, 179
San Carlos (mission): abandonment of, 38; archaeology of, 31; Chacato Indians and, 32, 33, 35, 36, 61; and Chacato rebellion inquiries, 36, 44; Chisca Indians and, 30, 38, 61, 63; Christian Indians at, 30, 46; church at, 30, 44; convent at, 44; council house, absence of, 44; Fernández de Florencia at, 35; Fray Barreda at, 32, 33–34; Fray Paiva at, 35; granary at, 44; leaders of, 30, 32, 33, 35, 36, 37, 39, 40, 42, 45; location of, 31; maps of, 46; and migration, 45; population of, 30, 46
San Carlos (settlement), 2, 72, 104, 169
San Carlos de Çabacola (Sauocola mission), 41, 46, 47, 104
San Carlos de los Chacatos (mission): attacks on, 47, 48, 68, 96, 128; location of, 68, 96
Sánchez Griñan, Pedro, 94
San Jorge. *See* Charles Town (Charleston), S.C.
San Juan (settlement), 162, 168, 176, 178
San Juan de Guacara (mission), 121, 122, 128

San Luis (settlement): Apalachee Indians and, 35, 50, 61; Chacato Indians and, 34, 36, 47–48, 49; Chief Pentecolo in, 117; council house at, 47; expeditions from, 47, 67; Florencia family in, 119; garrison at, 26; Gov. Torres y Ayala at, 126; leaders of, 46, 47–48, 61, 112, 129; location of, 28, 96; maps of, 2, 88; Matheos and, 113, 118; mentioned, 96, 108, 117; and missions, 26, 27; Pansacola Indians and, 72; plans to attack, 130; resettlement of, 182; settlements near, 46; spies at, 118; and St. Augustine, 131; stores at, 187; and trade, 49
San Luis de Apalachee, 92
San Luis de Talimali (settlement): Apalachee Indians and, 51; ceramics at, 51; Chacato Indians and, 38; and Chacato rebellion, 36, 44; Chisca Indians and, 41; council house at, 44; fort at, 129; leaders of, 38, 41; mission, 132; plaza at, 44
San Marcos. *See* St. Marks, Fla.
San Nicolás (mission): abandonment of, 38; Chacato Indians and, 33, 41; Chisca Indians and, 30, 32, 33, 37, 40; church at, 30, 44; convent at, 44; leaders at, 33, 34, 35, 36, 39, 45; location of, 31; and migration, 45; population of, 30
San Nicolás (on map), 2
San Nicolás de los Chacatos (mission), 46, 60, 104
San Pedro de los Chines (mission), 26–27
San Pedro de Medellin (mission), 27
San Simón (mission), 105
Santa Catalina (Guale mission), 120
Santa Catalina (mission), 105
Santa Catalina de Ajoica (Timucua mission), 106, 119
Santa Catharina de Guale (settlement), 140
Santa Cruz, river of, 96. *See also* Apalachicola River
Santa Cruz (settlement), 2, 34, 105
Santa Cruz de Sabacola (mission), 103
Santa Cruz de Sabacola el Menor or Lesser (settlement), 89, 95, 96, 97
Santa Cruz de Sauocola (mission), 33, 88, 95–96, 97, 113, 114
Santa Elena Province, 106, 118
Santa Fé or Fée (mission), 24, 49, 56, 130
Santa Lucia de Acuera (mission), 36, 43, 56

Santiago (Chacato Indian), 35, 36, 37, 45
Santo Domingo de Talaje (mission), 58
Sartouche forest, 167, 169, 171
Satiquicha (settlement), 193n2
Sauacola or Sauocola (Spanish term), 6, 10
Sauocola (mission): and Chacato mission, 103; and Chacato rebellion, 95–96; collapse of, 95, 104, 126; dangers to, 112; Delgado and, 104; friars at, 95; location of, 38, 93, 96, 103, 112; Matheos and, 107, 108, 114, 117; population of, 95, 104, 126; relocation of, 104. *See also* San Carlos de Çabacola (Sauocola mission)
Sauocola (settlement): Apalachicoli Indians and, 100; and Apalachicoli Province, 10; Christian Indians in, 100; council house at, 149; friars and, 35, 67; houses at, 149; Joseph Primo de Rivera and, 167; languages in, 151; leaders of, 100, 107, 149; location of, 46, 67, 87; maps of, 88, 94; and migration, 10; and missions, 100; Peña and, 149, 162; population of, 150; relocation of, 85
Sauocola chicasa (settlement), 87
Sauocola Chuba (settlement), 88
Sauocola el Grande (settlement), 95, 107
Sauocola El Menor (Spanish term), 6
Sauocola Indians: and Apalachee Indians, 11, 91; in Apalachee Province, 100; and Apalachicoli Indians, 104, 126; attacks by, 44, 47, 48, 68, 104, 128; and Caueta Indians, 46; and Chacato Indians, 50, 104; and Chisca Indians, 41, 67, 96; and Christianity, 10, 99; English names for, 10; European names for, 10; forebears of, 11; and friars, 46, 96; as interpreters, 10; languages of, 10, 91, 152; leaders of, 41, 95–96, 99, 100, 112; as messengers, 10, 11; and migration, 11, 46, 85, 95, 103, 126; and missions, 47, 48, 68, 95, 97, 100, 104, 128; and Peña expedition, 160; settlements of, 11, 46, 97, 148; and Spaniards, 10, 96; as spies, 107, 108
Sauocola River, 11, 45
Sauqoogolo (English variation of "Sauocola"), 10
Sauwoogaloochee (English term), 6
Sauwoogelo (English term), 6
Savacola (male Apalachee name), 91
Savacola (settlement), 2, 188
Savacola, the other (settlement), 188

Savacola Indians, 27
Savana Indians, 138–139
Savannah culture, 15
Savannah Indians, 106
Savannah River: Apalachee Indians and, 146; Apalachicoli Indians and, 82; Casapuya Indians and, 145; cultures along, 15; and migration, 119, 147; as settlement boundary, 160; settlements on, 81, 148; Shawnee Indians and, 147; Yuchee Indians and, 147
Savannah River district, 137
Savannah River Valley, 58
Savanna Indians, 135
Savocola (settlement), 153
Savocola Indians, 148
Sawokli (English term), 6
Sawokli (settlement), 90, 94, 153
Sawokli (variation of "Sauocola"), 10
Scalps, dancing of, 185
Schnell, Frank T., 3, 17, 19, 20
Seecoffee. *See* Ysipacafi (Caueta Indian)
Seepeycoffee. *See* Ysipacafi (Caueta Indian)
Seminole (language), 151
Seminole Indians: ballgames of, 65; forebears of, 3, 13, 94, 137, 181, 190–191; languages of, 7; origins of name of, 181, 190–191; scholarship on, 3
Shawnee (language), 8, 13
Shawnee Indians, 57, 66, 135, 147
Shells, 74, 75
Shinholser (archaeological site), 90, 144
Shipwrecks, 134, 188
Shoulderbone (archaeological site), 90, 144
Sigüenza y Góngora, Carlos, 73–75, 193n1 (chap. 4)
Silver, 169
Silver Bluff (location), 12
Sincapafi. *See* Ysipacafi (Caueta Indian)
Singer phase, 17
Sioux (langauge), 135
Slaves: children as, 139, 140, 141; Creek Indians and, 172; English and, 76, 126, 137, 139, 140, 141; Indians as, 48, 57, 58, 76, 104, 106, 107, 114, 126, 129, 132–133, 137, 139, 141, 165, 167, 172; runaway, 191; in South Carolina, 133; terms for, 191; in West Indies, 126; Westo Indians and, 57; women as, 139, 140, 141
Smith, Marvin T., 3, 4, 13, 90

Solana, Alonso, 26, 38, 46
Solana, Juan, 148
Solana, Manuel, 65, 67, 68
South Carolina: Casapuya Indians in, 145; and Creek Indians, 160; Cusabo Indians in, 177; Florida Indians in, 120; governors of, 129, 131, 133, 134, 141, 158, 160, 173, 194n3; Guale Indians in, 145; Indian allies of, 138, 173; Lower Yamasee Indians in, 15; population of, 133; slaves in, 133; Spanish delegations to, 174; trade with, 173; Yamasee Indians in, 140, 142; and Yamasee War, 137, 138
Sowoolla (English variation of "Sauocola"), 10
Spain: communication with, 84; Echagaray in, 71; and England, 158; and France, 158, 173, 177; friars in, 84, 98, 179; migration from, 171; and Quadruple Alliance, 166, 173; recall of Moral Sánchez to, 182; treaties with, 170, 173
Spaniards: and Apalachee Province, 58, 121–122; and Apalachicola Province, 10; as captives, 185; in Caribbean, 41; and Chacato Indians, 11, 25; and Chichimeco Indians, 12, 55, 58; and Chine Indians, 11, 24, 25; and Chisca Indians, 12, 56, 63; and contact outside Florida, 1; and Creek Indians, 143; and English, 138–140; exiled, 49; and French, 24, 138; and Indians spies, 7; and interpreters, 11, 12, 43; as interpreters, 10, 36, 150, 151, 152, 163–165; on languages, 43; in Lower Chattahoochee Valley, 4; and Lower Creeks, 6; and names of Indian groups, 4; names used by, 5–6, 10, 25; and Pansacola Indians, 72; and Sauocola Indians, 10; as scouts, 56; spellings used by, 26; on sympathetic magic, 61; and terms for Indian leaders, 41; and trade, 28; and Yamasee War, 139–140, 159
Spanish (language), 36, 51, 155, 181
Spanish Approach to Pensacola, 1689–93 (Leonard), 6
Spring Creek, 26, 96
St. Augustine, Fla.: Apalachee Indians and, 146, 168, 187; Apalachicoli Indians and, 12, 50, 81, 101; architecture at, 133, 154, 155, 156, 157; attacks and seiges at, 58, 131, 132, 133, 139, 174, 181, 182, 183–184, 185; Cacique Miguel at, 39, 40, 41; Caueta Indians at, 92, 101; censuses of, 142, 143; children at, 181; Chisca Indians and, 39, 55, 63; church at, 176; convent at, 176; Creek Indians and, 139; Cutca Martín at, 39; Diocsale at, 37, 38, 40; drunkenness at, 181; Emperor Brims at, 80, 152; English prisoners at, 134; epidemics at, 179; forts at and near, 39, 41, 84, 143, 153, 163, 164, 182; French at, 171; friars at, 23, 179, 181; government officials at, 140, 154, 163; Guale Indians at, 140; and hurricanes, 133; and Indian delegations, 140, 141, 148, 150, 152, 153–154, 155–158, 159, 179, 184, 186; Indian gift fund at, 140; inquiries held at, 32, 44, 52, 53; and Matheos expeditions, 108; mentioned, 125, 149, 158, 160, 161; and migration, 7, 8, 137, 141–143, 146, 181; military at, 71, 127, 143, 160; official buildings at, 153, 163, 164; pastors of, 64; and Peña expeditions, 152, 153, 162–164, 169; Pojoy Indians at, 22; population near, 133, 143; settlements near, 55, 118, 132, 133, 141–146, 168, 174–177, 178, 179, 181, 183; ships at, 167; shipwrecks near, 134; Spaniards exiled from, 49; and St. Marks expedition, 167; threats to, 143; Timucua Indians and, 55; trade with, 179; Uchise Indians and, 181, 188; vulnerability of, 127; weapons at, 143; women at, 181; Yamasee Indians at, 141–142, 177; Yllache Indians at, 164
St. Catherines Island, 105
St. Charles Borromeo, 29
Stetson Collection, 94
Stewart, John, 122, 125
Stewart phase, 17, 19, 79
St. George. *See* Charles Town (Charleston), S.C.
St. Helena, 15, 86
Stincard (language). *See* Hitchiti (language)
St. Johns River, 56, 132, 152, 182, 184, 191
St. Johns River Valley, 55
St. Josephs Bay, 51, 171–172, 178
St. Marks, Fla.: architecture at, 188; Chine Indians and, 24; church at, 176; Eufalan Indians at, 188; Fernández de Florencia and, 26; forts at and near, 157, 158, 162, 163, 164, 166–169, 170, 171, 172, 175, 176, 178–179, 180, 184, 187–188; friars at, 178, 179; Gov. Torres y Ayala at, 128; and hunting parties, 187; Indian delegations at, 167–168; Lower Creek Indians and, 180; and Matheos expedi-

tions, 71; and Peña expeditions, 169; pilots at, 188–189; as port, 26, 157, 158, 164, 167; settlements near, 167, 168–169, 170, 171, 175, 176, 178–179, 180, 187, 189; store at, 182, 184, 187–188, 189; Talapuse Indians at, 169; taverns at, 187; Yamasee Indians at, 176

St. Nicolas de Tolentino, 29

Stores, 181, 182, 184, 187–188, 189. *See also* Trade goods; Traders

St. Simons Island, 105, 152, 184

Summer house, Creek, 44

Suwannee River, 22, 152

Suwannee River Valley, 22

Swaglaw (English variation of "Sauocola"), 10

Swanton, John R., 3; on Altamaha language, 145; on Amacano Indians, 24, 43; on "Apalache," 90; on Apalachicoli village, 82; on Atasi Indians, 13; on Capecheque Indians, 43; on Casapuya/Cosahue/Cusabo Indians, 145; on Casista (settlement), 81; on Casiste (settlement), 90–91; on Chacato Indians, 28, 43; on "Chalaque," 135; on Chatot Indians, 24; on Chichimeco Indians, 12; on Chief Chislacaliche, 147; on Chiluque Indians, 106; on Chine Indians, 24, 43; on Chisca Indians, 12, 64; on Cosapuya Indians, 177; on Creek Confederacy, 80; on Cusabo Indians, 177; on derivation of "Hitchiti," 9; on Florida Indian languages, 42–43; on Green Corn Ceremony, 94; on Hillabee (settlement), 91; on Ilapi (settlement), 91; and Lamhatty manuscript, 86; on Mikasuki Indians, 145; on Muscogee terms, 135; on "Ochesee," 8; on Ocute language, 145; on Pacara Indians, 43; on Pansacola Indians, 77, 78; on Savanna Indians, 135; on Sioux speakers, 135; on Ticopache occupants, 13; on Uchi Indians, 9–10; variation of "Sauocola" by, 10; on west Florida Indians, 28; on Westo Indians, 64; on Yamasee Indians, 24, 43, 142, 145; on Yoa Indians, 145; on Yuchi Indians, 64

Tabasa Indians. *See* Tawasa Indians

Tabasa Province, 116

Tactipique (Talapus cacique), 157

Tacusa or Tacûsa (settlement), 91, 92, 93

Tacûsi (settlement), 87

Tacussa (settlement), 87, 88, 114

Tahogale (settlement), 94

Talapusa Indians, 167, 170, 173

Talapuse Indians: in Alabama Province, 169; and allegiance to Philip V, 169; and Apalachee Indians, 175, 177; attacks by, 175, 177; and Cherokee Indians, 189; and Christianity, 159; English and, 170, 175; leaders of, 169; mines of, 169; at Pensacola, 177, 179; as Seminole forebears, 190; settlements of, 159, 170; Spaniards and, 180; and Uchise Indians, 175, 189

Talapuse Province, 161, 169

Talapus Indians, 3, 80, 150

Talapus Province, 150, 153, 155

Talapuze Indians, 135

Talapuze Province, 134–135

Talasi (settlement), 166, 169

Talasje (fort), 174

Talespuche Indians, 137

Talessi, 159

Talichasliche. *See* Chislacaliche (Uchise chief)

Tali Indians, 94

Talipasle (settlement): languages in, 91; location of, 87, 91; maps of, 88; and Matheos expeditions, 107, 108, 109, 113

Talipasli (settlement), 94

Talipuse Indians, 158, 159, 165, 172

Talipuse Province, 165, 166

Talischasliche. *See* Chislacaliche (Uchise chief)

Talisi (Indian leader), 13

Talisi (settlement), 159, 180

Talisi Indians, 13, 15

Talisi Province, 13, 82, 91, 126

Talissi Indians, 137

Talissi Province, 115

Talladega County, Ala., 13

Tallahassee, Fla., 1, 167

Tallapoosa (region), 79, 80

Tallapoosa Indians, 4–5, 115, 116, 180

Tallapoosa River: and Coosa River, 90; cultures along, 15; Delgado expedition to, 87; Kolomi and, 150; lower, 5; maps of, 2, 88; and migration, 81; polities along, 92; settlements along, 5, 82, 148

Tallapoosa River Valley, 1, 5

Tallasse Indians, 190, 191

Talleboosee Indians, 138–139

Tama (mission), 144
Tama (settlement), 26, 27
Tamagitas (settlement), 134, 135
Tamahita Province, 134
Tama Indians: attacks on, 175; and Christianity, 175; farms of, 160; locations of, 15; and migration, 15; settlements of, 15, 44; Spaniards and, 98; as spies, 117, 118; and visitations, 44
Tamaja Indians, 144
Tama Province, 52, 57, 58, 85, 193n1 (chap. 7)
Tamasle (settlement): agriculture at, 189; attacks on, 175, 179, 187; English and, 175, 187; establishment of, 180; leaders of, 169, 170, 175, 177; location of, 175, 180; Peña and, 183; surrender of, 187; Uchise Indians and, 179; Yamasee Indians and, 170
Tamaxle New (settlement), 181
Tamaxle the Old (settlement), 181
Tama-Yamasee (territory), 12, 86
Tama-Yamasee Indians: in Apalachee Province, 85, 118, 119; in Apalachicoli Province, 119; and Chichimeco Indians, 85; and Chiluque Indians, 106; and friars, 85; and Hitchiti speakers, 86; languages of, 98; and migration, 85, 98; and missions, 24; raids against, 98; Spaniards and, 86; Spanish names for, 106; as spies, 117
Tampa Bay, 22, 70, 71, 152
Tampico, Mexico, 70, 84
Tapia, Francisco Milán, 45
Tarihica (mission), 56, 121
Tascaliche. *See* Chislacaliche (Uchise chief)
Taskiki Indians, 148
Tasquique (settlement): burning of, 71, 81, 86, 116, 117, 121, 129; English and, 109, 113, 117; languages in, 7, 91, 151; location of, 7, 87, 93, 129, 161; maps of, 88; and Matheos expeditions, 71, 81, 86, 110, 113, 116, 117–118, 121; and Peña expeditions, 150, 161; population of, 150; rebuilding of, 117, 118; and relocation, 87, 153; scholarship on, 7; Spaniards and, 119, 129
Tasquique (Spanish term), 6
Tasquique chief, 141
Tasquique Indians: and Chacato Indians, 49, 50; languages of, 89, 91, 162; Matheos and, 118; and migration, 89, 117; murders of, 49, 50; and Peña expeditions, 162; spies in, 118; as traders, 49, 50
Tatepique (Talapuse cacique), 155
Tawasa (settlement): Bacta Diego at, 37, 45; Cacique Miguel at, 37; Chacato Indians at, 35, 36, 44; Coquita Luis at, 37; Cutca Martín at, 37, 39; Diocsale at, 37; maps of, 2, 88. *See also* Ocatoses (settlement)
Tawasa Indians: in Apalachee, 27, 46; and Atasi Indians, 105; and Chacato Indians, 27–28, 33; Díaz Vara Calderón on, 69; Diocsale and, 66; Gov. Quiroga y Losada and, 127; leaders of, 46; and migration, 27–28, 50, 105; settlements of, 27; threats against, 105; and Tiquipache Indians, 105
Tawasa Province, 2, 45, 72, 104, 115
Teguala or Teguale (settlement), 165, 167
Tennessee, 1, 4, 18, 53
TePaske, John Jay, 3, 174
Terrazas, Juan Bauptista, 56
Thamasle (settlement), 183
Thick Greenbriar site, 21
Thomole (rebel Apalachee), 134
Ticopache (settlement), 13. *See also* Tiquepache (settlement)
Ticopache Province, 115. *See also* Tiquepache Province
Tiguale (settlement), 134, 135
Timucua (language), 106, 146, 152
Timucua Indians: and Alafae Indians, 176; and Apalachicoli Indians, 49; attacks on, 53, 175; and Chichimeco Indians, 58; and Chisca Indians, 53; and Christianity, 53, 55, 175, 176; immolation of, 49; as interpreters, 36, 43; leaders of, 41; and missions, 24; at Pocosapa, 144; revolt by, 98–99; settlements of, 1, 22, 55; Spaniards on, 41
Timucua Province: Apalachicoli Indians and, 128; attacks on, 33, 38, 60, 128, 132, 133; borders of, 28; Chichimeco Indians and, 60; Chisca Indians and, 33, 55, 56; Christianity in, 23, 55, 132; missions in, 49, 55, 56, 132; raiding parties from, 23; Spaniards and, 29, 46, 99; Westo Indians and, 86; Yamassee Indians and, 38
Tiquepache (settlement), 129
Tiquepachee (Spanish term), 6. *See also* Ticopache (settlement); Ticopache Province

Tiquepache Indians: in Apalachee Province, 129; attacks by, 48, 68, 128; attacks on, 129; Gov. Quiroga y Losada and, 127; and missions, 48, 68, 128; and Spanish captives, 137; treaties with, 159

Tiquepache Province, 46, 126

Tiquipache Indians, 104, 105, 129

Tiquipache Province, 124

Tiritera (ship), 127

Tixjana (Indian), 159, 165, 180

Toa Indians, 14–15

Toalli (settlement), 14, 15

Tocobaga Indians, 44, 85, 180

Tocopaca Indians, 167, 168–169

Togulki (Caueta Indian), 82

Tohepakaliga or Tohopekaliga Indians, 190, 191

Torres y Ayala, Laureano de (governor, 1693–1699): and Apalachicoli Indians, 48, 121, 128; background of, 126, 128; on Chattahoochee River fort, 121, 126; on Chief Chine, 24; on English, 128; expeditions by, 24, 47, 48, 75, 96; and Gov. Quiroga y Losada, 128; as governor-elect, 126; journal of, 25; and missions, 121; at Pensacola Bay, 126, 128; and Spanish retaliatory expedition, 129

Tospe (Yamasee cacique), 143

Totopotomoy (Pamunkey Indian), 54

Trade: Apalachee Indians and, 123; Apalachicoli Indians and, 28, 48, 81, 123; with Apalachicoli Province, 83; in Caribbean, 182; Chisca Indians and, 53; Creek Indians and, 8; English and, 8, 48; French and, 76; and Matheos expeditions, 123; Pansacola Indians and, 76; Spaniards and, 28, 81; Tasquique Indians and, 49; Uchise Indians and, 182–183; with Virginia, 54; Yamasee Indians and, 182–183

Trade goods: awls, 181; bans on, 130; beads, 72, 117, 181, 187; bearskins, 47, 120; beaver, 115, 119, 120; bezoar stones, 129; blankets, 154; body paints, 181–182; brass, 181; buffalo hides, 74, 120, 129; cauldrons, 181, 186; cloth, 115, 154, 159, 167, 172, 182, 186; coins, 172; combs, 74, 181; deerskins, 33, 45, 66, 111, 115, 117, 119, 120, 129, 135, 182, 184; dyes, 181–182, 186; and emancipation of Indian slaves, 165; English, 130, 181–182, 185, 188; English and, 178; European, 137; finger rings, 181; French and, 182; furs, 74, 173; and gift-giving, 154; as gifts, 160, 186–187; hawks bells, 181; horses, 130; knives, 117; losses of, 188; and military expeditions, 129; native goods, 130; needles, 181; otter pelts, 120; panther skins, 47; pelts and skins, 173, 182, 184, 187, 188; pipes, 182; quality of, 188; razors, 181; scissors, 181; shells, 54; shortages of, 174; silver, 130, 172; sources of, 137, 146; Spaniards and, 178; Spanish, 188; stealing of, 49; tobacco, 34, 57, 155, 182, 188; weapons, 130. *See also* Clothing and accessories; Weapons and ammunition

Traders: abuses by, 137, 139, 173; and Alabama Indians, 139; Apalachee Indians as, 49; and Apalachicoli Province, 106; Chisca Indians and, 54; and Creek Indians, 4; and Creek terms, 94; English as, 4, 15, 59, 86, 89, 103, 105, 106, 115, 119, 121, 124, 136, 137, 139, 173, 174, 177; French as, 174; and Henry Woodward, 106; and languages, 54; Matheos and, 119; murders of, 49, 50; Rickohockan Indians as, 54; and rum, 139; Scots as, 122; and slaves, 139; Tasquique Indians as, 49, 50; and Yamasee War, 137

Trees: bark of, 74; rotten, for canoes, 189. *See also* Crops; Plants

Truixillo, Agustín, census, 146

Tuckebatchee Indians, 133

Tukabahchee (settlement and polity), 13, 92

Tukabatche (English term), 6

Tulsa Indians. *See* Talisi Indians

Tuskegee (English term), 6

Tuskegee Indians, 91

Tynte, Edward (S.C. governor, 1703–1709), 134

Ubabesa, Luis, 31–32, 35, 36, 37–38, 45

Uchee (English term for Chisca), 6

Uchee (settlement), 93

Uchee Indians, 12, 64, 151. *See also* Chisca Indians; Yuchi Indians

Uchi (settlement), 9, 87, 150, 151, 162

Uchi Indians, 9–10, 12, 151, 162. *See also* Chisca Indians

Uchise (language), 152, 161, 162. *See also* Hitchiti (language)

Uchise Indians: and agriculture, 184, 189; and Apalachee Indians, 170, 182, 187; and Apalachicoli Indians, 121; attacks by, 121, 175, 179;

Uchise Indians—*continued*
and Cherokee Indians, 184, 185, 189; and Chickasaw Indians, 180, 186; and Christian Indians, 185; and Christianity, 190; and clothing, 185; council houses of, 185; delegations of, 181, 184, 186; and English, 133, 170, 177, 181, 182–183, 185–186; and foods, 184, 185; and forts, 188; and French, 185; Guale interpreter on, 184–186; and horses, 185; languages of, 148; leaders of, 146, 147, 148, 181, 184, 186, 188; and migration, 121; and missions, 121; and neutrality, 185; and resettlement of Apalachee Province, 189; settlements of, 181, 187, 188; and shortages, 184; and Spaniards, 182–183, 184–189; and Spanish supplies, 180; and Talapuse Indians, 175, 189; and trade, 182–183; and weapons and ammunition, 185; and Yamasee Indians, 169, 170, 171, 175, 182–183, 187

Uchise Province, 134, 155, 170
Uchises (Spanish term), 4
Uchisi (language), 9
Uchisi (term), 8
Uchisi Indians, 8–9, 167
Uchize Indians: and Apalachicoli Indians, 135, 154; attacks by, 49, 50, 65, 105; and English, 105; forebears of, 105, 106; languages of, 148; leaders of, 148; modern identification of, 105–106; scholarship on, 3; and Spanish captives, 135; and trade, 105
Uchize Province, 135, 154, 157
Ulibahali Indians, 15
Ullibahali Indians. *See* Atasi Indians
Ullibahau (settlement), 2
Upper Apalachicola River, 46
Upper Creek Indians: and agriculture, 94; archaeology of, 16; attacks by, 134; characteristics of, 94; clothing of, 94; cultural assemblages of, 5; cultures of, 15; Emperor Brims and, 137; and English, 134, 159; forebears of, 1, 4–5, 15, 174; and forts, 126; and French, 139; and Green Corn Ceremony, 94; Hilibi Indians as, 13; and hunting, 94; languages of, 7; leaders of, 180; and Lower Creek Indians, 102; and medicinal herbs, 94; origins of name of, 6; and Pensacola, 180; scholarship on, 1, 3–5, 16; as Seminole forebears, 190; settlements of, 4, 13, 80; and Spaniards, 173;

Spanish names for, 80, 155; Talapusa Indians as, 173; territories of, 15, 66, 93; and warfare, 94; and Yamasee Indians, 173
Upper Creek Province, 17, 88, 134
Upper Towns (of Yamasee), 141, 142, 145
Usichi Province, 60

Valverde, Miguel de, 29–30
Vargas, Juan Gabriel de, 134–135, 136
Vchichi (settlement), 129
Vchichicas (settlement), 183
Vchize Indians. *See* Uchize Indians
Vega Castro y Pardo, Damián (governor, 1639–1645), 23, 55, 81
Veracruz, Mexico, 49, 84
Vessels: boats, 58; canoes, 24, 58, 71, 72, 117, 149, 150, 169, 189; captured, 184; English, 86; fishing crafts, 74; in Florida, 84; French, 127, 172; half-galleys, 184; ketches, 24, 25; pirogues, 132, 171, 186; rafts, 58; schooners, 116; ships, 84, 86, 120, 127; sloops, 158, 167; Spanish, 84; supply frigates, 127
Viracocha, 183
Virginia, 12, 54, 57, 58
Vsachi (settlement), 87, 92

Wacissa (settlement), 167, 168, 180
Waddells Mill Pond, 31
Wakulla River, 27, 157
Walker, John, 86
Walls, of wattle and daub, 14
War of Jenkins Ear, 182
War of the Quadruple Alliance, 173
War of the Spanish Succession, 131
Waselkov, Gregory A., 3, 51
Wauchope, Alejandro, 173
Weapemeoc Indians, 54
Weapons and ammunition: Alabama Indians and, 134, 135; ammunition, 59, 186; Apalachee Indians and, 131; Apalachicoli Indians and, 131; Apica Indians and, 134; arms, 157, 162, 172, 174, 184; arquebuses, 72; arrows, 55, 62, 74, 155; balls, 72, 136, 141, 146, 154, 158, 159, 181, 185; bans on trade of, 130; bar-shot, 62; belt pistols, 181; bows, 55, 74, 118, 155; cannon, 158, 171, 172; cartridges, 62; Chalaque Indians and, 134; Chalique Indians and, 134; Chichimeco In-

dians and, 58–59, 61; Chisca Indians and, 60, 62, 131; Creek Indians and, 179; cutlasses, 106; English and, 58, 130; firearms, 55, 58, 59, 60, 61, 85, 86, 98, 106, 135; flint stones, 181; as gifts, 185, 186; gun-flints, 175; guns, 146, 150, 173, 185; harquebuses, 30, 34, 111; hatchets, 34; machetes, 118, 131; materials for, 74; munitions, 35, 157, 162, 171, 172, 184; muskets, 34, 118, 131, 155, 157–158, 167, 181, 186; from New Spain, 172; Pansacola Indians and, 72; pistols, 118, 131, 155; powder, 59, 72, 136, 141, 146, 154, 158, 159, 181, 185; quivers, 118, 155; rifles, 175; sabers, 181; shortages of, 179, 187; shot, 59; shotguns, 58; in South, 55; at St. Marks store, 188; Talapuze Indians and, 134; as trade goods, 59; Westo Indians and, 86, 131; Yamasee Indians and, 170, 179

Weeden Island cultures, 19

Weeden Island period, 79

Weisman, Brent R., 190–191

Wenhold, Lucy L., 97

Westo (English term), 6

Westo Indians: and Apalachee Province, 86; attacks by, 56, 63, 65, 105, 131; and cannibalism, 64; in Carolinas, 64; characteristics of, 63–64, 98, 106; and Chattahoochee Valley palisades, 111; and Chichimeco Indians, 53–54; and Chisca Indians, 63–64; and Chuchumeco Indians, 67; and English, 53, 64, 86, 102, 105, 106, 109, 141; and Erie Indians, 54; and firearms, 86, 98; in Georgia, 86; and Ichisi Indians, 106; languages of, 63, 64, 91; maps of, 91; and migration, 57, 64; along Oconee River, 85; and Savannah Indians, 106; scholarship on, 12; settlements of, 15, 57, 59, 91; and slaves, 57; and Tama Indians, 15; and Timucua Province, 86; in Virginia, 57; war against, 64; and weapons, 131; and Yuchi Indians, 151. *See also* Chichimeco Indians

Westo Indians: Slave Traders of the Early Colonial South, The (Bowne), 54

White, John, 54

White, Nancy M., 21

Williams, Mark, 3, 7, 9, 145

Witchcraft, 61. *See also* Rituals and ceremonies

Woodland period, 66

Woodward, Henry, 58, 59, 81, 106, 109, 120

Worth, John E.: on 1647 revolt, 55; on Achito (settlement), 93; on Alape (settlement), 93; on Amacano Indians, 22, 23; on Apalachicoli (settlement), 93; on Big Sauocola, 95; on Casista (settlement), 93; on ceramics, 17–18, 19; on Chicahuti (settlement), 91; on Chichimeco Indians, 12, 56, 59; on Chief Chislacaliche, 147; on Chiluque Indians, 106; on Chisca Indians, 12, 53, 55, 56; on Colone (settlement), 93; on Díaz Vara Calderón's list of Apalachicoli towns, 89–90; on Hitachi speakers, 90, 91; on Kolomi Indians, 150; on Lower Creek Indians, 3, 7, 16; on missions, 23; on Muscogee language, 91; on Osuche (settlement), 91; on Ricahecrian Indians, 85; on Saucola Indians, 91; on settlements, 93; on Tacusa (settlement), 91, 93; on Talipasle (settlement), 91; on Tasquique Indians, 91; on Timucua missions, 56; on Westo Indians, 12, 85, 91; on Ylapi (settlement), 91; on Yuchi Indians, 91

Wright, J. Leitch, Jr., 4, 8, 191

Yamasee (language): Chiluque Indians and, 106; and Hitchiti (language), 7, 9, 91; Ichisi Indians and, 9; Lower Creeks and, 6; Ocutes and, 7–8; places spoken, 7, 91, 143–144, 151, 162; Tasquique Indians and, 89

Yamasee (Spanish term), 4

Yamasee Indians: and agriculture, 167, 169, 171; and Apalachee Indians, 168, 176, 178; and Apalachicoli Indians, 124; in Apalachicoli Province, 86; and Apisca Indians, 170; attacks by, 38, 49, 65, 86, 106, 119, 121, 143, 147; attacks on, 175; characteristics of, 183, 187; and Chief Chislacaliche, 167; and Chiluque Indians, 106; and Christianity, 143–144, 170, 175, 176, 177; clothing of, 118; and Creek Indians, 174; and English, 15, 86, 118, 138, 143, 169–170, 173, 174–175, 177, 182–183, 187; and firearms, 118; and Fort Walton culture, 43; in Georgia, 89; and Gov. Quiroga y Losada, 123; and Guale Indians, 187; and interpreters, 12, 119; and Kuseetaw Indians, 15, 86; languages of, 7, 9, 43, 140; leaders of, 86, 143–144; locations of, 106; and Lower Creek Indians, 177, 183; and migration, 15, 89, 118,

Yamasee Indians—*continued*
124, 141–142, 145, 171, 189; and Mikasuki Indians, 9; and missions, 141, 144, 168; and neutrality, 179; as nomads, 89; at Ocuti, 124; orders to apprehend, 124; and Peña, 151, 152, 171; population of, 138–139, 143–144; post-1708, 183; and relocation to Apalachee Province, 169; scholarshp on, 24; as Seminole forebears, 190; settlements of, 89, 118, 138, 143–145, 168, 169, 171, 174–175, 176, 178, 180; and slaves, 106; in South Carolina, 142, 147; and Spaniards, 98, 174, 178, 182–183, 187; as spies, 7, 145, 177; at St. Augustine, 141–142; and St. Marks, 169, 176; and Talapusa Indians, 170, 173; and Talupuse Indians, 177; and trade, 179, 182–183; and Uchise Indians, 169, 170, 171, 175, 182–183, 187; and Uchisi Indians, 167; and Upper Creek Indians, 173; weapons of, 106; and Yamasee War, 138, 143, 179; and Yoa Indians, 142, 145; and Yuchi Indians, 170

Yamasee War: Achito Indians and, 148; Altamaja leaders and, 140; Apalachee Indians and, 137, 138, 146; Apalachicoli Indians and, 137, 148; Casista Indians and, 148; Caueta Indians and, 148; Cherokee Indians and, 137, 138; Chiaha Indians and, 148; Chief Chislacaliche and, 148; Chisca Indians and, 80; Choctaw Indians and, 137; Creek Indians and, 137–138, 179; English and, 138, 141, 159; French and, 159; Indian leaders of, 137, 139, 140–141; Indians' defeat during, 137; mentioned, 118, 154; and migration, 4, 7, 8, 80, 82, 87, 137, 138, 142, 146, 147–148, 179; munitions for, 141; origins of, 139, 169; outbreak of, 140; Savocola Indians and, 148; scholarship on, 137, 138, 139; Spaniards and, 139–140, 141, 158, 159; Taskiki Indians and, 148; Yamasee Indians and, 138, 143, 179

Yatcatane (settlement), 29
Yfallaquisca (Nicunapa Indian), 193n2
Ylapi (settlement), 87, 90, 91, 92
Yllache Indians, 163–165
Yoa (settlement), 145
Yoa Indians, 142, 145
Ysfane, Juan, 11, 107, 108, 112, 113
Ysica Indians, 80, 151

Ysipacafi (Caueta Indian): and alliegance to Spain, 172; and assaults on Pensacola, 172–173; and Christianity, 165; and delegations to St. Augustine, 155, 156–157, 159; and English, 159–160, 161, 162–163; and enslaved Indians, 172; and expedition to St. Marks, 166; and expedition to Talapuse Province, 169; father of, 159–160, 161, 165, 166, 183; and French, 172–173; gifts for, 167; and La Mobila Province, 168; as leader, 146, 155, 156–157, 165, 168; and Lower Creek Indians, 163; at Mobile, 172; mother of, 146, 165; and Orta, 165; and Pansacola Province, 162–163; and Peña expeditions, 160, 161, 165, 166; in Pensacola, 165; and rift with Emperor Brims, 159–160, 161; and Spaniards, 146, 148, 183; in St. Augustine, 165; synonyms for, 146; wife of, 146, 165; and Yamasee Indians, 183

Yslachamuque. *See* Brims (Caueta chief)
Ytorio, Clemente, 188–189
Yuchee or Yuche Indians, 147, 175, 177, 180
Yuches (settlement), 188
Yuchi (settlement), 153
Yuchi Indians: and Apalachee Indians, 170, 175; and Apalachicoli Indians, 64; ballgames of, 65–66; and Central Algonkian Indians, 66; in Chattahoochee Valley, 80; and Chisca Indians, 68; as cultural mediators, 66; and English, 147, 170, 175; forebears of, 64; languages of, 12, 66, 80, 91; leaders of, 65, 164; and Lower Creek Indians, 68; maps of, 91; Mark F. Boyd on, 64–65; and migration, 80; in Oklahoma, 68; and Peña, 162; rituals of, 65–66; scholarship on, 10, 12; as Seminole forebears, 190; settlements of, 91; and social organization, 66; and Uchi Indians, 151; and Westo Indians, 151; and Yamasee Indians, 170, 175. *See also* Uchee Indians; Uchize Indians

Yufala (settlement), 170, 188
Yupaha (legendary land), 14
Yustaga (missions), 132
Yustaga Province, 55

Zalacaxliches (settlement), 188
Zúñiga y Zerda, Joseph de (governor, 1699–1706), 23–24, 26, 67, 130

John H. Hann, historian at the San Luis Archaeological and Historic Site in Tallahassee, is a member of the Florida Department of State, Bureau of Archaeological Research. He is the author, coauthor, or translator of many books on the native peoples of Florida, including *Indians of Central and South Florida, 1513–1763* (UPF, 2003), *The Apalachee Indians and Mission San Luis* (with Bonnie McEwan, UPF, 1998) and *Hernando de Soto among the Apalachee: The Archaeology of the First Winter Encampment* (with Charles R. Ewen, UPF, 1998).

Ripley P. Bullen Series
Florida Museum of Natural History
Edited by Jerald T. Milanich

Tacachale: Essays on the Indians of Florida and Southeastern Georgia during the Historic Period, edited by Jerald T. Milanich and Samuel Proctor (1978); first paperback edition, 1994

Aboriginal Subsistence Technology on the Southeastern Coastal Plain during the Late Prehistoric Period, by Lewis H. Larson (1980)

Cemochechobee: Archaeology of a Mississippian Ceremonial Center on the Chattahoochee River, by Frank T. Schnell, Vernon J. Knight, Jr., and Gail S. Schnell (1981)

Fort Center: An Archaeological Site in the Lake Okeechobee Basin, by William H. Sears, with contributions by Elsie O'R. Sears and Karl T. Steinen (1982); first paperback edition, 1994

Perspectives on Gulf Coast Prehistory, edited by Dave D. Davis (1984)

Archaeology of Aboriginal Culture Change in the Interior Southeast: Depopulation during the Early Historic Period, by Marvin T. Smith (1987); first paperback edition, 1992

Apalachee: The Land between the Rivers, by John H. Hann (1988)

Key Marco's Buried Treasure: Archaeology and Adventure in the Nineteenth Century, by Marion Spjut Gilliland (1989)

First Encounters: Spanish Explorations in the Caribbean and the United States, 1492-1570, edited by Jerald T. Milanich and Susan Milbrath (1989)

Missions to the Calusa, edited and translated by John H. Hann, with an introduction by William H. Marquardt (1991)

Excavations on the Franciscan Frontier: Archaeology at the Fig Springs Mission, by Brent Richards Weisman (1992)

The People Who Discovered Columbus: The Prehistory of the Bahamas, by William F. Keegan (1992)

Hernando de Soto and the Indians of Florida, by Jerald T. Milanich and Charles Hudson (1993)

Foraging and Farming in the Eastern Woodlands, edited by C. Margaret Scarry (1993)

Puerto Real: The Archaeology of a Sixteenth-Century Spanish Town in Hispaniola, edited by Kathleen Deagan (1995)

Political Structure and Change in the Prehistoric Southeastern United States, edited by John F. Scarry (1996)

Bioarchaeology of Native American Adaptation in the Spanish Borderlands, edited by Brenda J. Baker and Lisa Kealhofer (1996)

A History of the Timucua Indians and Missions, by John H. Hann (1996)

Archaeology of the Mid-Holocene Southeast, edited by Kenneth E. Sassaman and David G. Anderson (1996)

The Indigenous People of the Caribbean, edited by Samuel M. Wilson (1997); first paperback edition, 1999

Hernando de Soto among the Apalachee: The Archaeology of the First Winter Encampment, by Charles R. Ewen and John H. Hann (1998)

The Timucuan Chiefdoms of Spanish Florida, by John E. Worth: vol. 1, *Assimilation*; vol. 2, *Resistance and Destruction* (1998)

Ancient Earthen Enclosures of the Eastern Woodlands, edited by Robert C. Mainfort, Jr., and Lynne P. Sullivan (1998)

An Environmental History of Northeast Florida, by James J. Miller (1998)

Precolumbian Architecture in Eastern North America, by William N. Morgan (1999)

Archaeology of Colonial Pensacola, edited by Judith A. Bense (1999)

Grit-Tempered: Early Women Archaeologists in the Southeastern United States, edited by Nancy Marie White, Lynne P. Sullivan, and Rochelle A. Marrinan (1999); first paperback edition, 2001

Coosa: The Rise and Fall of a Southeastern Mississippian Chiefdom, by Marvin T. Smith (2000)
Religion, Power, and Politics in Colonial St. Augustine, by Robert L. Kapitzke (2001)
Bioarchaeology of Spanish Florida: The Impact of Colonialism, edited by Clark Spencer Larsen (2001)
Archaeological Studies of Gender in the Southeastern United States, edited by Jane M. Eastman and Christopher B. Rodning (2001)
The Archaeology of Traditions: Agency and History Before and After Columbus, edited by Timothy R. Pauketat (2001)
Foraging, Farming, and Coastal Biocultural Adaptation in Late Prehistoric North Carolina, by Dale L. Hutchinson (2002)
Windover: Multidisciplinary Investigations of an Early Archaic Florida Cemetery, edited by Glen H. Doran (2002)
Archaeology of the Everglades, by John W. Griffin (2002)
Pioneer in Space and Time: John Mann Goggin and the Development of Florida Archaeology, by Brent Richards Weisman (2002)
Indians of Central and South Florida, 1513-1763, by John H. Hann (2003)
Presidio Santa Maria de Galve: A Struggle for Survival in Colonial Spanish Pensacola, edited by Judith A. Bense (2003)
Bioarchaeology of the Florida Gulf Coast: Adaptation, Conflict, and Change, by Dale L. Hutchinson (2004)
The Myth of Syphilis: The Natural History of Treponematosis in North America, edited by Mary Lucas Powell and Della Collins Cook (2005)
The Florida Journals of Frank Hamilton Cushing, edited by Phyllis E. Kolianos and Brent R. Weisman (2005)
The Lost Florida Manuscript of Frank Hamilton Cushing, edited by Phyllis E. Kolianos and Brent R. Weisman (2005)
The Native American World Beyond Apalachee: West Florida and the Chattahoochee Valley, by John H. Hann (2006)